DOROTHY L. SAYERS

Her Life and Soul

Also by Barbara Reynolds (as editor)

*The Letters of Dorothy L. Sayers
1899–1939: The Making of a Detective Novelist*

DOROTHY L. SAYERS

Her Life and Soul

BARBARA REYNOLDS

St. Martin's Griffin
New York

DOROTHY L. SAYERS: HER LIFE AND SOUL. Copyright © 1993
by Barbara Reynolds. All rights reserved. Printed in the United
States of America. No part of this book may be used or
reproduced in any manner whatsoever without written
permission except in the case of brief quotations embodied in
critical articles or reviews. For information, address St. Martin's
Press, 175 Fifth Avenue, New York, N.Y. 10010.

ISBN 0-312-15353-8

First published in Great Britain by Hodder & Stoughton Ltd.

First St. Martin's Griffin Edition: April 1997

10 9 8 7 6 5 4 3 2 1

Contents

Illustrations	viii
Foreword	ix
1 Childhood	1
2 School	27
3 Oxford	45
4 Return to Oxford	63
5 Adrift	85
6 London	97
7 John Cournos	107
8 A Man and a Motor-cycle	117
9 Behind the Scenes	129
10 John Anthony	141
11 Marriage	153
12 Enter Lord Peter Wimsey	171
13 Sometime Scholar of Somerville College	185
14 Family Ties	199
15 The Making of a Detective Story	213
16 Under Contract	225
17 A Labour of Love	237
18 A City Sanctified	247
19 Joy's Bonfire	261
20 Canterbury	273
21 Words of an Archangel	283
22 The Challenge of War	291
23 Creativeness	307
24 Incarnation	317

25 Reluctant Prophet   331
26 Seeing It Through   341
27 Gaudium   353
28 The Woman Who Was Dorothy L. Sayers   367
   Notes   373
   Appendix   385
   Principal Sources   387
   Acknowledgments   389
   Index   391

To all who have helped me to write this book

Illustrations

Group with Henry Sayers and Oscar Wilde	2
Dorothy's mother as a young woman	4
Dorothy aged four	8
Family group	19
Dorothy as Athos	20
Dorothy imitating Hugh Allen, 1915	46
Dorothy at Somerville	49
Roy Ridley	57
Leonard Hodgson	77
Eric Whelpton	86
John Cournos	107
Dorothy in London	113
Bill White	120
Dorothy's son as a schoolboy	120
Dorothy at Benson's	130
John Anthony as a baby	146
Mac in 1914	153
Mac with Dorothy's fan-mail	163
Dorothy the established writer	168
Dorothy's father as an old man	207
The house at Witham	209
Mac during World War II	232
Dorothy in 1937	280
Dorothy as an air-raid warden	297
Cartoon of Churchill by Dorothy	348
A page from a letter with drawings of kittens	357
Dorothy at Benson's in 1950	360
A scene from *The Just Vengeance*	362

Foreword

"Every biographical study is an interim report." (Ralph E. Hone)

No definitive biography of Dorothy L. Sayers can be written until her letters are published. The present work is based on a selection of the most personal and significant, from which ample quotations are provided. The result is that she largely tells her own story, and in her own voice. In theory, she would have approved, for she stated, in her unfinished work on Wilkie Collins, that the secret of success in biography was to allow the subject to speak for himself as far as possible in diaries and letters.

In fact, as far as she was concerned, she abhorred the personal approach. She expressed the hope that no account of her life would be written until fifty years after her death. She told her son that she intended to destroy all letters and private papers in her possession. But she did not do so; and she must have realised that the recipients of her own remarkable letters were unlikely to throw them away. Some use of them has already been made by previous biographers but the portraits of her that have emerged so far have left me dissatisfied.

I had the good fortune to know Dorothy Sayers. Over a period of eleven years we met and corresponded (mainly about Dante) and we became close friends. The person I knew is recognisable in her letters and I have retraced her there. Despite her vehement protestations to the contrary, all her writings — novels, plays, poems, theological articles, translations and literary criticism — are deeply and consistently personal. I have no doubt that the more we get to know and understand her, the more we will appreciate and comprehend her works.

That is my justification, if any is needed, for presenting this new — though still interim — biography of Dorothy L. Sayers in the centenary year of her birth.

Barbara Reynolds
March 1993

DOROTHY L. SAYERS

Her Life and Soul

CHAPTER 1

Childhood

Dorothy Leigh Sayers was born in Oxford in 1893, on 13 June, the day consecrated in the calendar of saints to St Anthony of Padua. Her father, the Reverend Henry Sayers, was nearly forty and her mother, Helen Mary, was thirty-seven. They had married on 9 August 1892 and Dorothy was their only child.

Henry Sayers was then headmaster of the Christ Church Choir School, a post which provided accommodation at 1 Brewer Street, a seventeenth-century house where Cardinal Wolsey is said to have lived. This was Dorothy's birthplace. On 15 July she was baptised in Christ Church Cathedral. Her father, who was chaplain, performed the ceremony. Early in 1894 the family and the school moved into a new building, 3 Brewer Street, which was to be Dorothy's home until she was four and half years old.

Henry, born on 19 July 1854, was the elder son of the Reverend Robert Sayers of Tittleshall, Norfolk. In 1866 he won a scholarship to Winchester, where he remained until 1871. The school magazine, *The Wykehamist*, contains a mention of him as a member of the scholars' rugger team in 1870, but his name does not appear in connection with athletics, rowing or cricket. From this it may be deduced that his prowess at sport was no more than moderate. From his later career it is known that he had musical gifts but there is no record of his having learnt music at Winchester. After a gap of five years he went up to Magdalen College as an academical clerk, or choral scholar, the oldest of his matriculation group. It is not known how he spent the years between Winchester and Oxford. His father was not a wealthy man and Henry may have taught music in order to earn money to help with expenses at Oxford. Among his contemporaries at Magdalen was Oscar Wilde, who graduated in 1878. Photographs show that they had friends in common and that they

1

took part in social events together. He rowed and played cricket for the college. He was six feet, two inches tall, blue-eyed and strikingly handsome, with a classical profile. It is evident from his photographs that he took an interest in his appearance. His clothes are elegant, the brim of his bowler hat is fashionably curly. His hair, which is beginning to recede (he lost it early), is expertly trimmed and parted down the middle. He wears beautifully shaped side-burns and a full moustache. Altogether he is something of a dandy.

He was not academically brilliant for he took only a pass degree in his chosen subject, Divinity, in 1879. He was ordained priest at Hereford in 1880. That same year he was appointed headmaster of St Michael's College, Tenbury, a school where boys are trained as choristers. He took up his post at Christ Church Choir School in 1884. It consisted only of the choirboys, sixteen in all, "small demons with angel voices", as his daughter was later to call them, to whom it was his responsibility to teach Latin. The following extracts from his account of his thirteen years at the school give some idea of his benign and gentle personality.

If the saying that the country which has no annals is happy may be extended to schools, I think that the Choir School, during the thirteen years that I was privileged to preside over it, must have its full share of happiness; for looking back after an interval of two years, I can recall but little of an eventful or exciting character . . . The old Choir House, No. 1 Brewer Street, an ancient building of some archaeological interest, [was] very ill-adapted for young

Henry Sayers, Oscar Wilde and friends. Henry is second on the right at the back, with Oscar Wilde seated in front of him.
(*Magdalen College, Oxford*)

boys, the rooms being small, low, and dark, and the house over-shadowed by other dwellings which closely surrounded it . . .

Behind the old Choir House was a small yard . . . where some most exciting cricket used to be played. Each boy had an india-rubber ball, and innings were taken in "school order". I have often stood to be bowled to by sixteen bowlers at 2d a wicket and 1d a catch, until the sport became too expensive, for if you succeeded in keeping the balls out of your wicket it was impossible to elude the multitude of hands that were on the alert to catch them . . .

Very happy days, on the whole, they were; and often, in the seclusion of my country rectory, I recall them with regret, and even in fancy seem to hear the booming of "Tom", the signal for putting lights out and saying "Goodnight!" May I take this opportunity of greeting again my former pupils who may chance to read these lines, of expressing the hope that they have long forgotten any instances, if such there were, of hastiness or severity in my treat-ment of them, and of assuring them of the pleasure it will give me to see any of them here, should they at any time be within reach, and to revive the memories of days "for ever fled".

A man of scholarly interests, whose favourite poet was Horace, Henry Sayers was also a competent musician, being not only a singer (probably a bass) but a violinist and a composer as well. He was a Mason, having been initiated at St Michael's Lodge in Tenbury, where he became Worshipful Master in 1883. In 1885, after taking up his post at Oxford, he joined the Apollo University Lodge, of which he became Worshipful Master in 1889. His progress was rapid; on average, one Mason out of four qualifies for such high office. He deferred marriage until his late thirties, whether from financial considerations or lack of inclination we do not know.

Helen Sayers, née Leigh, known always as Nellie or Nell, was the daughter of a solicitor and a niece of Percival Leigh, the humorist, who was also an amateur actor and a friend of Dickens and Thack-eray. Dorothy described her as a vivacious and attractive woman with an abundance of bright brown hair. "Her long upper lip, strong nose and wide mouth made her face too decided for actual beauty, in a day when regularity of feature was more highly esteemed than it is now, but her broad, intelligent forehead, speaking eyes and liveliness of expression must have made her admired at any period." She had an exceptional intellect and in different circumstances might have been a writer. Her letters were always lively and entertaining. She had a keen sense of humour and would sometimes laugh until the

Dorothy's mother as a young woman (*Estate of Anthony Fleming*)

tears ran down her cheeks, a characteristic which her daughter inherited. It seems surprising that so attractive a woman did not marry until she was thirty-six. It is said, however, by someone who knew her that she had suffered some illness in her youth which spoilt her looks.

Dorothy retained a vivid memory of her early years in Oxford. In a brief, unfinished autobiographical sketch, entitled *My Edwardian Childhood*, she recalls being taken for walks in Christ Church Meadow and playing peep-bo with her nurse among the elm-trees in the Broad Walk. On one occasion, when they were about to set out with the pram, Dorothy for some reason refused to go and rolled on the nursery floor, screaming. Retribution followed in the form of a spanking. This is her earliest distinct memory "and if that means anything to the psychoanalysts, I make them a present of it". It was perhaps this nurse who kept her out too long in a November fog, with the result that she developed bronchial pneumonia. The nurse was replaced by another, who looked after her during her illness. In those days before antibiotics there was a garment known as a "pneumonia jacket", padded with cotton wool. Her nurse removed

4

this piece by piece as the patient got better and finally said, "I don't think you need this old thing any more", and threw it on the fire. "I was horrified," Dorothy recalled, "expecting to drop dead instantly after such flagrant defiance of the doctor's orders."

Among her most vivid recollections was the sight in a dentist's shop front of a row of false teeth which slowly opened and shut. Years later, she recalled this entrancing spectacle in a sketch, entitled *The Tooth of Time*. She relates that she had visited her dentist in London and was about to take her leave when she caught sight of a complete set of dentures lying on his mantelpiece:

I was transported back over a quarter of a century. Once more I held my nurse's hand and walked with short steps within my native city of dreaming spires. Once again, all agog for mystery and adventure, we trod, she and I, the subtly sensuous curve of the High Street. As we drew near to the shrine of romance, an awful rapture of suspense agitated us. "Do you think it will be working today, Nurse?" I would say. And Nurse, successfully concealing her emotions, in the grown-up manner, would reply, "Very likely, dear."

It thrills me now – the recollection of the magic glass case, placed thoughtfully low upon the wall, as though with courteous consideration for the stature of childhood.

There must have been half a dozen of them, if my memory serves – half a dozen faultlessly gleaming double rows of teeth set in gums of coral. And if we were fortunate in our visit (that is, as I now suppose, if we had not carelessly chosen to go abroad upon a Sunday or early-closing day), they moved – instinct with a miraculous life. Slowly, meditatively, they opened and closed, chewing upon some unseen, ambrosial food – pearl-laden oysters, breathing antiphonally upon the bed of an enchanted ocean . . . I cannot bear to think that the passionless Barmecide feast of those rhythmical mouths is ended and the marvel of their mechanism cast out to moulder upon the dust-heap.

Although Dorothy had a nurse to look after her, her parents were not the remote figures described in many autobiographies of the period, visited formally in the drawing-room or seen briefly at bedtime. On the contrary, she was much loved by them and often in their company. Every morning she was brought down to her mother's room and put into bed beside her. Her mother then read aloud to her, and Dorothy, looking over her shoulder, herself learnt to read without realising that she was doing so. Her mother was thus, without knowing it, a pioneer of the "Look-and-Say" method of teaching children to read, which became renowned twenty years later.

Her two aunts, Mabel Leigh and Gertrude Sayers, also made much of her. She was welcome in the drawing-room, even when there were visitors, for whom she was encouraged to perform various childish tricks. Two generations separated her from these benevolent elders and from them she imbibed ways of speech and a social manner that were already out of date. It was rather similar to being raised by grandparents. She did have some young company from time to time: her cousin Margaret Leigh, who lived near by, and other children were invited in to play with her, but, she remembered later, she didn't care much for them, preferring the conversation of people older than herself.

She first saw the sea at Broadstairs, at the age of three and a half. There existed an old photograph, showing her as a solemn child with a fringe, wearing a sun-bonnet and striped bathing drawers, her frock bundled into them. Her mother and nurse were seated behind her on the sand, her mother wearing a linen blouse, a stiff collar and a hard sailor hat with a thick white veil. She remembered that she wandered along the beach and showed a crab she had found to a strange man, who carried her into the sea on his shoulder, and back to her mother, she calling out "Mummy! Mummy! I've found a new uncle!" "He was a very nice fellow," said Mrs Sayers, relating the event at home, "but he might have been *anybody*!" Picking up people, or diseases, or the wrong accent were risks against which children were anxiously guarded.

Other early Oxford memories included Scruggs, an Old English sheep-dog belonging to the school. (She was to give his name to a dog which makes a brief appearance in *The Five Red Herrings*.) The tolling of Tom – 101 strokes every night at five past nine – was a puzzle to her, for she had been told that no clock struck more than twelve, yet he would toll on and on till she had long lost count. The building next to the school, where Campion Hall now stands, was then a stable for the horses which pulled the trams. The noise of their hoofs and their whinnying, not to mention the stable smells, were part of her childhood, as was the noise of iron-clad wheels on cobblestones. Of her toys she recalled a beautiful jointed doll named Gladys with a trunkful of exquisite hand-made clothes. This she set aside with respect but did not play with. There were also Jumbo, a handsome elephant with real skin, Tommy the wooden horse and

Ajax the railway engine. But the toys she really liked were two furry monkeys, named Jacko and Jocko. Jacko was "puckish, mischievous, enterprising, always in disgrace, but enduringly beloved". Jocko, whose eyes "beamed with red and black glass", was "utterly virtuous and amiable". There was also a rag doll named Frenchman, embroidered in Harlequin-like lozenges of blue and red wool, "evidently intended by nature to play the villain's part". She wove many stories round these three characters.

Her father also read aloud to her. Curled up on his knee, in the evenings, she listened to the Uncle Remus stories, Grimm's fairy stories and, above all, the Alice books. She remembered being taken to the school library to borrow these: a boy took two red volumes off a shelf, slapped them together to dispel the dust and handed them to her father. She was then four years old, an early age at which to enter Lewis Carroll's wonderland and looking-glass world. She recalled the "sheer gorgeousness of Jabberwocky", which seemed to her a sequence of entrancing sounds. ("Many things that I could only dimly understand were delightful to me by reason of rhyme or rhythm," she later said.) Lewis Carroll (Charles Dodgson, the mathematician) was then a don at Christ Church, with rooms in Tom Quad, but her parents were not personally acquainted with him. "I never saw him," she wrote and yet she told friends that he had seen her in her perambulator. His books, as also the tales of Brer Rabbit, were to become a frequent source of reference and quotation in her own writings.

Towards the end of 1897, when Dorothy was four and a half, there was a sense of impending change in the household. She heard talk of the country and a new house; a large book appeared, full of wall-paper patterns, over which her mother and Aunt Mabel pored. Her father had been offered the living of Bluntisham-cum-Earith, in the county of Huntingdonshire in the fenland of East Anglia, one of the best livings in the gift of Christ Church. This was a welcome change for her father but it was a wrench for her mother, who enjoyed the social life of Oxford. The domestic staff were told about the move and about the very different life it would mean for them if they came. They all chose to accompany the family, "an immense tribute to my mother's character", said Dorothy; "she was always served with great devotion".

Her parents went on ahead to Bluntisham and Dorothy was left in her old home with her nurse for the last day or two. The little wooden cart belonging to Jacko and Jocko was taken down from the top of a cupboard and packed "under my anxious eye". Jacko had

Dorothy aged four with Jacko and Jocko *(Estate of Anthony Fleming)*

remained with her. She cut him out an elegant travelling jacket and cap from stiff blue material: "he looked very smart". She vividly remembered her first arrival at the rectory, "wearing a brown pelisse and bonnet trimmed with feathers". A photograph taken of her at this time shows her dressed as she describes and holding Jacko and Jocko on her lap. She did not remember the train journey from Oxford but she recalled walking up from Bluntisham station to find the new home, about ten minutes away. Aunt Mabel and Grand-mother Sayers must have joined her and her nurse at some point on the journey, for she remembered them walking ahead, her grand-mother dressed in widow's weeds and Aunt Mabel carrying a parrot in a travelling-cage. She walked beside her nurse. It was January and as they turned in at the rectory gate she saw that both sides of the drive were gold with winter aconites.

The rectory at Bluntisham, five minutes' walk from the church and set far back from the road, was a large ivy-covered house standing in two acres of garden. One day a visiting missionary, walking up from the station, passed the house and continued beyond the church for some way, looking in vain for the rectory and eventually turning back. Apologising for his late arrival, he explained that he had thought it was "a gentleman's house". "My father," said Dorothy, "placed his finger-tips together and said with a deprecating little bow, 'We *hope* it is'." This was a family joke for many years.

The house was large enough for Dorothy to have a night and a day nursery.There was room for Grandmother Sayers and Aunt Mabel Leigh, who both lived there permanently, and for Aunt Gertrude Sayers who came on long visits. The servants who had chosen to accompany them from Oxford comprised a cook, a manservant and three maids. There was also Dorothy's nurse, later to be replaced by a series of governesses. A gardener, John Chapman, was engaged locally. His wife Elizabeth was the laundry-maid and later took over as cook. Their son Bob was the houseboy and helped his father in the garden. Their daughter Annie was the same age as Dorothy and the two little girls sometimes had tea together.

The inhabitants of Bluntisham, numbering about 900, were mainly farmers and farm-labourers. There was no local squire and no resident doctor. Social life was therefore limited and very different from Oxford. Dorothy's cousin, Margaret Leigh, visited the rectory as a child and recalls in her autobiography, *The Fruit in the Seed*, that her "Aunt Nell", who had married a schoolmaster but had never anticipated having to perform the duties of a parson's wife in a country parish, nevertheless settled down to make the best of things:

> She was very popular with the poor, especially the old women, whom she visited frequently; but had no use for the farmers' wives, who . . . wore hats that made the church pews look like stalls at a country flower show. Teetotallers were an abomination to her, and she took a malicious pleasure in watching them at choir treats, lapping up the trifle she had plentifully doped with brandy.

Margaret Leigh confirms that Aunt Nell had been strikingly handsome in her youth and that her beautiful auburn hair was always impeccably dressed. She confirms also that she spent a lot of time writing "witty and closely packed letters".

Aunt Mabel took her share of parish duties, though, with an instinct for self-protection, managed not to be present at births and deaths. Grandmother Sayers, the widow of a parson and the mother of two more, had the church in her blood and took an active (sometimes an over-active) interest in the welfare of the parishioners. Thus the rector, an old-fashioned parson of the Broad Church type, was ably supported in the fulfilment of his pastoral responsibilities, which he managed, in a leisurely way, to combine with the life of a country gentleman.

9

The house was beautiful. Years later Dorothy recalled it in loving detail. Her mother, who had inherited a small legacy, spent it on repairs and redecoration, employing a first-rate Oxford firm, to the disappointment of the local craftsmen. The hall was long, with a square section in the centre, tapering to narrow passages at each end and divided by archways draped with heavy dark blue patterned curtains, looped back with thick, tasselled cords. The stone floor was covered with brown linoleum, patterned with squares to simulate parquet. A painting of the hall, unsigned but probably painted by Dorothy as a girl, still exists, showing all these details. The effect is light, colourful and welcoming.

A shallow staircase with frail Victorian banisters led to the first floor ("a poor staircase", Mrs Sayers called it). It was painted white, with a mahogany handrail. Under the staircase stood a large coke stove. When she was little, Dorothy liked to be lifted up to see the tortoise stamped on its lid, ringed with the words "Slow But Sure Combustion". In 1957, visiting Chichester Cathedral in her company, I drew attention to another such stove, saying the words always amused me, with their menace of hell fire. She laughed and said, "We had one just like that at Bluntisham."

The drawing-room on the south side, facing the garden, was the finest room in the house. Even as a small child Dorothy knew that it was beautiful. Two white fluted pillars supported a beam across the middle of the ceiling. It had three large windows which were secured at night with heavy shutters. One, the central window of the house, was framed by a handsome pillared doorway, which had been transferred from St Ives in 1848, when Slepe Hall, known as Oliver Cromwell's house, was pulled down. The drawing-room wall-paper was light blue, with a meandering pattern. The woodwork was also painted blue, with panels picked out in white. The room contained a particularly lovely oval mahogany table which Mr Sayers had had made to his specifications.

On one side of the drawing-room a door led into her father's study. This too was papered in blue, with a self-pattern of large poppies. Dorothy had always to knock before entering. Inside was an American organ which her father was fond of playing. She remembered also "a mysterious and lovely box" which contained his masonic regalia, in which he sometimes allowed her to dress up. "It was no doubt very irregular of him . . . but it happened only occasionally and was a particularly solemn treat." A narrow slip off the drawing-room was papered in light green and wainscoted in black. A pattern of yellow irises on a black ground adorned each side of the

hearth. Across the chimney-piece ran a legend in Old English letter-
ing: "Cheerful Hearts Make Cheerful Hearths", which Dorothy
thought must be a pun of some kind, though not so good, she
considered, as the puns in the Alice books. The panels of the door
were painted with designs of birds and flowers. In later years, when
she read Wilkie Collins' novel *The Moonstone*, she visualised this as
the door painted by Franklin Blake and Rachel Verinder.

A second drawing-room off the far end of the passage was seldom
used, being dark and rather gloomy. At some stage an extra window,
which had been blocked up, was opened to admit more light. It had
deep yellow wall-paper, a yellow carpet and green curtains. The
fireplace was draped, when not in use, with green velvet curtains
which ran on rods from each side of the hearth and the room was
crowded with little tables, covered with ornaments and knick-
knacks. It was here that visitors were received and Dorothy was
invited to meet them, wearing a mauve velvet frock or a red plush
one, each with a deep falling collar of lace. A photograph was taken
of her wearing one of these.

To the left side of the hall was Dorothy's day nursery, which later
became her schoolroom. Beyond a green baize door, which shut
automatically with a swishing sound, was the boot hall, pantry and
"servants' hall" (a small, dark room), and a palatial W.C. which
stood on a dais like a throne and had a willow-pattern china bowl.
Next came the back stairs and the kitchen. Beyond this were the
larder, scullery and laundry. The ceiling of the kitchen was studded
with hooks, left by previous occupants who had cured their own
hams and bacon. A cavernous range served for all the cooking and
for heating the water. Coal, which the range consumed at an alarming rate, was priced at eighteen shillings a ton, a heavy charge. There
was no gas or electricity. For lighting, the household depended on
paraffin lamps and candles. A row of shining brass candlesticks was
set out on the hall table every night for going up to bed.

The stone and brick flooring required frequent scrubbing. Every
drop of water had to be pumped by hand. The process began at a
quarter to eight each morning and continued for fifteen minutes. This
sufficed to fill the cistern for the day. Mrs Sayers was always afraid
that the water would run short and that there would be an explosion.
It was the period of wash-stands with jug and basin in the bedrooms,
and chamber pots. The housemaid carried cans of hot water up to the
bedrooms every morning. When baths were needed, hot water was
again carried up and poured into a hip bath. "Strangely enough, my
mother used to say," wrote Dorothy, "she never had a servant

complain of this colossal labour in all the twenty years we were at Bluntisham."

The garden was a place of delight, with two lawns, tall, shady trees and well-tended flower-beds. Some of the trees had been planted in the early nineteenth century. There was a mulberry so old it had to be held together with nuts and bolts. Lime trees and chestnuts were resonant in summer with the humming of bumble-bees. A Wellingtonia offered roosting holes for tree-creepers on the north and east sides, away from the prevailing winds. In January a striking feature were the winter aconites, which had caught the eye of the four-year-old Dorothy when she first arrived. From February onwards the garden was full of bird song as greenfinches, chaffinches, blackbirds and thrushes claimed their territories. The dawn chorus was clamorous. Colonies of rooks stripped the bark from the lime trees for lining their nests. There were goldcrests, wood pigeons and owls. Mallard and widgeon and sometimes wild geese flew over the garden and river swans were visible on the Ouse a quarter of a mile away to the south, with the peaceful, uninterrupted view of Over Church and village. When floods were out – and this was a danger every year – trees and church spires looked like ships at sea.

With the spring came mauve primroses and an abundant array of daffodils, tulips, wallflowers and forget-me-nots. An unusual plant, the dusky geranium, grew by a wicket gate. In May the copper beech on the upper lawn passed through wonderful shades of yellow, brown and pink, before settling into the heavy bronze of its later stage. In certain years an old tulip tree bore flowers. There were lilacs and laburnums. A photograph exists, showing Cook and a friend helping to mow the lawn. There is a sun-dial, there are flowering shrubs and tall hardy perennials; the impression is one of a luxuriant abundance. In August, when the golden corn tossed in the unceasing wind and clouds moved slowly across the vast spaces of fenland sky, the prospect was one of peace and plenty. Even in winter, which could be severe and desolate, there were moments of glory, as when pack ice shone scarlet in the setting sun.

Dorothy's childhood was thus spent amid beauty, first at Oxford and then in this exceptionally lovely rectory, unusual for the period in its light, colourful decoration. She spent a lot of time out of doors, playing in the garden, going for walks or drives, or running with her hoop. There was much anxiety about catching colds, a solicitude which she resented, but it was a constant worry in days before antibiotics, when to get one's feet wet or to be caught in a downpour could lead to serious illness. She was thought by her parents to be a delicate child but she grew sturdy and strong. Food was plentiful, though stodgy, as was usual then. She later recalled that all her relations seemed to suffer from constipation, dosing themselves everlastingly with laxatives. She herself escaped, she said, because she ate so much fruit from the garden, even though she was told not to: strawberries, mulberries, peaches, figs and plums. There were two vegetable gardens and three asparagus beds, which must have lightened the family diet.

There was a pony in the paddock named Jenny. It was the task of Bob, the gardener's son, to catch her and harness her to the trap if anyone wished to go for a drive. This took some time and departing guests driven to the station sometimes missed their trains. One of Dorothy's aunts suffered this misfortune and returned in the trap to wait for a later train. She found the maids dismantling the bed in which she had slept and turning back the mattress. She burst into tears and said: "No sooner do I leave the house than you get rid of all traces of me." "My poor mother", Dorothy commented, "was only doing her best to organise the work of the household and she had then to take the time to sit down and console my tearful aunt." Memories of the difficulty of catching a pony in a paddock remained in Dorothy's mind and she was to allude to the problem in her novel *Have His Carcase*, transferring the recollection to her alter-ego Harriet Vane:

Harriet had often wondered how people ever managed to catch horses in large fields. It seemed so silly of the creatures to allow themselves to be taken – and indeed, she remembered distinctly having once stayed in a country rectory where it always took at least an hour for "the boy" to catch the pony, with the result that the pony-trap frequently failed to catch the train.

It was a conventional household. The family gathered in the dining-room at eight-fifteen in the morning, the servants entered and the rector said prayers. Dorothy then withdrew and had her breakfast in the nursery. She was taught at home. Lessons took place at regular hours, with a governess, and the year was divided into terms and holidays, as though she was at school. In her early years her mother took charge of dictation. She had violin lessons, at first with her father, with whom she practised in the evenings, and later from a teacher in the neighbourhood. Bobs, the canary, used to join in when she practised and she had to cover up his cage in order to concentrate on the pitch of her own notes. She also went to dancing classes, which she enjoyed. Pattern was always something she delighted in.

She had learnt to read before she left Oxford and by the age of five her handwriting is large and well formed, obviously based on "copper plate", a formal pattern which children in those days were set to copy after they had practised "pothooks and hangers". Her earliest extant letter, dated February 1899, is addressed to her mother who had gone to Oxford to visit her brother Henry Leigh and his wife Maud, the parents of Margaret. It is written with a steel dip pen and is free from blots, which shows great skill in the management of ink at so early an age. The little girl misses her mother but exhibits a sturdy independence. She has been over to Earith – a mile from Bluntisham – ("I ran all the way with my hoop") – where Mrs Hard gave her an orange. She is looking forward to violin practice with her father and is "almost sorry" she has a holiday from dictation. (Dorothy was to say later that she was a priggish child; perhaps there is a sign of it here.) In another letter of the same period she sends her mother a little painting she has done and says she will remember "about being kind to Granny". In reply to her mother's enquiry she says that the length of her pinafores is twenty-five inches. From this it appears that at the age of five and a half Dorothy was over four feet tall.

In a letter dated February 1900 we have a glimpse of the Dorothy Sayers who loved to relate amusing episodes. Remembering her mother's injunction to be "kind to Granny", she had given her a piece of butterscotch. The old lady, who was reading something interesting, swallowed it whole and it got stuck in her throat. "Aunt Mab suggested a dose of cold water to wash it down which did no good, afterwards doses of hot to melt it which finally got it down."

While she was still six, her father began teaching her Latin. She has left a charming account of her first lesson:

I do not know whether my father missed his small choristers amid the new duties of a country parish, or whether he was actuated only by a sense of the fitness of things and a regard for his daughter's intellectual welfare. I know only that I was rising seven when he appeared one morning in the nursery, holding in his hand a shabby black book, which had already seen some service, and addressed to me the following memorable words: "I think, my dear, that you are now old enough to begin to learn Latin."

The shabby black book was Dr William Smith's *Principia*. Dorothy's father sat down in the big chair, put his arm firmly round his daughter to prevent her from wriggling, opened the book and confronted her with the declension of *mensa*:

> Presumably at this point he explained that the ancient Romans had had the un-English habit of altering the endings of their nouns according as the case was altered. I have no recollection of finding anything particularly odd about this: I was far too young. Life was full of odd things, which one accepted without protest, as simple facts. A dog had four legs, a beetle six, a spider eight: why not?

Together they got as far as part 2 of exercise I, translating simple sentences into Latin; whereupon her father rose to go, leaving the book with her and telling her to learn the declension of *mensa* by heart. This done, little Miss Dorothy skipped along the stone-flagged passage to show off her knowledge in the kitchen.

Thereafter she had Latin lessons with her father every day. He used the "old" pronunciation, as may be seen from the fact that he taught her the joke: "Why are Roman sailors wicked?" Answer: "Because they are *nautae*" (pronounced "naughty"). She evidently made rapid progress for in February 1900 she ends a letter to her mother announcing proudly that she has earned a penny for reciting the future simple of the irregular verb *malo*, "at the first guess". She also says she is pleased to hear the good news from the Front (it was the period of the Boer War; the tide was turning in favour of the British and Ladysmith was relieved on 28 February) and, "would you believe it?", she read the whole of the leading article in the newspaper to Granny and Aunt.Mab. She was then six and a half years old.

It is related that Maria Brontë, another child of a parsonage, read newspapers and periodicals at the age of seven and a half and discussed the articles with her father. Dorothy, it seems, was even more advanced. Children taught at home often develop fast and Dorothy had the advantage of being an only child. As she grew older, children from the neighbourhood were invited to share lessons with her. One of these was a girl named Betty Osborne, who became a friend. Occasionally one would be taken on as a boarder. In October 1901 there is mention of a boy named Guy, who joins Dorothy and Granny and Aunt Mab in games of spillikins and beggar-my-neighbour. This was Guy Cooke, the younger brother of one of Mr Sayers' pupils at the Choir School. Mr Sayers grew fond of him and Dorothy was naturally jealous. There were the usual quarrels and tale-bearing, as is normal between siblings, and were even more likely to occur in an assorted schoolroom in which up to then one little girl had reigned supreme.

In a later letter we learn that Dorothy and Guy have been given cardboard to make armour. She has devised a coat of arms out of blue paper, cut in the shape of a shield, with a golden heart on it and the motto "To Glory or to Death". (She developed a liking for the heroic early in life.) Guy joins her at the dancing lessons and in a letter to her mother dated 29 May 1902 she relates that at the breaking up of the class they always have Sir Roger de Coverley: " . . . and so we had it yesternoon, and Guy and two others prostrated themselves flat". She adds a complacent postscript: "Miss R. thought I danced as well as any of them yesterday."

She began writing poems and also plays, which were acted, in costume and with properties, which she made. She designed and decorated the programmes, with the cast list written in ornate script. She drew and painted well and made her own Christmas cards. Out of doors, she collected botanical specimens and insects and worked at classifying them. She had an appetite for exact information and enjoyed passing it on to other people. She also liked to know how things worked. Aunt Mabel, who was an expert knitter, taught her to knit. On being promoted to four needles, on which she made ribbing, she worked out for herself why the relation of plain and purl was different from that of knitting produced on two needles. When she communicated this (quite ingenious) discovery triumphantly to her aunt, she met with the calm reply, "Yes, of course, dear."

Something which greatly excited her was the discovery that "things joined up", that one subject was connected with or even identical to another. She twice described this experience. As a young child she had read about Cyrus the Persian, who was pigeon-holed in her mind with "classical times". Then one day, "with a shock as of sacrilege", she realised that Cyrus the Persian, who diverted the course of the Euphrates in order to march along the dry river-bed into Babylon, was the same Cyrus whose exploits are blazoned on the wall at Belshazzar's feast: ancient history and the Bible had joined up. This happened again when she realised that Xerxes and Ahasuerus were one and the same. From then on lessons ceased to be lessons, they were part of everything else, history was all of a piece, compartments of knowledge, no longer watertight, merged into one another.

She experienced a similar ecstasy when, applying the principles of geometry, she located the metal corners of the tennis court which had become overgrown. This gave her a sense of "the lovely satisfying unity of things – the wedding of the thing learnt and the thing done – the great intellectual fulfilment". She would never forget the "magnificent moment when the intersecting circles marched out of the Euclid book and met on the green grass in the sun-flecked shadow of the mulberry tree".

She played tennis and croquet in the garden, skated on the river in winter, went for country walks and rode a bicycle. She sang in the church choir and played her violin at village concerts. She began to learn French and progressed rapidly once she had a French governess, to the extent that at one time she spoke French almost as well as she spoke English. She also learnt German and could converse fluently in that language with her governess, with whom she read a good deal of German Romantic poetry.

Her childhood was active and varied, with plenty of space and opportunity for self-expression. Her creative imagination developed early. She told herself stories in bed at night, sometimes speaking the dialogue audibly, to the amusement of her elders. She enjoyed hearing the English classics read aloud. Grandmother Sayers' speciality was Scott; Aunt Mabel was a good performer in the works of Dickens. Both ladies read without skipping, with the result that Dorothy, who read voraciously herself, acquired the habit of reading continuously and attentively. She had a robust taste for murderous tales of ogres and the bloodiest parts of *Robinson Crusoe*, to which she thrilled with a purely literary horror, giving imaginative assent to what she knew was fiction. Similarly, she knew her own fantasies were deliberate creations, never losing touch with her own identity as "a child in a white pinafore with a big frill round the neck".

As regards books of instruction, she was brought up, as most children of that period were, on *Little Arthur's History of England*. She also read Robert Ball's *Starland* and *The Story of the Heavens*. In 1947 she recalled, in a letter to me, "a funny little old book called *The Peasant Philosopher* (about Wordsworth's period, I suppose, but which is lost and I have never met it again), in which an elderly sea-captain instructed the precocious young hero in the principles of clock-making and of navigation by the stars".

She said in later life that she was too much cosseted by her family. In 1929 she wrote in a letter to her cousin, Ivy Shrimpton: "When we had a fire in the kitchen beam at Bluntisham, I was pushed off to church — to church! — instead of being allowed to run round and help. I sometimes wish I'd been given the rough with the smooth when I was a kid." This solicitude gave her a resentment against anxiety for her safety or well-being, so that she could scarcely be civil to anyone who expressed it. Her parents were not always indulgent, however. In a letter to me, written in 1953, she said: "I remember myself [as a child] – a half-baked little animal, running eagerly after the first pleasure that presents itself, and finding its parents now 'formidable' and now protective, according as one behaves." And in 1949, commenting on the world into which my daughter had then just been born, she said:

> My childhood world was . . . hedged about . . . with moral restrictions (expressions like "duty", "self-control", "contentment with one's lot", "obedience", "children must be seen and not heard" and "want must be your master" had not yet been relegated to the category of morbid psychology), but the controls were imposed from inside and not outside – which makes a good deal of difference.

Her parents loved the theatre and took her to London at least once a year to see a production. They encouraged her in her play-acting and dressing up and sat through the performance of her plays, to which all the members of the household were invited. On one occasion, at Christmas time, a play was interrupted by the arrival of carol singers outside the house. "Blow the carol singers," said the usually mild-mannered rector.

She loved to identify herself with favourite characters in books. Her father had read aloud to her Charlotte M. Yonge's *The Little Duke* and at once she imagined herself in the title role. Her father was Osmond and other members of the family were other characters. Once, when rebuked, she replied, "You mustn't talk like that to me. I'm Duke Richard of Normandy." Her mother thought this was carrying play-acting too far and said she was becoming rude and pert. Dorothy was hurt by her mother's literal-mindedness. Commenting on this childhood habit, she later wrote:

> I dramatised myself, and have at all periods of my life continued to dramatise myself, into a great number of egotistical impersonations of a very common type, making myself the heroine (or more often the hero) of countless dramatic situations – but at all times with a perfect realisation that I was the creator, not the subject, of these fantasies.

Concerned that she lacked the companionship of other children, her parents not only arranged that her lessons were sometimes shared; they invited cousins to stay – Margaret Leigh and Gerald and Raymond Sayers. Her favourite cousin was Ivy Shrimpton, another

Dorothy at twelve with her family outside Bluntisham Rectory.
Standing, left to right: her father, Ivy Shrimpton, her mother; seated,
left to right: Aunt Gertrude Sayers, Grannie Sayers, Aunt Mabel Leigh.
(Marion E. Wade Center)

niece of her mother's, who had been brought up on a farm in
California. She was eight years older than Dorothy, "old enough to
seem like a grown-up person and young enough to be a real companion". Dorothy was five years old when she first saw her, but it was
not until she was eight and Ivy sixteen that they got to know each
other well. From then on Ivy was a regular visitor in August and
often at Christmas as well. She possessed a knack with younger
children, being full of a wisdom of a rough-and-ready kind, with a
talent for creating toys out of string and cut paper. Her great merit
was that she would discuss any question seriously and thoughtfully.
If she did not know the answer she said so, and would put forward a
theory as a theory, open to argument and refutation. This suited
Dorothy and the two cousins got on well. Ivy contributed to
Dorothy's literary education by introducing her to Louisa M.
Alcott's *Little Women* and, somewhat unexpectedly, Barham's
Ingoldsby Legends, which she was able to make intelligible and
enjoyable to the younger child. She herself wrote poems and stories,
contributing to a magazine which Dorothy produced with the help of
her governess. Although so much older, she treated Dorothy as an
equal and in some ways Dorothy was the more advanced. There

19

Dorothy as Athos *(Marion E. Wade Center)*

exists a remarkable letter in which Dorothy, aged fourteen, sends Ivy, at her request, an explanation of the minor scales, both the harmonic and the melodic. Dorothy calls it "a treatise", which is indeed what it is, astonishing in its clarity and grasp of musical theory. Perhaps her father taught her this as well as the violin (he assumed at an early stage that she would be a musician) and it may be that some of the phrases in the letter are his. In several of her letters there seem to be snatches of the conversation of grown-ups, which Dorothy takes over as her own, in the way that children often do, especially when they are trying to impress someone older than themselves.

An important aspect of Dorothy's friendship with Ivy was their shared imaginative and creative enjoyment of the novels of Alexandre Dumas. Dorothy began reading *The Three Musketeers* in French at the age of thirteen and was immediately captivated by the romantic tales of the picturesque heroes – Athos, Porthos, Aramis, d'Artagnan – loyal, gallant, always in love, ever ready to draw sword in defence of the king and to punish traitors. Dorothy surrendered wholly to the power of the narrative, the swift dialogue, the dashing adventures, above all to the charm of the apparel. As she had done earlier with the characters out of *The Little Duke*, so now, with even greater exuberance, she peopled the rectory with characters out of Dumas. She identified herself with Athos, the hopeless lover, hiding a broken heart behind a melancholy smile. (It is said that Thackeray would have liked to read about him from sunrise to sunset.)

The entire household and all her friends were enlisted in the game. Her father was King Louis XIII and her mother was Cardinal Richelieu. Betty Osborne was Aramis, a French girl who was staying at the rectory was Porthos – rather a heavily-built girl, one deduces. The governess, Miss Hamilton, was d'Artagnan. Aunt Gertrude Sayers played Madame de Bois-Tracy. Ivy, who at first took this part, later became Marie de Rohan-Montbazon, duchesse de Chevreuse, the beloved of Athos. The Chapmans (gardener and laundry-maid), the cook and the parlour-maid were all allotted suitable roles, such as grooms to the musketeers. The garden echoed to ferocious French oaths and the clashing of wooden swords.

It is not known how active a part the grown-ups consented to play in this creative fantasy. Mr Sayers, at least, went so far as to wear a false beard in his impersonation of Louis XIII. With Dorothy it was all-consuming. She *was* Athos, as an actress is a character on the stage. She acquired somehow, obviously with her parents' help, a magnificent costume, in which she was photographed – plumed hat, ruffles, slashed sleeves, bedizened walking-stick and a curled moustache, which she twirls with elegant nonchalance. The effect is most attractive and the pose struck is that of an accomplished actress. Other photographs of Dorothy as a child are not flattering but this one shows how pretty she could look. There also exist several snapshots of the same period, taken out of doors – one of two musketeers seated side by side on a bench and one of Dorothy, again as Athos, standing at her/his horse's head – even the pony, Linda by that time, was brought into the game.

The musketeer costumes were used occasionally for other dramatic productions. Writing to Ivy, she describes the preparations for a performance of a scene from a comedy by Molière:

> Do you remember, when you were here, our once acting a scene out of *Les Femmes Savantes* up here in my quarters? We are going to do that in costume. Porthos and I are the men in costume of the musketeer period, and Miss Hamilton and Aramis take the women's parts. We have been hard at work making a curly wig for Porthos, as, of course, his hair is too long; it was a job, but it is done at last. It is made of jute. I, of course, wear my own hair, curled at the ends. Miss Hamilton is in black, with a big lace ruff, standing out behind. My genius invented the ruff, or rather collar. It is on a cardboard foundation and is a great success. It should, of course, be wired but that was too much trouble. Then we did her hair up in long ringlets, like Henrietta Maria, with Mrs Chapman's goffering irons, the same that we used for my moustache. Miss Hamilton does look so nice – quite pretty, though she is not really so. She has a quaint Louis XV type of face that goes splendidly with curls.

As well as acting, producing plays and making costumes and props and programmes, in addition to regular lessons with her governess, Dorothy was also writing long narrative poems, some of which she illustrated in pen-and-ink or water-colour. She wishes Ivy were there to talk to about them. When she has time, she makes copies to send her. In a letter dated 23 February 1908 she says she is at work on a complex poem, "Songs of the Crown", divided into sections, one being entitled "Lyrics of War" and another "The Prisoner of War". The latter concerns the feelings of a prisoner in a dark and dismal dungeon. "He begins hopefully and cheerfully. He next relapses into despair with suicidal tendencies – abandoning these gloomy ideas after a while he decides to wait for his release."

In the same letter she gives a lively and detailed description of a concert held in the nearby village of Somersham:

> It was a lovely concert. They had got a splendid tenor rejoicing in the name of d'Arcy de Ferrars – down from London – he sang most beautifully. He was a stout, grey-haired, middle-aged person, with a seal-ring and a seraphic smile. Then there was an enormously fat lady, with an endless double chin, vanishing away into her neck . . .

Dorothy played the violin – three pieces and an encore . . . "for they encored me – they did indeed" – this in spite of the disconcertingly springy platform, laid across two trestles: "at every stroke of the bow the platform shook and danced and swung and sprang and jumped and rolled and tossed like a ship at sea". This sentence is perhaps typical of a schoolgirl's exuberant enjoyment of a string of words, but there is also something characteristically Sayersian about it in the triumphant swing of the rhythm.

We also learn from her letters to Ivy what books she is reading. On her thirteenth birthday her mother gave her *Roland Yorke* by Mrs Henry Wood, which she considers one of that writer's best books, "and that is saying a good deal". A year or so later she is enjoying "two lovely books by Stanley Weyman": *A Gentleman of France* and *Under the Red Robe*. The Conservative candidate, Oliver Locker-Lampson, stays the night and Dorothy has a delightful talk with him about books. He turns out to be an admirer of "the Master" (i.e. Dumas) and also of Molière. After a second visit, knowing that the family lacked a set of Molière's comedies, this perfect guest sent "a dear little (second-hand) edition, in seven volumes", as a present. At this period Dorothy has discovered Thomas Beddoes, whose favourite subject was death "treated in a gruesome manner". She finds his work "most curious and very ghastly" and is impressed by its grimness. Years later she was to cull quotations from Beddoes' unfinished drama, *Death's Jest Book*, as epigraphs for the chapters of *Have His Carcase*, and she devoted several pages of appreciation of the beauty of his fragmented work in *The Mind of the Maker*.

At the same age, rising fifteen, she is "diligently studying" seventeenth-century English poets, no doubt under the direction of her governess. She likes Milton, though she finds him difficult. At Easter her father gave her an edition of Pope and she is enjoying *The Rape of the Lock*, which must have been more fun for her than *Paradise Lost*. She has read the greater part of Butler's *Hudibras* and enjoyed it, "although, like all the productions of the period, it is spoilt by its coarseness in parts". This censorious comment sounds like an echo of the governess.

Her writing continues to be ambitious and prolific. She mentions ballads about a character named Sir Roland. She sends a few stanzas, descriptive of the approach of night: "The constellations are all in their right places; I used a star-map to be certain." She has several cantatas in her mind's eye, on the subject of the musketeers. "For a cantata one wants a nice, compact little story, like that of the queen's diamonds, and it is difficult to find." The structure is ambitious, with stanzas to be set to music for solo voices and for chorus. She has written one for the last of the series, with the death of Athos for its leading feature. She enjoys writing cantatas because they afford such facilities for varied versification: "One does not get tired of the same metre. That is my trouble with Sir Roland – I grow sick of the metre. Some day – not yet – I am going to write a story of adventure called *My Master's Son*, but I am not ready for that yet. The plot is still ripening in my mind." A rough draft of the first chapter of this work shows that it was to have been written in prose. Subtitled "A Romance of the 17th Century", it has a preface in verse.

She is also at work on what she calls *The Comediad*, composed of cantos and containing some "fine old Spenserian words". She is compiling notes to the poem. Another work of this period is a well-devised comedy entitled *The Wit*, in accomplished verse, displaying a mastery of rhyme and metre. *Aldovrando*, set in Spain, is a drama in verse and prose, with a rhymed prologue and a final chorus to be sung to the air of "Bonnie Dundee". Fair copies of these early works exist in notebooks, penned in elaborate script. She assumes the name of Athos and one of the cantatas is dedicated "To the Genius of the Master", namely Alexandre Dumas.

It is evident that already in her teens Dorothy intended to be a writer, preferably a poet, and that she was practising a variety of verse forms and techniques. She even looked forward, humorously, to being famous. When she was thirteen she wrote and produced a play entitled *Such is Fame*, in which a very young authoress (played by herself) has just written a successful book and gets into difficulties because she has drawn one of the characters from a combined portrait of two of her aunts. In one of her letters to Ivy, after signing herself "Dorothy (alias Athos)", she adds a facetious postscript:

You must keep this letter, for the signature will be valuable when the fame of "Athos" is spread throughout the world of letters. We shall see it in the *Strand* or some other mag, thus:

"Fig. 19 is a very interesting and unusual specimen taken from a most valuable autograph letter now in the possession of Miss Ivy Shrimpton."

An anecdote is related by someone who knew Dorothy at this period: "I mean to be famous", she is alleged to have said, "and I will let no-one stand in my way." Whether this was said seriously or self-mockingly is not known, but there is little doubt that she knew she had a creative imagination and a talent for writing.

Dorothy's budding sexuality is also reflected in her letters to Ivy. There are two distinct aspects of this. On the one hand she dramatises herself in the part of Athos, hopelessly enamoured of the fair duchesse de Chevreuse (Ivy), to whom she writes flowery love letters and poems in French. On the other hand, there is a young man in whom she takes an interest and her letters about him are different. His name was Cyril Hutchinson. He came regularly to spend the summer in the neighbourhood with his parents, who were on visiting terms with the Sayers family. Ivy met him and they all played croquet together on the rectory lawn. They nicknamed him "Dull Red", from the colour of the ball he played with. Dorothy flirts with him, holds long conversations with him standing by the garden gate, puts a rose in his button-hole, dreams of him and confides to Ivy that she is suffering from "Dull-Reditis". One summer, when he is expected, she wonders if he will propose: "Shouldn't we all be flabbergasted if he *did*!" Ivy responds in kind but after a while seems to think that Dorothy is perhaps dwelling too much on Cyril and he is thereafter referred to as "the Forbidden Subject".

This seems normal adolescent behaviour (as it was then). So too does the crush she developed for an unattainable Adonis, namely the actor Lewis Waller, a handsome matinée idol, much admired by many others besides Dorothy, for there was a Keen on Waller Club. A few days before Christmas in 1908, when Dorothy was fifteen and a half, her parents took her to London to see a performance of *Henry V*, in which Lewis Waller played the title role. (It was one of his great parts.) On Boxing Day Dorothy wrote to Ivy:

Just a line to tell you that I have fallen madly, hopelessly, desperately in love with the splendidest, handsomest, loveliest, most magnificent man in England. He has the most delicious voice you ever heard, and the most wonderful and glorious eyes ever seen. And his smile! Adorable! Ravishing! Exquisite! I have four photographs of him in my bedroom and I kiss them every night!

One way of managing the emotions is to pretend that they are more powerful than they actually are. Dorothy was to make use of this discovery on several occasions.

Some of her letters to Ivy touch on serious topics, such as religion and morality. In one of her longest, a letter covering several days, in a section dated 1 March 1908, she takes Ivy to task for intolerance and lack of charity. We do not know what remark of Ivy's prompted this but Dorothy's response seems inspired either by something she has read or, possibly, by one of her father's sermons. Professing great hesitation and fear of offending her cousin, she wrote:

> I think, old girl, that you are just a bit inclined to form a harsh judgment . . . of other people . . . I think you are a little apt to say, in effect: "What this man did was an offence against morality. It was therefore wrong and inexcusable . . . " Dear old girl, get out of the way of thinking that. It is terribly closely allied to Pharisaism, which, you know, is the one thing our Lord was always so down upon . . . I shouldn't like to feel, Ivy, that supposing some time I sinned a great sin, that I should be afraid to come to you for help. Only, unless you would try to make allowances for me, I'm afraid I should.

Dorothy was then only fourteen years old. Sixteen years later, she did indeed need Ivy's help and was not afraid to turn to her.

That, however, was far ahead. The immediate future was disturbing enough. The musketeers will walk no more side by side in the garden or fight together for the king. The grand bond will be broken for ever. Dorothy is going away to school.

CHAPTER 2

School

Dorothy's parents realised that their lively-minded and talented daughter would benefit from a university education. Oxford was the obvious choice, but how to get her there? To gain entry and preferably a scholarship to one of the recently-founded colleges for women (Somerville for choice) she would need more experienced teaching than a governess could provide. Accordingly they looked about them. A day-school was out of the question: there was no convenient transport between Bluntisham and nearby towns such as Huntingdon, Stamford or Cambridge, where high schools existed. Had they lived in or near London they would have had a range of excellent schools to choose from, the North London Collegiate, for example, or one of the schools set up in the late nineteenth century by the Girls' Public Day School Trust. St Paul's Girls' School, a relative newcomer, had opened in 1904. Some London schools took boarders but in the end Mr and Mrs Sayers decided on the Godolphin School in Salisbury, which had the advantage of the fresh air of Wiltshire and a beautiful prospect from its situation on the top of Milford Hill. The headmistress, Miss Alice Mary Douglas, had built it up from modest beginnings. She was helped by her sister, Miss Lucy Douglas, who became a house mistress. Together they assembled an experienced staff. When Dorothy joined there were about 200 pupils, over one half of whom were boarders. In many ways it was an excellent choice.

The decision had been taken in June 1908 but for some unknown reason it was arranged that Dorothy should join the school in the second term of the following year. Plans and preparations, the buying and making of school clothes went on all during the autumn, filling her with expectation and, no doubt, with some apprehension. She had never lived away from home before nor attended a school of any kind. As a farewell treat, her parents had taken her to London to see *Henry V* and she had had the exhilarating experience of falling in love from afar with Lewis Waller. Ivy had come to spend a few days with her after Christmas and Dorothy had written rapturously in advance of the long talks they would have together by the fireside, telling ghost stories, reading poems to each other, laughing at their old jokes and pledging to Dorothy's success at Salisbury. A few weeks later, kitted out and with recent happy experiences to cheer her, she arrived at the Godolphin on 17 January 1909.

In an unfinished, partly autobiographical novel, entitled *Cat o' Mary*, Dorothy describes the experience and feelings of Katherine Lammas, who, at a similar age, goes to boarding-school for the first time. In factual details the work bears a close similarity to Dorothy's early life and much can be learnt from it. Since it is partly a work of fiction, however, it would be a mistake to identify Dorothy and Katherine in every respect. Some allowance has to be made for selectivity and the process of self-dramatisation which formed a part of Dorothy's creative writing. At the very least the unhappiness and discomfort attributed to Katherine should be balanced against the letters which Dorothy wrote home to her parents. It has been suggested that these masked a deep unhappiness and it is true that in later life Dorothy said that as a schoolgirl she felt like a fish out of water. As an expression of her feelings *at the time*, however, the letters present a somewhat different picture.

From the first letter onwards, dated 24 January 1909, the tone is amused, happy, even enthusiastic, the description of people and events lively and entertaining. Of course she is looking forward to the holidays — what child does not? — and of course school is not the same as home, but she is finding it quite jolly. Her mistakes and confusion in the first few days are minimal and she describes them with a characteristic talent for comical self-portraiture. There is a very nice girl in her house, named Violet Christy, who was kind to her when she first arrived. She is fond of theatricals and books and Dorothy suspects that she writes. Please may she invite her to stay at Bluntisham during the Easter holidays? She is sure her parents will like her. And may she please have some sweets to hand round, as the others are always giving her chocs and things, and she'd like to return their favours.

Life at school is far from dull. She begins violin lessons and is at once invited to play first violin in the school orchestra: "They have really an awfully good band . . . We are at present learning a suite by Purcell and a Minuet by Schubert . . . It was great fun yesterday. I enjoyed it thoroughly." (In *Cat o' Mary*, Katherine is depicted as being less talented at the violin than she was led to believe and, to her father's disappointment, she asks permission to give it up. This did not occur in Dorothy's own case.) There is dancing in the hall on Saturday evenings and Dorothy joins in with gusto: "It was simply glorious. I had a scrumptious time, and a most killing dance with Fanny Maud" (the nickname of her form mistress, Miss White). Dorothy wrote out the dance programme, which she kept. Dated 28 March, it shows that she partnered Miss White in the Lancers, danced four waltzes, the two-step, and played the violin for two other items.

The mistresses produce a play, which turns out well, to Dorothy's surprised admiration. Her house mistress, Miss Payton, is putting on a house play, a variation of the story of Little Red Riding Hood, in which the wolf (to be played by Dorothy) turns out to be a prince in disguise. Will her mother please send her some scraps of her musketeer costume? The play is a great success. Violet Christy was "awfully good as the grandmother with her hair powdered with flour".

It has been said that she was unpopular at school and a misfit. It is true that she was not the conventional type of schoolgirl, good at games and experienced in communal living. Nevertheless, she had a great deal to offer. Her command of French was exceptional (this may have aroused resentment at first), she played the piano and the violin, she could sing, act and produce plays, she could write, she was lively and exuberant, above all, she enjoyed *sharing* enthusiasms with her friends – the very reverse of a loner. Hearing that her cousin Margaret Leigh is unhappy at boarding-school, she remarks that she was afraid Margaret would mind being parted from her mother. "If she can't even eat, I'm afraid she must be in rather a bad way." Not so Dorothy! She eats "enormously" and has two helpings of everything. "They feed you jolly well here; we had apple-tart today."

Her descriptions of the mistresses are in no way carping or hostile. She admires one for her figure (the games mistress), another for her lovely auburn hair, another for her command of language. She refers to them by their nicknames and uses the slang current among her fellow-pupils. One mistress, scornful of Dorothy's crush on Lewis Waller, reveals that she has a "crackation" on Forbes-Robertson, much to Dorothy's glee. She very much likes the "quaint little mathematics mistress", who is said to be a dissenter and a radical and to consider plays immoral, so much so that she wouldn't attend the mistresses' play or have anything to do with it.

29

Her parents are amused and tolerant about her adoration of Lewis Waller. They send her photographs of him, for which she thanks them, saying, "I am very much envied here because I get so many things by post." She has no inhibitions about telling them about her feelings towards Miss White. Here was a clear case of *schwärmerei*, in which other girls also indulged. Miss White was aware of it and evidently amused. She also seems to have known how to deal with it. When Violet Christy asked for her autograph she wrote the following inscription in a large hand which filled the page:

> "Laodamia"
> ll. 73-78
> Wordsworth

Violet and Dorothy thumbed a volume of Wordsworth and found the following lines:

> Be taught, O faithful Consort, to control
> Rebellious passion; for the Gods approve
> The depth, and not the tumult, of the soul;
> A fervent, not ungovernable, love.
> Thy transports moderate, and meekly mourn,
> When I depart, for brief is my sojourn.

"Miss W. was simply bursting with amusement over her little joke. We were all most frightfully amused." There was no sophisticated talk in those days of lesbians and gays. It is natural, Miss Climpson thinks to herself in *Unnatural Death*, for a schoolgirl to be *schwärmerisch* – in a young woman of twenty-two it is thoroughly undesirable. This would seem to have been Dorothy's own view of the matter. In *Cat o' Mary*, she comments on a corresponding stage in the life of Katherine Lammas:

> Katherine's pash ran its course with no more deviation from traditional lines than an L.C.C. tram. She suffered exquisite pangs and enjoyed herself enormously. Here she could dramatise life to her heart's content. The ridicule that she inevitably encountered she did not resent, for she was playing a chosen part, and the laughter of the audience was the world's tribute to the accomplished comédienne.

Life at the Godolphin offered many other excitements and enjoyments apart from emotional fixation. One of them was music. Early in her first term there was a lecture on the programme of a concert which the older girls were to attend. "Miss Mixer (consult prospectus) gave the lecture, and Fräulein Fehmer and Miss Atkinson played parts of the programme to illustrate the lecture. Fräulein Fehmer is my piano mistress. She is an old dear. I like her awfully." The concert was a piano recital by the fifteen-year-old pianist Ernst Lengyel: "Of course, he plays marvellously." What, one wonders, became of this "wonderful young pianist"?

Dorothy makes progress in her own piano lessons with Miss Fehmer and forms a great admiration for her, greater even, it would seem, than for the fifteen-year-old prodigy: "We had a lovely treat on Friday. Fräulein Fehmer . . . gave a Chopin concert in the Hall. It was simply lovely. She plays divinely. I never enjoyed a piano concert so much in my life, I think. She played such awfully pretty things. She is very fond of Chopin, and interprets him splendidly."

Years later, during World War II, Dorothy Sayers wrote a tribute to her German music mistress. She recalled her vividly:

> . . . stiffly built, with a strong square face, lionish, slightly blunted, as though the hand of the potter had given a gentle push to the damp clay; she wore eye-glasses, and a shawl round her shoulders in cold weather; her hair was straight and dark, combed back over a pad; she had strong square hands, grasping the keys easily from middle C to the major third above the octave, blunt finger-tips and wide flat knuckles; she used a rather unorthodox and very powerful action of the whole forearm, so that the wires sang under her touch like bells.

And in a poem entitled "Target Area", she imagined the Lancaster bombers over Frankfurt, where Fräulein Fehmer then lived. She had kept in touch with her during the years, sending her a copy of each of her novels as they came out. And now, in the poem, the memories of her playing Chopin at the Godolphin are recalled with poignancy and love:

> There is a particular nocturne
> that I cannot hear to this day without thinking of her;
> when it is rendered
> by celebrated musicians over the aether
> I see the red-brick walls, the games trophies,
> the rush-bottomed chairs, the row of aspidistras

that garnished the edge of the platform, and Fräulein Fehmer
gowned in an unbecoming dark-blue silk,
lifting the song from the strings with a squaring of her strong
shoulders;
the notes on the wireless are only an imperfect echo
of that performance . . .

After the war, Dorothy made enquiries and, discovering that Fräulein
Fehmer was still alive, arranged for food and clothing to be sent to
her until she died in 1948.

But that was far ahead. Dorothy evidently made good progress
with her piano lessons and her parents were sufficiently satisfied to
send her a "magnificent music-case". "Fräulein Fehmer was so
pleased, she nearly jumped out of the window for joy." Violin lessons
continue. In December 1910 her teacher asks her as a personal
favour if she will also learn the viola as she is organising an orchestra
in Salisbury and needs another viola player. Dorothy does so, even
though it means learning another clef. The following year the
Godolphin School orchestra is invited to join in a concert of all the
orchestras of London schools: "to the end of her days your daughter
will be able to say that she has played the violin in the Albert Hall".
The concert took place on 13 December 1911. It was evidently quite
an honour for the school, as "only two other country orchestras,
Oxford and Winchester, have been asked to play". At the end-of-
term concert she was asked to sing a solo, "so you see I am getting
quite a list of public engagements!"

There were school expeditions, to Old Sarum to view archaeological remains, picnics in the country, a visit to Bournemouth. On
24 May 1909, in celebration of Empire Day, the school marched four
abreast in forms to the market place in Salisbury to salute a flag
which had been sent by the children of Salisbury, New South Wales.
On the death of Edward VII the school attended a memorial service
in the cathedral: "The music was simply glorious – Beethoven's,
Chopin's and other Dead Marches and the Dead March in *Saul*. 'O
God our Help' was something too thrilling for words. I do think that
is without exception the finest hymn ever written." In the autumn
term of 1910 Sir Ernest Shackleton lectures on Antarctica in the
County Hall in Salisbury and the school troops down to hear him:
"It was simply wonderful – I had never seen a hero before, and it was
rather a thrilling experience. He is extraordinarily British – very quiet
and drawly-voiced and quite absolutely splendid. We are all in love
with him, and buying postcards of him." Dorothy writes a sonnet

about him and sends it to him – and receives a reply, which she duly copies out in a letter to her parents.

The girls were allowed to visit friends, with their parents' permission, on any Saturday or Sunday afternoon. Aunt Gertrude comes to visit her and takes her out to tea. She is hoping her father can come down for her birthday, which falls during a weekend in 1910. Instead, her parents arranged for her cousin Raymond to take her to see *The School for Scandal* performed by Tree's company in London. Dorothy thoroughly enjoyed herself and she found Raymond a delightful young man. He also took her to the White City and they finished up with the scenic railway. She wrote to her mother: "My dear! You would die if you went on. It's simply awful – we enjoyed it thoroughly. You've absolutely no idea of the terrific speed at which you rush down! I only squealed once, and that was because my hat nearly blew off." This was in 1909, when there were still horse-drawn buses in London, and the sensation of speed, such as we now take for granted, had yet to be experienced. Raymond evidently enjoyed his cousin's company for in a subsequent letter Dorothy tells her parents that he is coming to Salisbury to see her and is planning to stay over the weekend. "We are going to hire a bicycle if it's fine and go for a ride on Sunday." The house mistress, Miss Payton, asks if her parents know about it and they, in their turn, seem to have misgivings, which they express. Dorothy returns an aggrieved letter: "It really is absurd. As if one couldn't go for a bicycle ride with one's own cousin! If he could haul me over London on Tuesday surely he can see me in Salisbury on Sunday. Girls are always having cousins and people to see them."

The situation seems to have been resolved for Dorothy's next letter to her parents is once again affectionate and amiable. Throughout she is considerate, anxious not to run up bills beyond what is necessary, reassuring them about her health when she has any minor indisposition. In the autumn term of 1910 she begins to suffer from headaches and thinks she may need glasses: "I'm afraid I'm going to make you a bit worried, but it's much sensibler to write. Don't be alarmed – it's not very awful, only I've been having rather a nasty headache and run-down feeling the last few days. I went to bed and had a rest on Friday and I'm taking a tonic and I'm feeling all right again now."

She goes to have her eyes tested in Salisbury and finds that she has astigmatism in one eye, though she has "beautiful long sight". The upshot is, she is to wear spectacles for reading – "not for always, thank goodness!"

One of Dorothy's greatest joys was to be involved in putting on a play. Sometimes even plays she writes herself are considered good enough to perform:

> I am simply head over ears in the play – to say nothing of work. Every spare moment I am writing programmes for all I'm worth. I am doing simply lovely ones, in exact imitation of real theatre programmes. The play is written and the costumes have arrived, but there is still heaps and heaps to be done, and I am simply overwhelmed with business. You see, of course, I have to stage-manage as well. Violet helps, but I have most to do in the way of arranging and writing and painting things, to say nothing of writing the play, learning my part, etc, etc.

This letter has no date, but would seem to have been written during her second term. Her parents co-operate to the extent of sending off her swords "beautifully packed", though her father makes a mild enquiry as to whether all this time spent on the play might not interfere with work for her exams. Dorothy writes back reassuringly. Her confidence in her ability to manage several activities at the same time was not misplaced, as her examination results were to prove.

In a later letter, probably written during the autumn term of 1909, there is news that another play by Dorothy is to be produced. This is the melodrama, entitled *Aldovrando*, written at Bluntisham before she went to school. The characters have the romantic names of Rinaldo, Estella and Donna Marta; there is also the figure of a Chorus, who is to perform in a red robe, while Dorothy plays her fiddle softly. She needs a great number of properties, for which she apologetically asks her parents. "*Do* let me pay part at least of the carriage. I should feel *so* much happier and more comfortable if you would."

There was also the excitement of visits to Salisbury of a company of French actors. On 13 October 1909, during Dorothy's second term, they performed Molière's *L'Avare* in the County Hall: "What shall I say about Wednesday evening? That it was glorious? perfect? ripping? delightful? killing? splendid? beautiful? No adjective could properly describe the delightfulness of it all . . . It was too lovely for words! The only drawback is that . . . " The "drawback" was that Miss White asked Dorothy to write "a really racy account" of the production for the *Godolphin School Magazine*, which she did, in French. The following year, on 4 November, the French actors come again, this time to the school itself, where they perform another play by Molière, *Le Bourgeois Gentilhomme*. After the performance Dorothy has the delightful experience of conversing in French with the manager, Monsieur Roubaud. He makes her feel grown up (she is, after all, seventeen by this time):

> One gets sick of school sometimes and being "Dorothy" to everyone, and blown up by everybody, from Miss Douglas to one's Games Representative. You can't think how pleasant it is to be smiled and bowed to, and called "Mademoiselle", and paid compliments, and be told that you are *"si charmante"*, and that a pleasant and vivacious little Frenchman is *"ravi d'avoir fait votre connaissance"* and hopes to see you next year . . . and to be asked with an accent of polite incredulity whether you are really English, and told that "Mademoiselle" speaks French *"à ravir"*.

The following term Dorothy is busy stage-managing what she calls a "Molière festival", to commemorate the anniversary of his death on 17 February. It was her own idea and it met with the whole-hearted approval of the headmistress. There is to be a performance of the third act of *Les Femmes Savantes*. Dorothy is to play Trissotin: "Sweetest Mummykin, if you could make me a new pair of red sateen breeches, as wide as the yellow pair, I should never be able to thank you enough. I shall want the old red pair as well. Lastly, will you ask Daddy to send the Saint George Suite for 2 violins."

Whether this tribute to Molière ever took place is not known, for in the next letter, in which she encloses the programme, Dorothy mentions a case of measles: "I do hope nothing may happen to prevent the play coming off." The disease spread through the school and Dorothy too succumbed, contracted double pneumonia and almost died. Her mother came to help nurse her through the crisis. Sitting by the bedside she must have thought tearfully of the red sateen breeches, which she had perhaps made by then for her enthusiastic, stage-struck daughter, now lying delirious and close to death. A specialist was sent for but did not arrive. The local doctor, acting on his own initiative, administered a saline injection, and the crisis was passed.

Dorothy spent the first stage of her convalescence in the Spero Nursing Home in Salisbury. Her mother remained, and speeded her recovery by reading poetry to her, to the surprise of the doctor, who suggested a nice detective story instead. Before leaving she was well enough to give a dramatic reading of the part of Richard III to the nurses, her lack of breath lending verisimilitude to the agitated feelings of the character. She spent the remainder of the term at Bluntisham in order to recuperate further and did not return to school until the following autumn. The summer of 1911 was exceptionally hot, the hottest on record until the temperature of 98.2° Fahrenheit was surmounted in 1990. No doubt the rectory was cool, with its stone-flagged corridors, and the garden shady under the mulberry tree. Nevertheless, it must have been an enervating period and Dorothy's recovery was no doubt delayed. It is known that her hair fell out – she evidently inherited thin, frail hair from her father – and when she went back to school in the autumn of 1911, after a break of six months, she was obliged for a time to wear a wig. In all likelihood it was partly for this reason that her parents had deferred her return.

Ralph E. Hone is surely right when he stresses the embarrassment this must have caused her. "The chagrin of facing herself in the mirror in this condition, especially at this time of her life, must have been hardly bearable." The very fact that she did return is remarkable. James Brabazon comments: "There must have been much heart-searching before she went, for her parents knew, this time, what they were sending her back to and what she felt about it." If this was so, it is surprising that her letters *continue* to be cheerful. She was then eighteen, an age at which it is normal for a young woman to feel that she has had enough of school. And yet, on 22 October 1911, she writes excitedly about a production of *The Merchant of Venice*, in which she is to play Shylock:

Will you please send me Daddy's beard and 3 pairs of breeches and your little old brown cloak and a false nose some time before the end of the month – and bag Auntie's Shakespeare with the pictures of Irving and E. Terry and send it to me at once, please. I must have a nose – and I can't get one here, but if you, either of you, happen to be in Cambridge or London – oh! I beg and beseech that you will step into a make-up shop and ask for a Jewish (not a comic red) nose, and instructions how to put it on . . . and oh! could you step into the toyshop – Hill's – in St Ives and get me 3d. worth of grey jute for a moustache?

In the next letter, dated 29 October, she announces that all she asked for has arrived and adds: "I don't think I shall need a wig, unless I had a nice grey half-bald one; my own hair is rather thick on top for Shylock." From this it is evident that by the end of October her hair had grown sufficiently for it to be no longer necessary for her to wear a wig. The embarrassment, acute as it must have been, can have lasted only about six weeks.

An additional excitement this same term was that the French players were coming again. They were to perform Molière's *Les Précieuses Ridicules* and *La Poudre aux Yeux* by Labiche. She doesn't think she will have an opportunity to talk with Monsieur Roubaud this time as they are performing in a hall in the town. Nevertheless, after the performance Monsieur Roubaud, who had recognised her, waited at the door to greet her. One of the teachers forbade her to speak with him and Dorothy protested and did in fact reply when he addressed her, for which she was reprimanded. Seething with indignation, she went straight to the headmistress on her return. Miss Douglas took her part and said that other members of staff had misunderstood the situation. Dorothy was incensed, not so much by the needless anxiety on their part as by their snobbery towards the acting profession. She wrote a sonnet about it and further expressed her indignation to her parents:

> against those good, devout Christians (Heaven save the mark!) who applaud the play and scorn the player. They are as dangerous to their own religion as to the morality of the theatrical profession; they drive the one into reckless loss of self-respect, and bring the other into disrepute – Pharisees!

Dorothy took the standing of the theatrical profession very much to heart. She had been delighted to discover, the previous year, a kindred spirit, named Molly Edmondson, whose ambition was to go on the stage: "We exchanged ideas on the subject of the establishment of a National Theatre, and the elevation of the drama to its proper place as a noble and inspiring art." About this time Dorothy was thinking that she would like to train for the stage herself and she had been talking it over with some of the staff. One teacher was encouraging but Miss Douglas "rather thinks I should probably be a greater success as a dramatist than as an actor".

The scorn which Dorothy expresses for the pharisaical mistress who tried to prevent her from talking to Monsieur Roubaud raises the important question of her attitude to the religious atmosphere of the Godolphin, and particularly her feelings about her confirmation. The evidence on this matter is contradictory and requires scrutiny.

In 1930 Dorothy wrote to her cousin Ivy about the religious upbringing of her son John Anthony, who was then six years old. It appears that Ivy had asked if she would like him to be baptised and she replied:

> Being baptised against one's will is not nearly so harmful as being
> confirmed against one's will, which is what happened to me and
> gave me a resentment against religion which lasted a long time . . .
> The cultivation of religious emotion without philosophic basis is
> thoroughly pernicious – in my opinion.

In *Cat o' Mary*, on which Dorothy began working in 1934, the
feelings attributed to Katherine Lammas about religious teaching at
school are uncompromising in their hostility:

> The awkward stutter and hush that accompanied the word
> "Gawd" was even more indissolubly attached to the words
> "communion" and "sacrament" . . . To these rites, which were
> held in secret, a strong flavour of the indecent seemed to cling. Like
> the central act of marriage . . . the central mysteries of religion
> were by common consent exceedingly sacred and beautiful, but on
> the other hand indelicate, and only to be mentioned in periphrastic
> whispers.

Dorothy's letters home give no indication that she felt uncomfortable about the religious atmosphere of the school. It is not that she
remains silent on the subject; on the contrary, she goes out of her
way to volunteer that she likes what she finds there in that respect.
On hearing from her father that her cousin Margaret has to learn
collects every Sunday, she replies expressing sympathy and goes on:

> Which reminds me to tell you that that sort of thing is very nice
> here; one is not bothered a bit about religion etc., etc. We have
> prayers in the Hall every morning – just a psalm, a hymn, a short
> piece of gospel and a few prayers, not in the least long or tiring. We
> have no collects or anything of that sort to learn on Sundays.
> Evening prayers at school are quite short, too, and, then, just
> before we go to bed each house has a short reading and a prayer
> said by the house mistress – in our case, Miss Payton. So you see
> we aren't much bothered.

She then adds: "I am so glad you've got *Orthodoxy*. I am not
surprised to hear that Chesterton is a Christian. I expect, though,
that he is a very cheerful one and rather original in his views, eh?"
Religious observance at the Godolphin was organised in three ways.

First, there were the daily prayers in the school itself, as Dorothy described them to her father. For communal worship the school attended either St Martin's Church or the cathedral. She is critical of the way the litany is pointed at St Martin's and of the congregation's habit of dragging the prayers. But she loves the services in the cathedral. She is sentimental about the choir boys with "darling little ruffs round their necks – they're just sweet!" Please may she have her hymn book from home, as she wants to join in the singing of hymns on Sunday evenings and can't possibly sing treble. On one occasion one of her father's hymn tunes was sung at school and was "hugely admired".

On 5 November 1911, when she has returned to school after her illness and when, according to Brabazon, her true feelings about it have been admitted to her parents and she might be expected to write frankly if she has not done so before, she volunteers that she has a great admiration for a Mr Johnston, who preaches "so splendidly":

He possesses the gift of preaching in a rare degree, the power of using beautiful words and of delivering them with effect – Miss Douglas calls him a poet – I think she is right –; he has also a peculiarly "appealing" voice and a pleasant dignity of bearing. We are simply desolated to lose him.

It is unlikely that Dorothy's parents would have given instructions for her to be confirmed with other candidates at the Godolphin without consulting her. In *Cat o' Mary*, Katherine expresses reluctance about it to her parents and they disappoint her by persuading her to agree. This does not seem to have been Dorothy's case. In an undated letter, probably written early in 1910, she says without more ado: "There isn't any news this week, except one or two odds and ends about Miss White. I am to be confirmed this year – we go to Canon Miers' (if that's how he spells himself) Confirmation Classes on Tuesday and Friday." This reads like an untroubled reference to an arrangement she has taken for granted. Later she tells her mother that the school is providing the caps and veils and that the service will be on Wednesday in Holy Week, in the cathedral. And she adds light-heartedly, "Isn't it funny, it's the same day as the boat-race." In the same letter she says: "We've just been to Cathedral to hear the Dean preach – the darling! He always preaches on the first Sunday in the month – he was simply ripping this afternoon – angel! He is the most adorable old dear, he really is." Her description of the ceremony itself is wholly favourable and gives no hint of embarrassment:

39

It was an awfully nice service, and everything was most beautifully arranged . . . It was a huge affair – about 200 candidates [28 from the Godolphin] . . . the Cathedral was absolutely packed . . . we sat on the N. side, in the 3rd row from the pulpit – I was on the outside of our row. Our veils were most awfully nice – chiffon – very simple with just a little ruche at the top . . . I suppose one ought not to think about such things, but I do so like to see things in really good taste – ours most certainly were that. We went up to the altar a whole row at a time, and the Bishop moved along and did us in twos, only I was the odd one at the end of the row, so I was done alone . . . The Bishop's address was quite nice, but not awfully exciting – I wish our Dean were a Bishop! . . . I had a small talk with Canon Myers last night – he is ripping. [*In Cat o' Mary*, Canon "Tusher", who prepares Katherine for confirmation, is described as fat, wheezy and unappealing – anything but "ripping". This suggests that Katherine's experience belongs more to fiction than to truth.] We are all to make our Communion together on Easter Sunday – the whole (confirmed) School with us – I think, don't you, it would be nicest to have it then, with the School, and Miss Douglas would like it, especially as I am in the VI, etc. . . . You see, being at school, one feels rather out of it if one doesn't do things with the school.

The letter ends with a postscript: "I never can write about my feelings – that's why I haven't." This is a most uncharacteristic remark. Dorothy writes continually, effusively, about her feelings. What she must mean is that she can never write about her religious feelings. Possibly at the time of the ceremony she experienced none; or possibly she experienced a gush of pietism which disconcerted her.

In *Cat o' Mary*, Katherine Lammas' confirmation is dismissed coldly as follows: "She wrote in duty bound to her parents giving a detailed account of the ceremony. But that would not do by itself. She chewed her pen. 'I won't say anything about feelings', she wrote. 'I can't express those very well!'" These are almost the exact words of Dorothy's own postscript to her parents.

Brabazon is convinced that at the time of her confirmation Dorothy felt the same embarrassment and sense of hypocrisy which she later attributes to her fictitious character Katherine Lammas and that Katherine's distaste for the religiosity of her school was also Dorothy's. He is convinced, moreover, that *all* her letters from school are a sham:

In her letters home she found it quite impossible to speak of her mental and physical distress. She knew that her parents would want her first of all to be happy at school, and secondly to look forward to the holidays. She could say neither of these things with any truth, but these are what her letters said. And to cover her lack of candour she filled them with factual information about where she kept her books, the names of the girls in her dormitory, her lessons and her progress with the detested compulsory games.

Yet her letters contain far more than that. Her excitement about the plays she is writing and producing, her pleasure in playing her violin in the school orchestra, her delight in the visits of the French actors, her urgent requests for permission to invite her friends home to Bluntisham – can this be all pretence? If so, Dorothy's ability to create and sustain a fictional character began early.

The resentment against religion which Dorothy mentioned to Ivy in 1930 appears, if we are to rely on *Cat o' Mary* in this connection, to have been a distaste for the Evangelical pietism which characterised the religious atmosphere of the Godolphin. She seems to have sensed that there were two kinds of Christianity, the sentimental, which made her feel uncomfortable, and the Christianity she glimpsed in the lovely language of the Scriptures and in the great churches, where the name of God was surrounded "with scarlet and blue and gold and strange birds and flowers in painted missals . . . In the book called *Orthodoxy* there were glimpses of this other Christianity, which was beautiful and adventurous and queerly full of honour." And elsewhere in *Cat o' Mary* she wrote: "A strict course of exact and dogmatic theology might well provide the intellect with a good, strong bone to cut its teeth on; but . . . to worship with the understanding had already, in Katherine's school-days, become unfashionable." That is Dorothy L. Sayers writing in 1934, by which time she had long found her spiritual home in the Anglo-Catholic form of Christianity, and when it was indeed characteristic of her to worship with the understanding. It is unlikely that the sixteen-year-old Dorothy thought so clearly about the matter. That her feelings were confused at the time of her confirmation is not, after all, surprising.

One aspect of her school life has not been mentioned – namely work. She says very little about it in her letters. There are a few references to exams – she is taking German – in French literature lessons they are concentrating on Racine – Miss Douglas wants to talk with her mother about her Oxford scholarship. She expresses occasional boredom and anxiety but on the whole her allusions to work are off-hand. Nevertheless, she was not wasting her time. Each autumn term Miss Douglas read out the results of the Oxford and Cambridge Joint Board Higher Certificate Examinations. On 17 September 1909 she announced that six full certificates had been obtained, and six distinctions, three by one girl, D. Sayers. In the autumn term of 1910 she was again mentioned as having gained distinction. Finally, at the beginning of the spring term of 1911, Miss Douglas announced that Dorothy Sayers had come top in all England in the Cambridge Higher Local Examination, with distinction in French and spoken German.

These are the bare facts. Nothing is said in her letters of the imaginative and intellectual rapture she experienced in studying French literature under the guidance of Miss White. There are revealing sections in *Cat o' Mary* which suggest how Dorothy's critical and literary talent developed. The set texts for the Higher Certificate Examination were Molière's *Le Misanthrope*, Corneille's *Le Cid* and Racine's *Britannicus*:

> Ground in the slow mills of textual criticism, these works acquired a new and more luscious savour . . . When the work itself will stand the strain and when the mind to which it is presented for trituration happens to delight in that particular exercise . . . the result is satisfaction of a particularly rich kind. If once you have seen the wood as a whole, it will afford only an added delight to number and admire the trees. When Katherine sat down to prepare a passage from Molière she experienced the actual physical sensation of plaiting and weaving together innumerable threads to make a pattern, a tapestry, a created beauty.

One day in summer, as she sat revising *Le Misanthrope*, she was pierced with the unexpected beauty of a line in an ironic speech by Eliante (Act II, scene iv):

La pâle est aux jasmins en blancheur comparable

The meaning is that a lover will exaggeratedly compare the pallor of his lady to the whiteness of jasmine – not a likely context in which to find rapture. But find it Dorothy did. The symphony on the vowel "a" explained it partly and the fortuitous associations of the word *jasmins*:

She sat up. It was as though the whole scent of summer had poured suddenly through the open window and intoxicated her. For the first time she heard the mower, smelt the roses, noticed the rich buzz of the satisfied bees, became aware that the sky was blue and drenched in sunlight. One line with mysterious power to unlock the heart. Why? The old recurrent surging-up of some inner well-spring of strength and splendour flushed Katherine's cheeks, mounted to her head, made her instantaneously and unbearably happy. She held the world between her hands and turned it over and over, like some curious jewel.

This capacity for rapture, which is attributed here to Katherine Lammas, was indeed Dorothy's own and would carry her victorious through many a set-back in life. It was also to make her creatively responsive to the expression by poets such as Dante of what she was to call "the Beatrician Vision".

For an unknown reason she did not complete the autumn term of 1911. On 26 November she mentions a scarlet-fever scare. She is sick of school now and would like to catch the illness if it meant coming home. Perhaps she did, or showed signs of coming down with it. At the beginning of the next term Miss Douglas announced: "It was a great disappointment that Dorothy Sayers had to leave on account of illness. She is going to try at home to win her scholarship." It has been suggested that she suffered some form of nervous breakdown, but there is no evidence for this. She was certainly well enough to keep up her work at home, continuing to be tutored by Miss White by correspondence. In March 1912 she sat for the Gilchrist Scholarship to Somerville College and was successful. Her achievement (which was in large measure due to the inspired teaching of Miss White) was duly commemorated on a plaque in the school hall.

She returned in September 1912 for Commemoration (the annual Old Girls' reunion) to receive a prize for photography, a hobby she had pursued at school, in addition to all her other activities. As a farewell gesture she made a contribution to the Old Godolphin Girls' Scholarship Fund.

CHAPTER 3

Oxford

As a young woman Dorothy was very interested in her appearance and took a lot of pleasure in clothes. When she was eighteen her mother passed on to her a compliment about her looks. Dorothy replied:

> How *very* kind of *dear* Mrs Wilde to say I was good-looking! She's completely mistaken – but that's quite beside the point. It's only that when I am properly dressed I give a sort of spurious impression of good looks – it's more a kind of smartness than anything else – Heigh ho! I'm longing to put on a trimmed hat again!

She was also interested in the effect she made on young men. When her father takes a candidate for ordination as a pupil she longs to come home to meet him, but not in her school hat, that will never do: "I'm dying to break his celibate heart with a hopeless passion. How lucky I wasn't born beautiful – I should have been an awful flirt." As it happened, that young man proved quite uninteresting and she looked forward to better things at Oxford.

She went up on 11 October 1912, her trunks packed not only with books but also with as many pretty clothes as she could afford, including a costume for a fancy-dress party, which, she told her parents, was much admired. Indeed, the phrase "my dress was much admired" occurs almost as frequently in her letters as references to her work. She was tall and slim, with a long slender neck, dark hair and blue eyes. Her short, blunt nose and long upper lip troubled her, but she was pleased with her mouth, which was wide and well shaped and had a dimple at each side. Dorothy, like most young women, was realistic about her feminine charms, such as they were,

Dorothy imitating Hugh Allen, 1915 *(Marion E. Wade Center)*

and looked forward happily to using them. It was all part of being young, at a period when the art of flirtation was understood on both sides as an amusing game of badinage and witty repartee.

Her social life began with a swing. The fancy-dress party at Somerville broke the ice. In Oxford itself there were already a number of people who knew her: her Aunt Maud Leigh and cousin Margaret, who also won a scholarship to Somerville; two elderly Sayers cousins, Eleanor and Gertrude; and friends of her parents, Dr and Mrs Mee, Dr and Mrs Dixey, who had an undergraduate son named Giles; and Mr and Mrs Brabant, whose son Frank was also at Oxford. Most useful of all, her cousin Gerald Sayers was at Christ Church.

Gerald comes to tea with her at once and is "particularly amiable". She goes to tea with the Dixeys: "Giles was very nervous and dropped the scones into the ashes and the chocolate cakes on the hearth-rug. Otherwise all went well." She is invited back to have tea with Gerald at Christ Church, where anchovy toast is served. She meets the Brabants but they bore her rather: "They are so keen on Suffrage societies and activities in general." Their son Frank "is not bad, but, I fear, rather an earnest young man. I should think he got too many good works at home."

Dorothy was not an earnest young woman. Quite the contrary. Early in her first term, Cousin Eleanor calls on her and tries to interest her in the Christian Social Union and then writes to her about "the terrible social and economic evils of the present day . . . Up till now your clever young mind has been too much occupied with other matters to enable you to think of these matters . . . " Dorothy throws "the beastly thing" on the fire and writes a rude letter in reply. But Cousin Eleanor is not easily crushed and she returns several times to plague Dorothy with her well-meaning advice and concern for her spiritual welfare.

Her first two terms were plagued not only by Cousin Eleanor but also by certain examinations which she had to pass in order to be admitted to an Honours degree course. One of these was known as "Responsions" or "Smalls", for which Latin and Greek were required. Though she had begun Latin at an early age she had let it lapse in preference to French and German and now needed to be coached. Much later she described her tutor as follows:

> As soon as I took residence in Oxford, I was sent to a warrior called Mr Herbert May, with instructions that I was to be crammed through Smalls. Mr May lived in a narrow, semi-detached house in the gloomier purlieus of Oxford, in a perpetual atmosphere of snuff. With this he refreshed himself all through his coachings; and I would not grudge him a single pinch of it, for his life must have been a hard one. So far as I know, he spent all his time with people like me. He was the indefatigable seagull, for-ever winging his way through the clashing rocks of Latin Prose and Greek Unseens with a fleet of dismal and inexperienced Argonauts thrashing the seas at his tail. A kindlier and more imper-turbable man I never met. In two terms he accomplished what my school-teachers had not ventured to undertake in four years.

Dorothy disliked exams though she knew how to do well in them. (That was one thing which she later admitted she had learnt at the Godolphin.) To help her through "Smalls" she asks her father to send her a box of cigarettes she has left behind, for she has made "a grand discovery . . . There is absolutely no objection to smoking, except in Common Room. Isn't that grand? One better than Girton, eh?" It was somewhat advanced for a woman to smoke in 1912 but her parents had evidently raised no objection and her father duly sent the cigarettes. (Her mother also smoked.)

There was one other preliminary examination she had to pass, namely Divinity Moderations, known as "Divvers". For this she needed a knowledge of New Testament Greek, in order to translate from St Matthew and St John; she was also required to mug up the subject matter of the Acts of the Apostles:

> By the way, I hope you don't mind if I plough in Divvers, because I've only just begun to look at the work, and it's really very catchy and stupid – and what on earth *does* it matter whether it was S. Matthew or S. Luke who told the story of the Gadarene swine [it is related also in the Gospel of St Mark], or who the brethren of Our Lord precisely were? . . . Having read two Gospels with more attention than I had ever before given to the subject, I came to the conclusion that such a set of stupid, literal, pig-headed people never existed as Christ had to do with, including the disciples.

An amusing early comment from the future author of *The Man Born to be King*.

In her second term she is attending German classes, which she finds boring, except for the attractions of the teacher, Dr Willoughby, with whom she flirts and who is by no means unresponsive. When she takes her viva in German she quite deliberately uses her feminine charm and is not at all abashed in telling her friend Catherine Godfrey about it:

> Herr Jost was quite nice to me. I first of all got dreadfully muddled with some kings and dates. When he had disentangled them for me he said: "I was very much surprised" (my heart sank into my boots) "to see that you considered Schiller's *Robbers* a pleasing play". I thought to myself, "Now is the moment for an individual touch", and relying on the fact that I had put on my best coat and skirt and a becoming hat, I assumed my most womanly smile and said, "Oh! don't you think it is?" He smiled – I was encouraged to give my reasons – he smiled and agreed. At any rate he passed me.

Not all young women at that period took the trouble to dress attractively. Dorothy is disgusted at the pose of "naturalness" affected by her erstwhile school friend, Eleanor Chase, now at Girton College, Cambridge, who comes to stay with her in Bluntisham during the Easter vacation in 1913. Dorothy writes to Catherine Godfrey about her:

> We were all rather annoyed with her . . . because she has adopted

Friends at Somerville:
Dorothy is second
from the right
(*Marion E. Wade
Center*)

that dreadful "pose of being natural" which is the posiest pose I
know. You know what I mean. She dresses all anyhow and does
her hair hideously, and sprawls about all loose at the joints in ugly
attitudes and wears no stays. She is also loud in her assertions that
she "hates" nice clothes and "can't bear" jewellery and thinks it
"an awful bore" to make herself look decent. It is such a pity
because she is a very good-looking girl – and it's all put on, you
know. She's just as self-conscious in her ungainliness as the vainest
person in her elegance, and talks as persistently about clothes, to
abuse them, as other people do to gloat over them.

Dorothy, on the contrary, believes that "it is every woman's duty to
look as nice as she can, especially when brought under the eye of
undergraduates". Going to lectures at the Taylorian, she puts on a
"most useful" little round hat: "I find that one must be respectable
when one's the only woman or almost the only woman there, because one's so conspicuous." On returning to Oxford, immediately
after the visit of the depressing Eleanor Chase, she wrote home:

Everybody has come up fearfully smart in new clothing. Elsie

[Henderson] has got a very pretty fawn coat and skirt, with a coat rather like mine, and a new hat of which she is inordinately proud. We have been (all of us, I mean, not only Elsie and I) talking about nothing but clothes all the time . . .
2 o'clock Back from church. I took Elsie, and our skirts were so tight it took us about 10 minutes to kneel down . . . I wore my hat with the pink scarf, having got my hair just right for it and the brim at the right angle, and everybody admires it . . .

She seems to have gone to church regularly, even though her thoughts were not always on the sermon. She heartily agrees with a preacher at St Barnabas who is "sick to death of controversy". One Sunday she and Elsie go to church in Cowley (whether in the same tight skirts or not, is not recorded) and she is greatly taken with the "wonderful sweet quality" of the choirboys' voices, which she prefers to the choir at Magdalen. She often goes to evening service at New College Chapel but her reason for that has to do with worship of another kind.

The organist at New College was Dr Hugh Percy Allen, who was also the conductor of the Oxford Bach Choir. Dorothy joined this immediately on arrival. She had a good contralto voice and had had experience of choral singing at school. She had also been taking singing lessons in Bluntisham before going up to Oxford. The audition therefore presented no difficulty. At once a note of rapture is sounded and continues through her letters, not only about the music but especially about the conductor. A peak of excitement was reached in the summer term of 1914, when a festival of four concerts was held, dedicated exclusively to the works of J. S. Bach. Notice of this was served on the members of the choir a year in advance and Dorothy gives her parents details of the programme:

    I.   Three Cantatas
    II. Orchestral and Choral Concert to include the Magnificat
    III. Three Motets: "Be not afraid"
                     "Come, Jesu, come"
                     "Sing to the Lord"
    IV. The Mass in B minor

"Isn't it perfectly scrumptious?" she exclaims, using the same adjective she had used as a schoolgirl to describe a school dance. And she adds: "Will you please send me my 'Be not afraid'? I left it in my bedroom, or in the drawing-room."

50

Aesthetically, as well as emotionally, the Bach Choir seems to have been Dorothy's most enriching experience at Oxford. Her infatuation for Hugh Allen was demonstrated in an exaggerated manner and became something of a joke among her friends. Nevertheless, the experience of rehearsing under the baton of so expert and exacting a conductor, of taking part in the performance of works of such beauty and complexity gave a new dimension to her response to creativity and art. It was to remain with her all her life.

When the Bach festival eventually took place, a disaster occurred in the rendering of the third of the three motets, "Sing to the Lord":

> In one of those tiresome places where you come in fortissimo just off the beat, the whole of the first choir, including myself, got stage-fright together and never came in at all. I have never lived through such a ghastly moment . . . then everybody in desperation sang wildly whatever notes they could hit on, and the organ came in, and by a miracle the thing rightened itself.

But the Mass in B Minor was superb – "it was more exciting than you can possibly imagine . . . I don't know what the audience was doing at the end, but I know that the choir went simply mad."

Hugh Allen, later Sir Hugh Allen, K.C.V.O, became Oxford Professor of Music in 1918 and that same year Director of the Royal College of Music. Born in 1870, he was a married man of forty-two years of age when Dorothy first knew him. He seems to have taken a fancy to a number of his female choristers, Dorothy being among them, and it was his habit to invite them to join him in the New College organ loft. Dorothy accepted several times and made no bones about telling her parents. They for their part seem to have expressed some concern, for in one letter she says, "Don't be perturbed, and for Heaven's sake don't think anything horrid about him." His interest in what Dorothy calls "the long procession of little tame cats who have adorned his organ-loft in succession" seems to have been rather more than fatherly, however. On one occasion he took a ring from Dorothy's finger, "the chrysoprase ring Aunt Maud gave me" and, fooling about with it, nearly lost it by dropping it down between the organ-pedals. Dorothy seems to have thought she was in control of the situation. Probably it intrigued her to see how far she would trust herself to go with him. She undoubtedly flirted with him, made her admiration obvious and dressed deliberately to catch his eye. She makes herself "the most ravishing little cap to wear in New College chapel . . . executed in black ribbon and net, and it is so becoming the Bursar thinks it is quite unsuitable for a place of worship!" Her Aunt Maud gives her a beautiful red cloak for her birthday. When Dr Allen accepts an invitation to dine and lecture at Somerville, Dorothy asks her parents: "Do you think I had better have my red cloak to shine in? I'm told the Doctor has a very quick eye for women's clothing!" She will be dining with him that evening at High Table. Her parents send the cloak. "I mean to look jolly nice!" Dorothy says when she writes to thank them.

It is an amusing experience for a young woman to test her powers of attraction and no doubt Dr Allen was more of a challenge and more interesting than most of the undergraduates. She looked on it as quite a triumph to have got him to dine and lecture at Somerville and was satisfied that she had come out the winner of their equivocal and possibly dangerous game. His part in it was the more dubious. It would be interesting to know, if he later read her novels, whether he was made uncomfortable by the reference in *Gaudy Night* to the university rule forbidding "girling" by Senior Members, and whether he was reminded of the flirtatious young Dorothy in the scene in *Have His Carcase* in which Harriet Vane vamps Henry Weldon.

Dorothy's friendship with Giles Dixey became intense at one moment. They exchanged poems which they sought to improve by mutual appreciation and criticism but Dorothy wished the relationship to remain friendly only. Another undergraduate, named Arthur Forrest, who was a musician and a member of the Bach Choir, enjoyed talking with her about music and seemed to have serious intentions, of which Dorothy was aware. "Shall I make a bid for him?" she asks her parents, and from the levity of the question it is apparent that her feelings were not involved. When war was declared Arthur Forrest was sent out to the Dardanelles. Dorothy felt very anxious but when news of his death reached her, she was grieved but not heartbroken. Writing to Mrs Dixey on 17 December 1915, she said: "I suppose if he had lived he might have been quite good, musically, but it's all the same now." She composed a brief poem in memory of him, entitled "Epitaph for a Young Musician", which was published in the *Oxford Magazine*.

Her life at Oxford was active and varied. She takes dancing lessons and gets on well with a fashionable American dance known as the Boston. She learns to scull and to punt. She enjoys Eights Week (when the college boats compete) and is invited on to the Balliol barge. She goes to a lecture by G. K. Chesterton, whom she admires, and one by G. B. Shaw, whom she abominates for his "clever half-truths". She goes to lectures by J. A. J. Carlyle on the eighteenth-century novel. She attends a lecture on Dante by H. A. L. Fisher. Never having seen any Gilbert and Sullivan operas, she goes to five in one week. She does very little work and that with extreme reluctance. She has heard of a malady which if indulged in theologians term a sin – *aboulia*: "that is what I suffer from". By her third term she has made an alarming discovery, which she confesses to her parents: "Do you know, it is dreadful, but the longer I stay in Oxford, the more certain I am that I was never cut out for an academic career – I was really meant to be sociable."

She is certain she will fail the exam in German which is coming up, but she does not. Without realising it, she has been learning how to work and how not to work. Her friend, Elsie Henderson, on the other hand, over-works. Dorothy is convinced during one vacation that Elsie is working five hours a day, instead of puffing cigarette smoke into novels, as she herself is doing. "What a thing it is to have a well-regulated mind!" But Elsie suffers a breakdown and has to be nursed carefully back to health, in which process Dorothy assists.

In spite of social distractions, Dorothy's urge to write does not desert her. In her first term, she and a friend named Amphy Middlemore start a society

. . . among about six of the First-Years, for mutual admiration. We meet every week to read our own works. Our first meeting was last Wednesday. I read "Earl Ulfric" and "Peredux" and another girl read two things and Amphy provided the refreshments. It was really quite a success. I hope we shall be able to keep it up.

The date of this letter is 10 November 1912, that is, one month after the beginning of term. This is the earliest mention of the celebrated Mutual Admiration Society (M.A.S.), from which it is plain that it was started by Dorothy herself and one other girl and that the phrase "mutual admiration" was in her mind from the beginning. What Dorothy was obviously looking for was someone, or better several people, with whom to exchange and discuss work in progress, as she had done for so long with Ivy Shrimpton. She always needed this encouragement and stimulus. She was not a private, solitary person but a very gregarious one and this is particularly true of her as a writer.

Beneath all the frivolity runs a strong current of creativity. Quite soon the Mutual Admiration Society plan an album to contain their best compositions. One of Dorothy's contributions is to be "The Gates of Paradise", which she copies out to send to Muriel ("Jim")

Jaeger in July 1913. "I am not pleased with all of it, but I thought the twisty trees and Satan and the Head of the Crucified came out better than I expected." Strangely, the "twisty trees" and "the Head of the Crucified" disappeared from the final version, as published in her first volume of poems, *Op. I.* Another contribution from Dorothy (there were to be three) was a fragment from a long allegorical poem entitled "Sir Omez", on which she was then working. "He is going quite strong, by the way." She has an idea for a lovely incident with a vampire in it for the canto dealing with Lust:

> I wish there were a bit more variety about methods of tackling the seven deadly sins, but I think I'd better stick to them, because unless one has some sort of scheme, one can go wandering on for ever making up adventures and fights, and that becomes wearisome. Sir Omez is just preparing to meet Sir Maljoyous (gluttony – that is, I suppose, self-indulgence in general) . . . I do hate work – I wonder why. It is so inconvenient.

It is fascinating to see Dorothy Sayers concerning herself at this early date with an allegorical presentation of the seven deadly sins and discussing the advantage of a firm structure to prevent her poem from meandering. It is no wonder that she knew so well what she was dealing with when she came to translate Dante thirty years later.

A week after writing to "Jim" Jaeger, she sends another letter to Catherine Godfrey ("Tony"), telling her also about "Sir Omez" and confessing that she has done no academic work:

> Elsie [Henderson] makes me quite ill. She is steadily working through all those books we had to take home, and I simply daren't tell her I've done practically nothing! It's not exactly that I am idle, but I'm interested in something else the whole time. At present I am deep in the writing of an allegorical epic, of which I have completed the first canto. I began it last vac, and as it is distinctly Christian in tone I started out to mention it to Elsie, when she asked what I had been doing. I said: "I have started work on an epic" – she said: "What on earth do you want to do that for? Nobody wants to read epics." So I felt crushed and took my epic elsewhere. Then I have got to write something for M.A.S., and it has got to be in prose; I write prose uncommonly badly, and can't get ideas.

She says the same thing in her next letter to "Jim" Jaeger:

I cannot get any ideas for prose. Prose is a thing . . . I only write upon compulsion, and then badly. You have probably noticed already my tendency to periodic expression . . . in poetry I have to sit upon it, but in prose it ambles away with me.

She does not realise that in her letter-writing she reveals a decided talent for unselfconscious, lively prose, such as she will later use in her novels. Her description of the degree-giving ceremony in Oxford (the Encaenia) in her letter to Catherine Godfrey, is so good that it deserves to be quoted almost in full. Some of the details are of particular interest in connection with *Gaudy Night*.

We got to the theatre [the Sheldonian] about 11 o'clock . . . there was straw laid down in Broad Street as if someone was ill, and the streets were simply full of people . . . We gave up our tickets at a door, and panted, jostling each other, up a narrow staircase, emerging at length just behind one of the rostra. We got splendid places – couldn't have had better – we dodged the pillars, so that they blocked nothing. We could see the door, the whole of the area, the Vigger-Chagger's [Vice-Chancellor's] seat, both rostra and the organ . . . Till 12 o'clock we watched people coming in . . . and we listened to the organ, which varied a severely classical programme with "Hitchy Koo" (vociferously applauded) and "Auld Lang Syne". Then the procession arrived – very Oxfordy and scarlet and imposing – Spooner looking as mad as usual – Dr Dixey looking like a walrus – the (not yet) Poet Laureate frightfully distinguished and ornamental – among the doctors. The V. Chancellor looked ripping – most awfully refined and mediaeval, and he has a high, melancholy, well-bred voice that just exactly suits a scarlet gown and flat Tudor-looking black velvet cap. Then there were the new M.A.s in their robes – the Archbishop rather nice and humorous, Dillon and the other service man, looking pokerish and martial, the sweet old Regius Professor of Greek at Cambridge, very frail and doddery, with a queer, scrunched up face like an apple, and the German chap from Bonn, very German – his hair erected like a crest . . . Then Dr Heberden, with his proctors one on each side of him, started off in Latin, to open Convocation and propose the conferring of degrees. When he had finished, the Public Orator – namely Godley, the man who writes such screaming poetry you know – started off to "present" the Honorary doctors . . . When he'd finished, the Vigger-Chagger addressed all the assembled doctors in a sing-song little speech, beginning something about "Does it please you doctors of the University that so-and-so should be admitted to such-and-such a degree – *Placet-ne?*" and then he took off his cap; then said "*placet*" without leaving time for anyone to make an objection if he wanted to, and put it on again.

Her description of the winner of the Newdigate prize is particularly interesting:

His poem was on "Oxford", and he recited it so nicely. He had a very clear pleasant voice . . . He read from the rostrum close to us, so we saw and heard splendidly. His poem was not frightfully full of genius . . . but there was an appealing sort of youthfulness and pathos and Oxford feeling about it that made it quite charming . . . Charis and I fell head over ears in love with him on the spot. His name is Maurice Roy Ridley – isn't it a killing name, like the hero of a six-penny novelette? He has just gone down from Balliol, so I shall see him no more. My loves are always unsatisfactory, as you know.

But she did see him again and by then his image was famous all over the world. In 1935, while Dorothy and Muriel St Clare Byrne were working on the play *Busman's Honeymoon* and casting about in their minds for an actor to play the part of Lord Peter, Dorothy went to Oxford to deliver a lecture entitled "Aristotle and the Art of Detective Fiction". While there, she wrote to Muriel: "My dear, my heart is BROKEN! I have seen the *perfect* Peter Wimsey. Height, voice, charm, smile, manner, outline of features, everything – and he is – THE CHAPLAIN OF BALLIOL!!!" His name was Roy Ridley. He and Dorothy became friends and it is said that she grew irritated with his exploitation of his likeness to Wimsey. In truth, she had no right to be irritated, for his image had entered the deep recesses of her memory in 1913, to lodge there for nearly a decade, after which he rose into her conscious mind, she did not realise from where, and became, in outward form, Lord Peter Wimsey.

Among Dorothy's many raptures at Oxford religious ecstasy found no place. She had no experience of conversion, having always been "inside", as she later expressed it. Though she told Ivy Shrimpton that being confirmed "against her will" had given her a resentment towards religion, it is evident from her letters from Oxford that she made no formal break with religious observances. She was unresponsive to organisations such as the Christian Union.

Roy Ridley, the physical
original of Peter Wimsey
(Balliol College, Oxford)

Her cousin Eleanor Sayers had attempted to enlist her interest in it –
to her disgust – and her friend Catherine Godfrey appears to have
done the same. Writing to her from Bluntisham on Good Friday
1913, Dorothy says:

> Certainly not! Speaking as a baptised and more or less educated
> member of the Catholic Church of Christ as in England by law
> established, certainly not! The C.U. is no more a necessary cor-
> ollary of Christianity than the Inquisition. The only necessary
> products of Christianity are those which Christ appointed. He did
> not encourage misty theological discussion, but taught by author-
> ity and by example. The early Christians did the same. They met to
> pray and to exhort. Thus the Catholic Church in the Middle Ages.
> Discussion of beliefs and dogmas came in, I suppose, with the
> Renascence, but rested on the authority of the Church.
>
> The C.U. appears to me more like a product of Darwinism. Yes
> – you must aggressively save souls, but you will never do it by
> unprofitable argument. I know little about the C.U. but it seems to
> me, from all I hear of it, to begin from the wrong end. Christianity
> rests on Faith, not Faith on Christianity. If you have read *Ortho-
> doxy* you will see what I mean.

Her last comment is the key to her development in this respect. The previous term she had been reading Chesterton's *What's Wrong with the World*, parts of which she found "very pleasing". In later years she acknowledged her indebtedness to Chesterton. When she had read *Orthodoxy* at school she had been inspired by the image of Christendom as a heavenly chariot which "flies thundering through the ages, the dull heresies sprawling and prostrate, the wild truth reeling but erect". But for this invigorating vision, she told a friend long afterwards, she might in her schooldays have given up Christianity altogether. She puts the matter less vehemently, more gently, in 1915, when writing again to Catherine Godfrey, who has decided to go in for teaching: "I think you'll make a simply topping teacher. Be nice and sympathetic and like yourself to gawky young souls growing out of their spiritual clothing, like mine was when I was at school." The interesting point about this comment is her use of the past tense, which suggests that she had found spiritual clothing at Oxford which fitted her better. If so, it was of an intellectual kind. What she resented most was any attempt to persuade her into religious emotions she did not feel. Not only Cousin Eleanor but also Aunt Annie was concerned about her spiritual welfare. One Sunday in March 1914, Dorothy wrote as follows to her parents:

> Gloom has come upon me. I went to tea with the aunts at Leckford Road (Eleanor was not there) and Aunt Annie walked back with me, and thought it her duty to enquire after my soul's welfare. She will probably send you an account of my spiritual state, so I may as well prepare you. I do not at all mind discussing my soul – I do it every day – but I do not like doing it with very earnest people of narrow experience. They are so apt to be hurt, or shocked or surprised or worried. I let her down as gently as possible, but it's so difficult to make people see that what you have been taught counts for nothing, and that the only things worth having are the things you find out for yourself.

She explains that she finds it difficult to choose between the many different explanations and theories of life:

> There are more different brands offered to us than probably there ever were to Aunt Annie . . . Among them is the Christian religion in which you happen to have been brought up. Your friend so-and-so has been brought up in quite a different way of thinking; is a perfectly splendid person and thoroughly happy. What are you going to do about it? – I'm worrying it out quietly, and whatever I

get hold of will be valuable, because I've got it for myself; but really, you know, the whole question is not as simple as it looks. All this in case Aunt Annie should think fit to make any alarming statements about "contentedly living without the means of Grace", which sounds so horrid and mediaeval somehow.

She adds a postscript: "Don't worry about my soul – but above all, don't let anyone else worry you about it."

There are very few references to her academic work, and those few are laconic. She enjoys her tutorials with Miss Mildred Pope and finds the study of Old French and the sound changes from Classical to Vulgar Latin through into Old and Modern French "quite thrilling, but whirly-whirly". The first term of her second year is extremely busy, but Miss Pope is pleased with her progress and relaxes with her pupils enough to hold an All Hallows Eve party. "We bobbed for apples and chose husbands blind-fold (I am doomed to marry a widower) and jumped over candles to see which months would be happy." There is one delightful glimpse of Miss Pope (later to be immortalised as Miss Lydgate in *Gaudy Night*) enjoying philological problems which Dorothy has brought her: "I rejoiced Miss Pope's heart the other day by bringing her four puzzling constructions culled in the course of my reading. She couldn't explain any of them completely, and was scrumptiously happy piling up grammars and dictionaries and scratching her head over them." In her next letter she writes: "Miss Pope says she likes my method of work, which is encouraging of her. She is a nice person."

Socially, Dorothy's life at Somerville was a success. Vera Brittain, who went up in 1914, has left a delightful picture of her in her moving work, *Testament of Youth*. She found there were two classes of second- and third-year women students: those who examined every atom of you and those who pretended not to see you. Dorothy, who belonged to the former group, was friendly to first-years and Vera Brittain took an immediate liking to her: "A bouncing and exuberant young female who always seemed to be preparing for tea-parties, she could be seen at almost any hour of the day or night scuttling about the top floor of the new Maitland building with a kettle in her hand and a little checked apron fastened over her skirt." This tallies perfectly with the impression created by Dorothy's letters to her parents.

Her first two years at Oxford coincided with the last of the pre-war period. Life was never to be the same again, but realisation of this came slowly. Dorothy and two of her friends – Elsie Henderson and a Miss Lawrance (possibly a Senior Member to act as chaperon) – were so unaware of the international situation that they arranged to go on holiday to France in August 1914. The local chemist in Bluntisham at least said he hoped they would get back safely, but Dorothy went blithely off to Tours "for the next seven weeks". She crossed from Southampton to Le Havre on the night of 30-31 July. On 1 August Germany declared war on Russia and the following day invaded Luxembourg.

She wrote at once to say that they would probably find themselves back in England in a week. Madame Larnaudie, the landlady (39 rue Laponneraye), may find it impossible to get provisions, as "we are in a state of siege". Travel is impossible at the moment, because all trains have been stopped as far as ordinary passengers are concerned. She finds it intensely exciting. Tours is full of soldiers and sailors and groups of people on street corners talking about war. "In a restaurant it seemed odd to see the umbrella-stand stuck full of swords." Food is short and unofficial rationing has begun. Horses are being requisitioned and the milk-woman may not be able to deliver milk any more. She was writing on the first day of the mobilisation of the French army. The next day Germany declared war on France.

This thing is like a novel by H. G. Wells. The whole world is going to war, and it has happened in two days! On Wednesday, nobody here had any idea it was coming . . . or Mme Larnaudie would have sent to put us off. Nothing was really known till Thursday, when we had already started. Personally, I am delighted that she was not able to warn us. You have no idea how frightfully exciting it is being here, right in the middle of things.

Mobilisation will not be completed till 16 August, so there is no hope of returning until after that date. Dorothy is much impressed by the patriotism and organisation of the French. They are expecting great things of England. "One feels rather glad to be English." Two Germans and a French curé are shot for being spies: "I'm sure traitors *ought* to be shot." Troops keep passing through Tours. "It is simply marvellous how orderly and quiet everyone is here in France. One is really proud to be allied with them." She admires the resistance of the Belgians, " . . . immensely valuable to us because it gives us time". The French are enthused by the thought of regaining Alsace-Lorraine: "Mme Larnaudie is so thrilled at the idea of seeing the end of the German nightmare, as she saw the beginning in 1870, that sometimes — being by nature very excitable — she doesn't know what to do with herself." So the letters from France continue, one a day, filled with vivid detail and a delighted sense of being in the centre of things.

Elsie Henderson falls ill and Dorothy and Miss Lawrance behave towards her with the utmost consideration. When at last arrangements can be made for their return, Dorothy, always compassionate about illness, asks her mother if she may bring Elsie to Bluntisham to rest. She warns her that Elsie may be ill there, but her mother agrees and all three travellers arrive at the rectory on 25 August.

The Oxford to which they returned was filled with Belgian refugees and young men who had volunteered for the Forces and were waiting to be called up. Somerville College, being adjacent to the Radcliffe Infirmary, had been commandeered by the War Office as a hospital for the wounded and the students were accommodated in the St Mary Hall Quadrangle of Oriel College. They dined in what was Oriel's J.C.R. and their common room was one of the libraries.

Dorothy was busily involved at first with helping to find lodgings for Belgian refugees. She was struck by the rigid class distinction which prevented them from speaking to anybody they wouldn't "know" in their own country. One aristocratic Belgian lady said she could not associate with Miss Bruce, the head of the Committee for Belgian Relief, because she had seen her riding a bicycle, something done only by shop-girls in Belgium. It was explained that Miss Pamela Bruce was an "Honourable", being the daughter of a lord, and the Belgian lady was mollified.

> This has been a flurried week — yesterday I helped to see a family of nine Belgians with their two maids into a house which the Bursar and Miss Phillpotts, assisted by the Senior Student, Elsie and myself had furnished in a week with borrowed furniture. It was a humorous job. You should have seen Lady Mary Murray's cook explaining the kitchen range to us in English, Miss Jones and myself explaining to Madame Rüdder in French, and Madame Rüdder passing on the explanation in Flemish to the cook and housemaid. It was like a page out of *Punch*.

Apart from such initial public-spirited activities, Dorothy seems to have resumed her Oxford life relatively unconcerned about the war. It should be remembered that at first very little news from the Front was allowed to reach the public. Her friends are called up, but, unlike Vera Brittain, she had no brother or fiancé to agonise about. When bombs begin to be dropped she prays continually that Oxford may be spared. "I make a special point of praying this in New College Chapel, but I haven't been able to the last few times – there is no praying done in the organ-loft."

Dr Allen, concerts, talk of careers and exams, a fancy-dress ball, at which she impersonates Dr Allen, boating on the river, more conversations with Dr Allen, and, here and there, an occasional reference to "working hard" are the main contents of her letters. She thinks of training as a nurse and going out to France after her exams and talks the matter over with Miss Pope. It would be good to do something real for a change. But the chief excitement, quite eclipsing any other consideration, even the thought of finals – she achieved a first class Honours degree – was the going-down play, which she helped to write and to organise and in which, once again, she impersonated her beloved Dr Allen.

She seems at last, and perhaps by this very act, to have exorcised him. Not so Oxford. That would continue to hold her in its spell.

CHAPTER 4

Return to Oxford

It is evident that even with the emolument from the Gilchrist scholarship Dorothy's father had a fair amount to pay while she was at Oxford – fees for examinations, the extra cost of staying up after the end of term to take a viva, bills for books, her journeys to and fro, to say nothing of a personal allowance. Dorothy often expressed concern about this; her father was far from wealthy. From time to time he added to his stipend of about seven hundred pounds by taking pupils who boarded at the rectory, and there is occasional mention of a paying guest. This added to the responsibilities of her mother, who suffered from nervous attacks, anxiety or strain tending to make her lose control over her speech and limbs. This was always a worrying possibility and Dorothy found these attacks alarming to witness.

It seems remarkable nowadays how much Dorothy told her elderly parents. When she was a young adult they were in their sixties yet her letters home are no different from the letters she writes to close friends; indeed, as regards intimate feelings and affairs of the heart she sometimes told her parents more than she told her contemporaries. The telephone makes it possible now for the young to keep in touch with their elders without revealing too much of themselves. The weekly letter home, which earlier was quite usual, even in the case of sons, and was often continued well on into adult life, resulted in an emotional dependence which would probably be considered undesirable today. It may have retarded maturity, but, if so, Dorothy would have been no different from her female contemporaries in that respect. To their modern counterparts they would seem surprisingly unsophisticated and inexperienced.

Sexually this is undoubtedly the case. The strict rules about chaperons enforced in the women's colleges meant that men and women undergraduates seldom saw each other alone and quite a

63

flurry ensued if inadvertently they infringed the regulation. Dorothy describes an incident at a theatre, where she finds herself unintentionally sitting beside Giles Dixey. He is as worried as she is that she may get into trouble with her college authorities, so, to relieve both their minds, Dorothy clambers along several rows of seats to talk with the Senior Student of Somerville, who laughingly tells her not to worry. Dorothy relates such episodes and inconveniences with perfect good humour, evidently feeling no resentment but accepting the convention as a necessity.

In June 1919 Dorothy wrote an article for the magazine *Oxford Outlook*, entitled "Eros in Academe". Five years have passed since she took her Finals. The Great War has destroyed the world she knew. Looking back on herself as an undergraduate and also, perhaps, comparing the pre-war with the post-war scene, she says with a certain bitterness:

> When I lived in Academe I should never have thought of going to one of its guardians for advice in any social difficulty. I should have feared, not unkindness or unwillingness to help, but just blank want of knowledge. "This kind of thing never happened to me," says the guide, philosopher, and friend; "to a nice girl social difficulties do not occur." That is a cowardly lie. Things do happen; it is monstrous to pretend that they do not or ought not.

When she wrote that, she was twenty-six and had spent the last two years as a post-graduate in Oxford, working for Basil Blackwell. By then a certain disenchantment seems to have set in. Co-education, she continued, did not mean sitting beside a man at the same lecture; nor is it possible for a woman undergraduate to gain experience "in an atmosphere in which going to tea with a youth ranks as a thrilling dissipation, and inviting the same man twice in a term is considered too desperately exciting for all concerned". Social attitudes and sexual *mores* had changed during and after the war: "Flirtation was once a dignified and delicate affair, like whist; now it is more like poker ... We have advanced indeed so far that it is no longer considered indecent to understand Love (which we call Sex) [or] even to enjoy it." There seems to be a note of regret here that so little experience was available to her before. Perhaps incidents had occurred with which she did not know how to deal and it may be of herself that she is thinking when she writes: "Things do happen; and it is monstrous to pretend that they do not or ought not." Perhaps Dr Hugh Allen sometimes went further than she wished in the organ loft. Perhaps some undergraduate had been clumsy or experimental. Whatever the situation on which she might have welcomed advice, it is unlikely to have involved losing her virginity, or wishing to, except, perhaps, unconsciously.

In a letter to Ivy Shrimpton written from Bluntisham in March 1914 she naïvely relates a dream of "a passionate love-scene with the Forbidden Subject [Cyril Hutchinson] – in my room at college of all places – I don't know how he came there unchaperoned! It was very violent and exhausting – nearly broke my back – I must have been in an uncomfortable and screwed up position in bed."

In chapter 6 of *Gaudy Night*, Harriet Vane awakes reluctantly from a dream in which she was being embraced by Lord Peter: "'Peter,' said Harriet. And with the sound of her own voice she came drowsing and floating up out of the strong circle of his arms, through a green sea of sun-dappled beech-leaves into darkness. 'Oh, damn,' said Harriet softly to herself. 'Oh, damn. And I didn't want to wake up.'" By then Dorothy Sayers has read her Freud and ironically makes Harriet remark to herself: "It's disquieting to reflect that one's dreams never symbolise one's real wishes, but always something Much Worse ... I wonder what are the unthinkable depths of awfulness that can only be expressed by the polite symbol of Peter's embraces." It is unlikely, however, that Dorothy's dream of Cyril Hutchinson signified anything more than the normal urges of her twenty-year-old, unfulfilled body. It is perhaps significant that it is to Ivy that she relates the dream, not her parents, and it may be that Ivy had always been her confidante in matters of such intimacy.

The stimulus of continual companionship, albeit chaperoned, of young men, must have left the women undergraduates uncertain of themselves and dissatisfied. The male undergraduates had outlets, if they cared to look for them. Women friends living in Oxford or visiting were not subject to college discipline. Touring companies came to the theatre, performing tuneful musical comedies such as *Our Miss Gibbs*, *The Arcadians*, *The Chocolate Soldier*. Dorothy does not mention any of these shows, but the men went to see them and some of them invited attractive young singers and dancers out to dinner and to their rooms, unchaperoned. Sometimes they proposed marriage to them.

During and after the war, the behaviour of the women changed. Not only members of touring companies but women members of colleges too were less likely to lead restricted lives. "We were none of us chaste," the writer Eric Whelpton said, when speaking of these years, some of which he spent at Oxford, when Dorothy got to know him. Although the chaperon rule no longer applied to her (she was herself a chaperon then!), it is unlikely (in view of later events) that Dorothy went to bed with any of her men friends at this period, but she must have known what was going on around her.

In 1915, however, the enchantment of Oxford was still bright. When her last year was drawing to a close her father offered her the chance of staying up for another year. Dorothy replied:

> Daddy dear – you are most awfully good and generous to me – I don't quite know what to do about it. The difficulty is, getting something which will enable one to put away a little money for one's declining years, so to speak – and there are no jobs in Oxford that I can hear of – and it's a question whether it's worth while wasting (so to speak) a year. If I worked for a B.Litt. or anything, it would mean fees, and expense – and even then wouldn't lead to anything very paying ... But ever so many thanks – and if of course I could stay in Oxford a bit longer, I should be very glad.

In many ways Dorothy would have loved to stay on at Oxford. Whenever she went back she felt she was going home. "I that am twice thy child", she wrote in a poem apostrophising Oxford. In the summer vacation of 1913 she wrote to Catherine Godfrey:

> Do you know – you're the only person to whom I dare confess it – for a bit after I got home, I was simply homesick for Oxford – not for college – but for that curve in the High and Radcliffe Square by moonlight, and for the people in the street and the stories about Varsity life ... I'm getting gradually reconciled to being in the depths of the country with no one to speak to – and of course, it is jolly to be home – but I wish Oxford were within bicycling distance.

And writing to "Jim" Jaeger in September 1915 she said: "While we keep on writing to each other about the good old days and thinking about them, it doesn't do to spend one's whole time planning to get back to Oxford or to see each other again. Not that any of us is likely to do that, unless it is I." She was to speak in *Gaudy Night* of Mary Stokes "who haunted the College with a sick persistence". Harriet Vane did not do so, but her creator, it seems, did.

Her father's generous offer must, therefore, have been very tempting, but her sense of public duty proved stronger. After hearing that there was a demand in France for nurses who could speak French she wrote to her parents: "I propose, if possible, if you will allow me, and if I find that I am physically fit, to take a month's training in August at any hospital that will take me. This would cost, I suppose, from £10-15 – then I could go abroad in September."

She asks a friend to find her a post in France, conditionally upon her being accepted for training. She hopes very much that there is no permanent weakness left in her lungs by the double pneumonia she suffered three years before. (She had also had bronchial pneumonia as a small child.) She realises she would hate the hard labour and horrors of nursing, but she would be glad to have done something real for the first time in her life. In the meantime she is happy organising a concert for the wounded recuperating in the temporary hospital at Somerville.

She applies to the French Red Cross, but they will not take people under the age of twenty-three. Several people consider she is quite sensible enough to look after herself so she is going to see what personal influence will do. This leads to nothing: "The fact is, the Red Cross is so very badly organised, both here and in France, that there is no means of getting information centrally." She thinks of applying to the matron at the Radcliffe Infirmary to see if they will train her there. On the other hand, she has also heard that there is need of women to teach in boys' schools: "If I thought I should be more use in that line than nursing I should not mind trying to teach for a year, say – but here again, there is no organisation, and one has to hear about things privately."

Whatever Dorothy's amorous dissatisfactions, conscious or un-conscious, the great love of her life at this period was Oxford. She finds it painful to leave. To make the parting easier, she asks her mother if she may invite three of her friends to spend a few days with her at Bluntisham:

> Would it be possible, when I'm home this vac. and before I go to France – if I go – to have a few of my Somerville friends down to Bluntisham together, before we all go our ways? I know it's an awful trouble and expense – but we should be so glad to rough it and "do" for ourselves a bit, if we could come together. Three or four of us could have such a jolly time, and go on the river, and do lots more than if it was just me and one friend. Dear, sweet, darling Mummy, think what can be done about it.

The three friends in question were Dorothy Rowe, Muriel Jaeger and Catherine Godfrey. Dorothy's mother agreed and towards the end of

June they spent a happy few days together, talking about poetry — they were all members of the Mutual Admiration Society — arguing and laughing. Mrs Sayers must have found them more cheerful company than her brother-in-law Major Sayers and her nephew Raymond, Dorothy's charming cousin who had escorted her in London when she was a schoolgirl. They each paid a visit to Bluntisham in July, with their respective wives. Both men, Dorothy relates in a letter to Muriel Jaeger,

> have got nervous breakdown, one has neuritis and the other has damaged his eye gazing at aeroplanes. Jolly business, war. Both seem uncommonly gloomy over the prospect, but I don't know how far they can really judge. I'm rather glad they're gone, because I do so hate everlasting war-talk, and I'm always in terror of Mother getting another of her nervous attacks. She was on the verge of one the night my uncle arrived.

With the rectory now emptied of nerve-shattered officers from the Front, Dorothy could give thought to what concerned her most of all, the expression in poetry of her passionate love of Oxford. She sends drafts of her poems to Catherine Godfrey ("a bulky package") and to Muriel Jaeger, who in return sends Dorothy a complimentary sonnet. The foundation members of the Mutual Admiration Society, like the musketeers of Bluntisham, are scattered, but still joined by correspondence. For Dorothy especially the link continued to be important and productive.

Basil Blackwell, the son of the Oxford bookseller, then a young man in his twenties, had started a series of little volumes entitled *Oxford Poetry*, of which the first had appeared in 1913. His aim was to discover and launch talented young poets. G. D. H. Cole was one of the editors of the first volume and Gilbert Murray contributed the Introduction. The second volume, published in 1914, had an Introduction by Walter Raleigh. Blackwell also started a series of volumes entitled *Adventurers All*, each containing the poems of a single author. Eight of these had been published by 1914; one, entitled *The Burning Wheel*, was by Aldous Huxley.

Dorothy was interested in both ventures. While still at Somerville she had been working on a lay, a complex structure of twelve poems, distinct but metrically interlaced, on the subject of the beauty and enchantment of Oxford. She submitted it to the editors of the 1915 volume of *Oxford Poetry*, G. D. H. Cole and T. W. Earp, who accepted it. The volume came out in December 1915. By then

Dorothy was busy revising and putting together a collection of poems, including the lay, which she had written during the summer and autumn of 1915. She offered this to Basil Blackwell as Number 9 in his series *Adventurers All*. He accepted it and the volume, *Op. I*, was published on 28 December 1916 in a limited edition of 350 copies.

In its most obvious meaning, the title stands for Opus I, namely, the first of many works which the author hopes to write. This is evident from the prefatory poem:

> I will build up my house from the stark foundations,
>   If God will give me time enough,
> And search unwearying over the seas and nations
>   For stones or better stuff.

> Though here be only the mortar and rough-hewn granite,
>   I will lay on and not desist
> Till it stand and shine as I dreamed it when I began it
>   Emerald, amethyst.

There is, perhaps, another, subtle meaning underlying the obvious. Since almost all the poems are inspired by Oxford, "Op." may stand for "Oxford Poetry".

The volume is dedicated to her closest Oxford friends: to "the Stage-Manager of the *Admiral Guinea*" (i.e. Dorothy Rowe, who stage-managed the going-down play), to "the Conductor of the Bach Choir" (her beloved Dr Hugh Percy Allen), and to "the Members of the Mutual Admiration Society". This dedication sums up what Dorothy then felt were her most important Oxford experiences: the joy of comradeship in organising and acting a play, the glory of singing with the Bach Choir, and the creative stimulus of exchanging and discussing poetry with fellow enthusiasts. The first of the poems also contains a tribute to her friend Giles Dixey, with whom she had exchanged poetry in her first year – a quotation from a sonnet he had written on Oxford:

> . . . Far beneath
> My holier passion, in their eyes and ears
> Enchantment vast but foolish lingereth.

It is noteworthy that themes such as academic endeavour and

intellectual integrity, aspects of Oxford which she was later to proclaim as so valuable, do not stir her creatively at this period.

At the end of July 1915 Dorothy writes to Muriel Jaeger:

> Just at present I'm simply struggling with Oxford fever, with the help of Franz Schubert and J. S. Bach. I feel a strong repulsion from all books, but am attracted by music, so I'm practising violently. One can't sit glooming while trying to play a Bach prelude correctly – at least not when one plays the piano as rottenly as I do. I have also found Betty Osborne very willing to play classical stuff with me, so I've taken the fiddle up again. But oh! my dear! I do want Oxford! If I've not got a job which keeps me stuck elsewhere this autumn I shan't be able to keep away from the place.

With the same letter she sends a copy of *The Last Castle*, a series of poems in different styles; they would be included in *Op. I*:

> A word about *The Last Castle*. I've sent it just as it is, because you know what it's all about, and for outside consumption it would want lots and lots of expanding and altering. I've only cast in some more lyrics, and added the scoffing labels of the various "schools" which we used to patronise. Good old M.A.S. We got some fun out of it, didn't we?

In October 1915 she wrote to Dorothy Rowe, who lived in Bournemouth, to tell her she had been practising writing rondeaux and other technical exercises, "trying different shapes and models with different lengths of line and arrangements of time and refrain". These make up part of the "bulky package", which also includes a poem entitled "The Matter of Brittany", ultimately included in *Op. I*. It was written, she says,

> mainly for enjoyment. I thought I was tired of "Oxfords" and "Alma Maters" and "Going-downs" and "To a Leader of Men"s and things that mean a powerful lot, and terseness and pregnancy and dignity and so on, so I thought I'd just revel a bit in the dear old obvious glories of scarlet cloaks and dragons and Otherworld Journeys, and the clank and gurgle of alliteration, and the gorgeousness of proper names. So you are to read it in this spirit, please, if possible at night and by the fire.

It is interesting to note that W. H. Auden, in his Inaugural Lecture in

1956 as Professor of Poetry at Oxford, set the following qualifications for a critic:

> Do you like, and by like I really mean like, not approve of on principle:
> 1. Long lists of proper names?
> 2. Riddles and all other ways of not calling a spade a spade?
> 3. Complicated verse forms of great technical difficulty?
> 4. Conscious theatrical exaggeration?
>
> If a critic could truthfully answer "yes" to all four, then I should trust his judgment implicitly in all literary matters.

Dorothy quoted this to me in a letter dated 19 June 1956, adding in glee:

> There now! I can truthfully answer "yes" to all four – consequently, the Oxford Professor of Poetry would, believe it or not, implicitly trust my judgment on all literary matters! There's glory for you! – And to think that I always felt rather apologetic about these addictions of mine; not that I was ashamed of them, but that I felt them to be the kind of thing that exposed me to withering criticism from the right-minded. It just shows.

How gratified and amazed she would have been in 1915 to know that a future Oxford Professor of Poetry and a foremost poet would trust her judgment implicitly in all literary matters!

There had been another reunion of Oxford friends in September of that year, this time in London, in the house of Charis Barnett (later Mrs Sydney Frankenburg), whose brother Donald had recently been killed in France. Catherine Godfrey, who had begun teaching at Blackheath High School, joined them and they all bedded down on the floor, "round a gas-stove with no gas in it for fear of zepps . . . and talked late, and pretended we were at college". She went shopping with Charis and her sister-in-law Hilda, and with their expert help bought a coat and skirt:

> It is all black, with a short front and long straight back to the coat and high collar; the skirt is simply fascinating – band, and deep hip-yoke, and wide skirt with two most attractive little pleats in front and full pleats at the back. 5½ guineas, reduced for me from 6½. Then we bought a black velvet hat at Whiteley's for 7/– and a pink rose for eighteen pence and Hilda did the trimming in a most fetching manner.

The visit to London was further enlivened by Dorothy's first experience of a moving staircase:

> I'd never been on one before, so Charis told me how to step on to it, which I did, and she stood beside me, holding my arm, lest I should get giddy or anything. So, standing still abreast, we took up rather a lot of room and blocked up the stairs. Suddenly an old lady pushed violently past me from behind, and muttering "I must get down this thing quickly – I'm always sick if I don't" – hurled herself to the bottom in a series of goat-like leaps. Anything more reassuring to a neophyte!

But the great news is that she has been invited by the librarian of Somerville to spend a few weeks in college free of charge, helping with the library. She is the more delighted because "Jim" Jaeger is staying up for a fourth year and Dorothy will be able to help her to settle in.

This brief return to Oxford must have helped her to make up her mind. Nothing had come of her attempts to train as a nurse; she had applied for a post with the Board of Trade, but that too was unsuccessful. On 23 November she wrote to Catherine Godfrey: "I got sick of hanging about, and I thought it wouldn't do any harm to try, say, a year of teaching, so I sent to the Joint Agency for notices of Boys' and Girls' schools." She received two invitations for interview, one for a school in Harrow and another for a school in Hull. She wanted to be near London but she preferred the headmistress of the school in Hull and the conditions of the post as they were described. She went to London for the interview, which took place at the Berners Hotel in Berners Street.

> I asked for Miss Elliott, and a tall person in a musquash coat and becoming hat flew out, and caught me, and carried me into the drawing-room, and began to talk. She said that the High School at Hull had been run by the same H.M. with no ideas for 26 years, and had suffered in consequence, and that the London Council which runs it (it is some kind of church school) had now appointed her (Miss Elliott) and she had had to begin by making a clean sweep of the fossilised staff (all unqualified!), and was beginning in January to re-organise the whole thing and work it up again . . . She then said that I was the sort of person she wanted, experience or none – that she was starting off with practically a whole new staff of young, qualified women, that she would want me to

arrange and take the whole of the French – and in short, offered me the post straight off – £120 p.a. non-resident.

Among the advantages of the post which Dorothy stressed was the fact that she would be helping to create a tradition and that if Miss Elliott made a success with the school, "it wouldn't be a bad thing to have done".

She has some misgivings, but on the whole her attitude is positive and optimistic. Miss Elliott must have been pleased with her catch: the twenty-two-year-old Oxford graduate, with a First in French, dressed for the interview, we may be sure, in the new coat and skirt with the attractive pleats and the black velvet hat, fetchingly trimmed with a pink rose.

Having accepted the post, Dorothy went to Yarmouth, where she spent a delightful week with her cousin Raymond and his wife, and where, she said, she did her best to forget all about the decision she had made. After Christmas she visited Dorothy Rowe in Bournemouth. Here, no doubt, the pros and cons of the job were discussed, especially as Miss Rowe had by then had experience of teaching. Finally on 18 January 1916, as she expressed it, she went north to seek her fortune.

Her lodgings were at 80 Westbourne Avenue. She was pleasantly surprised to find some quite good shops in Hull and at least one decent café. The staff were all young and there was much laughter and good comradeship. This must have helped to make up to Dorothy for the separation from her Oxford friends. Miss Elliott had promised that the staff would be introduced to "nice people in Hull", especially "some charming members of the advisory committee", so the social life available may also have been something of a consolation. We know from her letters that she amused herself putting in some practice exerting her charms on the local curate.

She was shocked to find her pupils accustomed to learning by rote without understanding what it was they were reciting. She set about awakening their minds, trying to show them the relatedness of one subject to another. But she was, after all, exceptional in this awareness. Even at Oxford she had noticed that fellow students of Romance philology were satisfied with learning bits and pieces of the subject by heart and had said to herself, "These people don't know what they're doing." She was vividly remembered by her Hull ex-pupils, who found her different from the rest of the staff. She was gay and attractive; she dressed well and moved quickly. Her smile, with the deep dimples, was reassuring and her laughter infectious.

Recalling her own schooldays, which were not far off, she encouraged her pupils to write and act little plays in French. To their surprise, they found they could, even though they made ridiculous mistakes, such as confusing a *"cochon"* (pig) with a *"cocher"* (coachman). She even got the class to act Molière's *Les Précieuses Ridicules*, the proceeds being given to the Red Cross. She organised a school choir, which she conducted herself. She was persuaded by Miss Elliott to take a class in German, which she did not enjoy as much as teaching French. Possibly the war had something to do with this.

There were frequent zeppelin raids on Hull, the target being, of course, the port. "William [i.e. the Kaiser] was over last night," she writes to her parents, as people used to say of Hitler during World War II. During one raid her landlady, who was not very strong, had a shaking fit. "I thought she would be ill," Dorothy wrote to Muriel Jaeger. "I had never seen fear before – believe me, it is brutal, bestial and utterly degrading – I should say it is the one experience which is neither good for man nor beast." Fortunately, Dorothy had some spirits in her room, which she administered to the landlady to settle her nerves. It does not seem from the letter that she herself was frightened, though she said that raids were "hell".

She disliked teaching and it has been related that one of her pupils overheard her saying, "I'd rather sweep streets than teach children." It may be that the prospect of re-organisation and creation of a new tradition, held out enticingly by Miss Elliott at the interview, did not materialise. The fact remains, however, that Dorothy stayed the course better than Catherine Godfrey, whose health broke down under the strain of teaching in Blackheath.

She went on writing poetry. In February 1916 a poem dedicated "To Members of the Bach Choir on Active Service" was published in the *Oxford Magazine*. (By then conditions of trench warfare were known to the civilian population and a note of realism entered some of her poetry.) Muriel Jaeger wrote to tell her that Dr Allen had laid down his baton in the middle of a rehearsal and in poignant tones had urged the choir to read it. In March of that year she heard that *Op. I* had been accepted for publication. Other poems were published in the *Oxford Magazine*, among them a translation of a sonnet on the subject of Icarus by the sixteenth-century poet Desportes:

> Here fell young Icarus, that dared to climb
> Heaven, and, audacious, cleave the starry plain;
> Here dropped his wingless body; hearts remain

All envy at a failure thus sublime . . .

The note strikes false in the context of the page, filled as it is with notices of undergraduates killed in action. One member of Magdalen College, Lt. Archibald McNair, who was awarded a V.C., was present when a German mine exploded and buried several of his men. (She was to give the war-time fate of being buried in a trench-hole to Lord Peter Wimsey.) She won a poetry competition in the *Saturday Westminster Review* for a poem in imitation of Browning. Her pseudonym for this was H. P. Rallentando, the name under which she had impersonated Dr Allen in the going-down play.

In the summer vacation of 1916 her thoughts turned to the work she had done at Oxford with Miss Mildred Pope. On 3 August she wrote to the librarian of the Cambridge University Library (F. J. H. Jenkinson) to ask whether and on what terms she could be admitted as a reader. For the next seven weeks, she says, she would like to have access to early French texts, from the *Chanson de Roland* to the Renaissance, and to the studies of Joseph Bédier and Gaston Paris on the mediaeval period. This is the moment when she began translating the *Chanson de Roland* into rhymed couplets, a version she later declared to be "very bad" and which she subsequently replaced by her translation of the same work into assonance, published in Penguin Classics in 1957. Permission to read was granted, but she would not have had permission to borrow. The University Library was then in the building known as Old Schools, behind the Senate House, in the centre of Cambridge. No doubt she took time to browse in the bookshops near by and to visit Mr Heffer in Petty Cury, who was a friend of her parents. Once, when she visited him between trains, she wrote to say she had found him as "amiable and witty as usual".

She returned to Hull for the autumn term of 1916, refreshed in mind and spirit by her renewed scholarly interest in the literature of Old French. The year ended triumphantly with the publication of *Op. I*. This was her first book and she must have felt exhilarated. She knew now more than ever that she wanted to be a writer and that teaching could never be a career for her. She talked matters over with her father, who had earlier suggested that she should stay on in Oxford for a fourth year. He himself had been offered a new living, as rector of Christchurch in the Isle of Ely (now Cambridgeshire), with a considerably larger stipend. He was consequently in a position to propose an arrangement with Basil Blackwell, whereby his daughter would be taught publishing in return for a down payment of one hundred pounds. For her work as an apprentice she was to be paid a wage of two pounds a week. To Dorothy this must have seemed an ideal solution: it got her out of teaching and it enabled her to return to Oxford. She blithely gave notice to Miss Elliott and arranged to leave at Easter. "There is *no future* in teaching," she wrote to her father; "I might really make something of publishing." The new job was to begin on 1 May 1917.

She spent part of her fourth term at Hull learning about technique from a friendly local printer: "He says I may go and potter about there and ask any questions I like. Today I watched a forme being locked up ready for printing." In February she went to Oxford to meet Basil Blackwell. She visited her friends the Dixeys and learnt that Giles, "poor boy", was being sent out to the Front. She asks her mother to write to him, "just one of those nice letters you write so charmingly". She also runs across Miss Penrose, the Principal of Somerville, and tells her about her job. "I don't think she liked it because publishing isn't work of national importance."

By the end of April she is installed in rooms at 17 Long Wall Street, with a beautiful view of the deer park from her bedroom window. Muriel St Clare Byrne (a younger friend and member of the M.A.S.) is up, completing her final year. They have decided to go shares in hiring a punt. (They were to become life-long friends and, in 1937, co-authors of the detective comedy, *Busman's Honeymoon*.)

The job suits her very well. She loves the quaint little office, where she works from 9.30 till 1 and from 2.15 till 6. She often has to run round to the printers and so is getting "quite sleek and pink". She is overjoyed to be back: "Life is such fun. I don't know what right I have to be enjoying myself so much." Doreen Wallace, the future novelist, who knew her well at this time, wrote of her:

> I have never known anyone so brimful of the energy of a well-stocked mind: even at 24, when I knew her first, she knew an enormous amount about all sorts of subjects ... and nothing would content her but fact. There was, however, a lighter side to this impressive character. Long and slim in those days, small head held alert on slender neck, she loped round Oxford looking for fun. Some of the fun was our Rhyme Club – one minute to produce the rhyming line, no matter whether sense or nonsense.

Ralph E. Hone's phrase aptly conveys her state of mind: "She set out ˀ˅ make Oxford her demesne of joy." And she succeeded.

went on the river with old M.A.S. friends, Amphy Middlemore, "Tony" Godfrey and "Jim" Jaeger. Soon afterwards she picked up "two perfectly charming Australian Tommies" in the Botanical Gardens and invited them to go punting:

> They are perfect dears – such absolute natural gentlemen, making themselves perfectly at home, without the least familiarity and with no stupid shyness. I took them again on Friday, and pretty weary I was at the end of it, as I couldn't get hold of anyone else, and so of course I had to do all the punting.

On the next occasion she enlisted the help of "a perfectly delightful padre, the Vice-Principal of Teddy [St Edmund] Hall . . . He is most charming, and won my heart yesterday by coming into the office and telling me how much he liked *Op. I* – which (good man!) he had bought."

The "perfectly delightful and charming padre" was the Reverend Leonard Hodgson. He and Dorothy met several times. One evening he arrived unexpectedly at Basil Blackwell's house, where Dorothy had been invited to supper. She described the occasion to her parents. After dropping innumerable knives and forks while helping to clear the table,

> he succeeded in cornering me in the drawing-room after supper,

Leonard Hodgson in 1920
(Magdalen College, Oxford)

while Basil and Christine were making coffee . . . and informed me that he loved me with his whole heart and would I marry him?!!! My elegant and maidenly reply, to the best of my recollection, was "Oh Lord!" – and I very nearly fainted into the nearest chair – seeing that I've met him four or five times at most, and only twice to talk to at any length.

She told him she had never considered him in that connection and certainly did not love him. She remembered to say that he had done her a great honour, "when enter Basil, innocently, with the cigarettes".

Leonard Hodgson departed but waited with his bicycle outside the house until Dorothy also took her leave; whereupon the conversation was reopened and he apologised for being so precipitate. "And so ends the story of my first proposal . . . After all, it's nice to think anybody should care for one so much." She adds a postscript: "Don't get agitated! I'll never marry a man I don't care for."

Her suitor, however, refuses to take "no" for an answer and a week later Dorothy tells her parents she has written to tell him she cannot marry him:

Beastly job, but it had to be done. I can't tell you why I can't, because he's very nice and extremely good, but I don't love him, and there's an end. You know the way you worry about a thing and suddenly one morning you wake up and find that it has gone and settled itself irrevocably, apparently without your own interference.

Nevertheless, he still persisted and Dorothy became irritated:

It bores me dreadfully to have him perpetually coming to tea in the office and looking like a Good Friday cod. You never would believe me when I dissected my character for your benefit but I was right about myself. To have somebody devoted to me arouses all my worst feelings. I *loathe* being deferred to. I *abominate* being waited on. It *infuriates* me to feel that my words are numbered and my actions watched. I want somebody to fight with!

Leonard Hodgson was to go on to achieve distinction as a theologian. He became a Doctor of Divinity, Canon of Winchester, and ultimately Regius Professor of Divinity at Oxford and Canon of Christ Church. Had Dorothy married him she would have been spared much anguish. She would also have become quite a different person – the wife of an Oxford professor and mother, probably, of several children. With her energy she might have kept up her studies in Old French, tutoring for Somerville and perhaps even being elected a Fellow. Hodgson published an impressive number of books. In one, *The Doctrine of the Trinity* (1943), he refers to Dorothy's work, *The Mind of the Maker*, which he calls a "fascinating little book" and "a very illuminating aid to the understanding of the faith". The tone is perhaps somewhat patronising, ironically so, since her book is now so much better known than his, but the comment comes graciously from a man whose love and devotion had been rejected twenty-six years before.

In July of that year, 1917, she fell ill with appendicitis and entered the Acland Nursing Home in Oxford to have her appendix removed. The surgeon, Major Whitelock, became flirtatious. Dorothy was amused by his banter and the give-and-take of daring repartee. "I love having someone to fool with," she told her mother, "meeting on equal terms, seeing which can joke the other down." The terms were hardly equal, since Major Whitelock was a stout, middle-aged, married man with a grown-up daughter. He told Dorothy she was a wicked little girl with the face of a mediaeval saint: "He followed this up by hugging me. Perhaps he will kiss me next time and I shall box his ears – and we shall part on the best of terms." Major (soon afterwards promoted Colonel) Whitelock continued to take advantage of his position even after Dorothy had left hospital. He called at her lodgings unannounced one day, but found her "in a brisk, unkissable mood", having spent an hour and a half practising a Beethoven violin sonata with a woman friend. The game of flirtation, she found, "is only for idle moments; it fades and palls when one has other excitements".

Another of her conquests at the nursing home was "a dear little boy of about 7 or 8 years old", with whom she played a game of snap. She related that at the end of it he turned to her "with the sweetest smile and asked in the most grown-up way, 'Shall I see you again?'"

Music continues to play an important part in her life. She joins the Bach Choir again and resumes contact with Dr Allen. She finds him older and rather tired. The glamour has departed somewhat: "A strange man – symbolic of something enormous . . . a statue of a god, flawed in the smelting, poor dear!" In March 1918 he asks her to sing four bars solo at a performance by the choir, "with full orchestra for the first time since the war". She asks to have her violin sent up by

passenger train. "I think I must join the orchestra, if I can still play."
Her standard is judged good enough and she sings on Mondays and
plays on Wednesdays, taking part as an alto in combined concerts
and as a violinist in orchestral concerts. She has begun to learn the
flageolet and is becoming "rather a dab at it". She is thinking of
going on to the oboe or the flute. She hires a piano, as she finds it is
nice to have something handy to strum on. A small orchestra, in
which she plays second fiddle, is organised to give concerts for
wounded men. Early in 1919 she is asked to sing in a private
performance of Parry's six motets, "Songs of Farewell", by the
combined Christ Church and New College choirs, Dr Allen conducting. "It's really very jolly – they are beautiful little works – one or
two of them quite great little works." Dr Allen delivers his Inaugural
Lecture as Professor of Music and Dorothy is again invited to help.
She plays the violin in the illustrations and sings two chorales "prac-
tically at sight in a singular little quartet", composed of herself, two
other women and Dr Allen. "It's nice to be picked out to do these
little stunts."

Her enjoyment of music was often connected with religious celebrations and festivals. She goes with Aunt Maud to hear Tenebrae
at Cowley, "an office which always sounds extraordinarily thrilling
and beautiful". In December 1917 she excuses herself from going
home at Christmas and hopes her father will not be hurt. She wants
to be, for the first time, "in a place where Christmas is really kept".
She has never heard a real festival Mass – one of the big festivals – in
her life. The following Easter she says, "I intend to hear as many as
possible of the Holy Week offices this year. They sing them very
beautifully at Cowley."

Her resentment against Christianity, a phase of which she spoke
later in life, was certainly not in evidence at this period. Basil Blackwell recalled that she always had a crucifix on her desk and that she
crossed herself when saying grace at meals. Doreen Wallace found it
irritating that Dorothy was "so bloody religious". Her chief production in 1917 was the poems which she later published as
Catholic Tales and Christian Songs. Writing to her parents about this
volume, she said:

> Some people think it "wonderful" and some think it "blasphem-
> ous" . . . Some mugwumps may object to it like anything. You
> won't mind being the parents and aunt of a notoriety, if that
> should happen, will you? I can assure you that it is intended at any
> rate to be the expression of reverent belief, but some people find it

hard to allow that faith, if lively, can be reverent.

This book, Dorothy's second in two years, was published by Blackwell in September 1918. She had offered it previously to G. K. Chesterton, hoping he would accept it for *The New Witness*. The poems are much in his style and to a large extent inspired by his own robust and hearty expressions of faith. Technically they are an advance on *Op. I*. In content also they are more mature. The most original is a brilliant satirical mystery play, *The Mocking of Christ*, with its witty epigraph, "So man made God in his own image". This little drama contains many of the elements Dorothy later developed in her articles on the Christian faith. Christ is mocked daily by ecclesiastical wrangling, by insistence on certain details of ritual, by arguments about the choice of church music, by religiosity, trivialities, respectability, muscular Christianity, self-righteousness, war, sentimentality and the facile identification of Christianity with pagan faiths and Greek philosophy.

The volume also includes another lay, *The House of the Soul*, more ambitious in scope than her previous attempt at this elaborate structure and more assured. The promise in the prefatory poem to *Op.I*, "I will build up my house from the stark foundations", is being fulfilled.

Dorothy heard in advance that Theodore Maynard, a Catholic poet of some prominence at the time, intended to review the poems unfavourably in *The New Witness*. He based his criticism on theological grounds, asserting that the poems equated Christianity with paganism. On the principle that "to say anything is better than to say nothing", Dorothy asked her friend Muriel Jaeger to reply to the review under an assumed name, agreeing with Maynard, and then to follow this with another letter putting the opposite view. Dorothy herself would write in at a later stage and there would be "a scrumptious row", which would make the book "go like wildfire".

Muriel entered into the spirit of the game. Her first pseudonym was H. Hunter ("heresy-hunter"); her next was M. James (a combination of her initial M and her nickname "Jim"). "Very wicked of you," said Dorothy; "they'll take you for M. R. James." Several genuine correspondents joined in, among them Wilfred Rowland Childe, a volume of whose poems had preceded Dorothy's *Op. I* in Basil Blackwell's series, *Adventurers All*. He objected to Maynard's "patronising clericalism", saying that he had noticed the same attitude towards "Mr Charles Williams, whose truly noble poetry he vilified from the same standpoint".

This brought Charles Williams, in all innocence, into the manufactured controversy. He and Dorothy later became close friends, but at this period they had not even met. In 1937 he was to suggest her name to the organisers of the Canterbury Festival as someone who might write a religious drama. This has seemed surprising up to now as Dorothy was not then known as a dramatist. However, Williams' letter to *The New Witness*, dated 12 January 1919, confirms the hypothesis which I put forward in *The Passionate Intellect: Dorothy L. Sayers' Encounter with Dante*, namely, that he had read *The Mocking of Christ*. I give below the relevant passages from his letter:

Perhaps Mr Childe's too kind reference to me may excuse an interference in this controversy, although I have no place from which to criticise either Miss Sayers' book, most of which I liked, or Mr Maynard's review, with most of which I agreed ... Theology can criticise poetry from its own standpoint; or better, it can contribute its science as a help to criticism. If a book is issued called *Catholic Tales*, obviously its Catholic readers have a right to decide whether or not it is in accord with their accepted theology ...

What criticism has to guard against ... is the substitution for [a new and sincere artistic appeal] of any kind of artistic trick. I think there is a certain danger of this trick, of the use of such names as Osiris and of such mythologies without proper coordination of them with Christian theology. To say this is not necessarily to say that Miss Sayers has used the trick and not made the appeal ... I certainly read *The Mocking of Christ* as in part a warning against that trick ...

I may perhaps be allowed to add that, having read the correspondence, I read Miss Sayers' book again and liked it more.

Dorothy could not have hoped for a better result than this. She had, in fact, hooked a bigger fish than she knew. The whole episode is characteristic of her high-spirited and mischievous sense of fun. By January 1919 she had tired of it. "The Maynard controversy," she wrote to her parents, "can stew in its own juice ... Controversy is bad for the spirit, however enlivening to the wits."

Her letters during this period radiate happiness. She signs two of them "yours merrily", and "your ever-loving and very happy Dorothy". She spends a delightful evening with the Dixeys – the younger son, Roger, is home on leave. They sing songs from Gilbert and Sullivan operas and behave boisterously. The next morning

Roger bursts into her office and takes her off to join a lunch party at Wadham College. She spends another jolly evening with two friends. "We occupied ourselves in the construction of nonsense verses before a large wood-fire, and were exceedingly merry."

There are war-time food and fuel restrictions, but her landlady does her best for her and she keeps well. Occasionally her mother sends some butter, or fruit, or asparagus and many times she sends flowers, especially daffodils which grow plentifully at Christchurch. Dorothy takes great pleasure in making her room attractive. She has bought a Medici print of Botticelli's "Birth of Venus" — "it cost an awful lot, but one must have some one really glorious thing to look at." She has made her room beautiful with "the most glorious armful of yellow and scarlet autumn foliage . . . which shows wonderfully against my brown door-curtain."

Her parents also send clothes. She has a "gorgeous warm khaki wool jersey with pockets" which "makes [her] feel most warm and happy". She has blued ten shillings on a pair of old pinchbeck ear-rings, which look exactly like chandeliers — "frightfully fascinating". They will be the very thing to wear with her black and gold tunic. Her parents respond by sending her a silver-gilt brooch, which she will wear with the ear-rings at the Brabants', where she will meet the Dixeys again and they will have a little music: "Dear Mamma, I'm going to look very nice, thanks to you." She earns some extra money for such extavagances by teaching French at three guineas a term to a six-year-old child. "He is a dear little boy and amazingly intelligent and no trouble whatever."

In January 1919 she finds "a most charming little set of three rooms in 5 Bath Place, where the landlady is generous with food and cooks quite well". She plans to establish a salon there every Thursday evening. For this she needs an evening dress, not having had one for six years. She is having one made of blue charmeuse with a ninon top and a wide silver belt with a fringed end. Her red cloak is being re-lined in primrose and done up with a black fur collar. (Her fur stole, named Percival, was sacrificed for this purpose.)

One evening she entertains "two advanced young poets, Osbert and Sacheverell Sitwell": "They came into Blackwell's . . . and looked such fearful bloods that I had to invite them quickly before I got frightened. I believe they are very good company, and anyway B.H.B. [Basil Blackwell] wants to get hold of Sachie and I think I can do that for him." They came, in uniform, to a meeting of the Rhyme Club, but were silent and aloof, having no heart for nonsense.

She loves her new sitting-room. It is small, but seems larger than it is. The pictures look perfect and she is having shelves put up. "I'm thoroughly established here now and feel as if I'd lived here all my Oxford life, except that I am still too much in love with my room to be quite an old stager. I bid fair to become quite silly about it! It is really delightful and absolutely all my own." Her landlady looks after her well and leaves her alone. She can come in unquestioned at any time of the day or night: "There's glory for you!"

She holds one particularly successful musical evening: "Mrs Molyneux played the fiddle, Mr Shaw of Keble [Francis Shaw, who had replaced Dr Allen as conductor of the Bach Choir], who is one of the most brilliant pianists I know, played the piano . . . " There were about five or six other guests. Among them was a certain Captain Whelpton, who much admired the colour scheme of her blue evening dress and her red cloak, trimmed with black fur and lined with primrose. "By the way," she writes, "I don't believe I ever told you about Whelpton. He lives in the house."

CHAPTER 5

Adrift

The war was over but before the Armistice another disaster had struck, which killed, it is estimated, even more people: Spanish influenza. Dorothy got a mild form of it and was immune to the worst. A defiant gaiety in the midst of calamity seems to have been the current mood among the young, but even Dorothy, blithe-spirited as she usually was, felt she must cancel an All Hallows Eve party in 1918, at which guests were to have told ghost stories. After all, as she wrote to her mother: "One cannot give hilarious parties when people are dropping dead all round one! Lots and lots of people are dropping dead – they get pneumonia and are never seen alive again. It's like being in London when the plague was on."

Men began to drift back from the Forces. Frank Brabant and Giles Dixey were demobilised. Giles was suffering from depression; his younger brother Roger, who not long before had sung songs from Gilbert and Sullivan at an evening party and had breezily carried Dorothy off to lunch at Wadham, "has come home", she reported, "with frightfully bad shell-shock . . . he is terrifed to see anybody".

Early in 1919, Dorothy caught German measles. She did not feel ill but it was a notifiable disease and she could not at once return to the office. She wrote home: "I'm going to seize this God-sent opportunity for going into Retreat for a few days. I'm getting so dusty and scuffling in the spiritual region I really thought I never should get straight again – so it's just as well. I never thought I'd get time for such a thing, but doubtless all is for the best." She spent five days at the Convent of the Holy Name, in Malvern.

In May, after working for two years for Blackwell's, Dorothy cut loose. She had begun to find office work tedious and the firm was now mainly publishing school text-books, which did not call for her literary talents. Basil Blackwell said later that she had seemed to him

Eric Whelpton *(Barbara
Whelpton)*

like a racehorse harnessed to a cart. She continued to edit for him on
a basis of piece-work, which she supplemented by free-lance journalism and coaching. The lack of regular work soon depressed her and
she grew short of money. She felt she was no use to anyone. Even her
friends, she said, were tired of her.

In the meantime she had fallen in love with Captain Eric Whelpton. Tall, dark and very good-looking, he had been invalided out of
the army and returned to Oxford in May 1918. He first met Dorothy
when she had rooms in Long Wall Street. Doreen Wallace introduced

them, unwisely, as she was herself in love with him. Whelpton's
illness, believed at first to be epilepsy but later diagnosed as polio,
had left him subject to fainting fits. He also had periods of amnesia (a
condition Dorothy would later use in connection with the character
George Fentiman in *The Unpleasantness at the Bellona Club*). His
frail state of health, combined with his good looks, made him a
romantic figure and he had many women admirers. He lived at 5
Bath Place, where he had a sitting-room on the ground floor and a
bedroom above. He had told Dorothy that the landlady was generous with food and cooked well. Perhaps interpreting this as
encouragement, she had moved into three rooms in the same house
when they fell vacant. The delight she felt at being there, which she
had expressed in such rapturous terms to her parents, was no doubt
heightened by the presence of Captain Whelpton. He soon became a
member of her circle and a guest at her coffee parties and salons.

Whelpton says in his autobiography, *The Making of a European*,
that Dorothy's attitude to him was protective and maternal. Her
feelings were stronger than that. At Easter that year she confided to
Muriel Jaeger that she was in love with him; indeed, in her usual self-
dramatising manner, she proclaimed her enamourment to a number
of friends, including Doreen Wallace, who felt aggrieved, and said
later that Dorothy had "nobbled" him. She was over twenty-five
when they met; he was twenty-four. She was already a graduate, had
published two volumes of poetry and had been earning her living for
three years. He had now to return to undergraduate status and to
recover his health, if he could. He admitted readily that she was his
superior in talent and intelligence and that she did a great deal to
educate him. They had in common an interest in French literature, in
which he was well read, and he spoke French fluently, having been
brought up in France. Looking back on himself in later years, he said
he was conceited and gave himself airs as a man-about-town. This
may well have added to his attractiveness. Sexually, he was already
quite experienced and sophisticated enough to arrange for a woman
friend to stay at the Randolph Hotel from time to time.

He has described an evening party in Dorothy's sitting-room, at
which he sat on the floor in the firelight, leaning against her knees
while she caressed him discreetly in the darkness. On another occasion he fell in a faint on her floor and Dorothy, according to
Doreen Wallace, "nursed his head and cooed over him". Unable to
bring him round, she ran to fetch a friend and neighbour, Dr Alice
Chance, who administered an injection, and together they put him to
bed.

The inconclusive nature of this relationship, combined with a lack of direction in her career, made her feel increasingly unsettled. She told her parents she was thinking of sub-letting her rooms, but the landlady would not agree to this and said she would now prefer to let to a man. "They pay more," commented Dorothy bitterly:

I shouldn't be surprised if I cut Oxford before long. I want a thorough change. Look here, should you mind awfully if I went to France for a bit, supposing I can get a job? . . . I'll hate leaving Oxford for some things – the place, and some of the people, and the music and so on . . . but it's the everlasting bother of how and where to live.

Her restlessness was increased by her knowledge that Whelpton was leaving Oxford. He had been awarded a war degree at the end of 1918 and though he thought of continuing to read history, with a view to trying for the Foreign Office, he found the English climate too harsh and his health was not improving. Consequently, in May 1919 he accepted a post teaching English at a school in Normandy. Rather pointedly, Dorothy wrote to ask him if he could find her a job in France. At the end of June she wrote to Muriel Jaeger:

I am going down next week – it may be for ever – I don't know. I am negotiating for various things just at present – possibly a year in France. It is nearly impossible to get anywhere to live in Oxford – I'm turned out of here next term and feel that a complete change would be a good thing. At present all is confusion as regards plans, and I should like to cut my throat.

She often used this exaggerated expression, sometimes for quite trivial reasons, so it need not be taken literally here. Nevertheless, she knew now that it would be a mistake to stay on longer in Oxford and this depressed her.

L'Ecole des Roches, the boarding school where Whelpton was teaching, is situated in spacious surroundings near Verneuil in Eure, in the south of Normandy. Soon after he arrived, the headmaster invited him to organise a bureau for the exchange of French and English pupils. For this purpose he would need an assistant who was fluent in both languages. Whelpton, remembering Dorothy's letter, offered her the job. On 22 July she wrote again to Muriel Jaeger:

Last night I had to decide several things in a great hurry, and lost my head. France has materialised very suddenly. After our conversations of last Easter, you will be amused to know that I am going out to be Mr Whelpton's secretary. He is running a sort of Educational Bureau out there.

The formal use of the surname seems surprising nowadays, when people are so quickly on Christian-name terms. At that period, even between women, surnames were used for a long time until a stage of friendship was reached when the change was judged to be welcome. Writing to her mother to ask if her three Somerville friends may come to stay at Bluntisham, Dorothy refers to them as Miss Jaeger, Miss Godfrey and Miss Rowe. And although, according to Doreen Wallace, Whelpton had fainted in Dorothy's sitting-room and she had "cooed over him", they still addressed each other as Mr Whelpton and Miss Sayers. This is shown by a letter from Dorothy, dated 29 July 1919, arranging for him to visit her parents before she went to France:

Dear Mr Whelpton,
Many thanks for your kind letter, in which you seem to have thought of everything. I was just going to ask you about the bicycle. I will track the Cycle Touring Club to its lair without delay, and cope with the passports and things.
This is just to say that I feel sure the family will be charmed to inspect you at Christchurch on the 16th. – Are you aware that the 17th is a Sunday, and that you will have to hear Dad preach (being the 3rd Sunday in the month)? – No! I recollect, you never go to church, so it's all right. If you really don't mind coping with a Sunday in our midst, of course we shall simply love to have you, and then I will return with you on Monday, if that pleases you. I will tell them about it at home, and will you please let me know in good time where you will be coming from on the 16th, so that Dad can arrange to fetch you from the nearest available point. Christchurch is the last place God made, and when He'd finished he found He'd forgotten the stair-case! . . .
Very sincerely yours,
Dorothy L. Sayers

Although she was then twenty-six years old, it was thought desirable for her parents to meet the man for whom she would be working abroad. Whelpton has described his visit to Christchurch:

Mr Sayers was an excellent host, a fine scholar and a well-bred gentleman . . . As he was obviously anxious to find out whether he could entrust his daughter to my care, I saved him some embarrassment by telling him my affections were already engaged, that I had no romantic intentions whatsoever with regard to Dorothy, that she would be lodged in a different house and I should see very little of her outside office hours since, otherwise, in the social conditions that prevailed in provincial France at that time, we should be compromised . . .

Dinner was served in a pre-war atmosphere; a trim maid waited on us, and both Dorothy and her mother wore evening dress; I wore a dinner jacket, a garment still considered rather informal.

Dorothy was not entirely at her ease, for I do not think that she would have accepted the job at Les Roches if her parents had disapproved of me. Her grey-haired mother wore a dark dress trimmed with beautiful old lace, and impressed me as being a distinguished gentlewoman, very far from being worn down by her duties as a vicar's wife.

L'Ecole des Roches consisted then of six main houses, scattered over an estate in peaceful countryside. The panorama, still unspoilt, must have reminded Dorothy of the views round Bluntisham, which it much resembles. It was founded at the end of the nineteenth century by Edmond de Moleyns. Pupils were drawn mainly from the French élite – aristocrats, titled landowners, prosperous shipbuilders, railway tycoons and merchant bankers. The sons, and also the daughters, of members of the staff were accepted as pupils. There were several women teachers and Madame de Moleyns, the widow of the founder, was the house mother.

Dorothy crossed from Southampton to Le Havre and travelled to Verneuil by train via Paris. She took her bicycle with her, as Whelpton had advised. It was indeed necessary for getting to and fro between the buildings. Whelpton lived in the house known as la Guichardière. Dorothy was lodged some way off in le Vallon, the house of the deputy headmaster, Count Marty. The office of the Bureau, where Dorothy and Whelpton worked together, was in a building facing a small wood. To reach it they had to cross meadows starred in the spring with cowslips and buttercups. Dorothy at once wrote happily to Muriel Jaeger:

I think this adventure is going to be quite amusing . . . The "Boojum" [Muriel's word for Whelpton] met me at Verneuil and we drove out to the school under a most romantic moon, in a strange little foreign cart with a sort of tilt. So here we are established! – and it's a lovely place – woods all round, and a delightful little old-fashioned town about two miles off. What do you want to know about the "Snark"? [This was Dorothy's alternative word for Whelpton.] He is much better in health than he was, anyhow, though he did have a heart-attack the other day – and handsomer than ever. But that does not interest you. As an employer – just what I expected – brilliant in some ways – I really admire his grasp of things and his amazing dexterity in handling people. Feckless in others, and has to be thoroughly nurse-maided as regards office routine.

She had to supply him with everything and show him how to manage carbon paper in the typewriter. He even asked her to cut his hair; she refused, not regarding that as part of a secretary's duties.

Writing to Ivy Shrimpton she reports that the school "is a very jolly place. The boys are charming and so are all the teaching crowd, and I get on fine with I think I may say all of them." Whelpton, she says, is "a pretty groggy specimen and I have occasionally to cope with faints and ague and heart-attacks and all sorts – However, he's a really good sort and we get along well together on the whole." He had thoughtfully chosen the most agreeable of the school houses for her to live in and took the trouble to introduce her to local families. She tells her parents she is making "heaps of friends". She works at her viola in her spare time, hoping to be good enough to play in the school orchestra, which she proves to be. She also takes part in chamber music, a new experience which she finds "very jolly". Francis Hill, the music teacher, and his wife, who is a violinist, want her to join in quartets with them.

In October Whelpton fainted and fell off his bicycle, or fell off and then fainted (he could not remember which). He landed on his right shoulder and dislocated it:

He has had doctors and people pulling him about all day. It must hurt like the devil. He is very plucky about pain, but if it gets too bad he faints, and of course he can't sleep at all, so we're in for a pretty cheerful week. It's like Bath Place over again, except that I'd fifty times rather have to deal with a sprained shoulder than with nameless nervous attacks.

It appears that after this episode Whelpton began to respond to

91

Dorothy's obvious interest in him. He complimented her on her hair style and on her black jumper adorned with a Tudor rose (stitched on in an obliging moment by Doreen Wallace in Oxford). He told her she had pretty hands, a nice neck, beautiful shoulders, good legs, good ankles, a good temper and "a bit of the devil in [her]". All this she reports to her parents, adding that he is quite wrong about the legs and ankles, otherwise "the rest is true". She seems to have had some moral scruples, perhaps about her feelings towards him, for she says in the same letter that she is hoping to get to Oxford for a few days: "It's convenient for confessions and things – awful arrears to be made up after all these excommunicate months!" There was an English chapel in the school grounds, but Dorothy, by then a High Anglican, evidently did not find it adequate for her spiritual needs.

In warm weather she played bridge with her colleagues at a table set out under the trees among the cow parsley. One of the group was an old Etonian and ex-cavalry officer named Charles Crichton. He regaled the company with stories of his club, his adventures during the London season and at country-house parties and of the eccentric gentleman's gentleman who looked after him in his flat in Jermyn Street. Bates by name, he had formerly been a footman in a ducal house. At the outbreak of war he enlisted in Crichton's regiment and became his batman. Crichton had been impoverished by the war and was obliged to earn his living. He still managed to dress well. He possessed three dress suits, three winter overcoats, three coats for the spring and three raincoats. He held that suits and overcoats should never be worn two days in succession. He once said to Whelpton: "Do you know, I bought these shoes ready-made at Harrods. I could not wear them in England: everyone would be staring at my feet."

He lodged in the same house as Dorothy and, according to Whelpton, for some reason they disliked each other intensely. However that may be, since they met daily at meals, she must have absorbed a good deal of information from him concerning social behaviour in high life which was to prove useful to her when she created Lord Peter Wimsey and his entourage. Bates was clearly a model for Bunter.

When Dorothy first arrived she was asked to teach a class of boys to act an English play. She accepted merrily and wrote for advice to her theatrically experienced friend, Dorothy Rowe. When Whelpton fell ill or was away she took over his classes and corrected his pupils' essays. She herself often accompanied groups of boys to and fro across the Channel, thus having an occasional few days in London at the Bureau's expense and seeing her friends. Sometimes her parents travelled down to London to meet her.

The work in the office was not demanding and she and Whelpton spent much time talking to each other. He held forth to her on the difference between the French and the English attitude to sex, a question she was to introduce into her novels. He told her about an unhappy love affair, about his anxiety concerning his health, his fears that he could never marry, and never obtain the work he wanted — "all this", she wrote to her parents, "with his head buried on my knees and making me smell of brilliantine in the most compromising manner!"

They talked about books and writing. She spent much of her spare time reading crime stories. When he teased her about this, she told him that she and some Oxford friends were thinking of forming a syndicate to write detective stories, for which they believed they could create a market. She had in fact discussed the matter with Michael Sadleir; G. D. H. Cole and his wife Margaret were also said to be interested. She invited Whelpton to join with them and make his fortune. He declined, having no liking for such books. Sad to say, he admitted in later life that he had never been able to finish any of her detective novels. Of her works, the one he admired most was her translation, *Tristan in Brittany*, which he had discussed with her in Oxford; she had daringly drawn his attention to the episode of Iseult of the White Hands and the water which splashed her thighs.

Looking back, Whelpton said later that he had the impression that the figure of a detective (as yet unnamed) was taking shape in her mind at Verneuil, based partly on Charles Crichton and partly on himself. He had many of the attributes of Lord Peter Wimsey. He bought his suits in Savile Row, his shirts from Hall, his shoes in Jermyn Street. He was widely travelled and knew the world of high society in London and Paris. He was a connoisseur of food and wine. He talked to Dorothy about many such matters. He also told her about his mother's aristocratic forebears and their Elizabethan family manor house near Ruthin, in Wales, which had a mile-long drive; and about one of his ancestors who had saved the life of Charles I at the Battle of Naseby. If Whelpton's surmise is correct, and it is plausible, then several traits of Crichton and himself were blended in Dorothy's imagination to form a character who was to have the physical appearance of Roy Ridley, the Newdigate prize-winner of six years before.

An event occurred which threw Dorothy and Whelpton closely together, literally at one moment into each other's arms. A young unmarried woman on the staff, named Adèle, became pregnant. Her mother refused to help her and, in her desperation, she was considering an abortion. Horrified, Dorothy turned to Whelpton for advice, knowing that he had relatives in Paris who were involved in charitable work. Telling him about the case, she burst into tears. He took her in his arms and promised to do what he could. Dorothy wrote grandiloquently to her parents: "So you see we two irresponsible young people are resolutely founding a family, in a morganatic kind of way! However, we are not going to have any crimes committed, that's the chief thing." She referred to the girl's plight as "a long and very silly story . . . these stories are always so trivial – nothing at all inspiring about them". The father (by a strange anticipation of Dorothy's later involvement, he was a Russian Jew) had no intention of marrying the girl; and Dorothy would not "with any conscience force a man into a marriage he doesn't want; nothing but misery could come of it".

Having taken an interest, she does not let the matter drop. She goes several times to visit Adèle in Paris: "I dread loneliness for her. I must make a point of seeing her whenever I go and I shall stay a couple of nights with her at Christmas . . . She has now a number of very good friends . . . and a good prospect of work and assistance . . . A friend has lent her a flat and will look after her 'when her time comes'."

By the turn of the year Dorothy's relations with Whelpton had reached a crisis. As he himself later admitted, working together alone in a small room for five or six hours a day was a situation which was bound to lead to some degree of intimacy. He knew then that Dorothy was in love with him: she openly admired him, wrote poems to him which she left secreted in his blotter and frequently put her arms round him. Being the gentleman he was, he exercised self-restraint, but he was not entirely unresponsive:

During our hours together in France there was a charming and intimate companionship, punctuated at times when I did yield a little to her physical transports . . . I had a deep affection for her and I did my best not to hurt her . . . The disaster for both of us was that she was so physically attracted, otherwise our marvellous friendship would have continued for forty years, to our mutual benefit.

Towards the end of 1919 Whelpton went to London for a few days. While at a theatre he met someone with whom he fell deeply in love. They hoped to marry but were obliged to keep their engagement a secret because the lady, already married, was trying to divorce her husband and discretion was essential. Nevertheless, letters arrived from her at the office almost daily and Dorothy suffered all the torments of jealousy. At one point the situation became so tense that she offered to leave. They settled things between them but Whelpton had already begun to lose interest in the Bureau and was spending more time in London. Dorothy's spirits drooped and she succumbed to an epidemic of mumps.

This was a tedious set-back. However, she was spirited and well enough to write to Muriel Jaeger, asking her to send all the Sexton Blake books she could lay hands on, "in discreet packages of about two at a time, for I am doomed to 21 days' solitary confinement with nothing to read . . . isolated from my office and my employer". Together they conducted a brilliant spoof analysis of the Sexton Blake saga, tracing its origins to solar mythology, resurrection legends and folk rituals. Muriel wrote learned letters under the name of "Hunter" (continuing the pseudonym of H. Hunter which she had assumed in the *The New Witness* hoax). Dorothy signed herself "Alexander Mitchingham": ("this seems to me a nice, scratchy sort of name for a professor of comparative religion, so I hereby adopt it"). In this *persona*, she argued that the Sexton Blake stories were connected with the Osiris mysteries and possibly with the Mithraic solar ritual and with Oriental Jesus-cults, "whose solar origins have been so indisputably established by Drews and Robertson". (She was to make Charles Parker refer solemnly to these authors when he discusses theology with Lord Peter in *Whose Body?*) The Sexton Blake romp was an anticipation of the contributions she was later to make to the "higher criticism" of the saga of Sherlock Holmes.

As a result of her illness her hair began to fall out again. She spent a few days in Paris, where she visited Adèle and also had an enjoyable time visiting museums and going to a "ripping concert" at the Châtelet. She also consulted a hair specialist who told her she had no specific disease but was in generally poor health; he prescribed a number of lotions and ointments.

Whelpton, who had been job-hunting in London, decided to become a partner in a house agency in Florence. He was eager now to live in Italy, a country which had enchanted him as a child. He hoped also to set up home there with the woman he wished to marry. (Sadly, this was not to be, for Frances, as she was named, died mysteriously, probably of tuberculosis, a few months later.) Before leaving, he offered Dorothy the chance to take over his interest in the Bureau for the money he had put into it, namely forty pounds. For some time she considered the possibility quite seriously: "It's not every day one can buy a show of one's own for £40!" The work of the Bureau was increasing and the outlook seemed promising. She made contact with the Anglo-French Society in London, hoping they might set up an office and employ her to run it from there. In the meantime, "I seem to play the viola all day long . . . The Hills very much want me to go on tour with them in a quartet at Christmas if they can get one up. Of course I should like nothing better. I hope it comes off." They advise her to keep on with her violin, and say she could make money as an orchestral player, but she is more inclined to stick to the viola and to look out for quartet playing in London.

She has occasional "black times", but they do not last long and her hair is growing again. She sticks loyally to her responsibilities. With Whelpton away she has all his English classes to cope with. The headmaster too will be away in August, so it will be necessary for her to stay on, especially as Whelpton will have left by then. She even considers collaborating with the headmaster to produce an Anglo-French textbook for schools.

Adèle's baby was born in June: "It's a boy, I'm glad to say . . . she can really make good, and will have something to fill her life." She will have to find work and Dorothy hopes to help her in this. She even asks her mother if she could take her on at Christchurch – "she cooks splendidly". Could she offer her shelter, if need be? "I'm determined to make a good job of Adèle, and it's *after* the crisis that people need help most – which is what so many people won't understand." It is not known how Mrs Sayers responded to this suggestion or what further steps Dorothy took to find Adèle work in England. A year or two later she reports that Adèle is in London teaching at the Berlitz School of Languages. The little boy is being cared for somewhere in the country. That is the last mention of them, except that Dorothy gives the name Adèle to the French maid of Mademoiselle Vonderaa in *Clouds of Witness* – not a very attractive character.

Finally, by the end of September 1920 the headmaster had found a replacement for her; she was free to pack her trunks, tie a label on her bicycle and make her farewells. She had no job, no prospects – just a strong urge to write and a determination to avoid teaching if she could. London beckoned.

CHAPTER 6

London

It was 1920 – a time of economic depression, widespread unemployment, and ex-service men selling matches in the street. The loss of life in the war had upset the demographic balance and there were two million "surplus" women, as they were called. Dorothy was one of them. She was also unemployed.

Aged twenty-seven, she had published two volumes of poetry and had held three jobs in the space of four years, none of them leading anywhere. She had received a proposal of marriage, unwelcome, and several men had sought her company, one or two with serious intentions which she had not encouraged. She was in love with Eric Whelpton, who was fond of her but no more. A farewell lunch in London before he went to Italy had ended in humiliation: she had asked him back to her lodgings for "coffee" and he had refused.

She had a number of very good women friends who would continue to be important to her all her life. Several had been members of the Mutual Admiration Society, whose bonds, like those of the Inklings, were enduring. She had no money, apart from what her father could afford to send her and what little, if anything, she had been able to save from her salary.

In October she received a boost to her morale. Oxford University had consented to regularise the position concerning degrees for women. Up till then they had been eligible only for the title to a degree: they were not officially graduates. (This remained the situation at Cambridge University until 1947.) On 14 October 1920 a ceremony was held in the Sheldonian at which the first batch of qualified women – Dorothy L. Sayers among them – were formally invested first with a B.A. and immediately afterwards with an M.A. (the requisite minimum of five years having elapsed since the graduands had taken their final exams). It was the first time in

Oxford that a woman had been addressed by the academic title *domina*, the feminine of *dominus*, representing the status of B.A., or *magistra*, the feminine of *magister*, representing the status of M.A.

Dorothy had chosen to take part in the first of the ceremonies: "It will be so much more amusing". It did have its amusing moments (the Vice-Chancellor in his embarrassment tapped one graduand on the head with his mortar-board instead of with the Testament, as he should have done), but it was also solemn and historically momentous. From now on all Oxford women graduates would be entitled to write B.A., or M.A.,(Oxon.) after their names. For the first time women undergraduates would wear gowns and soft peaked caps (the shape of headgear chosen as the equivalent of mortar-boards) – a sight to stir "even the unchanging passivity of Oxford", as Vera Brittain expressed it. Not all were pleasurably stirred. A facetious undergraduate, writing for an Oxford journal, described the "strange vision" of a woman in cap and gown alighting from a bicycle: "I realised with a pang that I was in the presence of my equal and Schools assumed a new terror for me. The woman undergraduate stood revealed. Two senile, placid dons passed me. '*Monstrum horrendum informe*', I heard one murmur – " "a monster fearful and hideous" – Virgil's description of Polyphemus. If Dorothy read this article in 1920 or Vera Brittain's reference to it in *Testament of Youth*, published in 1933, it perhaps suggested to her another term of abuse for female intruders upon male territory, namely harpies. If so, this may be the origin of the quotation, also from Virgil, found pinned to the dummy hanging in Shrewsbury College Chapel in *Gaudy Night*.

The academic prospects of Dorothy L. Sayers, M.A. (Oxon.) were far from bleak. With her first class Oxford degree in French she was eminently qualified to teach and could have obtained a post at one of the best schools in London. No teaching diploma was required at that time and she had in any case had four terms' experience in Hull. But she was determined to avoid a teaching career if possible. There was another avenue open to her: she could have applied to Somerville College to enter for a post-graduate degree in mediaeval French literature. This would have meant further expense for her father, but it is possible that Miss Pope would have been able to put some lecturing and tutoring in her way. Her interest in the subject was still alive in 1916, when she applied for a reader's ticket to Cambridge University Library; and she had already translated part at least of the romance of Tristan by the Anglo-Norman poet Thomas, two long sections of which were published in the journal *Modern Languages* in 1920. (The complete translation was not published until 1929.) She had, therefore, some hankering after scholarly work but she always denied, in later life, that she had ever wanted an academic career. Her creative urge was far stronger and she preferred the company of writers and artists to that of dons. From now on Bohemian London would be her sphere.

On one of her journeys between France and England she had met a film producer named Cyril Mannering. He suggested that she should write a screen scenario of a successful novel by Vincent Blasco Ibañez, *Blood and Sand*. Dorothy's optimism was always exuberant. She wrote excitedly to Muriel Jaeger: "Supposing one could sell, say, £250 or £300 worth of scenarios per annum, one could live where one liked." In Italy, for instance, she day-dreamed; the exchange rate was favourable ... and Eric Whelpton was in Florence. She asked Dorothy Rowe to collaborate and went several times to stay with her in Bournemouth. Together they worked out a viable script entitled *The Matador*. Mr Mannering declared himself "immensely pleased" with it, but unfortunately he had omitted to find out whether the rights of the book were free. Nothing more is heard of *The Matador*, so possibly they were not. This did not diminish Dorothy's zest. Still encouraged by Mannering, she went on writing film scenarios and found them "very amusing to construct". It may even be that she sold some.

Accommodation in London was a problem. She thought first of sharing a flat with Muriel Jaeger, who proved a staunch and valuable friend at this period. Her prospects, however, were uncertain and she tended to throw up jobs without warning. A flat was in any case difficult to find and Dorothy settled for an unfurnished room at the top of a women's club at 36 St George's Square, Pimlico. (She was to locate Lord Peter Wimsey's assistant, Miss Climpson, in a top-storey flat in the same square.) The only furniture she had was a camp bed, which she bought for thirty-five shillings, and a table and an arm-chair lent by Muriel. Fortunately, her father continued to send her a monthly allowance; and through a contact with some unspecified Polish organisation he was able also to pass on French documents to be translated into English. At a shilling a page the work was quite well paid. Blithely optimistic once again, Dorothy saw herself earning as much as ten pounds a week. The work did not materialise at that quantity but her situation eased a little. She made her room more comfortable – her parents sent furniture from Christchurch – and she splashed out on a bed-cover "of a sort of futurist pattern in orange, black and violet".

At the end of October she allowed herself another visit to Dorothy Rowe, who was busy with a production of Pinero's *Trelawney of the Wells*. Several beautiful early Victorian costumes were stored in her house. Dorothy, who loved clothes, tried them on: "There is an evening dress of flowered puce silk which suits me down to the ground. When I have made my pile out of Poland I shall have an evening dress like that – slipping off one's shoulders, and with a crinoline – It would be such a sensation when everybody else was in hobbled skirts!"

She continued to apply for various jobs, without success. At the end of the year, despite her dislike of teaching, she accepted a temporary post at Clapham High School. Florence Barry, head of the English department there, whom she had known at Somerville, had been given leave of absence in the winter term of 1921 to complete her thesis for a B. Litt., entitled "A Century of Children's Literature". She asked Dorothy if she would deputise for her. English was not her professional field but she felt she could rise to the occasion. It would require some preparation, though, "and if another Polish book comes along it will make things a bit of a rush", she commented.

Over sixty years later, three former pupils of Clapham High School still recalled her as "a memorable bird of passage". The girl who was door monitress on Miss Sayers' first morning remembered her approach down the corridor "looking rather ungainly, pale-faced, hair crimped back into a bun, pince-nez dangling round her neck, wearing a shapeless black dress down which it looked as if she had dropped half her breakfast". (This may have been the black jumper with the Tudor rose, seen from a distance. If so, she was making her clothes last a long time.) The door monitress gave a disparaging signal and the class made up its collective mind it could safely ignore the substitute mistress. Their passive resistance lasted five minutes at most. "We were transfixed, eyes staring, ears listening to the pearls that began to fall from her lips." Her teaching methods were unusual. Ignoring a seat, she would lie stretched out on one of the benches along the wall, feet up, her chin propped on an elbow. On one occasion she seized a sword suspended above the classroom mantelpiece and "stumped up and down between the desks brandishing it above her head, quoting meantime from *The Pirates of Penzance*: 'with cat-like tread upon our prey we steal'". She left on her pupils the impression of a startling personality.

Her Hull pupils, who had known her five years before, remembered her as attractively dressed, gay and laughing. The Clapham girls recalled her deep voice, piercing blue eyes and daunting look.

The merry, self-confident young Oxford graduate with the dimpled smile has gone. She is five years older, working hard and worried about money. Evidently she can no longer afford to dress well.

Before taking the job at Clapham, she had moved to 44 Mecklenburg Square, where she had "a lovely Georgian room, with three great windows and a balcony looking into the square". (She later gave this room to Harriet Vane, who sits at her desk, gazing out with unseeing eyes at a game of tennis, trying to make up her mind whether to attend the Shrewsbury Gaudy.) Her father helped with the removal expenses and the cost of new equipment. The landlady did not provide board so Dorothy had now to learn to cook. She began with eggs and a frying-pan. She also relied on modest restaurants. "Food is my most sinful extravagance," she wrote; "I am just going out to get a huge dinner in Soho for two shillings and three pence (beer extra!)" She worked long hours in her spare time, translating documents for "the Poles". On Saturdays she studied books on criminology in the Reading Room of the British Museum.

This must have been the period when she was planning her first detective novel. On 22 January 1921 she wrote to her mother:

> I have chosen this moment to be visited with ideas for a detective story and a Grand Guignol play ... My detective story begins brightly, with a fat lady found dead in her bath with nothing on but her pince-nez. Now why did she wear pince-nez in her bath? If you can guess, you will be in a position to lay hands upon the murderer, but he's a very cool and cunning fellow. The Grand Guignol play ends with a poisoned kiss!

Nothing more is heard of the Grand Guignol play but the novel turned into *Whose Body?*, in which Lord Peter Wimsey made his first public appearance in 1923. Dorothy said later that the idea of a body in the bath began at a party at Oxford at which one person had to set a story going, the others then continuing it in turn. In *Whose Body?*, the corpse is not that of a fat lady but of a man with Semitic-type features, also wearing pince-nez. He is mistaken by a police Inspector for a Jewish financier who has at that moment disappeared. Lord Peter knows at once "by the evidence of [his] own eyes" that this cannot be – a discreet allusion to the fact that the body in the bath is uncircumcised. In an early version she had made this detail explicit. The publishers asked her to censor it and she complied. However, she left a number of hints on the matter, including one which must have appealed to her mischievous sense of humour. Lord Peter's friend,

Detective Inspector Charles Parker, enjoys studying theology in his spare time. At one point Lord Peter comes upon him reading a commentary on the Epistle to the Galatians. Why the Epistle to the Galatians? Because it contains St Paul's views on the subject of circumcision. The literary clues in her novels are always subtle. Parker, however, does not make the connection. He still thinks the body in the bath may be the Jewish financier.

She was obviously over-working. Muriel Jaeger appears to have thought so for one Saturday morning she picked her up at the British Museum and carried her off to the Regent's Park Zoo. On another occasion she took her to the National Portrait Gallery. "I had no idea it was so interesting," Dorothy commented. (Years later her own portrait, by Sir William Hutchison, was to hang there.) Muriel encouraged her and urged her on when the novel got stuck and Dorothy was to dedicate it to her when it was published.

In the summer of 1921 Dorothy went home to the rectory in Christchurch and completed her novel there. She also earned some money coaching pupils in French at a nearby rectory in Upwell, which was to serve in part as the setting for *The Nine Tailors*. Her parents continued to help and encourage her and her letters to them show what her life was like from week to week. They send her fresh eggs from the country, and daffodils to decorate her room – once even some budding twigs. She sends her washing home to save laundry bills. And she is trying hard to get a job. In April 1921 she wrote to her cousin Ivy: "My life is dull really just at present – but I can't see how it's to be mended. I don't want a career and careers don't want me . . . Still, I'm no worse off than lots of other unmarried women, and a lot better off than many, so it doesn't do to grouse too much." She wants very much to hang on in London, even though hope of a job is faint. "I love it in spite of everything."

In November 1921 "Lord Peter", as she then referred to her first novel, was being typed: "I expect he'll cost about £7, curse him!"; and she thinks gloomily of how little chance there is of ever selling him. Nevertheless, she has already begun on her second novel, *Clouds of Witness*: "I spend all my time reading or writing crimes in the Museum! Nice life, isn't it? I've done the coroner's direction to the jury today and I feel quite exhausted." She has been promised introductions to publishers. This is another reason why she wants to stay in London:

After spending so much time on him [i.e. Lord Peter], and getting him typed (and I'm afraid the bill for that will have to go home too) it would be absurd not to make some energetic effort to place him. The typist is dawdling over him, it seems to me . . . If only he'd sell! . . . I'm afraid he can never be "a jolly extra" [as her father had suggested] because as a matter of fact it takes all one's time and energy to invent even bad sensational stories . . . Every time I look at him he seems more feeble.

A publisher's reader shows interest and by the end of November she is talking of negotiating terms. She does not want to sell the copyright, even though that would bring in some much needed money. It would damage the series "if I produced subsequent Lord Peters . . . I am quite sure now there is money in him. I was worried for fear I might have produced a complete white elephant!" She is hopeful that within the next three months she will get some definite offer, and on 19 December she writes decisively to her parents:

Nobody can feel more acutely than I do the unsatisfactoriness of my financial position . . . If you like I'll make a sporting offer — that if you can manage to help me to "keep going" until next summer, then, if Lord Peter is still unsold I will chuck the whole thing, confess myself beaten and take a permanent teaching job.

The offer was genuine. Surprisingly, in view of her attitude, she had by then had an enjoyable experience of teaching. That autumn she had accepted a temporary post at a high school for girls at Acton, in West London. In November she had written to her parents while sitting in a classroom, supervising girls doing their preparation:

I am writing this in prep! I like this school, as schools go; they feed you well and treat you well. The headmistress and staff are particularly nice, and I like the girls, though one or two forms have obviously been giving my unhappy predecessor a hell of a time. At 10 minutes past 12 precisely I shall proceed to mete out frightfulness in Upper IV A where it is badly needed. The Upper V German division, supposed to be tartars, have come to heel in the most charming way; I wonder if they have anything in pickle for me!

Her pupils evidently liked her, for she told Ivy that "dozens of schoolgirls" wrote her "long rigmaroles" about literature and expected her to answer. "They think me 'Oh! so charming' and I wish they wouldn't." By the end of three months, she tells her parents, "there will be a [permanent] Modern Languages post vacant at

Acton, and I feel certain that if I were to apply for it, Miss Sprule would give me the preference over any other candidate, and I have liked teaching in Acton better than in any other school I have ever struck." She hopes, however, it will not come to that: "One reason why I am so keen about Lord Peter is that writing him keeps my mind thoroughly occupied, and prevents me from wanting too badly the kind of life I do want, and see no chance of getting."

In the meantime she has moved again, to a flat in 24 Great James Street, found for her by Muriel Jaeger. This was to be her London address for the rest of her life. At the end of December 1921 she wrote to tell Ivy that she had been plunged into the horrors of house moving. She had to leave Mecklenburg Square on 14 December and could not take vacant possession of the new flat until Christmas Eve. In the interval she stayed with friends and set about buying pots and pans and curtains and kitchen towels and knife powder and hearth brooms and gas fittings:

> Domestic work is very strenuous when you are not used to it. I've got a whole little flat now – three rooms and use of bathroom on my floor – and very pretty it all is, white-panelled everywhere, except in the kitchen, and all done up fresh by the landlord. I've taken it on a 3-years' lease.

The rent was seventy pounds a year. Her father suggested coming to see the flat, which was prudent of him, since he had agreed to pay the rent in advance. At her request he brought up her reproduction of Perugino's *Crucifixion* which hung in the drawing-room at Christchurch. Her mother sent up some cutlery. In thanking her Dorothy recalls the boot-boy at Bluntisham (was his name Eric Wallace?) who used to produce odd shapes of knives by polishing them on the knifeboard – "a thin waist and a blob on the end". She looks forward eagerly to her father's visit: "I'm really in love with [the flat]. I hope he will be, too, though it's so tiny he will hardly be able to stand upright in it." She has bought curtains at Barker's; her pictures will look lovely on the white panelled walls; she has been staining the sitting-room floor. "You'd laugh to see me tackling all these domestic jobs – the worst job was cleaning the gas-stove." She is now cooking an Irish stew.

Her father was evidently satisfied with what he saw for in January he sent a generous cheque. This enabled her to buy "a nice little black coat-frock of beautiful gaberdine and a splendid black corduroy skirt". Aunt Gertrude comes to lunch: the roast ribs of beef with roast potatoes, followed by a rice pudding, turn out very well. She has bought a multiple steamer and a patent claw for lifting tins out of the oven. She feels she has a "bent" for domesticity after all. She possessed in fact all the instincts of a home-maker and was rapturously happy every time she moved into new accommodation.

In January 1922 Ward, Lock and Co. were considering Lord Peter but hanging fire. She continued, however, with *Clouds of Witness* and in March she had a piece of good fortune. She had gone to Bournemouth to stay with Dorothy Rowe, whose company she always found congenial for her writing. While there she met Sir Arthur Marshall, a barrister and a Liberal politician:

> I pumped him for all sorts of information for the new story I'm writing, which has been hung up for some time for lack of legal details. He is being simply sweet about it, and taking a tremendous interest in working out the details. It's a very unusual case – a peer tried for murder – of course before the House of Lords – and he didn't know the procedure himself when I asked; but he made a point of finding out all about it yesterday from Lord Russell (who was tried for bigamy some time ago), and took me out to coffee this morning and simply filled me up with priceless information. Also he has promised to take me some time when there is an interesting case on in the Lords to show me what it looks like. He says it's very jolly to see – all the Lords in their robes, and counsel in full dress with full-bottomed wigs!

(Dorothy partly drew on him as a model for Sir Impey Biggs, the handsome barrister who makes his first appearance in *Clouds of Witness*.)

By April she has found an agent – Andrew Dakers – "who simply loves my Lord Peter and is certain of selling him . . . I do hope something will come of it . . . I have plenty of ideas for other books if this first one gets taken. After all, I'm sure writing is much more my job than office work or teaching." Hutchinson's are considering Lord Peter, "humming and hawing over him". They have asked for a synopsis of the second novel before deciding about the first.

Finally in July 1922 an offer arrives by cable from an American publishing house, Boni and Liveright. Hutchinson's have withdrawn and she must now begin all over again in the U.K., but with the prestige of the American offer behind her. She is to receive two hundred and fifty dollars in advance of royalties and has hopes that the story will be published as a serial first: "That is where the money is." The book itself will be published within the next twelve months. The title has now been chosen – *WHOSE BODY?* – a brain-wave of the American publishers. To celebrate, Dorothy gave a dinner in her flat for a woman friend and her agent Andrew Dakers, who honoured the occasion by coming in evening dress.

Despite her penury, Dorothy's social life in London had been lively. If she could only find a job, she said, she would be more or less permanently in high spirits. She has gone to lots of parties, theatres and even once to a night-club. Someone, she will not say who ("It's so nice to have a little mystery"), has taken her to tea and to lunch at the Ritz. J. C. Squire, who accepted one of her poems for *The London Mercury*, comes to tea and expresses interest in her translation of the *Romance of Tristan*. She gets to know Norman Davey, whose book, *The Pilgrim of a Smile*, she much admires. He takes her out several times and gives her presents: "I hope Norman isn't going to get devoted – that would be the culmination of all tiresomeness." She spends a jolly evening with him and Charles Scott-Stokes, the brother of a Somerville friend:

> I dined with Norman at Isola Bella and we went to see the Grand Guignol at the Little Theatre (my treat to him – because he had really given me such a lot of hospitality and small presents) and Charles [Scott-Stokes] joined us at the theatre. I'd been gloomy and grinding away at a new story and poverty-stricken and bothered for ever so long, and it was good to let out for one night and look nice and be taken everywhere in taxis.

Nothing is wrong, she told her parents, but the financial side. That was about to right itself. In March she had applied for a vacancy as a copy-writer with the advertising firm of S. H. Benson but had heard nothing. Then, in May, she was offered a job for a trial period of a month, at a salary of four pounds a week. In June the appointment was confirmed.

She wrote to tell her parents, thanking them rapturously for all their help. At last she was independent. The work was fun and would make an excellent stop-gap, enabling her to get on with her writing in her spare time. Benson's, situated in Kingsway, were only ten minutes' walk from where she lived. Everything, as she loved to say, was "gas and gaiters". But was it?

CHAPTER 7

John Cournos

During the years 1921 and 1922, while Dorothy was desperately trying to find a footing in London, writing her first two detective novels, translating, teaching and going about when she could with friends, her sexual life was in turmoil. She had fallen in love again, this time with consequences that were almost to destroy her.

Among the many events recorded in her letters home the name John crops up from time to time, but with no indication that he means anything more to her than her other male acquaintances. She was in fact bewitched by him.

John Cournos, a Russian Jew, was born in Kiev in 1881. His father's name was Korshoon, but when John was five years old his parents were divorced and his mother married again. John was given his stepfather's name of Cournos. When he was ten the family

John Cournos *(Alfred Satterthwaite)*

emigrated to the United States. Other children were born and times were hard. John attended school in Philadelphia but was obliged to sell newspapers to help the family to make ends meet. At the age of twelve he left school and worked in a spinning factory, first as a bobbin boy, then as a piecer for two dollars fifty a week. This was raised to three dollars when he was put in charge of a spinning mule with 500 spindles. When he was fourteen he walked into the building of the *Philadelphia Record* and happened to see that newspaper's proprietor, William M. Singerley, pacing up and down the hall. John handed him a note in which he had set out his circumstances and his need to earn money to help his family. Mr Singerley gave him a dollar bill. The boy said he did not want money but a job. Mr Singerley, impressed, engaged him on the spot as office-boy to the managing editor.

This was Cournos' introduction to the world of journalism. In the best American tradition, he rose to be assistant editor. In 1912 he decided to go to England to try his fortune as a free-lance. He interviewed H. G. Wells, G. K. Chesterton, John Masefield and Gordon Craig. The last-named invited him to become a member of his Theatre Committee, which included W. B. Yeats, Ezra Pound and Ralph Hodgson.

During the war he worked at Marconi House as a translator for the Russian Government and in 1917 he was appointed a member of the Anglo-Russian Commission to Petrograd, which included Hugh Walpole and Harold Williams, the foreign correspondent of *The Times*. On his return to London he worked for the Foreign Office and the Ministry of Information.

His first novel, *The Mask*, was published in 1919. Admired by celebrities such as W. B. Yeats, Ford Madox Ford and President Masaryk, it was awarded the Hawthornden Prize. He was a regular contributor to the *Criterion, The Times Literary Supplement, John o' London's Weekly* and other journals. As a poet he had won recognition as a member of the Imagist school. A volume of his poems, written in London and Petrograd, entitled *In Exile*, was published in the U.S.A. by Boni and Liveright in 1923.

He was in touch with literary and Bohemian London and he and Dorothy may have had friends in common. She was bound to find him attractive. He was tall and dark and somewhat like Eric Whelpton in appearance, but with the slanting cheek-bones of the Slav. He had the authority of an experienced, older man and could speak impressively of his travels and contacts. His voice was American with the remains of a Russian accent. He held passionate beliefs about life, literature and love. He had written two novels and was at work on a third – a vast would-be masterpiece in the tradition of Tolstoy. Dorothy's horizons were widened; she had never met anyone like him. His deprived and heroic childhood also stirred her admiration and compassion.

They met and talked and made love, though stopping short of consummation. Cournos told her he was resolved never to marry. It was against his principles as an adherent of the philosophy of free love, so much nobler, in his view, than matrimony, with its legal trammels and signing of documents. Dorothy, passionately in love, wanted to marry him and have children by him.

A comment thrown off in a letter to her mother, written in March 1921, is significant of her state of mind at this time. Her cousin Gwen is pregnant and Dorothy says admiringly: "If I can spin about and build rockeries when (or if ever) I'm seven months with child, I shall consider myself fortunate . . . I notice that the people like Christine Blackwell and Madame Marty, who skip around till the last moment, always have the jolliest babies." This is written by a woman who can imagine herself happily pregnant. A little while later she says: "I am really awfully domesticated when I like." She takes up sewing and cheerfully makes herself clothes, economically, out of remnants – a black camisole and "delightful underclothes all over little purple parrots". She takes pleasure in cooking. At the age of twenty-eight she is beginning to visualise herself as a competent wife and home-maker.

All during the time when she is planning and writing *Whose Body?* John Cournos is a foremost figure in her life. In the summer of 1921, when she plans to go home to Christchurch to finish the book, she asks if she may invite him to come with her: "He'll be no trouble, if he does come, being used to living under pretty uncomfortable conditions and asking nothing but kind treatment. – He is *not* the young man who entertains me at the Ritz." He did not come, but while she was at home she told her parents about him and induced them to read *The Mask*, which they liked. She told Cournos this and he replied: "Your mother and dad appear to be quite charming people from your accounts and I shall certainly contrive to meet them some day. But perhaps they won't like *The Wall* [his second novel] as well, or the handwriting on it may prove to be a little terrifying." Quoting this to her parents, Dorothy comments: "Personally, I think *The Wall* is not nearly so alarming as John thinks it is. Why do men love to make themselves out such wonderful devils when they aren't anything of the sort? John imagines he's a terrible person!" He suffers from depression and his moods are uncertain. As in the case of Whelpton, Dorothy believes she can cajole and rally him with kindness and good sense: "John came up to town for a day on Friday and I dined with him. He seemed more cheerful about his book [his third novel, *Babel*] than I have ever seen him. He really wants to know you. Perhaps I could get hold of him at Christmas, but he is really devoted to his work and finds it hard to get away." There is something touching about her attempts to introduce this elusive and moody foreigner into the bosom of an English country parsonage. Nor was he the companion for her that she looked for:

John was "nice" enough Friday week in a general way, but I fear he has no sympathy with Lord Peter, being the kind of man who takes his writing seriously and spells Art with a capital A. Norman [Davey], on the other hand, is very helpful. I was delighted with a dictum of Philip Guedalla's in the *Daily News*: "The detective story is the normal recreation of noble minds." It makes me feel ever so noble.

Dorothy, made to feel inferior by Cournos, took some reassurance from the opinions of others. Another and more serious disagreement threatened to bring the relationship to an end. On 18 January 1922 she wrote: "John turned up the other day and was all right, though deeply buried in *Babel*. He and I have had a difference, though, on a point of practical Christianity (to which he strongly objects!) and I may hear no more of him." The difference concerned the use of contraceptives, to which Dorothy would not agree. But she did hear more of him, almost at once, for on 14 February she wrote to say that he would be staying in her flat while she was away in Bournemouth visiting Dorothy Rowe and working on *Clouds of Witness*. From this it is plain that her second novel also belongs to what may be called her Cournos-ridden period.

I am leaving Cournos (who has finished the great work at last – 130,000 words – good gad!) to keep the flat warm in my absence. I couldn't let it for so short a time, and it will save his money, so it seems a convenient arrangement . . . I've got a pair of sheets for John, and pillow-cases which I bought cheap in the sales.

On her return from Bournemouth she mentions him again:

John was here to dinner last night – a very dainty dinner, though I say it; though he was too tired to do it full justice. He is exhausted with his work on *Babel*, and was hoping to be able to take a complete rest. Unhappily, his American sales of *The Wall* have turned out badly – owing, as he says, to the slackness, deliberate or otherwise, of the publisher – he is short of the money he had counted on, and has to go on working. He has no kind parents to fall back on, you see – in fact all his people do is clamour for money. And he has worked so hard, and suffered so much – he deserves something better of life.

In the midst of her own anxieties she finds it possible to sympathise with his and to offer what help she can. She writes again on 17 March: "I saw John yesterday; he is just off to spend a few months at work in Oxford. He is still tired out, but seemed really grateful to have a place of his own to lay his head while he was in town." She still longs for her parents to know him. In May she writes: "John is in Oxford [where her mother was also staying] – you may meet without knowing it. I'd ask him to call on you, but he's such an odd bird, you would probably find him a little difficult." In June she goes to Oxford herself and sees Cournos there; he is planning "a vast poem" and another novel. By then Dorothy's own fortunes have taken a turn for the better: she has landed the job with Benson's, which calls for a celebration: "I had John to dinner on Saturday – and the dinner was perfect. I had five courses, and they were all thoroughly successful and none of them came out of tins, except the jelly mixture, of course." And she copies out the menu:

Wines and Liqueurs
Vermouth – French *Noilly Prat*, Italian *Martinazzi*
Wine – Red Spanish Burgundy
Dinner
Hors d'Oeuvre – Grapefruit *rafraîchi* on ice with whipped cream
Potage – *Consommé au vermicelle*
Rôti – Beefsteak *à l'Anglaise*, potatoes and salad
Dessert – Fruit jelly with cream (natural fruit in calves' foot orange
    jelly)
Savoury – Baked mushrooms *en casserole* with coffee and *Grand
    Marnier Cordon Rouge*

She adds a postscript: "Aren't I a little wonder? I do like cooking nice dinners."

There are only two further references to Cournos after that. On 18

September 1922 she writes that he is returning to America in October; and on 13 November: "John hasn't so much as sent me a postcard since he went away." As she was later to discover, he had married somebody else.

Her parents probably breathed a sigh of relief. Even from these brief allusions it must have been evident to them that Dorothy was being made use of. The only thing she would seem to have gained from him was an introduction to Andrew Dakers, who proved to be an excellent agent. In fact, what was really happening between their cherished daughter and this unknown foreigner would have deeply distressed and horrified them.

The evidence can be pieced together from three sources: the letters which Dorothy later wrote to Cournos, the episode of Philip Boyes in *Strong Poison* and a novel by Cournos, *The Devil is an English Gentleman*.

With his high-flown ideals of love, Cournos hoped that Dorothy would agree to intercourse without a commitment to marriage. She would not agree and her chief objection was not to the act itself but to the use of contraceptives. Her attitude is not easy to understand. Religious scruples were not the problem for she was not a Roman Catholic. It is true that the work of Marie Stopes and other pioneers in birth control was sternly opposed by some Anglican clergy and by rigid moralists who feared that such measures would lead to promiscuity. Dorothy was a High Anglican but she was not a rigid moralist. She must have heard the subject discussed at Somerville. One of her close friends, Charis Barnett, was to become well known as the author of books and articles on contraception. Another contemporary, Margaret Chubb (later Mrs Geoffrey Pyke), became Secretary of the National Birth Control Association. The importance of such work in the liberation of women from the slavery of frequent child-bearing must have been obvious to someone of Dorothy's robust common sense. Yet she was to reproach Cournos, in a letter written after the affair was ended, with soiling their love by suggesting the use "of every dirty trick invented by civilisation to avoid the natural result . . . there is always that taint of the rubber-shop now".

It must be that her passionate desire to marry Cournos and become the mother of his children confused her normally rational mind; or perhaps she thought that if she yielded to him he would be less likely to marry her. Cournos said afterwards that he would have married her if she had yielded: he was waiting for her to prove her devotion. In their love-making they went so far as to undress and lie naked on a couch together, but no further. Either he was impotent or he took

Dorothy's Leonardo smile. She gave a copy of this photograph, by Dorothy Wilding, to John Cournos.

pleasure in the power that he, the son of impoverished Jewish immigrants, could thus exercise over an Oxford-educated, still virginal daughter of the Church of England. Whatever his motives, and he no doubt rationalised them to his satisfaction, the sexual torment he inflicted was an intolerable burden added to Dorothy's already harassed life. That she could maintain her equilibrium and an outward semblance of control is a measure of the strength of her inner creative powers.

When she was able to look back with detachment on this experience she dealt with it in the novelist's way: she objectified it in fiction. The relationship in *Strong Poison* between Philip Boyes and Harriet Vane has many similarities. Boyes, like Cournos, proclaims belief in the philosophy of free love. Harriet, thinking him sincere, consents to live with him. The situation continues for a year and then breaks down. Explaining matters to Lord Peter Wimsey, Harriet says:

"Philip wasn't the sort of man to make a friend of a woman. He wanted devotion. I gave him that. I did, you know. But I couldn't stand being put on probation like an office-boy, to see if I was good enough to be condescended to. I quite thought he was honest when he said he didn't believe in marriage – and then it turned out that it was a test, to see whether my devotion was abject enough.

113

Well, it wasn't. I didn't like having matrimony offered as a bad-conduct prize."

Strong Poison was published in 1930. John Cournos read it in America. He could hardly fail to recognise the parallel. It must have irked him exceedingly to read Harriet's off-hand dismissal of the character of Boyes: "rather a defeatist sort of person . . . apt to think people were in league to spoil his chances . . . his idea was that great artists deserved to be boarded and lodged at the expense of the ordinary man". Two years later he took his revenge.

The Devil is an English Gentleman, John Cournos' seventh novel, was published by Farrar and Rinehart, New York, in 1932. In two volumes, it relates the fortunes of three generations of an English county family. In Volume 2 Cournos tells the whole story of his affair with Dorothy, reproducing part of their conversation and even phrases from her letters. A character named Richard Thorley represents himself. The woman in the affair is Stella Thurston – Dorothy to the life, except that she has fair hair, instead of dark, and is a graduate of Girton College, Cambridge, instead of Somerville College, Oxford. All her other traits are so close as to be photographic. She is long-necked, her eyes are blue, her hair is parted in the middle (as Dorothy's was when Cournos knew her), she is tall and slender and walks with a bold swing; her arms are slim and shapely. In personality she is frank and direct, with a come-hither look and a line in witty badinage. Her "Leonardo smile" is subtly and tantalisingly flirtatious, but her veneer of sophistication conceals sexual inexperience – she is "a provincial virgin".

Richard Thorley does not believe in marriage. The war has made him a fierce hater of institutions and conventions. Nevertheless, tired of philandering, he is beginning, after all, to consider marriage. Stella has awakened his sexual desire but he is not sure of his feelings. He both likes and dislikes her. He much prefers her Leonardo smile to her conversation: "She insisted on talking, on being heard, and indulged in an excess of badinage . . . doubtless she would get by St Peter with a pert phrase."

Stella likes Richard at once from their first meeting. Her experience of men has been limited to a few casual liberties taken at a picnic or at a dance. He has awakened the woman in her; nobody has ever gone so far in making passionate love to her before. She feels that she is entering on the great adventure of her life.

Richard is inclined to marry her, but feels he must test her first. He has always looked for understanding and generosity in women. Does Stella have what he requires?

She invites him to dinner, which she cooks herself. It is delicious, accompanied by wine and ending with black coffee and a liqueur. They leave the table and retire to a couch piled with cushions. They caress each other. Slowly he undresses her. She makes no resistance. Then he removes his own clothes and she looks at him with interest. It is the first time she has seen a man naked. (Cournos, being a Jew, was circumcised – like the victim in *Whose Body?*)

Richard and Stella lie side by side on the couch.

They caressed one another with languid passion, deliberately restrained, as if in fear of the consequences of excess. She did not resist him, and he might have taken her. Though she desired to be taken, she inwardly held out against him and refrained from speaking the magic word he waited to hear.

He reads her secret thoughts: "If I give myself to him, he'll forsake me. I must have him forever or not at all." This he holds against her:

He wanted a woman capable of giving abundantly, unstinting, thoughtless of tomorrow; if he were assured of Stella being capable of this, he would take her for his own forever. He waited for the generous gesture, for a token of abandonment on her part; it did not come.

Stella does not understand what he wants. After a while, she pushes him away and cries bitterly. She feels ashamed to have been cheap in his eyes. She says: "I love you . . . and if you married me you'd have no cause for regret. I'd look after you. I'd do my best for you." But he wants surrender there and then, freely offered, not prompted by him. She asks him what he expects of her but he is unwilling to tell her. At one o'clock he leaves the flat and spends the rest of the night in a hotel.

A week later a frantic note arrives, pleading with him to come and see her. Again she cooks him a meal, again it is excellent, with wine, black coffee and Benedictine. Once more they undress and lie on the couch; again they torment each other with unfulfilled desire. They talk of marriage but Richard says he is not sure of himself – a way of saying he is not sure of her.

They continue to meet, to have meals together in Soho and in her flat. Sometimes they go to the theatre, which he loves, sometimes, for her sake, to the "pictures", which he loathes. They repeat the mutual nakedness, increasing their mutual frustration. They quarrel. He grows peevish, on one occasion refusing to stand in a long queue for some theatrical performance she was anxious to see.

She asks, "How will it end?"

He replies, "I don't want to marry. I'm afraid I'm not the marrying kind."

She asks, "What would you like me to do?"

He says, "You might become my mistress . . . if we pull along all right for a space we can discuss marriage." It is no longer a case of her voluntary surrender, but of probation.

She says, "Let me think it over."

Three days later, in response to a note, he calls at her flat. She says, "Why don't you marry me? If you ever get tired of me, I shall be quite willing to give you a divorce. That's fair enough, don't you think?"

He replies, "It's fair enough as far as it goes . . . But divorce is not to be had for the asking – not in this country. Why marry in the first place?"

She answers, "Because a woman must be careful. A woman with a lover cuts herself off from the world and from having children. She must wholly depend upon him and his companionship. But a woman with a husband can make her man's interests her own, and can look after his home. She can look the whole world in the face . . . I'm not sure I can stand the restrictions of 'free love'."

He replies, "And I of married love!"

Few readers of this pretentious novel, if they got this far, can have imagined that the description of so abnormal a relationship was anything but fiction – and strangely aberrant fiction at that. Set side by side with Dorothy's letters to Cournos, however, it is confirmed as true in every important detail. In the abortive love affair of these two novelists, fact was indeed stranger than fiction.

CHAPTER 8

A Man and a Motor-cycle

For all her satisfaction with her job at Benson's – her salary was soon raised to five pounds a week – Dorothy's emotional life was in ruins. At twenty-nine she had twice suffered rejection by men she loved. Her sexual feelings had been powerfully aroused and left unsatisfied. She could not long continue in this unnatural state; nor did she.

In December 1922, two months after Cournos had departed, she wrote home:

Dearest Mother,
Don't faint – I am coming home for Xmas on Saturday, with a man and a motor-cycle, with request that you will kindly give same a kind welcome and a few words of kindly cheer.

It's not anyone you know – it's a poor devil who has been staying with the people above me, and whom I chummed up with one weekend, finding him left lonely, so to speak, and he's been prettily grateful and has taken me out a lot on the bike. But he simply has not a red cent or a roof, and his job has gone bankrupt for the moment – the job being motors – so that, though he can always get petrol for nothing – he can get nothing else – and one can't eat petrol or sleep in it. That being so, and his friends departing for Xmas, and the poor blighter's own home being in some ungodly and far-off place, and him obliged to be in town again after Xmas – and so on – I said, would he save me my train fares home in exchange for his board and lodging, so to speak. He was really extraordinarily grateful! – My God! I've been lonely and poor enough alone in London to know what it feels like – and I know you'll have a fellow-feeling for the jobless. – So expect us some time Saturday. – Don't be alarmed – he's an absolute rock-bottom, first-class driver with safety attachment and all that.

Brooklands is his native heath, so to speak – engine-trouble an agreeable excuse for a wayside cigarette – no more.

His name is Bill White and I can vouch for his behaviour. Intellect isn't exactly his strong point – I mean, literary intellect – he knows all about cars, and how to sail a boat and so on – and in fact he's the last person you'd ever expect me to bring home, but he's really quite amiable, and will be desperately grateful for a roof over his head.

So it was Bill White, the motor-cyclist and car-salesman, not John Cournos, the high-brow novelist, whom the rector, Mrs Sayers and Aunt Mabel assembled to welcome as their guest that Christmas. He arrived clad in a leather jacket, leggings and boots, helmet and goggles. He was of medium height, spare and wiry, assertively masculine, with a look of determination on his plain, no-nonsense face. Dorothy had ridden pillion, clinging to his back, her arms round his waist, revelling in the speed, the vibration of the engine and the wind in her face. She had said she could vouch for his behaviour. This was a way of letting her mother know that though out of work he was socially presentable. The new motor-car business was attracting a fair number of young men of good address, though many of them were of limited financial resources. Some were successful and made money. Others came to grief.

The family no doubt received the invasion with competent tranquillity and a maid was instructed to conduct their guest to the spare bedroom. Whatever clothes he had brought in his saddle-bags, a formal suit, at least, would have been included, if not a dinner-jacket.

The Sayers family were always festive at Christmas. The house was decorated, there were log fires, a Christmas tree, carols, the exchange of presents, games, and chestnuts round the fire. Bill will have gone to church on Christmas morning and heard the rector preach. Dorothy, as she quite often did, may have sung a solo, in her fine contralto. Then back to the rectory for a traditional Christmas lunch, with turkey and plum-pudding. Left alone with the rector over the port, Bill was perhaps steered gracefully into a conversation about cars – the rector had a T-model Ford sedan. Bill may have told him about competing in the Tourist-Trophy motor-cycle races on the Isle of Man. On Boxing Day the local tradesmen will have called for their customary tips. Dorothy and Bill may have strolled in the garden or taken Tinker, the dog, for a walk round the village.

The next day came the bustling departure, Bill in motor-cycling kit once more, Dorothy well wrapped up – two figures waving from the sputtering, roaring machine as it disappeared down the road. We may imagine the rector waving after them and possibly wondering what, if anything, would come of *this* new relationship. He was never to know. Bill was a physical type, not literary and not intellectual. Unlike Cournos, he had no sexual hang-ups. He and Dorothy were not in love, but she was more than ready for sex and they were sufficiently attracted to each other to make it agreeable to both of them. She enjoyed his company and they had fun together. He was a good dancer and he taught her the up-to-date steps of the twenties – the bunny-hug, the shimmy and the black bottom. When there was a dance at Benson's, she asked him to go as her partner. He accepted and "did his duty nobly", she told her parents, which implies that she introduced him to her colleagues and that he had the social grace to dance with other women present. This occasion surely called for a dinner-jacket; possibly, since "he had not a red cent", they managed to hire or borrow one. She tells her parents that he has a job as a fitter on a small weekly wage, "enough to pay for an attic in a revolting slum off Theobald's Road. My neighbourhood is aristocratic in comparison!" She often gives him meals:

> I'm getting more and more ingenious in the cookery line. Honestly, if I didn't feed him pretty regularly, I don't know what would happen to him, poor wretch! However, he's a good little soul, and very easily kept amused, and has promised to stain my sitting-room floor for me, which is a great joy.

He does so and she reports that it looks wonderful. She has bought "two beautiful Persian rugs and an armchair nearly as big as the flat".

She introduces him to her friend Norman Davey, who had previously been her regular escort. A woman friend named Laura and one or two others persuade Norman to have dancing lessons and Dorothy and Bill arrange to go with them to a dance hall one evening in Cricklewood:

> So Bill, after a hard day's manual labour at his shop, and I, after the usual office grind, came home, washed and changed, had our dinner quickly and went round to pick up the others. Lo! and behold! There they were, lounging round the fire in an atmosphere you could cut with a knife, saying "Oh! it was such a foggy evening, and the dance hall was so far", and they didn't want to go and they weren't dressed, and they'd quite decided in their own

Left: Bill White on his motor-cycle in the Isle of Man *(Estate of Anthony Fleming)*

Above: Dorothy's son as a schoolboy; his resemblance to Bill White is marked. *(Estate of Anthony Fleming)*

minds that we shouldn't want to go either and "do be matey, Dorothy, and sit down and be comfortable with us". And Norman, roasting his posterior before the fire and looking all sleek and oily, saying in a haw-haw voice that it really was horrid out of doors – this to Bill, who had been testing motor-cycles all day in fog and rain and inches deep in liquid mud. I was so angry I could hardly speak and I found afterwards that Bill was just as bad. And I told Norman not to come the heavy over me, and the whole lot of them that they were damned unsporting, and Bill and I slammed out of the house and went to the Hammersmith Palais de Danse alone.

By now Bill has made her other friends seem effete – "soft-gutted", she called them, perhaps borrowing the phrase from Bill. In contrast, he was virile, tough and foul-mouthed. He told her dirty stories and recited limericks; and she, sitting on his knee in the big armchair, invented others, "each obscener than the last". (She was to give this coarseness to her aristocratic Lord Peter in *Clouds of Witness*, where he teases the middle-class Charles Parker by referring to the limerick about the young man at the War Office and the story of the young wife and the travelling salesman in bicycle pumps.) Bill liked pubs

120

and cinemas. He did not despise her (as Cournos had done) for doing crossword puzzles. He showed her how a motor-cycle worked. His enthusiasm was infectious. She learnt from him how pleasant it was "to feel the engine purring along in the lovely velvety way that means that everything is exquisitely adjusted and happy together". When she had a motor-cycle of her own, she enjoyed riding it and knew how to repair it. She owed to Bill her understanding of an air-lock in the petrol feed, which she was to use as a clue in *Unnatural Death*, her third novel.

On 22 May she tells her parents that Bill has got a job out of London and has gone away for a bit, "which is a good thing, as his late occupation was going steadily to the demnation bow-wows". There will be only one more mention of him in her letters home.

By then she knew she was pregnant. She had refused to use contraceptives with Cournos because she wanted children by him. Now, ironically, having used precautions with Bill, by whom she did not want a child, she had conceived by accident. It was a terrible shock. Everything had been going so well. She was enjoying her job at Benson's, where they thought highly of her. Only a year before she had written to thank her parents for all their patience and generous help in enabling her to lead an independent life in London. She could not bear to tell them what had happened. She sought the advice of a woman doctor, Alice Chance, her neighbour in Bath Place, Oxford, who had remained a friend. After Dorothy's death, Dr Chance told Eric Whelpton that they had discussed the possibility of abortion. If this is so, Dr Chance may have dissuaded her, for the methods then used were dangerous as well as illegal; or Dorothy herself may have decided against it. That she considered it at all, if she did, is a measure of her despair.

In June she went away for a fortnight's holiday to a cottage in Bovingdon, Hertfordshire. She had "a beast of a cold", she told her parents and she wanted a quiet place to write in. She described herself as setting off with a bag of books in one hand and her cat in the other – "the perfect travelling spinster!" This was disingenuous indeed.

She spent the two weeks in the cottage, with only her cat for company, thinking out her problem. When she returned to London she had made a crucial decision: she would keep her pregnancy secret from her parents. Had she decided otherwise, some of her difficulties would have been eased and her life might have been happier. But she was convinced that the news would cause them immense distress. They were both nearly seventy. Aunt Mabel was even older. Her mother suffered from a nervous complaint which was brought on by strain and worry. She thought of the embarrassment it would cause her father if word got out in the parish. She imagined the gossip among her aunts, uncles and cousins. Much better to face the thing alone.

This decision meant that she could not confide in any of her friends, for even the most discreet of them might let slip a word which would get back to Christchurch. This, for someone who always needed to relate what was happening and to share her thoughts and feelings, was a heavy price. The one exception was Dr Alice Chance but the secret was safe with her, for she had been consulted professionally.

There were other matters to be decided. What arrangements could she make for the child? Bill had stormed out, "in rage and misery", she later said, when she told him she was pregnant. But if he came round and was willing to share the responsibility, did she want to marry him? How would they live on his meagre wage if she had to give up her job? Should she part with the baby to an orphanage or to a society for the protection of waifs and strays? In England adoption was not made legal until 1926 and was unknown to common law; but a guardian might be appointed, if she could find one; or the child might be given into the care of foster parents. Dr Chance is someone she would be likely to consult about such things and she may have made enquiries on Dorothy's behalf.

There is a mystery about the maternity home. Of all places in England, Dorothy chose one in Southbourne, Hampshire, a seaside resort near Bournemouth, where her friend Dorothy Rowe lived. The explanation which leaps to mind is that she did, after all, confide in this one friend and ask her advice. But Miss Rowe, when questioned, denied categorically that she had known anything about it. The explanation must therefore lie elsewhere.

Ralph E. Hone suggests in his biography that Dorothy turned to a relative on her mother's side of the family, some members of which still lived in Hampshire. He may be right. Her unpublished novel, *Cat o' Mary*, contains an intriguing clue which seems to point in that direction. In this fictional but factually based work, every character is plainly identifiable as an actual person – except one: Katherine Lammas' Great-Aunt Agatha, her mother's aunt. This strong-minded, forthright, sensible woman wins Katherine's trust, for she never asks unnecessary questions and can be relied on in emergencies. When Katherine, grown up and married, is about to have a baby, she goes to stay with her in order to escape the tiresome and unnecessary fussing of her husband and her mother. Later, when Katherine's husband is involved with a mistress and asks for a divorce, it is again Great-Aunt Agatha to whom she turns, for the bracing effect of her unsentimental and realistic views on life.

The robust, forthright personality of an elderly lady, who has about her a faint suggestion of a racy past, is a recurrent minor figure in Dorothy's fiction. There is even a trace of her in one of her last works, the unfinished novel about Dante and his daughter. A search through the genealogy of the Leigh family reveals no aunt of the right age, unless the widow of Great-Uncle Percival was still alive in 1923. Someone there must have been, a relative or a family friend, of whom Dorothy asked advice and who recommended the maternity home in Southbourne because she lived near by and could be on hand.

This person, or possibly Dr Chance, may have suggested arrangements for the care of the baby – arrangements which must have broken down at a late stage; for it was only at the last moment, two days before the birth, that Dorothy took what must have seemed from the beginning an obvious step: she wrote to her cousin Ivy.

Aunt Amy Shrimpton, her mother's widowed sister, and her daughter Ivy supported themselves by fostering children in their house in Cowley, near Oxford. Such arrangements had been regularised by the Act of 1908, which protected infants maintained for pay by foster parents. Aunt Amy and Ivy were no baby-farmers. Their little charges thrived and were well taught. As recently as June 1922 Dorothy's mother had visited their house and sent a glowing account of what she saw; the children, she said, were great advertisements of the Shrimptons' good management. Dorothy, therefore, had no doubts as to the competence of her aunt and cousin as foster parents. What led her to try other resources first was the fear that as they were such close relations her mother would be bound to learn the truth.

She returned from Bovingdon in the last week in June and resumed her job at Benson's. She corrected the proofs of the English edition of *Whose Body?*, and continued work on *Clouds of Witness*. She wrote her usual letters home. In one, perhaps in reply to an enquiry, she said that Bill had a job in a bank. She reported that "Lord Peter" was not selling as well as she hoped and she must stick to advertising for a few years more. Her salary had gone up again, to six pounds, ten shillings a week, and she was now eligible for a bonus when there was one. She was still anxious about money (more than ever now): "I wish I could write a good detective play – that's where the money is!"

At the end of November she took eight weeks' leave of absence, on the grounds of illness. She was then seven months with child. It is surprising that her colleagues at Benson's were unaware of her condition. Either they were tactful or the change in her outline was successfully disguised by loose, flowing garments. She let her flat in Great James Street to a woman friend, who sent on her post. This enabled her to head her own letters with that address and to have them posted from there.

Some time in the autumn her mother had suggested coming up to London to see her. Dorothy replied, heading this letter "Kingsway" (the address of Benson's):

Look here – I'm awfully rushed and rather bothered. Don't come up till the Spring. I want to get things straightened out, and I can't do that till I get my accounts from America and England and have got my new book into the Press both sides of the Atlantic. Just now I simply couldn't give my mind to anybody or anything. Don't expect me at Xmas. – At Easter I hope to see you with a settled scheme of things, but just at present I'm too "hot and bothered" to cope. I've got all sorts of irons in the fire – When I'm clear, come up by all means – at present you'd hardly see me.

She evidently thought that her condition would not escape her mother's eye.

She must have spent December in Hampshire, her whereabouts known only to the friend or relative who had suggested the nursing home and with whom she may have been staying. She wrote letters and tried to make progress with her book. Remembering her admiration for her cousin Gwen, no doubt she kept active physically. She later told Cournos, with pride, that she had been extremely well all during her pregnancy.

On 3 January 1924, in Tuckton Lodge, Ilford Lane, Southbourne, she gave birth to a son. His birth was registered on 28 January in Christchurch, a suburb of Bournemouth. She identified herself as Dorothy L. Sayers, authoress, of 24 Great James Street, London. The space for the father's name was left vacant. The place of registration, echoing Christ Church, Oxford, where she had been christened, and Christchurch, Cambridgeshire, where her father was now rector, must have chimed poignantly in her ears. She named the baby John Anthony – John for the son she had wanted by Cournos and Anthony perhaps for St Anthony of Padua, whose day of commemoration was her own birthday, 13 June.

It was not an easy birth (she described it as "a hard job"); she was, after all, over thirty and a primipara. It was usual then for mothers to remain in hospital for at least a fortnight after a birth. Dorothy stayed three weeks, during which time she breast-fed the baby, on the doctor's advice. There were no telegrams, no letters of congratulation, no flowers and presents from delighted grandparents. Above all, no visit from a proud and beaming father. The loneliness of her situation had just begun.

Her letter to Ivy, dated 1 January 1924 and headed 24 Great James Street, does not yet tell the exact truth. She begins by thanking her for a letter and a Christmas present, which have evidently been sent on from London by her tenant:

Dearest Ivy,

Thank you very much for your letter and the delightful pussy. I have been meaning for some time to write to you on a matter of business. There's an infant I'm very anxious you should have the charge of, and I hope very much indeed you'll be able to take it. It isn't actually there yet, but it will be before many days are over. It won't have any legal father, poor little soul, but I know you would be all the more willing to help give it the best possible start in life on that account. The parents want to do the very best for it, and will be ready to pay whatever your usual terms are, and probably something over. They especially want it to have affection rather than pomp! I know that nobody could do better for it in that way than you. I am very personally interested in the matter, and will tell you more about it later on, or when I see you as I hope to do before too long. The point is – what would be the earliest possible moment at which you could take it? At present everything depends on the girl's not losing her job. Everything has been most discreetly managed – her retirement from public life is accounted for by "illness" – but naturally she can't turn up back at work plus a baby – at least, not without letting stacks and stacks of people into the secret, which might then leak out. So you see, the sooner she could dump the infant on you and clear back to work, the more chance there [is] of there being money to support it, as both parents are working and one of them alone couldn't do much to support it. From the mother's history it should be an extremely healthy child, having given not the slightest trouble or bad time so far, and I understand the doctor thinks everything should go easily. It will be a little gent (or lady as the case may be) on both sides and would probably be in your charge for some years – till circumstances enable the mother to take it herself. I think you would find it a paying proposition, and I do very much hope that you will be able to help in the matter, as I feel that nobody could do better for it than you. Indeed, I'd ask you to make a very special effort in the matter – and it is so great a relief to feel that somebody really trustworthy will have the child, and its mother is counting much on my cousin!

Please let me know by return of post whether you can manage it by hook or by crook – and if so, the earliest moment at which you could take it, and what your terms would be. I can guarantee the payments – and you would be given an entirely free hand in such matters as doctors, clothing, and necessaries of every kind.

I am rather in a hurry, as usual, so can only say how glad I am you like Lord Peter. There will be a new adventure of his very soon. Why do you want that wretched pretty girl? She is the ruin of any detective story! However, there is a love-affair (of a sort) in the new book.

My very best love to Aunt Amy – and don't fail us over the baby!

Your loving Dorothy.

Ivy replied at once, in the affirmative. Dorothy must have received the letter a few days after the baby was born. On 16 January she wrote again, and once again the letter is headed with the London address:

Dearest Ivy,

Excuse hasty note. Have been waiting to give you definite news. Your baby arrived on January 3rd – a sturdy little boy – and will be brought to you with all paraphernalia and particulars on or about January 30th. Terms quite satisfactory. Ever so glad you can take him. Will let you know further.

Best love,

Dorothy.

On 27 January she wrote again, this time heading the letter from the nursing home and telling the truth. She was bringing the baby herself on the thirtieth, probably by road, as there was threat of a rail strike. She had intended to tell Ivy face to face that she was the baby's mother. Instead, she includes a separate confidential statement, which Ivy is to share with Aunt Amy if she thinks fit. "I know you are the most discreet woman in the world . . . I trust your discretion absolutely." The statement was contained in an envelope marked "Strictly Confidential. Particulars about Baby."

My dear, everything I told you about the boy is absolutely true – only I didn't tell you he was my own! I won't go into the whole story – think the best you can of me – I know it won't make you love the boy any the less. He is really a fine little chap, – and I can't feel too bad about it myself now, because it will be so jolly to have him later on. I am 30 now, and it didn't seem at all likely I should marry – I shall have something for my latter age, anyway. But never mind me – don't think about it, but just be fond of the little chap. I wouldn't like to send him to anybody but you, because I know I can trust you absolutely to give him everything which I can't give him these first years.

I didn't tell you straight away for two reasons: 1) I thought you would be able to tell me more frankly about terms, and whether it would be convenient for you to have him, if you thought he was somebody else's. 2) I have no idea what Aunt Amy will feel about it. If you think it would distress her very much there is no need to tell her – you have a quite plausible story to account for my interest in him. Please use your own judgment. Whatever you do will be right.

They know nothing about it at home, and they must know nothing. It would grieve them quite unnecessarily. You know, it's not the kind of ill-doing Mother has any sympathy for, – she isn't either a man-lover or a baby-worshipper, – so I see no reason whatever for distressing them. So please, not a word of any kind to Christchurch. By the time I want the boy, they will be too old, if they are still alive, to worry much about anything, and they must have these last years in peace. I know you can be as silent as the grave, and I trust you to be so in this case.

The boy will have to be registered in my name, of course, but I think he may as well be known by his father's, which is as non-committal and common as blackberries – so to you and the world he'll be John Anthony White. For certain reasons, that isn't the name I've been using here, so I haven't been able to mark his things.

I'm afraid you'll have a job with him at first – food, etc., because he has been breast-fed. They said it would be better to give him a good start in the natural way and then let him struggle with the change of food than to bottle-feed him from the beginning. He is very greedy and seems to have a pretty sturdy little inside, so I hope you'll be able to get him started without too much trouble. You will know what to try. If you need anything more expensive, for doctors or advice, or anything in the world for him, let me know. I can manage it. He is rather noisy and excitable – you'll find it doesn't do to nurse him or pet him much, or he'll keep you at it day and night. He's accustomed to be tucked down in bed when he yowls and taken no notice of – so be stern with him.

He has been circumcised, by the doctor's advice, and I think you will find his little insides in working order.

I'll tell you anything else there's time for when I see you. Goodbye till then, my dear, and be good to my son!

Dorothy.

By the beginning of February she was back at work.

CHAPTER 9

Behind the Scenes

Dorothy now had a son but no husband. She hoped for a time that she and Bill might make some sort of a go of it together. In February, writing to Ivy, she said, "I must find out whether his father wants anything to do with him." Evidently he did not and expressed no desire even to see his child. He was terrified of becoming further involved and made this plain. By the end of April Dorothy had told him, as she put it, "to go to Hell". Before long he had taken up with someone else.

Her colleagues at Benson's welcomed her back and remarked that she had put on weight. This often happens after childbirth. In fact, from then on her metabolism changed. After being slender, she began to grow corpulent and, as time went on, with increasing indulgence in good food and wine, she finally became grossly overweight. Another consequence of her pregnancy and, no doubt, of her anxieties, was that her hair fell out again. To deal with this, she wore a spectacular silver wig. This suited her very well and she continued to wear it for many years. A portrait of her by John (later Sir John) Gilroy, which is dated 1929, shows how attractive she looked in it.

The atmosphere of Benson's, some of her colleagues even, and the nature of the work are amusingly depicted in her novel *Murder Must Advertise*. In some ways it reminded her of Oxford, where essays mysteriously got written in a welter of talk and other activities. Brabazon has commented on Dorothy's flair for this work:

Nothing in the commercial world could have suited her better than the work she was doing for Benson's. She was in the company of draughtsmen, designers and printers, as well as fellow writers; and she was earning her living by performing her favourite activity, playing with words. The enjoyment of one's own skill is part of the

A drawing of Dorothy at Benson's by John Gilroy *(Estate of Sir John Gilroy)*

fun of writing for any writer, and for Dorothy it was particularly so. Whether she was composing an advertisement for stockings or writing a sonnet or a villanelle, ideas still had to be fitted into a neat, predetermined form and expressed with the maximum possible impact. Dorothy loved problems like this, and to be paid for spending one's time solving them must ... have seemed like heaven on earth.

And so indeed it must have seemed, in her first year. Her rapture was modified thereafter and she developed misgivings as to the ethics of advertising, which she was to touch on in *Murder Must Advertise* — lightly, however, for that novel recaptures a great deal of the fun and enjoyment to which Brabazon refers.

In 1924 no one at work knew what her private feelings were; nor did her parents or any of her friends — not even Ivy, to whom she was writing regularly about John Anthony. They are dramatically revealed, however, in a series of anguished letters which she wrote to none other than John Cournos.

In August news reached her that he had married. His wife had had two previous husbands and was the mother of two children. An American, named Helen Kestner Satterthwaite, she was the author of detective stories published under the pseudonym of Sybil Norton. This must have been yet another painful blow to Dorothy. She had believed Cournos when he said it was against his principles to marry, and now, like Philip Boyes in *Strong Poison*, he was revealed as an empty theorist. Like Harriet Vane, Dorothy had been made a fool of.

Nevertheless, on 22 August 1924 she wrote to wish him joy:

Dear John,

I've heard you're married. I hope you are very, very happy, with someone you can really love.

I went over the rocks. As you know, I was going there rapidly, but I preferred it shouldn't be with you, but with somebody I didn't really care twopence for. I couldn't have stood a catastrophe with you. It was a worse catastrophe than I intended, because I went and had a young son (thank God, it wasn't a daughter!) and the man's affection couldn't stand the strain and he chucked me and went off with someone else! So I don't quite know what I'm going to do with the infant, but he's a very nice one!

Both of us did what we swore we'd never do, you see — I do hope your experiment turned out better than mine. You needn't bother about answering this unless you like, but somehow I've always felt

I should like you to know. I hope you're ever so happy.
Dorothy

I say – wasn't I clever? Nobody knew – and don't tell anybody, please. Didn't even have to chuck my job!

Cournos did reply but in a manner that angered Dorothy so much that she did not trust herself to answer for several weeks. His first reaction on hearing that she had yielded sexually to another man was one of wounded vanity: "Why not me?" he asked. "Because", she replied, "the one thing worse than bearing the child of a man you hate would be being condemned to be childless by the man you loved."

Cournos' side of the correspondence does not, apparently, exist (Dorothy probably destroyed it), but from her letters to him (which he prudently deposited in the Houghton Library of Harvard University) and from the use he made of them in his novel, *The Devil is an English Gentleman*, it is possible to follow, as on a lighted stage, every move in the denouement of this unhappy relationship.

The passages in the novel describing the unconsummated love-making of Stella and Richard clarify certain allusions in Dorothy's letters. These in turn substantiate the veracity of the narrative, to the degree that some of her very words are quoted.

Richard, like Cournos in real life, renounces his principles and marries. Stella, like Dorothy, finds relief in an affair with a man named Jimmy, who, like Bill, is a motor-cyclist. Cournos was well aware of the sexual significance of this. "For some reason," he wrote, "Stella's favourite diversion was pillion riding." Describing Jimmy, he shows that he understands why:

Attired in his motoring costume, his large frame appeared so masculine, so efficient in a male way. She had often seen him on his machine and he seemed so at one with it. She thought the motor-cycle a beautiful mechanism, and the sight of one awakened in her a series of pleasurable associations. To be sitting on the hind seat, clinging tightly to a man, the machine flying at top speed, gave her a thrill and an exhilaration such as, before meeting Richard, nothing else gave her.

In his first letter, Cournos had asked if he and Dorothy might meet. She replied: "Now why in the world should you want to meet me? Last time we met, you told me with brutal frankness that you had no use for my conversation. Do you think my misfortunes will have added new lustre to my wit?" ("Have you come to crow over me?" Stella asks when Richard goes to see her.)

Dorothy agreed to meet Cournos, but

it's going to hurt like hell to see you, because Judah with all thy faults I love thee still, and as you've no use for me I must be in a very stupid and false and painful position. And I won't be made to cry in teashops. But if you like to come here, I will see you. And ask any questions you like. – I can't imagine the question I would not readily and frankly answer.

It is evident that she had a great need to talk to someone about her predicament. Their conversation can be reconstructed from the novel as well as from subsequent letters.

Richard calls to see Stella. He is full of remorse and prepared to receive her reproaches. He wonders if he can help her in some way.

Cournos asked Dorothy if there was anything he could do for her. She said, "Spare me your maxims, I don't want any of your sermons." Stella likewise says, "Don't preach me one of your sermons." Dorothy asked his opinion: should she look out for a husband, or take a lover as a companion? Could he introduce her to somebody? She wrote: "I asked you to help me, and I still want help, you don't know how badly ... If you can help me, I shall be very grateful." They discussed the question and Cournos evidently undertook to look out for someone for her. Dorothy, with her habit of linking everything to literary allusions, dubbed Cournos "Uncle Pandarus" and the desired companion "Troilus", a sad little jest which they kept up for some time.

Richard/Cournos asks why she agreed to be Jimmy's/Bill's mistress when she had sworn that was something she would never do. Stella/Dorothy replies: "You misunderstood me. I said I would never become *your* mistress. I loved you too much for that. I wanted to be your wife." Richard/Cournos asks: "How can a woman deny to a man she loves what she freely offers to a man she loathes?"

Stella, speaking almost Dorothy's very words, says:

Do you suppose I preferred having a child by a man I hold in contempt to having one by the man I loved? Let me explain to you. If a woman truly loves a man, she wants children by him. She doesn't want any of those nasty rubber-shop contrivances to

133

humiliate her love, make it the filthy thing that results where men and women resort to such things.

Richard/Cournos interrupts her: "I still don't understand. You had a child by this man." Stella replies: "Yes, my dear man. If you must know, it was one of those unavoidable accidents which occur in the best of families." The real Dorothy had written in her letter of 27 October: "God bless you, man, I didn't want *his* son – that I've got one only goes to show that Nature refuses to be driven out, even with pitch-forks – or other implements." Stella did not love Jimmy, so she "consented to the patronage of the rubber-shop. He was the means of gratifying my sexual hunger. It was not a question of love or passion." She no longer wants love; she wants the decencies of life. Dorothy, writing to Cournos, said, "Romantic love is not important, but bodily comfort and decency is . . . I really did want to live decently, and spare my parents (they still know nothing)." Stella, too, says that her parents know nothing.

Stella reproaches Richard for his self-esteem: "You are perfect. You are infallible. You are God." Dorothy wrote to Cournos, "Come off Mount Sinai"; in another letter she addressed him tauntingly as "divine Perfection".

Stella reproaches Richard for his dishonesty in the matter of marriage: "I loved you the best I knew how. But I can't forgive you for being a cheat. You said you were not the marrying sort. And the first thing I hear is that you're married. What do you call that if not downright cheating?" These words, though brief, are in substance identical to those in which Dorothy accused Cournos of having lied to her:

> I did [love you] in the only way I know. I paid you the biggest compliment I knew how; and you stood to me for something jolly fine – only there is always that taint of the "rubber-shop" now . . . You broke your own image in my heart, you see. You stood to me for beauty and truth – and you demanded ugliness, barrenness – and it seems now that even in doing so, you were just lying. You told me over and over again, "I cannot marry anyone", "I will not be responsible for anybody's life", "I will not be responsible for bringing any lives into the world".

Cournos had now wounded her even more deeply by telling her that he would after all have married her if she had given herself to him freely, "without threat or persuasion" – a situation he exactly reproduces in his novel.

Dorothy's feelings were in turmoil. Though she saw through Cournos now and had only unhappy memories of their time together, she could not free herself of her obsession for him, or, rather, for the person she once thought he was.

She is at the mercy of her emotions. If she sees either Bill or Cournos, she "howls all night" and is violently sick. Her work is suffering:

I hope Anthony and I don't come to the workhouse! But it's so hard to work. It frightens me to be so unhappy – I thought it would get better, but I think every day is worse than the last, and I'm always afraid they'll chuck me out of the office because I'm working so badly. And I haven't even the last resort of doing away with myself, because what would poor Anthony do then, poor thing?

In the novel, Stella actually threatens to commit suicide.

In the midst of so much misery, some measure of self-respect begins to emerge. She asserts her own value. Cournos had patronised her and drilled her wit out of existence, scorning her conversation, her detective stories and her taste in entertainment. But she knows she can be witty and entertaining at times. Bill found her so and she will not allow Cournos to abuse him. (An interesting point about Bill emerges here: he read Cournos' novel *Babel* – between 120,000 and 130,000 words long – and enjoyed it.) Her name for him is "the Beast" (and Stella, too, refers to Jimmy as a beast), not in disparagement but because he was sexually a man of action rather than words.

Unlike Cournos, she was honest and sincere, and would have been faithful if he had married her, while leaving him to have affairs had he so wished. She had even offered to marry him according to the law of England only, so that he could get a divorce in America if he tired of her. "I swear that if you had offered me love – or even asked for love – you should have had everything. Not easily, because I did not want to commit so bitter a sin." Even now she would rather be married than take another lover:

I become impatient of the beastly restrictions which "free love" imposes. I have a careless rage for life, and secrecy tends to make me bad-tempered . . . Give me a man that's human and careless and loves life, and one who can enjoy the rough-and-tumble of passion. I like to die spitting and swearing, you know, and I'm no mean wrestler! But there again – precautionary measures cramp the style, Bah! if you had chosen I would have given you three sons by this time.

She has become a different person from the one he knew. In his novel, Cournos writes of Stella: "Grief had put a stamp upon her features, a larger experience had added knowledge to the eyes." Dorothy has now had the maturing experience of giving birth. This puts her in a position from which *she* can now talk down to *him*.

I *know* now, what I was only sure of before, that the difference between the fruitful and the barren body is just that between conscious health and unconscious – what shall I call it? – uneasiness, discomfort, something that isn't quite health. Please take this from me – I have bought the right to say it to you.

She was not ashamed of what she had done. She was proud of the baby: "He is a fine little fellow . . . a sturdy little boy . . . he really is a fine little chap" are phrases that recur. She felt physically, creatively fulfilled, a sensation she did not forget, as can be seen from something she wrote sixteen years later in an article entitled "What Do We Believe?":

The men who create with their minds and those who create (not merely labour) with their hands, will, I think, agree that their periods of creative activity are those in which they feel right with themselves and the world. *And those who bring life into the world will tell you the same thing.* [My italics]

When Cournos talks of his wife's children as though they were his, Dorothy replies: "No, no, it's no use your trying to lay claim to them by proxy – not the slightest credit attaches to you in the matter – I may say 'my son' but you must not say 'my daughter'."
Towards the end of the episode of Stella and Richard in Cournos' novel, Richard acknowledges that he was in the wrong and says, "Let us be friends, Stella." She replies, "I wonder if a man and a woman could ever be friends." Cournos too hoped that he and Dorothy would count themselves friends and, taking rather too much for granted, said that he felt they were back on the old footing. She replied: "I know of no very happy sort of footing we ever were on."
Several of her letters reveal the depressing effect he had on her:

You were a rotten companion for a poor girl. You wouldn't go to the theatre and you wouldn't talk nonsense . . . Yes, I admit that you went to cinemas (and that it was a fearful job to find a piece you would condescend to see, as I remember excellently on one occasion, having tramped half London with a bad blister on my heel before you would settle down) – but I seldom remember your being very cheery there . . . You never asked me to go and do anything with you, or for you – never told me anything – I don't know now what your interests are really . . . I have always been strained and uncomfortable when you've seen me . . . I was really fond of you and afraid of you . . . As a companion you aren't my choice.

These letters suggest someone on the verge of a nervous break-down. They are written at a high pitch of tension – of grief, defiance and anger – all except one, which is the last. The tone of this is utterly different. It is as though a storm has raged, to be followed by calm, as if her circumstances had suddenly altered. In October 1925, Cournos, after a brief visit to the United States, returned to London once again. Finding an article by G. K. Chesterton on the writing of a detective story, he sent it to Dorothy, thinking it would interest her. It did, very much. She wrote to thank him:

Dear John,
    Many thanks – My attention had, as a matter of fact, already been drawn to it and I was intending to purchase it, so that I am indebted to you for saving me six useful pennies.

Cournos had told her that he despised detective fiction, but now he has the grace to send her something which will be of use to her in the practice of her craft. In response, she sends four pages of detailed commentary, analysing the technique of constructing a detective story, writing as though from one craftsman to another. The fact that she could be on such terms with him so soon after her previous letters suggests that their earlier relationship had not been devoid of the exchange of ideas or of good comradeship. The letter is also of very great interest as evidence of her growing mastery of her craft and as a prelude to the outstanding essay she was soon to write on the history of detective fiction, in the Introduction to her anthology, *Great Short Stories of Detection, Mystery and Horror*.
    She finds the article "one of the soundest and most useful pieces of constructive criticism" she has met for a long time: "G.K.C. has put his finger at once on the central difficulty", that of making the

solution neither too obscure nor too obvious. Though on the whole she does not care for a love-interest in a detective story, she admits that there is a great deal in what Chesterton says about its usefulness as camouflage. The stories in which it is most successful, she considers, are those in which it forms an integral part of the plot, as in Wilkie Collins' *The Moonstone* and E. C. Bentley's *Trent's Last Case*. She applauds Chesterton for upholding the strictly classic form of detective story and quotes his recommendation: "The thing that we realise must be the thing that we recognise; that is, it must be something previously known, and it ought to be prominently displayed." And she continues: "That excellent sentence should be illuminated in letters of gold and hung above the desk of every mystery-story writer." She cites as an excellent example one of Chesterton's own Father Brown stories, *The Invisible Man*. "But there! once started on the fascinating subject of technique, one could go on for hours."

She touches on the problem of characterisation. It is best done, she considers "in the flat and on rather broad lines". The story she is at present preparing to start on, *Unnatural Death*, is showing signs of becoming "round" (that is to say, the characters are becoming more life-like and credible than the structure of the form can bear), and for that reason she is rather nervous of it. She will try to keep it at no more than high relief, which means "combining the appeal to the emotions with the appeal to the intellect".

This, she concludes, with just a touch of her former mocking asperity, "means forgoing the appeal to the Tired Business Man and the Tired Journalist who, like yourself, do not want to flog their jaded intellects over the craftily-constructed detective story!"

John Cournos had made her deeply unhappy; but he was, after all, a man of unusual ability and a distinguished writer. He published nine novels, two plays, an autobiography (in which, however, there is no mention of Dorothy), fifteen volumes of translation and eight anthologies. *A Modern Plutarch*, a collection of biographical essays, reveals him as civilised and well-read. An arresting and original work, *Hear, O Israel*, published by Methuen in 1938, is an appeal to Jews to recognise Jesus as their greatest prophet and teacher:

We as Jews cannot afford to let Christianity fall before cohorts of Fascist and Communist barbarians. If Christianity falls we fall with it . . . If the historical resilience [of the Jews], only allowed them to rediscover Jesus, that rediscovery might be attended with a renaissance of creation and faith not less significant in its world-wide effects than the rediscovery of Greece by the Italians during the Quattrocento.

Did Dorothy know this work, one wonders? Was he keeping up with hers? Is he echoing her in the following passage, or did she later echo him? Had they, perhaps, discussed such matters?

If you go to the Gospels to learn about Christ, and compare the astonishingly virile figure of the original four biographies with the latter-day effeminate confections which pass as portraits of Christ, you begin to see that the discrepancy between them is as immense as the time that separates the present epoch in which the original figure walked, and acted, and spoke . . .

Or in this, also by Cournos:

The very language in which men speak of Jesus has become stereotyped, "stale, flat and unprofitable" . . . to see freshly, one must . . . begin from the beginning, see the matter historically, realistically. One must devise a new vocabulary, such as one might use if Jesus had only just come to earth for the first time . . .

This is a very striking anticipation of the stand Dorothy was to take when she wrote *The Man Born to be King*. It also gives, perhaps, a more balanced picture than her frenzied letters do, of the man she once wanted desperately to marry.

CHAPTER 10

John Anthony

Much has been made of the burden of guilt which Dorothy L. Sayers, the celebrated detective novelist and pillar of the Church, supposedly carried because of her illegitimate son. This is to disregard the fact that she was an Anglo-Catholic and that, as it has been shown, it was her practice to go to confession.

Since this is the case, the word "guilt", when used in connection with her, has a precise theological meaning. In one of her letters to John Cournos she spoke of sex outside marriage as "a bitter sin"; in another she said that God had punished her "bitterly". As long as she continued in a state of sin, as she regarded it, with Bill White, she could not, with true penitence, make confession; nor could she receive communion. The shock of her pregnancy brought about a change of heart.

Whenever it was that she entered into a state of repentance, her recourse then was to make confession and seek absolution. When she did so, the burden of guilt was lifted. There remained, however, the question of reparation. She may have asked for spiritual counselling about this. She may also have required it for any residue of psychological guilt which still troubled her. In any event, as an instructed Catholic, she would know that she must individually take responsibility for what had occurred.

In 1948, when Dorothy, then well-read in theology, had been studying and translating Dante for four years, she delivered a lecture entitled "The Meaning of Purgatory". It contains a passage which shows how clear a grasp she had of the theology of guilt, confession and absolution. She is explaining what the doctrine of Purgatory means "in purely human terms":

We will suppose that in a fit of anger or resentment or merely sheer wicked carelessness you damage something belonging to your friend – we will call it a valuable china teapot . . . We shall take it that, seeing the fragments of the teapot at your feet, you are overcome with shame and horror at what you have done and want to put matters right so far as possible. Obviously, there are two things to be done: the first is to restore the right relationship with your friend which has been broken up by your anger or negligence or whatever the sin was. You go to her at once and confess your sinful feeling and the guilty act to which it led; you say how dreadfully sorry you are, and you beg her to forgive you, and promise that you will try to make it up to her in future. That is, you make an act of penitence: confession, contrition and atonement. She forgives you at once, you kiss and make friends; and that restores the relationship. You are now released at once from the *guilt* of what you did: in technical terms, you have purged the *culpa*.

But, she goes on to say, something remains to be done, without which the atonement will not be complete:

You will want, that is, to make an act of compensation, and the technical term for that is purging the *reatus* . . . and if the sinner is truly penitent, he will be eager to purge it in any way God may appoint . . . if we are ever to be happy in His presence again, it is something in us that has to be altered.

In 1924 Dorothy would not have used the technical term, "purging the *reatus*", if indeed she had even heard of it then. The Latin word *reatus*, meaning a charge of which one is accused, has been adopted by theologians to represent the stain of sin which remains when the guilt, or *culpa*, has been purged by absolution. Dorothy Sayers did not believe in the Roman Catholic doctrine of Purgatory. Her purpose in this lecture was simply to make clear to an audience interested in Dante what that doctrine was. In doing so, she provided a lucid picture of her intellectual understanding of her own spiritual experience. Her soul was at peace. She had made an act of confession, contrition and atonement. The burden of guilt was at once lifted. What remained for her was a burden of responsibility. In practical terms, this meant supporting and educating John Anthony and providing him, as best she could, with maternal love and concern for his welfare. This responsibility she amply fulfilled and continued to fulfil, for the rest of her life.

To achieve this, she had the help and sympathy of her cousin Ivy. Her arrival at Cowley from Bournemouth with her three-week-old son in a Moses basket, snugly wrapped against the January cold, is not difficult to visualise. She could not stay long. She had to return to London that evening, by bus, for there was a rail strike. Conversation was probably restricted to the baby's immediate needs; what was left unsaid was no less eloquent. Aunt Amy (who may not have been told the truth) and her daughter Ivy received the newcomer with practised competence. There were other small children in the house who gathered round. In particular, there was a six-year-old named Isobel, who felt all a little girl's delight in the arrival of a living doll. Beyond doubt, John Anthony had been received into a loving home. Dorothy left and caught the bus to London.

Ivy wrote the following morning to let her know that the baby had passed a good night. On 1 February Dorothy replied: "It was a great relief . . . as I couldn't help thinking of poor little Algy perhaps yelling himself into fits and being sick, and all kinds of horrors! But I really think he's a determined kid and means to live!" She asks Ivy to be careful to see that "his little works work regular". She is convinced that the reason why the Leighs — especially her mother — take such a pessimistic view of life is that they are everlastingly tied up inside or dosing themselves. She concludes: "Send me a report from time to time." Ivy faithfully does so.

Her first anxiety is about a discharge from the baby's navel. Dorothy says that the nurse had told her this might happen; perhaps he should continue wearing his binder. She adds: "Never hesitate to call in advice when you're the least worried or puzzled about anything . . . Get the doctor whenever you like (it won't break me!)" She will wait a month or so before coming to see him. She reports that she is back into her stride at the office, where they were all charmed to see her and very sympathetic about her "illness".

Ivy had asked what she should do about the child in the event of Dorothy's premature decease. She replied:

If it should occur before that of my people, I think they will have to be told, because in that case they would probably wish to do what they could — and they might even be glad of John in my absence. Otherwise, I am arranging for guardians, but I must wait a little till I find out whether his father wants to have anything to do with him. He can't do anything material, but when he gets over his present feeling of helpless rage and misery about the matter, he may wish for a certain measure of recognition. I hope to get this settled up before long – but if I rush things I may ruin everything!

After three weeks Ivy reports that the baby has gained a whole pound and that the health visitor has called. In her reply Dorothy expresses a measure of maternal pride: "I hope you've observed what nice, flat ears I've made him. I gave special thought and trouble to their construction – so if I catch you putting him into round caps that give him elephant flaps there'll be *such* trouble!!!" Isobel is taking a fond interest in him and Ivy fears he is getting spoilt. Dorothy utters a warning not to let this happen: "I rather think he means to turn out a handful." Isobel was to become like an older sister to the little boy and Dorothy grew very fond of her, often enquiring after her, writing her letters and sending her presents.

Ivy's terms for fostering an infant were three pounds a month. Dorothy sent this regularly and sometimes added a little extra for additional expenses such as doctor's fees. She was earning over six pounds a week at Benson's. In her spare time she slaved at writing short stories, which brought in fees when magazines accepted them. She also worked continually at her novels and negotiated serial rights, which were lucrative. She lived economically and saved as much as possible for John Anthony's future and her own.

By the end of February she was feeling run down. This emerges in a letter to her parents, in which she tells them her hair is falling out again and that she has been taking a "tonic" – syrup of hypophosphates was the usual remedy at that period. She has also, as women often do when they are depressed, bought herself some new clothes. No doubt she badly needed some since her size had increased.

She continued for a time to be hopeful about the attitude of Bill. Writing to Ivy, she said: "John's father is, exactly as I hoped, beginning to feel less sore and take a little pride and interest, so I think my 'don't rush' attitude is justifying itself. I showed him your last letter, and he said, 'What an awfully nice woman she must be!'" Since these are the only recorded words of John Anthony's father, it is perhaps worth while to pause and consider what they reveal about him. First, he was decently grateful in his feelings towards Ivy. Secondly, his comment, brief as it is, has the unmistakable stamp of an educated person. In other words, to use the phraseology of the period, he spoke like a gentleman.

Dorothy continued to be hopeful: "He is really coming round quicker than I thought he ever would – after all, small babies aren't in themselves very attractive to the male mind." By the end of April all such hope had vanished.

On her first visit to see her son, she was astonished to find that the scarlet infant she had left was now so white. This may have caused the bad dream she relates in a letter of 10 April, in which the baby seemed to have grown elvish and wizened and to be decaying away. "Dreams go by opposites: you'll get that vaccinating done, won't you?"

After her second visit, she wrote:

I'm so glad I came down and saw the young man last Sunday, and saw him getting so big and looking so jolly . . . Whoever suffers over this business I'm quite clear it mustn't be John Anthony. If the poor little soul has to be fatherless, at least he mustn't be motherless. I think Isobel had better suppose I've adopted him or something of that kind, and if she does let anything out to Aunt Maud or anyone it can't be helped. They can suppose I "take an interest" in him – it wouldn't be the first time. [She may have been thinking of Adèle's baby.] As regards J.A. himself, I daresay he won't give things away himself just at present! If he does, it can't be helped – I've done what I could to spare people's feelings, but it can't be carried to the point of letting the kid lose anything he might be having. The father side of the question can wait; it's not likely to become acute for some time. Let me know what you think; but I do very strongly feel that as the boy *has* got a mother, he should have one properly, so to speak.

At Easter she went to Christchurch to see her parents and Aunt Mabel. She wrote to Ivy on 29 April:

I nearly told Mother, but Aunt M. makes everything so difficult. Better to wait – besides, things are being very rotten here for the time being. Thank you for your unfailing sympathy and discretion. "Bide the time" is a good motto . . . Poor little J.A. – I hardly know whether I love him or hate him – but he's happy enough so far, anyhow.

This last remark so distressed Ivy that Dorothy hastened to reply: "Don't take any notice of my moods. I had just told J.'s father to go to hell – he's always behaved fairly badly and finally became intolerable, so I thought he'd better push off." She had also been upset by her visit to Christchurch, her first since the baby's birth:

Of course, I knew going home would be rather a trial, but it had to be done, so there it was. I can't see that I should be doing any good by telling them at the present moment. It would be a great worry and embarrassment to *them* and *I* should have to answer a lot of questions which are better left alone. Everybody has not your valuable gift of silence . . . As it is, I can't see that anyone suffers but myself so far, and therefore, so far so good!

Ivy's loyal discretion was to be one of the consolations of Dorothy's life for many years. She was to prove a very competent foster mother and teacher to her little first-cousin-once-removed, who grew up to do her great credit.

In May, Ivy writes to say that the baby, now five months old, is getting quite active. Dorothy replies:

Glad J. is progressing – I don't know why he should kick you in the face or pull Isobel's hair, but if he bites the hand that feeds him, it's probably hereditary (she said bitterly!) His interest in the kitchen clock is intriguing. Is it the tick? I wish he'd be a mechanically-minded child – I hope he doesn't intend to be musical or artistic. – I'm so bored with writers and people like that. He's got a big head – he ought to have something in it, oughtn't he? Anyhow, there doesn't seem to be any fear that he's deaf, blind or imbecile, though I'm sure, considering the little pampering he got before he was born and the worry I was in, I wonder he has any faculties at all! Let me know when he wants clothes or anything.

John Anthony as a baby *(Marion E. Wade Center)*

In June she took a fortnight's holiday, in North Yorkshire, "to get Lord Peter finished amid his proper surroundings". She went with a friend, probably Muriel Jaeger, who lived in Yorkshire. They cycled up steep hills and walked, sometimes for five hours a day, braving the powerful winds on the moors. In the evenings she worked on her novel, *Clouds of Witness*, and was able to report to her mother "Lord Peter nearly done, thank the Lord!"

He had been giving trouble for some time. In December 1923 she had said that she was stuck at a point where Lord Peter required a piece of evidence and she could not see how to work it in. On 22 January, while still in the maternity home, with the baby two and a half weeks old, she said she had had to rewrite a couple of chapters owing to a change of plan.

The first section in which "the proper surroundings" of Yorkshire are relevant is chapter 4, in which Lord Peter visits Grimethorpe's farm at Grider's Hole –

a lonely outpost on the edge of the moor, in a valley of fertile land between two wide swells of heather. The track wound down from the height called Whemmeling Fell, skirted a vile swamp, and crossed the little River Ridd . . . The path was marked with stout white posts at regular intervals, and presently with hurdles. The reason for this was apparent as one came to the bottom of the valley, for only a few yards on the left began the stretch of rough, reedy tussocks, with a slobbering black bog between them, in which anything heavier than a water-wagtail would speedily suffer change into a succession of little bubbles.

This is a "snapshot" from one of their excursions. The feeling of depression which afflicts Lord Peter at this point is a clear enough indication of her own state of mind:

With that instinct which prompts one, when depressed, to wallow in every circumstance of gloom, Peter leaned sadly upon the hurdles and abandoned himself to a variety of shallow considerations upon (1) The vanity of human wishes; (2) Mutability; (3) First love; (4) The decay of idealism; (5) The aftermath of the Great War; (6) Birth-control; and (7) The fallacy of free-will.

One can trace through all seven topics of gloom the stages of Dorothy's own recent experiences.

The sight of the "slobbering bog" gave her an idea of how to solve her problem. In chapter 11 Lord Peter, this time accompanied by Bunter, sets out for Grider's Hole again, rashly leaving behind his handsome malacca walking stick with the compass in its head. They are overtaken by fog, "the great white menace rolling silently down through the November dusk from the wide loneliness of Whemmeling Fell". Ruthlessly, she sacrifices her valuable property, Lord Peter, who falls into the bog. It is very nearly the end of him, but he is rescued by stout Yorkshiremen, helped by Bunter, who haul him out with ropes – the description of this could stand as an allegory of Dorothy's own painful emergence from an abyss of wretchedness. In a fainting condition, he is carried into Grimethorpe's farmhouse, where he spends the night. In the morning he discovers the required evidence, the missing letter from Tommy Freeborn.

She returned to London, refreshed and fit, her novel well on the way to completion. In July, Ivy reports that her son has cut several teeth, both top and bottom. Dorothy bursts out into competitive maternal pride: "How perfectly brilliant of John Anthony! The much inferior child of one of my friends has only just managed the top ones with much difficulty at 10 months, having produced the bottom two at 8. I do hope I haven't perpetrated an infant phenomenon or anything." She has taken up photography again and hopes to get to Oxford while the light is still good in order to take some snaps of the baby, which she does. Her moods continue to swing and she lets some time go by before visiting Cowley again. Ivy urges her to come. She replies: "I will really try to come along before long – afraid I'm being rather a callous parent! J.A. seems to have faded out a bit with the rest of the nightmare, but I do quite like him really!" It was not long after this that she entered into correspondence with Cournos, to whom she several times mentioned the baby, and with pride. She badly needed someone to talk to about him: "It is very irritating to have no one to whom I can boast about him, but I'm afraid you don't sound as though you would be a very sympathetic listener." So great was her need that one day she confided in a total stranger:

I met a woman the other day, who has just divorced her husband. She has a boy of 10. She was a complete stranger, so I told her about my Anthony. She merely envied me having no father to lay claim to the child! I really began to feel it was rather enviable. I suppose the contemplation of other people's misfortunes is a really delightful occupation for I'm sure we both felt happier after that exchange of confidence.

Her life in London was not all gloom and anguish. In August her cousin Gerald took her out and she dined and danced with him. She told her mother he had become less stiff and had even unbent enough to exchange improper stories with her. On Election night in November she went out with friends to Trafalgar Square and remained until 2.45 a.m. Her mind keeps active and lively. She reads Monypenny and Buckle's biography of Disraeli with "real pleasure and excitement". She does crossword puzzles. She and her colleagues amuse themselves by inventing "stinkers" for each other. *Clouds of Witness* is still not quite finished: "It will need a lot of revision. It will not be as successful as the first. The subject is a bit too big and cumbersome. I am now considering the plot for a play – to begin cheerfully with two corpses and end with a stolen diamond." She went to stay with friends at Sevenoaks for Christmas – "very rich people and very rich food". She had sent a "mixed bag" of presents to all Ivy's children. Remembering Ivy's "remarkable success in making *The Ingoldsby Legends* intelligible and delightful" to her as a child, she sends Isobel some History-Rhyme books, which she is sure Ivy will help her to enjoy. She hopes "the Imp" is being good.

John Anthony was now one year old. Ivy loved him and was taking excellent care of him. He was among other children, a ready-made family, in the midst of whom he flourished and rapidly progressed. At Easter 1925, having received some money for the serial rights of *Clouds of Witness*, Dorothy plans to send the children presents. She finds a rubber-crawler for "the Terror" for when he wants to crawl in the garden. She also, at great expense, indulges in a musical rabbit, "Parisian and costly", which she buys at Hamley's, the famous London toy-shop: "My small cousin – Gwen's eldest boy – had one and it gave him enormous pleasure at J.A.'s age . . . Let me know if and at what age it attracts his attention."

In April 1925 a crisis occurred. Aunt Amy, who had not been well for some time, suddenly died. Dorothy wrote to express her sympathy, saying how jolly and lively she always was and recalling her sitting on the sofa playing with John Anthony. Her death raised problems, both immediate and long-term:

Look here – is J.A. going to be in the way? Because if so, I will hunt round and try to stick him somewhere else – *pro tem*, I hope, as I shouldn't feel half so cheery about him with anybody but you? I don't know if I can find anything at short notice, but I expect it's possible. I thought that if Mother should ask you to go down to Christchurch for a time or anything, you might feel you'd like to get rid of him. Please let me know.

Mrs Sayers went to Cowley to help Ivy over the funeral and other arrangements. She then saw, for the first and only time, the little boy who was her grandson. "Tell me what Mother thinks of him!" said Dorothy. Of all the sad aspects of the situation, this is perhaps the most poignant.

In a way, she longed to tell her mother the truth and was several times tempted to do so. It must have been a great temptation to Ivy, also, when her Aunt Nell came to stay, but she did not yield to it. Pondering Ivy's problems, Dorothy imagined herself divulging the truth: "If things should become acutely difficult, you can always shove J.A. off onto Mother and tell her, and I'll weigh in and explain, only I felt it would be a nuisance, what with Aunt Mab and the parish and everything, and I'd really rather wait till later on, if possible." She continues to weigh the pros and cons but decides, once again, in the negative:

If you can hang on a bit, I'll try and see if there's a possibility of dumping him somewhere. It should be possible, and there are one or two people I can ask. If we told Mother, she'd want to help, and I don't want to be helped. J.'s my look-out entirely, and it's feeble if I can't manage without help – financially and that, I mean.

A few days later she says that she has written to an old college friend, "who is a sort of trained authority on babies, and who might know of some person who would take charge of him in case you found it impossible".

In the meantime she had written to her mother:

I expect you had a very trying time down at Cowley. I have written to Ivy, and hope to go and see her soon. My advice, for what it is worth, would differ from yours, I think. I fear that, except with the very poorest and most uncomfortable sort of people, Ivy would find it extremely difficult to get a job as nurse or anything to do with children, as training is of paramount importance now-a-days. Nor do I think she would take readily to the yoke of servitude after so many years of independence. If she can possibly carry on, and get enough children to take care of to enable her to employ some help in the house, I think she would probably do better, as she undoubtedly has a marked talent for that kind of work.

After visiting Ivy, she writes again to her mother, on 24 April: "I think she would be sorry to give up the children and the girl [Isobel] would hate leaving her – though no doubt she will have to sometime. The baby, I gather, can, if necessary, be disposed of, if time is given to make arrangements."

She writes calmly and with assumed detachment. The crisis was in reality upsetting her greatly. She could not say so to Ivy and she longed to tell someone about it. She came near to doing so at the end of June, when she wrote again to her mother, who had said that her father was not sleeping well: "I've been sleeping rottenly too just lately – I think it's the heat. Anyway, after some weeks of being depressed well-nigh to tears, the coolth set in and I revived completely." It was not only the coolth that revived her. Ivy had reviewed her circumstances and decided that she would rather continue looking after children in her own home than in someone else's. She was only too happy to keep John Anthony.

The crisis was over. The necessity to tell her parents that they had a grandson had passed, and would never arise again.

CHAPTER 11

Marriage

"Fleming, that's my man," said the Duke of Denver in the witness-box, in *Clouds of Witness*.

Some time in the second half of 1925 a man named Fleming entered Dorothy's life. He was a journalist, working for the *News of the World*, a member of that tough, masculine society she had come to know in Bill's company, the world of pubs, of car salesmen, racing motorists and journalists. Fleming was of medium height, good-looking and sturdily built, a hearty, virile type, popular with other men and attractive to women. His wife had recently divorced him.

He had been through the war and had risen to the substantive rank of captain, which meant that he held the temporary rank of major

Mac in about 1914, before Dorothy knew him *(Estate of Ann Schreurs)*

and was usually addressed as such. Like many veterans, he had been gassed and still suffered from the effects of what was then called shell-shock. Born in 1881, being therefore twelve years older than Dorothy, he had served also in the Boer War, during which, like Winston Churchill in his youth, he had functioned as a war correspondent. In World War I he served with the Royal Army Service Corps in France, helping to transport ammunition to the Royal Artillery and acting at the same time as special correspondent to the *Sunday Chronicle*.

He was a Scot and people called him Mac. His real Christian names were Oswold Arthur, but for reasons unknown he adopted the name Atherton Fleming, which he used professionally. In 1911 he had married Winifred Meyrick, by whom he had two daughters. He lived first at Kenilworth and worked at Coventry for Daimler's as a publicity agent, and later in Hartfield, Sussex.

After the war his marriage collapsed. His wife, as reported by his younger daughter, the late Mrs Ann Schreurs, thought that his personality had changed, as though he had been damaged psychologically by the war. Two of his brothers, Edmund and Edward, had been killed and a third, Edgar, survived but was badly injured. Mac cut himself off from his wife and family, who had moved to a cottage in Gloucestershire, and by 1924 he was no longer sending any money to support them. His wife reluctantly sued for divorce on the grounds of adultery and desertion. When Dorothy got to know him he was matrimonially at a loose end.

He was doing well as a reporter on crime and motor-racing for the *News of the World* and a fair amount of freelance writing – some of it in advertising – also came his way. In 1919 he had published an excellent little book, *How to See the Battlefields*, containing a vivid account of the conditions under which the R.A.S.C. had to function in the field. He had a number of talents apart from writing: he painted well, he was a photographer, which in those days entailed developing plates in a dark-room (as Bunter does), and he was an expert cook. He was an amusing raconteur and fun to be with – the good companion Dorothy told Cournos she was looking for. Sexually adventurous himself, he made no bones about Dorothy's previous affair or the fact that she had a child born out of wedlock. On 13 April 1926 they were married in a registrar's office. Dorothy was dressed in green.

She had spared her parents the shock of her maternity. She could not spare them the pain of knowing that she was marrying a divorced man whose wife was still alive. She had put herself right with the world but wrong with the Church. Most painful too for her parents, and no doubt also for her, was the fact that she and Mac had to be married by a registrar – the remarriage in church of divorced persons being then inadmissible.

She put off telling them until the last possible moment. She did, however, inform Ivy, to whom she wrote on 15 March:

Something has (in Mr Micawber's phrase) "turned up" which seems to promise a solution for one part of our problem, though not of your immediate bother. [Ivy was having to look for somewhere else to live.] I am getting married to a man . . . who seems quite satisfied to throw the eye of affection and responsibility over John Anthony in the future. This seems to settle the difficulty as to his needing a boys' school, and a firm hand in a month or two! It doesn't mean that we can do with him as a permanent resident yet-a-while, because we shall both be keeping on working, so we want you to carry on as at present, please. But it will mean that there is somebody else to look to in a case of accident and so forth – I'm hoping we shall get down to see you ere long and jaw the whole matter over.

In the meantime we shall all have to turn our minds to the housing problem – we too, as there's no room for two in my flat. But when we meet we'll go over the whole question. One can't really do it on paper. The whole thing has happened very suddenly, and I haven't told anybody but you, not wanting a fuss, so pray say nothing until you hear further. I *will not* have Aunt G. all over us. Anyhow, marriages are one's own business . . . By the way, the name is Fleming. It goes quite nicely with both mine and J.A.'s, I think, though I shall probably still use my maiden name for most things – e.g. books and business.

Ivy wrote a long and sympathetic letter by return of post, for which Dorothy thanked her on 18 March, saying that they planned to get "hooked up" in about three weeks. "Mac is perfectly get-on-able-with and disposed to think the world of you for being so decent to me." She has not yet told them at Christchurch: "I don't want a fuss – and oh, lord! what about Aunt G. when it *does* come out! I'll tell them presently all right."

On 7 April she reports, again only to Ivy, that she is getting married the following week, on the thirteenth. She will let her parents know in a day or two, "Aunt G. and Aunt Maud having cleared off from Christchurch!"

155

No doubt she felt there was enough family gossip going on for the time being. Uncle Cecil, her father's brother, and his wife Flo were getting a judicial separation,

> him havin' been caught a-carryin' on with a female in the back garden – naughty old man! I feel rather inclined to congratulate him on retaining so much youthful energy. At his time of life, a romantic affair in the potting shed when everyone has gone to bed seems such a damp, rheumatic kind of job!

Ivy sent a wedding-present of a "beautiful little set of chessmen, handy to take about and pack away". Dorothy adds – the letter is dated 9 April – "I exploded the bomb at home yesterday – I hope they won't get too excited and proclaim it everywhere triumphantly. I begged them not to! Anyway, there it is, and we are now definitely committed to it, so I only hope it'll turn out pretty well." Her letter was as off-hand as she could make it:

> I am getting married on Tuesday (weather permitting!) to a man named Fleming, who is at the moment motoring correspondent to the *News of the World* and otherwise engaged in journalism. No money, but a good job, forty-two and otherwise eminently suitable and all that. I think you will rather like him. He was Special War Correspondent to the *Sunday Chronicle* during the war and to *Black and White* during the Boer War ... and is therefore quite the "old soldier". I didn't mention this before because it's our own business and I don't want an avalanche of interrogation from all sorts of people ... For God's sake don't "announce" it to Osbornes and Godfreys and people – just let it trickle out casually at subsequent times. No flowers by request!

She enclosed "a grubby press photograph" of Mac, wearing plus-fours, presenting a cup after a motor-race.

Such a casual way of announcing this important event was bound to cause dismay to both her parents, especially to her father, for whom marriage was a religious sacrament. He had himself performed the christening ceremony of his infant daughter in the cathedral in Oxford; she had been confirmed in Salisbury Cathedral. He must have hoped to preside at the ceremony of her wedding, whenever that was to be. Her mother, too, must have looked forward, at least in earlier years, to seeing her daughter married from her home in the rectory, with the usual gathering of relations and the participation of the parish. On the other hand, she may by then have become accustomed to her daughter's independent and unconventional way of conducting her life. As is often the way in circumstances of this nature, it was the mother who saw that the sooner she accepted the situation the better. She mastered her feelings and replied composedly, suffering no recurrence of her nervous disorder. This suggests that she might have taken the news of her grandchild more calmly than Dorothy feared. It is to her that Dorothy writes the day after the marriage.

Dear Mother,
    Meant to send you a card last night, but nobody had any stamps and we had all overeaten and over-drunk ourselves. I understand that, the news having seeped out, the whole of Fleet Street, incapably drunk, decorated the bar of the Falstaff last night, and for all I know they are still there.
    We were "turned off", as the hangman says, in the salubrious purlieus of the registrar's office of the Clerkenwell Road [No. 53], which was decorated with aged posters, headed WARNING and CAUTION and threatening fines and imprisonment. However, this seemed chiefly to concern persons under 21 years of age.

This is about as unsentimental an account of a wedding feast as it is possible to imagine. It also provides a glimpse of the hearty world of bibulous newspapermen Dorothy was now frequenting and, it appears, enjoying. (Several of them were to appear in her novels.)
    She was delighted with the way her mother had taken the news and replied at once: "You are a very sensible woman and your attitude in this matter is all I could desire!! That is just what I wanted you to do – keep things quiet till it's all over. It's our funeral! . . . Mac says he's sure from your letter that you are just the sort of woman he likes." Her father had sent a cheque as a wedding present, for which she is most grateful: "It seems that one cannot get married, even in the quietest way, without expense." It is strange that she did not write a letter of thanks to her father himself; perhaps she felt a little guilty in his regard. He had asked whether they would like an announcement made in *The Times*. Dorothy wrote:

Tell Dad I'm afraid a notice in *The Times* would be the very last thing we should think of having. It would bring a horde of the very people we particularly wish to avoid – Mac's Fleet Street acquaintances and family friends and all the imbeciles who were ever at school and college with me. Sorry and all that!

On the day of the marriage her parents had drunk to their health and happiness in champagne. Dorothy wrote: "I'm glad you had champagne on the 13th – not that it's a wine I've much use for personally; it's too thin and windy and you can't get nearly as much exhilaration out of it as you can from a good Burgundy . . . I'm glad your hand has not lost the art of drawing corks." Aunt Mabel, it appears, did not have any of the champagne. Dorothy cannot imagine why not, since it would have done her no harm. Perhaps she took the news of Dorothy's marriage harder than her parents did or perhaps she would have preferred Burgundy. (Dorothy was to give this preference to Ann Dorland in *The Unpleasantness at the Bellona Club*.)

At Whitsun Dorothy and Mac drove to Christchurch on a motor-cycle and for the first time the Reverend and Mrs Henry Sayers met their son-in-law. The visit was a success. Dorothy reported to Ivy that they had three days of gorgeous weather and that she had taken her mother out on the motor-cycle for a short run: "and she was ever so sporting – seemed thoroughly to enjoy going fast".

Eric Whelpton has described the formal style in which they dined when he visited them in 1919. We may be sure that Mrs Sayers made a special effort on this occasion also. Mac would have appreciated the good cooking, being himself a gourmet. He told Dorothy it was the best organised house he had ever stayed in and Dorothy delightedly passed this compliment on to her mother. This suggests Edwardian standards of hospitality. In *Cat o' Mary* Dorothy refers to "the seemly beauty of crystal and silver and fine starched linen" – a memory of her childhood at Bluntisham. No doubt it was the same at Christchurch. Village fêtes were held in the garden, which was beautifully tended by Bob Chapman, the son of the gardener at Bluntisham, whose job it had been to catch the pony years before. His wife Edith was employed as a maid, assisted by a girl from the village, Evelyn Compline, then in her teens. She was later to work for Dorothy and Mac.

Mac had pretensions to aristocratic birth. His father had held a modest position as Customs Officer in the Orkneys, where Mac was born, but the Fleming family had owned land at Biggar and Cumbernauld since the twelfth century. A Malcolm Fleming appears in Walter Scott's novel *Castle Dangerous*. His son, another Malcolm, was created Earl of Wigton by King David II of Scotland, the son of

Robert Bruce. The earldom died out but was re-created by James VI. Mac maintained that if everyone had their rights he would be the fourteenth Earl of Wigton. A genealogical tree in his handwriting traces his descent. It is not known how seriously Dorothy took this, nor indeed how much reliance Mac himself placed on it. So far as is known, he never pressed his claim. (Dorothy was to make play with a genealogical tree in *Unnatural Death* and with another in *Have His Carcase*, showing the alleged descent of the unfortunate Paul Alexis from the Tsar of Russia.)

Like the Irish who trace their descent from ancient kings of Erin, Mac no doubt felt he could hold up his head with the highest and is unlikely to have felt abashed in the company of the gentle, stately rector, with his now-white moustache and slight stoop, or of Mrs Sayers, a gentlewoman of distinguished manners, who nevertheless unbent sufficiently to smoke a clay pipe containing a cigarette – an unusual form of cigarette holder which must have endeared her to him. Dorothy had shocked the villagers by smoking in public, unashamedly buying her cigarettes at the village shop, kept by a Mr Jordan, who was also the postman. She was observed going for walks accompanied by Tinker, the rectory dog, her hair done up in a red kerchief, gypsy fashion, or sitting on the bank of a canal, smoking and writing. The villagers thought her distant and reserved, not friendly like her father, and it was their impression that her visits were a matter of duty rather than pleasure.

Her marriage took them all by surprise. She had seemed too studious to be the marrying kind. Mac's arrival created quite a flurry of interest and excitement. He was remembered as a handsome man, with a moustache, a flamboyant personality, who enjoyed a drink. He went to church on Sundays with the family and the congregation were amused to notice that he was always the first to leave, striding through the west gate, across two fields and straight into a pub called the Dun Cow. No doubt he missed his Fleet Street cronies. So, probably, did Dorothy.

Her parents took to Mac and he liked them He called her father "the guv'nor" (as Jack Munting refers to Elizabeth Drake's father in *The Documents in the Case*); in his letters he addressed Mrs Sayers as "Dearest Mother", sometimes "Darling Mother", and signed them "with much love". He told Dorothy that he found her mother a most entertaining person and said "there's no doubt which side of the family [your] turn for writing comes from". He even got on well with Aunt Mabel, who liked him and once wrote him a letter – an unusual mark of favour.

They settled down together in the flat in 24 Great James Street. Dorothy's parents sent presents: table linen, napkin rings, a rug, a fireside chair and several large bath-towels ("that's what I call a *real* bath-towel," said Mac). In August 1928, when the flat on the floor above fell vacant, they took it over as well, thus extending their premises into a maisonette, as Charles Parker and Lady Mary were to do when they married and settled down together in Great Ormond Street. Dorothy wrote to Victor Gollancz:

> The carpets are up. The floor is up ... The white-washers are washing ceilings as per estimate. The painters are giving two coats of paint as per estimate ... The cat is investigating the mysterious cavities between the joints of the flooring, with a view to getting nailed down under the floor if possible.
>
> My husband is giving his celebrated impersonation of the Mayor and Corporation of Ypres surveying the ruins of the Cloth Hall.
>
> I am trying to look like Dido building Carthage, and hoping (as I daresay she did) that the hammering will soon be over.
>
> Life is very wonderful.

And so it was. Dorothy enjoyed being married. Her physical needs were taken care of. Mac was sexually experienced and she learnt from him that a woman's fulfilment was not limited to bearing children, as she had strangely implied in her letters to Cournos. From asides in her novels and other writings, it is evident that this had come as something of a revelation.

Another shared enjoyment was good food. Mac knew a lot about cooking and wrote articles on the subject, and later on a book, entitled *Gourmet's Book of Food and Drink*, which he dedicated to his wife "who can make an omelette". In a letter to the *Evening Standard* about man-servants, Dorothy wrote:

> I have a first-class, experienced male chef, capable of turning out a perfect dinner for any number of people, who not only demands no salary, but also contributes to the support of the household. I came across this paragon some years ago, and, having sampled his cooking and ascertained that he held sound opinions on veal (which I detest) and garlic (which I appreciate), married him. So far, the arrangement seems to work very well, and, since giving me notice would be a troublesome and expensive matter, I am hoping he will stay.

The good food soon caused Dorothy to put on still more weight, to her dismay. She outgrew her clothes and began to notice that she was developing a double chin. About a year after her marriage she attended a family wedding, at which she met Uncle Cecil, who told her he hardly recognised her, she had grown so fat in the face. There is no mention, however, of any resolve to diet.

In September 1926 Dorothy's parents went to visit them, staying overnight in a nearby hotel. They had dinner in the flat, and Mac did the cooking. He was well in advance of his time, evidently regarding their marriage as a partnership between professional equals, which for several years it was. After the visit Dorothy wrote: "Mac and I enjoyed having you up here enormously and we hope you will come again and stay several days. I am sure Mac likes having such a nice mother to look after – he does do the looking-after business rather pleasingly, don't you think?" In October of that year Dorothy fell ill with a bad cold which caused her to turn yellow "like a canary" (presumably an attack of hepatitis). The doctor prescribed a diet of fish:

> Mac is a splendid person to have about when one is ill, looking after one in the most noble and devoted way and cooking everything most beautifully, though he has been having a horrid cold himself, poor dear . . . Anyway, I'm much better now, thanks to Mac, who is the sort of person that the poor call "a good husband".

Dorothy likewise was a good wife. She knitted Mac stockings with fancy turn-down tops, following Aunt Mabel's patent method of picking up stitches when turning the heel and inventing a pattern inspired by the coat of the tabby cat, as Miss Milsom does in *The Documents in the Case*. She was concerned about his health. He suffered from stomach upsets and bad coughs in winter (the after-effects of being gassed in the war). She insisted on taking holidays in places where the climate suited him, such as Cornwall or Kirkcudbright in Scotland.

They both worked hard. Benson's took a lot of Dorothy's energy and she was also writing novels and short stories in her spare time. Mac too had a number of assignments. On one occasion she wrote: "Both Mac and I have a big lot of work on hand and are hoping to make our fortunes – if only we can get it all done!" And on 12 December 1927 she wrote: "We are both working so strenuously that we haven't time to go anywhere or see anybody." But they did have an enjoyable evening out together at a dinner at the Press Club on 21 January 1928, when Mrs (later Dame) Laura Knight was one of the chief guests. John Drinkwater and his wife were also present and signed their menu for them.

Dorothy accompanied Mac to Brooklands ("I am becoming quite an habituée," she said), where he organised race meetings, as well as reporting on them for the *News of the World*. In earlier years he had himself taken part in motor-racing, mainly testing Daimlers, at Caerphilly and elsewhere. As a former resident of Hammersmith, at 153 Hammersmith Road, he would have known the French racing driver and car salesman Louis Contamin, who lived a few streets away, at 9 Wingate Road, and likewise frequented the company of newspapermen in Fleet Street and Soho. He was a partner in the firm of Millward and Contamin, one of those short-lived car-sales concerns of the period, such as Bill White had been involved in and which feature in *The Unpleasantness at the Bellona Club*. Contamin and Mac had more than motor-racing in common. They would have swapped stories of trench warfare (Contamin had been a stretcher-bearer and was decorated with the Croix de Guerre). As Mac's wife, Dorothy had many opportunities of lending an attentive ear to war anecdotes, of which she made use in her stories.

Ghoulish events occurred in motor-racing too. In March 1927 Mac's friend, Parry Thomas, was decapitated by the broken driving chain of his car while trying to establish a new speed record at Pendine Sands. Mac had to write an account of the accident. He also reported on other sensational cases. Dorothy went with him to Boulogne where he followed up the discovery of an English nurse named Daniels found dead in a field near the town, with a hypodermic syringe at her side. (*Unnatural Death* had been written previously, but contains an allusion to the Daniels case which was added at a late stage.) At the same time he was reporting on the arrest in Boulogne of Lord Terrington on bankruptcy charges. The case was the more sensational in that Lord Terrington was accompanied by a woman who was not his wife and that he collapsed and died of a heart attack a few moments after his arrest. Quite a scoop for Mac and for *John Bull*, the paper which commissioned the report! Dorothy thoroughly enjoyed the trip. She wrote to her mother on 20 March from the Hotel Meurice in Boulogne-sur-Mer:

> We rushed violently over here yesterday afternoon at about half an hour's notice. Mac is investigating the Daniels case and I am fooling about, hoping that an opportunity may present itself to ask

Mac with Dorothy's fan-mail at 24 Great James Street. The seated figure may be Andrew Dakers. (*Marion E. Wade Center*)

leading questions! Anyway, it was a very jolly trip over – simply glorious weather, sunshine and the cafés open till 2 in the morning. We rolled into bed about 2.30 and feel all the better for it, in spite of an intensive course of mixed drinks during the evening. Mac seems to have pals in every corner of Boulogne – taxi-drivers, pub-keepers, interpreters, ex-detectives etc. – and of course, what with the "affaire Daniels" and the Terrington case, the place is swarming with English journalists . . . This sort of life suits Mac.

It was a good partnership. Mac helped Dorothy with the anthology of short stories she was preparing for Gollancz. He acted as her unofficial press agent, getting advance notices of her books into various newspapers. Above all, they had fun together. They both had gusto for life. They both loved London. Dorothy had no snobbery in her taste for entertainment; neither had Mac. They enjoyed music halls – Maskelyne and Devant, the conjurors, and George Robey at the Holborn Empire delighted them. They enjoyed the cinema – the "talkies" were just coming in. (Cournos had been above such amusements.) They were also theatre-goers. As a former resident of Hammersmith, Mac would have been familiar with the Lyric Theatre, which had sprung to new life under the management of Nigel (later Sir Nigel) Playfair with the revival of *The Beggar's Opera* in 1921. Dorothy had seen this production – Charles Parker asks Lord Peter to play the music from it in *Whose Body?* In 1926, at the same theatre, she also saw the brilliantly original revue *Riverside Nights*, with sketches by A. P. Herbert and music by Frederick Austin and Alfred Reynolds. Mac still had friends in Hammersmith (they had to rush there one evening to comfort a deserted wife whose husband had disappeared, rather as George Fentiman disappears in *The Unpleasantness at the Bellona Club*), and they went to parties there, down by the river, as the short story "Nebuchadnezzar" shows:

> Bob Lester was having a birthday party – his mother and sister and about twenty intimate friends squashed into the little flat at Hammersmith. Everybody was either a writer or a painter or an actor of sorts, or did something or the other quite entertaining for a living, and they were fairly well accustomed to amusing themselves with sing-songs and games. They could fool wittily and behave like children, and get merry on invisible quantities of claret-cup, and they were all rather clever . . .

This is the kind of company Dorothy now frequented. She would have met people like this at the famous little pub, The Dove, on the river near Hammersmith Bridge, and at A. P. Herbert's house in Hammersmith Terrace or on his boat the *Water Gypsy*. (She knew A.P.H. and admired his contributions to *Punch* and was later to collaborate with him.) She and Mac may also have been guests at the house in Hammersmith Mall belonging to Nigel Playfair, who gave parties such as she describes. They may have watched the Oxford and Cambridge boat race from there. Another of her short stories, "The Queen's Square", written about this time contains a character named Playfair, not a common name, but prominent then and evidently to the forefront of her mind.

The General Strike of 1926 kept Mac busy, his headphones clamped to his ears all day, listening to news on the cat's-whisker wireless set. Dorothy herself was immensely busy. Her work at Benson's was becoming more and more entertaining. The celebrated advertising stunt of the Mustard Club began that year. Mac helped her with some of the copy, contributing to the club's Recipe Book. The campaign was Benson's greatest success to date and Dorothy's creative enthusiasm was largely responsible for it. Colman's mustard boomed and the Mustard Club was a household joke all over the country. London buses sported the fascia: "Have you joined the Mustard Club?" Hoardings queried, "Where's Father? At the

Mustard Club." "What is a canary? A sparrow that has joined the Mustard Club." The campaign was a joint effort and copy was anonymous. Nevertheless, Dorothy's humour and love of word-play can be spotted in the creation of such characters as Miss Di Gester, Lord Bacon of Cookham, the Baron of Beef. An elaborate prospectus of the Club proclaimed that it was originally founded by Aesculapius, the god of medicine, in the days of Ham and Shem. Nebuchadnezzar was one of the earliest members, finding mustard a welcome addition to his diet of grass. This is Dorothy of the Oxford days, frivolling among her witty friends, her happy and creative self again.

Her pleasure in domestic life is abundantly shown in the letters to her mother in which she describes the arrangements they are making about their extended premises. The sitting-room upstairs is to be Dorothy's work-room – the colour scheme is golden brown, with a touch of rich blue. Mac's study, "which we are trying to remember to call the library", is downstairs. He has found "a very beautiful little refectory table which exactly suits the dining-room". He got it at a great bargain: "He is wonderfully good at buying things like that and knows a lot about furniture." The upstairs kitchen will be his work-room for photography and carpentering. Her mother has sent two beautiful rugs (Mac intends to write a rapturous letter about them), a small yellow table, a chest-of-drawers, bed and bedding for the spare room ("you are always sending us presents") and a very lovely blue squat cushion which "will grace my room". The kitchen downstairs has been fitted with a beautiful new sink, complete with splasher and draining board.

We know exactly how the kitchen was arranged. She has described it in "The Vindictive Story of the Footsteps That Ran". This short story is set in a flat which looks out on to Great James Street. A murder has been committed and Lord Peter feels that there is a clue somewhere in the kitchen. He runs over the lay-out and contents in conversation with Bunter:

"Now let's remember the kitchen . . . Begin at the door. Fryin'-pans and saucepans on the wall. Gas-stove . . . Rack of wooden spoons on the wall, gas-lighter, pan-lifter . . . Mantelpiece. Spice-boxes and stuff . . . Dresser. Plates. Knives and forks . . . flour dredger – milk jug – sieve on the wall – nutmeg-grater. Three-tier steamer . . . Knife-board. Kitchen table. Choppin' board."

Unfortunately, they are troubled by mice and Dorothy confides to her mother that they cannot decide where to put the meat safe. They install a cat, named Adelbert. They have a cleaner named Miss Quick, who is reluctant to use a vacuum sweeper, preferring to get down on her hands and knees with a dust-pan and brush; but she is being gradually won round to up-to-date ways.

She writes joyfully about something she has bought for herself at "TREMENDOUS AND SELF-INDULGENT EXTRAVAGANCE":

> . . . a wonderful trick chair, with a back which reclines at all kinds of angles on pressure of a button, an extension to put one's feet up on at a greater or less incline, and a wonderful assortment of polished tables, book-rests and things attached to it which adjust themselves in all manner of positions. The idea is that when I come home tired in the legs after a day at the office, I should be able to sit in it with my feet comfortably up and write stories about Lord Peter. Up to the present, the insinuating ease with which it converts itself into a couch has (strange to say) induced more sleep than energy in its owner; but I am writing this in it – the back being, for the moment, severely upright – and hope presently to overcome the temptations it offers to laziness.

Mac made fun of it, calling it her "invalid chair", but she noticed, as in the story of Goldilocks, that when she came home from the office there were signs that someone had been sitting in it.

In June 1926, two months after their marriage, they had a disagreement. They had gone on holiday in the New Forest, travelling by means of Dorothy's motor-cycle, known as a "Ner-a-Car". Mac insisted on driving and "a little friction arose now and then" (as Dorothy expressed it to her mother) because, although Mac was the better and bolder driver, "taking corners in racing style and boring alarmingly through traffic", she reserved the right to drive her own bike occasionally, with Mac riding pillion: "I've seen enough of the results in your case of not being able to get about independently to hang on like grim death to my own liberties." (Her father had discouraged his wife from learning to drive when he first bought a car in Bluntisham.) In July they sold the Ner-a-Car "while the going was good" and in August they bought a small car, a two-three-seater coupé Belsize-Bradshaw. Dorothy preferred the motor-bike but Mac disliked it. She thinks the car will be a dreadful drain on their finances, with garage, tax, insurance, oil and petrol to pay for. "However, anything for a quiet life!" She dislikes cars because they are draught-traps. A windscreen is a mistake, she considers. The human face is adapted to receive a rush of air, but a windscreen sends the draught circling round the passenger's back, which is not adapted for it. The solo two-stroke motor-bike, which she first bought in March 1925, she is keeping for her own use.

In spite of occasional differences of opinion, Dorothy was obviously very happy. A great change had come over her life. Mac too seemed happy and confident, professionally in demand. There is no mention in Dorothy's letters of his former wife or of his daughters. For him it is as though his marital past has been wiped out. For Dorothy, however, there still remained the problem of her son.

Six weeks after their marriage, at the end of May 1926, they went to Cowley so that Mac could meet Ivy and see John Anthony, who was then two and a half years old. Any idea of having the child to live with them was out of the question then and, even when they acquired the upstairs flat, the accommodation was less suitable for a child than his present environment. Furthermore, Dorothy would have had to give up her job to look after him or else engage a nurse, neither of which she could have afforded to do. And there, in the meantime, was John Anthony, happy and well looked after by Ivy, living in a house with a garden, in the company of other children. He knew his mother as "Cousin Dorothy", who came to visit him now and then and brought him presents. And now there was "Cousin Mac". The situation was obviously best left alone for the time being.

Dorothy's marriage had given her equilibrium. The crisis of disillusionment caused by Cournos was over, like a bad dream. Never again would she be at the mercy of her emotions. She knew now exactly what she had to do. She had to keep on at her job at Benson's; and she had to write novels and short stories which would sell. John Anthony's upkeep would become more and more expensive. She was determined to give him as good an education as she could afford and did, in fact, earn enough to send him to a preparatory school when he was eleven, then to Malvern College at thirteen (he helped by winning a scholarship) and later to Oxford, where he entered Lord Peter Wimsey's College, Balliol, again winning a scholarship, and took a first class degree. But that was a long way ahead. In the meantime there was work to be done. And work she did! The early years of her marriage are extremely prolific, despite the increasing demands made on her energy during the day at Benson's. Between 1923 and 1928 she published four novels, twelve short stories, and edited the first volume of *Great Short Stories of Detection, Mystery and Horror*. She must have worked late into the night, sitting up at a table, "her elbows squared to the job", as she said she

Dorothy the established writer, photographed by Mac Fleming
(*Marion E. Wade Center*)

always preferred to do, rather than in the insidious trick chair.

She had several other enterprises on hand at this time. One was a biography of Wilkie Collins, whose detective novel, *The Moonstone*, she regarded as near perfection. She had learnt from him, as well as from Conan Doyle, that the way to lend an air of verisimilitude to an otherwise unconvincing narrative was to introduce precise, realistic detail. Lord Peter Wimsey is pure fantasy but almost all the novels and short stories in which he appears are firmly bolstered with familiar, factual detail, drawn from everyday life – her own life. Among the pages of her unfinished Collins biography we find the following:

> In order . . . to gain the reader's attention in the first place, and in order to secure his belief in far more astonishing parts of the narrative, the writer, if he knows his business, will strive for the utmost and most exact realism in the details of everything that happens "within the reader's own experience".

And she quotes Collins' own words: "Fancy and Imagination, Grace and Beauty, all these qualities which are to the work of Art what scent and colour are to the flower, can only grow toward Heaven by taking root in earth." The key-word here is earth. After her marriage to Mac, an earthy realism became, in fact, Dorothy's most sturdy characteristic. It was as though she was determined to distance herself as far as possible from the empty, specious theorising and patronising superiority of John Cournos, by whom she had been so misled and who had caused her so much grief. "Come off Mount Sinai," she once said to him. Whether he ever did is not known. She at any rate now had her feet on the ground.

CHAPTER 12

Enter Lord Peter Wimsey

Dorothy now had two men in her life: her husband and Lord Peter Wimsey. When she married Mac in April 1926, Lord Peter was already well established in two published novels (*Whose Body?* and *Clouds of Witness*), another in preparation (*Unnatural Death*), and four short stories: "The Problem of Uncle Meleager's Will", "The Entertaining Episode of the Article in Question", "Beyond the Reach of the Law", and "The Learned Adventure of the Dragon's Head".

He had started life as the son of the Duke of Peterborough. The first mention of him occurs in an unpublished short story, probably sketched out in France in 1920, in which he plays a minor role. His name first occurs in a conversation between two other characters:

> "Well, Monsieur Briffault was living in a flat in Piccadilly, lent him by Lord Peter Wimsey."
> "Who's Lord Peter Wimsey?"
> "I looked him up in *Who's Who*. Younger son of the Duke of Peterborough. Harmless sort of fellow, I think. Distinguished himself in the war. Rides his own horse in the Grand National. Authority on first editions. At present visiting the Duchess in Herts. I've seen his photo somewhere. Fair-haired, big nose, aristocratic sort of man whose socks match his tie. No politics."

From a synopsis in Dorothy's handwriting it is apparent that the story was intended as a contribution to the series of Sexton Blake stories, which were written by a syndicate. The plot is outlined as follows. A distinguished French politician, Monsieur Briffault, is found murdered in Lord Peter Wimsey's flat in Piccadilly and there are signs of a robbery. Sexton Blake is called in to investigate. Suspicion points to a young French actor named Jean Renault, who

171

had accompanied Monsieur Briffault home the previous night. The French Ambassador, however, suspects treachery on the part of Britain and insists on further investigation. Blake's boy assistant, Tinker, discovers a cipher among Monsieur Briffault's papers, based on a code book, which is missing. Lord Peter's flat is entered by a Belgian workman who tells the man-servant (unnamed) that he has come to clean the windows. The Belgian is Renault in disguise, who sets about searching for the cipher. He is discovered doing so by the man-servant, there is a fight and Renault escapes. Blake and Tinker chase him through London but he gives them the slip. Baffled, they wander into Westminster Cathedral. It is Holy Week and the office of Tenebrae is in progress. Tinker grows bored and his wandering eye singles out a member of the congregation who, he is sure, is Renault. He points him out to Blake who moves towards him, but at that point in the service the lights are dimmed and in the darkness Renault escapes again.

In the meantime word has come from the Paris Sûreté that Renault has given instructions for a large sum of money to be sent to Rome, to be paid into the account of a Contessa Malaspina. Blake and Tinker catch up with him in Paris at the Gare de Lyon disguised as a young French woman, who gives "herself" away by using a masculine French word in relation to "herself". (Dorothy was to use this idea later for the short story, "The Entertaining Episode of the Article in Question".)

Renault again escapes and Lord Peter is drawn into the chase. He pursues Renault to Rome by aeroplane and finds him there, this time disguised as the Contessa Malaspina, a frail, elderly lady, who announces "her" intention of travelling to England via Germany. By an ingenious trick Lord Peter diverts "her" luggage to Paris, where it is seized and opened by the police. It contains the code book and the cipher can at last be read. Renault is revealed as a thief, who had been employed by Monsieur Briffault (who was much in debt) to gain possession of a valuable jewel, of which the whereabouts are disclosed in the cipher. Sexton Blake lays a trap for Renault, who leads him to the jewel and at the same time falls into the hands of the police. The jewel is restored to an impoverished ducal family, to whom it rightfully belongs. The story was to end with the arrest, death or disappearance of Renault.

Dorothy was reading the Sexton Blake stories during her year at Verneuil and when she had to retire to bed with mumps she and Muriel Jaeger, as has been said, exchanged letters in which they indulged in spoof higher criticism of the saga. It may have occurred to her then to try her hand at a Sexton Blake story herself, casually introducing a fair-haired aristocrat as a secondary character. If so, then Lord Peter Wimsey was conceived in Normandy, as Eric Whelpton surmised, his background the chance result of sundry anecdotes of high life related by Charles Crichton, his basic appearance an unconscious remembrance of Ridley, whom he was to resemble physically more and more as he developed in her imagination, until, in 1935, she recognised the chaplain of Balliol as perfect for the part of Lord Peter Wimsey in *Busman's Honeymoon*, if only he had been an actor!

In 1936 Dorothy Sayers published an article entitled "How I came to Invent the Character of Lord Peter". She says there that she does not remember inventing him at all. Her impression is that she was thinking of writing a detective story and that he walked in, "complete with spats", and applied for the job. He was then, she said, the brother of the Earl of Denver and she later decided to give the family a step up by making the brother a duke. This suggests that by 1936 she had forgotten her Sexton Blake story (or chose to disregard it), in which Peter Wimsey is already the son of a duke, though at that time the Duke of Peterborough.

The surname Wimsey is rare but not unknown. Twice Dorothy was sent obituary notices of men called Peter Wimsey. "It is curious", she wrote to her friend Wilfrid Scott-Giles, "that one can never invent a surname which does not exist." She chose the name (believing she had invented it) for its associative sub-meaning of "whimsy". This is borne out by the family motto, "As my whimsy takes me", sometimes given as "I hold by my whimsy". Since he probably first came into her mind early in 1920, it is relevant to consider that she was then daily thinking and speaking in French. The French for "whimsy" is *boutade*. *Travailler par boutades* means "to work by fits and starts". Lord Peter's character is so far only dimly outlined in the unfinished story but his name already suggests, whether in English or in French, someone whose activity is governed by intuition and imagination, rather than by routine application.

When she returned to England in September 1920 the half-sketched figure of Lord Peter came with her at the back of her mind. Already he has a flat in Piccadilly; since the murder takes place there, he is drawn into the pursuit of the criminal; he has served with distinction in the war; he is an authority on first editions; he is also a man of unusual physical skill, since he rides his own horse in the Grand National. If he wants to travel quickly he thinks nothing of taking an aeroplane (in 1920). He is good at French for he spots the error made by Renault. He is something of a dandy, since he likes his socks to match his tie. He is said to look harmless and to have no politics.

By January 1921, as Dorothy told her mother, she had an idea for a detective story which began with the discovery of a naked body in a bath. She rummaged in the cupboard of her mind and found this young sprig of the nobility, ready to hand. She decided to see what she could make of him. After all, he had already assisted Sexton Blake in one case and a son of a duke would have many advantages – wealth, freedom, useful contacts and privileges. He would also be something quite new in detective fiction.

She first auditioned him, so to speak, for a part in a play, entitled *The Mousehole: A Detective Fantasia in Three Flats*. In this unfinished sketch, a husband and wife are found dead in a flat above Lord Peter's in Piccadilly. He makes his appearance on the scene with the following stage-direction: "Enter R. Lord Peter Wimsey, sleek, fair, monocle, dressed in a grey suit, with the exception of his coat, whose place is taken by a luxurious dressing-gown." Constable Sugg, large and red-faced, is next to arrive. "Lord P.: 'Ah, here comes the law. I'm afraid he looks rather a stupid one.'" Sugg and Lord Peter, who are old enemies in *Whose Body?*, do not yet know each other. When asked for his particulars, Lord Peter replies: "Lord Peter Wimsey. Thirty-two, unmarried; no occupation; residence, first floor; hobby, other people's business." *The Mousehole* got no further than a few pages. The plot of *Whose Body?*, however, took shape and so did Lord Peter. In May 1923 he made his first public appearance: "'Oh, damn!' said Lord Peter at Piccadilly Circus. 'Hi, driver!'"

As we have seen, Lord Peter was already in *Who's Who* in 1920. By 1923 his particulars were more detailed and the revised entry is as follows:

WIMSEY, PETER DEATH BREDON, D.S.O.; *born* 1890, *2nd* son of Mortimer Gerald Bredon Wimsey, 15th Duke of Denver, and of Honoria Lucasta, *daughter* of Francis Delagardie of Bellingham Manor, Hants. *Educated*: Eton College and Balliol College, Oxford (1st class honours, Sch. of Mod. Hist. 1912); served with H.M.Forces 1914/18 (Major, Rifle Brigade). *Author of*: "Notes on the Collecting of Incunabula", "The Murderer's Vade-Mecum", etc. *Recreations*: Criminology; bibliophily; music; cricket. *Clubs*: Marlborough; Egoists'. *Residences*: 110A Piccadilly, W.; Bredon Hall, Duke's Denver, Norfolk. *Arms*: Sable, 3 mice courant, argent, crest, a domestic cat couched as to spring, proper; *motto*: As my Whimsy takes me.

By now Lord Peter has acquired two other names: Death and Bredon. The surname Death (usually spelled De'Ath or D'Aeth and pronounced to rhyme either with "teeth" or "breath") is playfully adroit for a detective. The family name of Bredon, which his brother Gerald shares, has no obvious connotation, unless it is intended to echo the theme of hanging which occurs in the poetry of A. E. Housman, the immediate literary association being Housman's poem "On Bredon Hill". (A poem by Housman is one of the clues which enable Lord Peter to solve the murder in *Strong Poison* and reference is made to the Housman association in *Murder Must Advertise*.) The Christian name Peter, "so old-world and full of homely virtue", as its owner says in *Whose Body?*, has no apparently relevant meaning, though attempts have been made to discover one.

The earth in which this sprig of fantasy was planted was in great part Dorothy's own. He was almost her exact contemporary. He was up at Oxford. He has recreations which she shares: books and music; and she will become knowledgeable about cricket. To equip him as a detective she sets herself to learn about criminology. His bubbling cheerfulness, his habit of literary quotation, his manner of prattling, sometimes wittily, sometimes foolishly, his tendency to burst into song or whistle a passage of Bach, his blithe impetuosity, his mental agility and energy, his untiring capacity to engage in exuberant flights of fancy in pursuit of an idea are all characteristic of his creator. But not of her alone. Some of these traits of personality also have fictional antecedence, particularly in the character of Philip Trent in E. C. Bentley's detective novel, *Trent's Last Case*, a book she greatly admired and the influence of which she readily acknowledged. Some of Lord Peter's mannerisms are also deliberately evocative of P. G. Wodehouse's Bertie Wooster. She used them because they entertained her.

She also enjoyed sprinkling her stories with fragments of her own life, her own interests and even her own possessions. An intriguing example occurs in *Whose Body?* On Sir Reuben Levy's bedside table is a small volume, entitled *Letters from a Self-Made Merchant to his Son*, a work by the American humorist George Horace Lorimer. Dorothy possessed the sequel to this, *Old Gorgon Graham: More Letters from a Self-Made Merchant to his Son*, and no doubt also the first volume. Her copy of the sequel (which I now possess) is, like Sir Reuben's book, a small octavo volume, bound in soft blue leather, marbled, however, whereas Sir Reuben's copy is bound in polished morocco, for the better retention of finger-prints. On the fly-leaf is Dorothy's signature, "D. L. Sayers", in the handwriting of her late teens or early twenties. The "self-made merchant" is John Graham, head of the house of Graham and Company, pork-packers in Chicago. His rhythms of speech and some of his down-to-earth sayings provided the basis for the personality of John P. Milligan, the American financier in *Whose Body?* Even the name Milligan occurs in Lorimer's work. (Dorothy was also to give the name Tod Milligan to the dope-peddler in *Murder Must Advertise.*)

The plot of her first novel occurred to her at a time when she was depressed, hard up and undecided about her future. Her friend Muriel ("Jim") Jaeger was in London and Dorothy was seeing a good deal of her. No doubt they talked about their correspondence of the previous year in which they had discussed the Sexton Blake saga. If so, Lord Peter may have surfaced in conversation, particularly if Dorothy told Muriel about the unfinished story in which he appears. Muriel certainly played a crucial part in his realisation, for there were times when Dorothy's creative energy flagged and Muriel encouraged her to persevere. This is apparent from the dedication.

TO M.J.

Dear Jim:

This book is your fault. If it had not been for your brutal insistence, Lord Peter would never have staggered through to the end of this enquiry. Pray consider that he thanks you with his accustomed suavity.

Yours ever,
D.L.S.

The idea for the story came into her mind at the same time as an idea for a Grand Guignol play. What the play would have been about we do not know, except that it was to end with a poisoned kiss, but from its category it would necessarily have been gruesome. *Whose Body?* is, in fact, the most gruesome of all her novels, involving the substitution of the body of a murdered man for the body of a pauper intended for dissection by medical students. There is also an exhumation scene, in which dissected portions of the murdered man's body are identified by his widow.

Behind the horror of this story lies the nightmare of the recent war. Lord Peter's experiences, which included being blown up and buried in a shell hole, enable him to take a hardened view of the idea that a corpse was shaved and manicured after death. Charles Parker, his friend from Scotland Yard, is disturbed at the thought. Lord Peter says: "Here, sit down, man, and don't be an ass, stumpin' about the room like that. Worse things happen in war. This is only a blinkin' old shilling shocker."

The Grand Guignol gruesomeness of *Whose Body?* is offset by the flippancy of the dialogue. (This was also E. C. Bentley's formula.) When Parker remarks that Lord Peter is expressing himself very dramatically about the disappearance of Sir Reuben Levy, Lord Peter replies: "You recall me to the nursery rhymes of my youth – the sacred duty of flippancy – " And he quotes the lines by Edward Lear:

> There was an old man of Whitehaven
> Who danced a quadrille with a raven.
> They said, "It's absurd
> To encourage that bird",
> So they smashed that old man of Whitehaven.

But flippancy does not dispel Lord Peter's disquiet: "That's the correct attitude, Parker. Here's a poor old buffer spirited away – such a joke – and I don't believe he'd hurt a fly himself – that makes it funnier. D'you know, Parker, I don't care frightfully about this case after all."

The change of sex of the mysterious body in the bath, from "a fat lady" to a man of about fifty, with Semitic-type features, was dictated by the choice of the murder victim. But why did Dorothy make the victim a Jew? The body in the bath is at first mistaken for that of the financier Sir Reuben Levy, who has disappeared, but Lord Peter knows at once that this cannot be, for the body is uncircumcised, a detail which both Inspector Sugg and Detective Inspector Parker fail to notice. There are enough indications on the body to make the identification with a prominent financier improbable – the flea-bites, the bad teeth, the bitten finger-nails, the blistered feet and neglected toe-nails – without the need to bring in the matter of circumcision.

Dorothy had already met John Cournos when she was planning *Whose Body?* Jewishness and the attitude to Jews in English society were, therefore, uppermost in her mind; so, too, was the possibility of a mixed marriage. What would her status have been as the wife of a Jew? How would her parents have reacted? Her delineation of Sir Reuben Levy is kindly. A man of humble origin, of handsome appearance in his youth, he attracted the love of Christine Ford, a young Gentile girl of good Hampshire family. (Like Dorothy's mother, both the Dowager Duchess and Miss Ford come from Hampshire.) The Ford family objected to the match but it proved happy and Reuben Levy, having made a fortune, had been knighted. He is shown to be ruthless in business but a loving husband and father in private life. Lord Peter's friend, the Hon. Freddy Arbuthnot, falls in love with Sir Reuben's daughter Rachel, and ultimately marries her.

The defiant vulgarity of the opening discovery of a naked male body suggests that the author wanted to make it clear from the outset that, though a woman, she intended no simpering evasion of reality. She also introduced touches of the dark side of London life: prostitution, and a seedy night club, which is raided by the police. The description by Mr Piggott, the medical student, of the routine procedures of a dissecting room is unsparing. The horror of the exhumation scene, heightened by the piteous presence of Sir Reuben's widow, is economically but powerfully suggested. Dorothy had always had a robust imagination. Looking back on herself from the age of sixty-two, she wrote in a letter to me, dated 10 February 1956: "I was a very tough-minded beast of a child, and always insisted on having all the bloodthirsty bits read to me, to the great horror of my elders. (If they refused, I got the book for myself, which was good for my reading, if not for my morals.)" Though she attributed tough-mindedness to herself from childhood on, she nevertheless regarded detachment as a modern characteristic in women. In an unfinished short story, also about Lord Peter and dated probably about 1929, she wrote of "the callous-seeming man-to-mannishness of the completely post-war woman, carving surgeon-like into difficulties without repugnance or surprise". By the time she wrote *Whose Body?* she had become, at least as regards the writing of detective fiction, just such a post-war woman. As regards her personal life, however, it would be some time before she achieved anything approaching detachment.

One of the ways in which she did so was to mingle factual details of her own life with the fiction of her creation. This tendency increases and deepens as the novels proceed but it is apparent from the first. In the beginning this was little more than a game played for her own amusement. The placing of one of her own books on Sir Reuben's bedside table is a case in point. A pair of gold-rimmed pince-nez had been balanced on the nose of the dead body in the bath. She herself wore pince-nez at this period of her life. The rightful owner of the pince-nez is revealed as an elderly solicitor, a Mr Crimplesham. (Crimplesham is the name of a small village in

Norfolk.) Where does she locate him? In Salisbury, where she was at school. Why? Primarily, it saved her the trouble of invention; but it must also have amused her to make Lord Peter Wimsey and Bunter walk along the streets she knew so well:

> It was its comparative proximity to Milford Hill [on the top of which Godolphin School is situated] that induced Lord Peter to lunch at the Minster Hotel rather than at the White Hart or some other more picturesquely situated hostel. It was not a lunch calculated to cheer his mind; as in all Cathedral cities, the atmosphere of the Close pervades every nook and corner of Salisbury, and no food in that city but seems faintly flavoured with prayer-books. As he sat sadly consuming that impassive pale substance known to the English as "cheese" unqualified (for there are cheeses which go openly by their names, as Stilton, Camembert, Gruyère, Wensley-dale or Gorgonzola, but "cheese" is cheese and everywhere the same), he inquired of the waiter the whereabouts of Mr Crimple-sham's office.

This is surely reminiscent of lunch at the Minster Hotel with her parents or one of her aunts when they came to visit her at the Godolphin and seems even to echo scraps of family conversation.

The waiter replies: "You'll find the house easy. Just afore you come to Penny-farthing Street, sir, about two turnings off, on the right hand side opposite." Lord Peter and Bunter walk up the street together. Lord Peter recognises the office across the way and instructs Bunter to step into a little shop and buy a sporting paper. After the embarrassing interview, Lord Peter enters the cathedral to attend Evensong. The whole scene is vividly present to Dorothy's mind; it is as though she is there walking beside the character she has created, showing him the way.

She amuses herself also in endowing Lord Peter with a gift for logical disputation. This was one of her own attributes, which had been sharpened at Oxford in playful arguments with her friends. She has said that the idea of the body in the bath came originally from a game she had played at Oxford. This consisted of starting off with a mysterious situation, which each player had to develop in turn. We can learn just what such games were like by following the elaborate parody of the Oxford method of argumentation in which Lord Peter indulges. It was a game calling for mental agility and the ability to spot flaws in an argument. Dorothy's exuberant inventiveness led her to introduce such mental exercise into more than one of her novels purely for the fun of it. It is apparent at once that Crimplesham and his pince-nez are red herrings, yet the possibility that he may be the villain is pedantically divided into Hypotheses I and II, the former being subdivided in its turn into Alternatives A and B. Lord Peter blithely explores the suggestions arising from the sub-divisions, "following the methods inculcated at that University of which [he has] the honour to be a member". After two and a half pages of this, Parker patiently asks, "How about the first possibility of all, misunderstanding or accident?" Lord Peter replies: "Well! Well, for purposes of discussion, nothing, because it really doesn't afford any data for discussion." Quite so.

At the very beginning of this novel the author seems to send out a signal to the reader that Lord Peter is not to be taken too seriously. Seated in the taxi and asking the driver to turn back to 110A Piccadilly, he is described as follows: "His long amiable face looked as if it had generated spontaneously from his top hat, as white maggots breed from Gorgonzola." It was customary in the early 1920s, despite the post-war depression, for a gentleman attending a function such as Sir Ralph Brocklebury's sale of books to wear a frock-coat and a top hat. The simile of maggots breeding from Gorgonzola suggests that Dorothy, impoverished and unemployed, looked on such formality with amused contempt, regarding those who adhered to it in the light of parasites. But her social criticism, if it is that, is light and uncensorious. When Lord Peter changes his clothes to visit Mr Thipps, in whose bath the body has been discovered, she causes him to make fun of himself:

> "Can I have the heart to fluster the flustered Thipps further" (he asks himself) — "that's very difficult to say quickly — by appearing in a top-hat and frock-coat? I think not. Ten to one he will overlook my trousers and take me for the undertaker. A grey suit, I fancy, neat but not gaudy, with a hat to tone, suits my other self better. Exit the amateur of first editions: new motive introduced by solo bassoon; enter Sherlock Holmes, disguised as a walking gentleman."

He selects a dark-green tie to match his socks and substitutes a pair of brown shoes for his black ones. Though accustomed to be valeted, he makes the changes "with a rapidity one might not have expected from a man of his mannerisms", tying his tie "accurately without hesitation or the slightest compression of the lips".

The dandyism of the man-about-town is here coupled with the

controlled expertise of a detective, equipped with magnifying glass, disguised as a monocle, a small torch, disguised as a silver matchbox, and a beautiful malacca walking-stick, marked off in inches, containing a sword down the middle and a compass in the silver head. The elegance of Lord Peter and the insouciance with which he examines the body, "with his head on one side, bringing his monocle into play with the air of the late Joseph Chamberlain approving a rare orchid", is reflected, as in a distorting mirror, in the grotesque dandyism of the corpse, his bitten nails manicured and his hair, expertly cut and parted, exuding Parma violet scent.

The expensive world inhabited by Lord Peter was remote from Dorothy's experience but its denizens were to be seen in Mayfair and the West End, entering the Savile Club, leaving the Ritz, hailing taxis, top-hatted, wearing morning or evening dress and opulent overcoats with astrakhan collars. Eric Whelpton and Charles Crichton had mingled with such people. Dorothy herself was escorted to lunch and tea at the Ritz. The writer Michael Arlen, who specialised in figures of high life, was himself an example. Always immaculately attired by the best hatters, tailors and shoemakers in London, his slight, elegant figure was seen at every fashionable event. He drove an enormous yellow Rolls Royce and assumed a pose of wearied sophistication. He might easily have joined Lord Peter and Freddy Arbuthnot for lunch at Wyndham's.

> Lord Peter and the Honourable Freddy Arbuthnot, looking together like an advertisement for gents' trouserings, strolled into the dining-room at Wyndham's.
>
> "Haven't seen you for an age," said the Honourable Freddy, "what have you been doin' with yourself?"
>
> "Oh, foolin' about," said Lord Peter, languidly.
>
> "Thick or clear, sir?" inquired the waiter of the Honourable Freddy.
>
> "Which'll you have, Wimsey?" said that gentleman, transferring the burden of selection to his guest, "they're both equally poisonous."
>
> "Well, clear's less trouble to lick out of the spoon," said Lord Peter.

Beneath the frivolous and at times nonsensical surface of *Whose Body?* are several strata of serious import. The most profound and far-reaching of these is the question of good and evil. Lord Peter's flippancy conceals a vulnerable social conscience. He finds the initial challenge of investigation exciting and enjoyable but when the chase closes in on the quarry he loses pleasure in the pursuit and questions his right to intervene. Detective-Inspector Charles Parker points out that it is every citizen's duty to bring a criminal to justice; but Lord Peter cannot disengage his personal feelings. When he realises who the guilty man is, he suffers a relapse of a nervous malady caused by war-time experiences.

He solves the mystery not by logical analysis or argument but by the unconscious correlation of apparently disparate data. The mental process by which this occurs was something which Dorothy herself occasionally experienced. She compares it to a game of anagrams, in which a jumbled assortment of letters is presented, such as C O S S S S R I. It sometimes happens that "by no logical process that the conscious mind can detect, or under some adventitious external stimulus", the solution S C I S S O R S "presents itself with calm certainty". Just so did Lord Peter's mind assemble the scattered facts of the double mystery:

> He remembered – not one thing, not another thing, nor a logical succession of things, but everything – the whole thing, perfect, complete, in all its dimensions as it were and instantaneously; as if he stood outside the world and saw it suspended in infinitely dimensional space. He no longer needed to reason about it, or even to think about it. He knew it.

Whose Body? is concerned with more than the solution of a complex problem. The "adventitious stimulus" which prompted Lord Peter's unconscious mind was a remark by Charles Parker: "You're a responsible person." Lord Peter goes home and to take, as he thinks, his mind off the problem, settles down to read a recent book entitled *The Physiological Bases of the Conscience*:

> Mind and matter were one thing, that was the theme . . . Matter could erupt, as it were, into ideas. You could carve passions in the brain with a knife. You could get rid of imagination with drugs and cure an outworn convention like a disease. "The knowledge of good and evil is an observed phenomenon, attendant upon a certain condition of the brain-cells, which is removable."

He then knows how Sir Reuben has died and who has killed him.

After recovering from the nervous collapse which this realisation causes, and having set in motion arrangements for the exhumation,

Lord Peter, perusing the folio edition of Dante's *Divina Commedia*, which Bunter has bought for him at the sale — a work which inexorably proclaims individual responsibility and the freedom of the will — decides to give the murderer the choice between confessing his guilt or leaving the country.

Lord Peter's uncertainties and sensitivity, masked by a flippant nonchalance, make him, from the beginning, a potentially interesting character. He was to develop through the novels (though scarcely at all in the short stories), until readers who respond positively to him (and there are many who do not) amuse themselves by imagining that he really existed. This immortality he shares with Sherlock Holmes.

His creator was to say that Lord Peter became more real to her than many living persons. This is partly because she wove the threads of her own experience, thoughts and feelings into the fabric of his character. As she developed, so did he. As her interests grew, his mind became more congenial to hers. As a companion he would become more and more rewarding, both imaginatively and financially. Sadly, this ceased gradually to be true of her husband.

CHAPTER 13

Sometime Scholar of Somerville College

Dorothy now had many reasons to be happy. Life with Mac was fun. They both had work to do and could afford to live well. Her novels sold. Her short stories were accepted by magazine editors and published in collected volumes. She was appreciated at Benson's where the work, though sometimes exhausting, was an enjoyable challenge to her creative energy and talent.

The construction of detective fiction required inventiveness and skill. Dorothy found it, she had told Cournos, almost as satisfying as working with her hands, rather like laying a mosaic. But the full strength and depth of her intellect remained as yet untested. The training she had received at Oxford lay dormant.

But not entirely. Her interest in Old French literature revived, as we have seen, while she was teaching in Hull. She began translating the *Chanson de Roland*, into rhymed couplets. She wrote from Hull to tell Muriel Jaeger that someone called "Jack" liked it (probably another Somerville friend) and so she felt encouraged to go on with it. (In 1957, the last year of her life, she referred to this unfinished version. "I still have it," she wrote, "it is very bad. I completed the task much later – in assonance this time, and I hope with better results.")

Among the books she read in 1916 in the Cambridge University Library was Joseph Bédier's study of the manuscripts of *Tristan*, a narrative poem by the Anglo-Norman poet Thomas. She had studied it at Somerville with her tutor, Mildred Pope, and was now seized with the desire to translate this also. It was a task which required close scholarly application, for the poem exists only in fragments, which have been supplemented by prose renderings by Bédier of linking sections taken from sundry other manuscripts. She found this, she said, a "delightful and intensely interesting study". She

185

communicated her enthusiasm to her pupils in Hull. In a letter to Muriel Jaeger, she wrote: "I've only time for a line this evening. I'm awfully busy preparing an experiment for the VIth form. We are going to make texts – whole families of them – and see how they work out."

In October 1919 she was elected a member of the recently founded Modern Language Association. Miss Pope was on the Council and had founded an Oxford branch in September of that year. It seems an unlikely body for Dorothy to join, since the majority – about 90 per cent, it was estimated – were members of the teaching profession. It was probably Miss Pope's persuasion which decided her to do so. (The subscription was seven shillings and sixpence, increased the following year to fifteen shillings.) By the time Dorothy joined the Association she had translated the greater part of *Tristan*, having submitted it to Miss Pope for advice and guidance. (The manuscript still exists, with Miss Pope's corrections and suggestions.) In October 1919 the Association launched a new journal, entitled *Modern Languages*, to be published every two months. Miss Pope encouraged Dorothy to send a section of her translation to the editor, Eric G. Underwood, and no doubt wrote a letter in support of it.

Dorothy followed her advice. Her contribution was accepted and appeared in two parts, in the issues of June and August 1920, the first being preceded by a brief scholarly note on the poet Thomas and his work. The Editorial of the June issue contained the following announcement:

> The present number of *Modern Languages* contains a translation from the pen of Miss Dorothy L. Sayers of Somerville College, Oxford, of passages from Thomas's *Tristan*. We feel convinced that this translation will send many readers back, as it has ourselves, to refresh their memory in the original of this fascinating poet. In her English version of *Tristan*, of which a further extract will be printed in our next issue, Miss Sayers has to our mind attained a double achievement. She has not only caught with singular freshness and simplicity the grace and pathos of the original, but she has also produced – a thing seldom achieved by even the most skilful of translators – a rendering which is in itself a poem.

Arrival of the two numbers of the journal while she was still in Verneuil must have boosted Dorothy's self-esteem at that uncertain period. She may even have received payment, though the relevant rubric strikes a somewhat insecure note: "Contributions are welcome and will, wherever possible, be paid for."

Though Dorothy had made up her mind not to return to teaching if she could avoid it, she was probably in sympathy with the high ideals of the Association. Its aim was not to be a trade union of teachers nor an exclusively learned society, but to promote peace and amity in international relations by means of culture and an improved knowledge of foreign languages. The full title of the journal was *Modern Languages: A Review of Foreign Letters, Science and the Arts*. By culture was meant training which develops the higher faculties, the imagination, a sense of beauty and intellectual comprehension: "clearer vision, mental harmony, a just sense of proportion, higher illumination – these are the gifts which culture ought to bring". There had recently been a Report of the Prime Minister's Committee on Modern Languages, in which reference was made to "Classical Education [which] means scholarship with its passion for accuracy, discipline of taste, training in form and order". It was the purpose of the Modern Language Association and the editorial policy of the journal to ensure that the national needs outlined in the Report were provided for.

Adrift Dorothy was during this period, but she had at least temporary anchorage as a member of this high-minded body of scholars and teachers, whose hopes for a better world were encouraged by the founding in 1920 of the League of Nations. Years later, in 1938, when she had become famous, she was invited to be the President of the Association for the ensuing year, an honorific position which she accepted.

While she was teaching in Hull, she prepared a lecture on the Celtic tradition of Other-World journeys. The manuscript in which this exists is incomplete and has been much damaged by damp. It has no title, but a letter to Muriel Jaeger, dated 14 November 1916, reveals that it was to have been intriguingly called "The Way to the Other World" and that it was read to a meeting of the Association of Assistant Mistresses.

One of her sources is the learned work by Sir John Rhys, *Celtic Folklore, Welsh and Manx*, from which she quotes. She also draws on her Oxford study of mediaeval French romances derived from the Celtic tradition. The subject is vast and diffuse. In her compression of it to the dimensions of a brief address, the young Dorothy L. Sayers already exhibits characteristics which will make her a compelling lecturer in later years: an orderliness of mind enabling her to perceive a pattern in seemingly shapeless material, as well as an engaging desire to communicate delight. Here, for instance, is her comment on the story of Oisin (the Gaelic warrior also known as Ossian): "It is an almost perfect tale of the fairy-mistress type . . . Anyone who has not read it has missed one of the loveliest things on earth."

Her imaginative response to the mysterious powers of fairyland lends a delicately eerie quality to her writing. It is almost as though she believes in the perils and pleasures of the heroes who find themselves in thrall to praeternatural beings. After all, "it needs even today but a very slight action to put one into their power . . . Everybody remembers . . . how Burd Ellen got into the power of the elfin-king by walking incautiously round a church widdershins". We cannot be too careful, as Lord Peter is well aware in *The Nine Tailors*.

> In any story of adventure, however of the earth earthy the characters may seem to be, if the adventure occurs beside a river or fountain, and more particularly if there should be wonderful singing birds on or near the pine-trees beside the fountain, then you should be very careful to sign and shrive you, for you are dealing with faery, and that earthly-seeming knight is a phantom sent by the fay to woo you to Tir-nan-Og, where a thousand years are but as yesterday.

Particularly interesting, in connection with her later writings on time and eternity, is what she says about planes of being:

> One must remember that though in one sense the Other World was a definite place, somewhere beyond the Atlantic Ocean, yet in another the kingdom of gods was within one. Earth and fairy-land co-exist upon the same foot of ground. It was all a matter of the seeing eye . . . The dweller in this world can become aware of an existence on a totally different plane. To go from earth to faery is like passing from this time to eternity; it is not a journey in space, but a change of mental outlook.

She finds modern instances, in relation to Christian mythology, in the short stories of Monsignor R. H. Benson, "The Light Invisible" and "A Mirror of Shallott", and remarks: "The ancient Celt would undoubtedly find those tales much more possible and understandable than the average modern Christian — they deal with a set of phenomena with which he was quite familiar." She was to include one of R. H. Benson's stories in the anthology she edited for Gollancz.

She is entranced by the under-water adventures of Celtic folk-lore:

The fairy messenger chooses, as a rule, some spot at which to manifest her or himself . . . Very often it is enough to walk by the sea, or along the banks of a river. Thus Lanval meets with the fairies, walking by the river . . . In Denmark, Little Claus tells Great Claus of the maiden who met him at the bottom of the river . . . Both Condla and Cuchulain . . . pass over the sea to fairy-land, the one in a boat of glass, the other in a boat of bronze. In . . . the Imnam Bran, we have a description of the Under-sea country . . . And in the lovely "Voyage of Maelduin" we have many descriptions of these exquisite under-sea islands. In one case the water seems thin and mist-like above the tree-tops, and the voyagers are afraid lest they should sink through the unsubstantial sea and remain stranded in the faery country.

From this early lecture we gain some idea of the kind of student Dorothy Sayers was at Somerville: a mixture of the intellectual and the romantic. Her introduction to her complete translation of *Tristan*, which was published in 1929, shows the same combination of scholarly pleasure in research and imaginative response to a powerful love-story. She admires Professor Bédier – "that distinguished mediaevalist, who by rare good fortune combines profound scholarship with fine poetic insight", and finds his work on the manuscripts intensely interesting. She even gave Lord Peter Wimsey, somewhat improbably, a taste for collating the manuscripts of *Tristan* (in *Unnatural Death*). He might, more plausibly, have shared with her a response to the passionate love-story, on which she comments so revealingly:

The fatal love of Tristan and Iseult is an absorbing passion, before which every other consideration must give way; but the exasperating behaviour of the lovers conforms to the ordinary, human developments of that exasperating passion . . . There is a kind of desperate beauty in this mutual passion, faithful through years of sin and unfaith on both sides, and careless of lies and shifts and incredible dishonour.

Lewis Thorpe, the Arthurian scholar, commented: "The uncontrolled violence and the unremitting strength of the passion of Tristan and Iseult appealed to something strong and primitive that lay beneath Dorothy Sayers' scholarly intellect." She also admired the passages in which the poet, "a thoughtful and competent psychologist", analyses the feelings of Tristan and Iseult for each other:

Unlike many poets of his day, he is not really interested in fights with giants, magical marvels and adventures by sea and land; he scrambles hurriedly over these incidents, to spread himself with loving care over long dialogues and monologues containing elaborate analysis of feelings, motives and problems of morality.

Tristan in Brittany, published by Ernest Benn in July 1929, bore beneath the title the following paragraph:

Being the fragments of The
Romance of Tristan, written
in the XII century, by Thomas
the Anglo-Norman. Drawn
out of the French into the
English by Dorothy Leigh
Sayers, M.A., sometime scholar
of Somerville College, Oxford.

By then she was well established as an author of detective fiction, but she had not forgotten, nor did she wish her public to forget, her status as a scholar at Oxford.

At the same time, she allowed her imaginative and romantic tendencies plenty of scope. She indulged a life-long love of fairy-stories and over the years she gradually acquired a collection of the Fairy Book Series edited by Andrew Lang. In 1956, she was lacking two out of the twelve and said how much she wished she could obtain them. In June of that year, I was lucky enough to find *The Olive Fairy Book* in Deighton and Bell's bookshop in Cambridge and sent it to her as a birthday present. This spurred her Witham bookseller into action and he obtained *The Grey Fairy Book* for her, to her great delight. "I mark this day with a white stone", she wrote. Two years previously, in 1954, she had been reading Boiardo's *Orlando Innamorato*, in Italian, and was enthralled by his simple enjoyment of marvels, particularly the under-water realm of Fata Morgana and the enchanted garden of Orgagna, which she found "a riot of Arabian Nights fantasy". She adapted the Orgagna episode into a story for children; it was to have been illustrated by Fritz Wegner, but remained unpublished. In fact, she thought that the whole story of *Orlando Innamorato* would make "a wonderful book for children, with lots and lots of lovely illustrations". She was perhaps thinking of the illustrations by H. J. Ford and Lancelot Speed which had helped to make reading the Andrew Lang volumes such a pleasure to her in childhood. It is noteworthy that the collective title of her plays on the life of Christ, *The Man Born to be King*, is the title of a fairy-tale, chosen at the time when the B.B.C. had commissioned the plays for Children's Hour and inspired, perhaps, by the use of it by William Morris as a title for one of his poetic legends.

"If anyone will tell me a story I will listen," she said once to me. And indeed her response to story-telling was one of her most enduring and creative characteristics. Victor Gollancz chose the right person when he suggested that she should compile an anthology of short stories of detection, mystery and horror. Her wide reading in detective fiction of all kinds (about which Eric Whelpton had teased her) enabled her to make her selection without much difficulty. But she was also well-read in tales of the macabre and other-worldly experiences, and the tales of mystery and horror make up half of the anthology. Her comments on this section in the Introduction are brief but they show that even in 1928, when she had passed the mid-point of life, she still confessed, unashamedly, to experiencing a frisson in reading horror stories:

> In nothing is individual fancy so varied and capricious as in its perception of the horrible. To one person, E. L. White's *Lukundoo* is terrible beyond all imagination; to another, this story seems merely grotesque, and it is the imbecile endearments of the thing whose love "came to Professor Guildea" in Robert Hitchens's story which arouse in him that delicious nausea we look for in a horror yarn. One cannot argue about these things. I remember reading somewhere about an old sundial, around whose face was written: IT IS LATER THAN YOU THINK. If that motto does not give you a "cauld grue", then nothing that I or any other person can say will convince you of its soul-shaking ghastliness.

The section of the Introduction which deals with detective fiction is recognised as a masterpiece by connoisseurs in this *genre*. The first edition of the anthology was published in September 1928. Two years later, in June 1930, it was re-issued in a cheaper edition, at five shillings. This was reviewed in the *Evening News* of 6 June by Frank Swinnerton, who called the Introduction "the best essay upon the literature of fictitious crime and its unravelling that I have ever read". Strange to say, though he was a reviewer of detective fiction, he had not at that time read any of the Sayers novels: " . . . but if they are as good as her introduction here they must be very good indeed". He remedied his omission immediately: in July, when *The Documents in the Case* was chosen as the Book Guild detective story, he enthusiastically approved, and in his book, *The Georgian Literary Scene*, he expressed the view that her novels represented "the farthest point yet reached in the development of detective stories towards complete sophistication".

Dorothy's experience of teaching, uncongenial though she found it, had led her to experiment with unexpected comparisons and analogies. A manuscript exists which reveals something of her skill in this respect. It is an outline and the beginning of a course entitled "Lectures on Poetic Form", intended, judging from the simplicity of the style, for a young audience, possibly a school literary society or a sixth form. It may have been planned for pupils at l'Ecole des Roches, since the notebook containing the manuscript is inscribed with that address. On the other hand, the notebook may have been used later in England, perhaps in 1921, when she was teaching at Clapham High School, or later in Acton.

Six lectures were planned, in which accent, rhyme, assonance, alliteration and quantity were to be illustrated, from the origins of English poetic form to the present day. An intriguingly entitled section was to have been "The Suggestive Value of Verse-Forms and Formulae", which seems to anticipate the importance she later attached to the original form of poetry which she translated. In the opening fragment of the first lecture, it is seen that she identified pattern as the very essence of poetic form:

I think the best definition [of verse] is words put into a pattern. We know that all art must have form of some kind – merely mixing up all the paints in the paint-box together will not give us a picture – but pattern is something more. To have a pattern we must have some kind of repetition. It may be exact repetition as in wall-paper, or only the merest suggestion of repetition. For instance, in the great frieze of sculptures that runs round the Parthenon, the panels all differ very much in subject and treatment – there is a general similarity and they are all the same size and contain the same kind of figures, so that even they form a kind of pattern. Or take a well-known form in music – the waltz: e.g. Subject A, Subject B, each repeated, then a trio C and a return to A, B. This is a pattern. Or a fugue is a kind of pattern, in which the same subject occurs over and over with varying treatment and sung at different pitches. So with verse. The pattern may be very formal or so free as hardly to be a pattern at all, but pattern there must be of some sort, or it would not be verse at all.

She adopted Shelley's division of literary art into "the literature of knowledge" and "the literature of power". When she describes the latter she communicates her own response to it, revealing at the same time the resources on which she will herself draw as a creative writer and critic:

> The literature of power ... does not tell us anything we didn't know before but it works upon the great emotional forces which are in us already, and by suggestion and illusion and by the splendour of noble sound it stirs us up to respond to its stimulus, so that we really feel greater, wiser, more enthusiastic and altogether bigger people, just in the same way that great music does.

There can be little doubt that when she wrote that last phrase she was thinking of the effect on her of Bach's B Minor Mass. It is interesting that over forty years later C. S. Lewis was to say almost exactly the same thing about the effect on the reader of great literature. In *An Experiment in Criticism*, published in 1961, he wrote:

> Those of us who have been true readers all our life seldom realise the enormous debt we owe to authors ... In reading great literature I become a thousand men and yet remain myself ... Here, as in worship, in love, in moral action, and in knowing, I transcend myself: and am never more myself than when I do.

The intellectual features which this early manuscript of Dorothy's reveals are also found – reinforced – in the Introduction to the anthology: firmness of outline, clear distinctions and definitions, and the search for the connecting thread which binds disparate data into a coherent unity. Detective fiction was a comparatively new field when she undertook to become its cartographer. She had only one predecessor: E. M. Wrong, whose *Preface to Tales of Crime and Detection* was published in 1924. She refers handsomely to this as "a brilliant little study". Her own is longer, more comprehensive, and, for its time, definitive.

Who but Dorothy Sayers would have thought of beginning a selection of detective fiction with four stories from antiquity – two from the Apocrypha, one from the *Aeneid* and one from Herodotus? She even finds a germ of the detective story in Aesop's Fables:

"Why do you not come to pay your respects to me?" says Aesop's lion to the fox. "I beg your Majesty's pardon," says the fox, "but I have noticed the track of the animals that have already come to you; and while I see many hoof-marks going in, I see none coming out. Till the animals that have entered your cave come out again, I prefer to remain in the open air." Sherlock Holmes could not have reasoned more lucidly from the premises.

In the story of Bel and the Dragon, the first of the examples from the Apocrypha, she recognises an instance of the science of deduction from material clues "in the popular Scotland Yard manner", though reduced to its simplest expression, with its motif of ashes spread on the floor, reproduced, she notes, in the story of Tristan, where King Mark spreads flour between Tristan's bed and that of Iseult. (Tristan defeats the plot by leaping from one bed to the other.) In the story of Susanna and the Elders we have an example of the analysis of testimony and the confrontation of witnesses, "foreshadowing the Gallic method of eliciting the truth". Cacus the robber, in the story from the *Aeneid*, was apparently the first criminal to use the device of forged footprints, "though it is a long development from his primitive methods to the horses shod with cow-shoes in Conan Doyle's *Adventures of the Priory School*". The story of Rhampsinitus, taken from Herodotus, she identifies as an instance of the psychological method of detection and of the interplay of plot and counterplot.

Why, she asks, did the modern detective story take so long to develop? E. M. Wrong suggested that "a faulty law of evidence was to blame, for detectives cannot flourish until the public has an idea of what constitutes proof, and while a common criminal procedure is arrest, torture, confession and death". Dorothy Sayers points out that though detective fiction began with Edgar Allen Poe, crime stories had flourished ever since the story of Jacob and Esau, the tendency in early crime literature being to admire the cleverness of the criminal, as in the tales of Reynard the Fox and the ballads of Robin Hood. The detective-story proper could not develop until public sympathy had veered round to the side of law and order. Much depended, too, on the establishment of effective police organisation. By then, the defender of the weak was no longer the knight errant but the detective – "the latest of the popular heroes, the true successor of Roland and Lancelot".

In saying this she again displays the romantic element in her personality. Fairy-stories sometimes came true. The ordinary could be transfigured. A writer of detective fiction could win the love of a duke's son. A chief inspector could marry a duke's daughter. But there was also a strong rational bent to her mind which delighted in the intellectual side of detective fiction, as it delighted in puzzles of all kinds – cryptograms, codes, and especially crossword puzzles, a new craze in the 1920s to which she at once became addicted. Her first short story, "The Fascinating Story of Uncle Meleager's Will", turns on the solving of a crossword puzzle, which she herself invents.

In the Introduction to the anthology, her critical faculty, trained in the School of *Litterae Humaniores* at Oxford University, is brought to bear upon somewhat slender material, but to substantial effect. By a feat of creative criticism, the subject is set in order and transformed. It acquires organic life, obeying principles of growth and derivation. It happens that for the convenience of the reader the stories in the anthology are arranged under two headings: 1) Detection and Mystery, 2) Mystery and Horror. But these categories, it is shown, are not distinct: they have a common origin in the fiction of Edgar Allan Poe. He it was who between 1840 and 1845, in *The Murders in the Rue Morgue* and in *Thou Art the Man*, fused the story of horror with the story of detection, thereby creating, she affirms, the story of mystery. Since Poe's time, all three branches have flourished, in varying blends and combinations.

Poe also anticipated the general principles of what has come to be called detective fiction. In Dupin he created the eccentric and brilliant private detective, whose achievements are recorded by an admiring friend. From this pair descend Sherlock Holmes and Watson, Martin Hewitt and Brett, Hanaud and Mr Ricardo, Poirot and Hastings, Philo Vance and Van Dine. It is not surprising, Sayers remarks, that the formula has been used so often since it is so convenient for the writer. (It is not, however, a formula she used herself.)

Eccentricity in detectives became traditional, especially after Sherlock Holmes, to be followed by quirks or lovable traits of personality, and ultimately by a determined ordinariness. Her own detective ("if I may refer to him without immodesty") collects incunabula and "has a pretty taste in wines and haberdashery". His advantages of birth and position set him apart from other detectives, but his mannerisms may be said to derive from the tradition of eccentricity.

After a cursory and somewhat dismissive survey of women fictional detectives ("the really brilliant woman detective has yet to be created"), she introduces what would seem to be a quite marginal series of stories and gives them unexpected relevance. This is another example of her desire to reveal hidden poetry in the seemingly ordinary. The Sexton Blake cycle, "crossed with the Buffalo Bill adventure story", is, she maintains, in the Holmes tradition. Blake and his boy assistant Tinker even have an address in Baker Street. So far so good, but she goes further:

> The really interesting point about them is that they present the nearest modern approach to a national folk-lore, conceived as the centre for a cycle of loosely connected romances in the Arthurian manner. Their significance in popular literature and education would richly repay scientific investigation.

This is surely an echo of the "higher criticism" of the series in which she and Muriel Jaeger indulged in 1920, and a provocative challenge to the serious-minded.

Another unexpected ingredient which she brings to light from popular literature are the novels of Fenimore Cooper, who

> revealed to the delighted youth of two hemispheres the Red Indian's patient skill in tracking his quarry by footprints, in interrogating a broken twig, a mossy trunk, a fallen leaf . . . In the 'sixties the generation who had read Fenimore Cooper in boyhood turned, as novelists and readers, to tracing the spoor of the criminal upon their own native heath.

Both these instances are characteristic of her perception of similarity where none has been seen before. The effect is startling and shows both terms of the comparison in a new light.

On the rational side, it is evident that she welcomes the development of the *genre* along logical and intellectual lines. She is also strict in the matter of the "fair play rule", namely, that the reader should be shown the same clues as the detective. Sherlock Holmes, she regrets to say, does not always play fair – he "pounces upon a minute object" and draws a brilliant deduction from it. The rigour of the game requires that the reader should be told what the object is and given a chance to make the same brilliant deduction.

It may have been Victor Gollancz who suggested that she should write a biography of Wilkie Collins. Certainly, she was collecting material for it in 1921. The bookseller Myles Radford wrote to her on 15 June of that year: "When are you going to get your 'Life' finished? I really think you ought to have it out shortly, and I feel sure you have as much information about Wilkie as is likely to come to light, and a great deal more than most 'Memoirs' contain." She put off the actual writing of the biography until 1931 and never, in the end, finished it, though she always hoped to. E. R. Gregory, who edited the incomplete work, considers that her study of Collins made her a better novelist and a better critic than she might otherwise have become. This is probably true. Attitudes engendered by reading Collins stayed with her. His passion for factual accuracy, for instance, and his accumulation of precise, prosaic detail, by which a reader is brought to believe a tale of marvels, became part of her own formula. Like herself, Collins admired good story-telling and the ability to create characters of believable and enduring personality.

As may be seen from his memorial of his father, Wilkie Collins combined liveliness with scholarship. Dorothy L. Sayers also became a skilled practitioner of the art of appealing to the imagination as well as to the intellect. In later years, she sometimes spoke of herself as "a scholar spoiled", which suggests that she had a lingering nostalgia for the academic life, as Harriet Vane is shown to have, in *Gaudy Night*. But her scholarly training was not wasted. It gave solidity and depth to her critical writings as well as to her novels. To both she brought a creative exuberance of mind.

CHAPTER 14

Family Ties

"It's funny, but I don't think 'family ties' have ever meant anything at all to me. I only like people as individuals, apart from who they are." Thus Dorothy to Ivy in 1928.

She was never sentimental, which to her meant trying to deceive herself into believing that she felt what other people thought she should feel. She resisted this all her life, not only in personal relationships but also as regards her religious belief. She had noticed that people who assumed the feelings expected of them were the ones who were deemed sincere. This was an affront to her innate honesty and her respect for integrity, both of mind and heart.

She especially refused to be sentimental about her motherhood. Ivy sent her some photos of John Anthony at the age of four. She wrote: "[He] looks quite a credit to us! I must really try to feel thrilled about him — but I don't believe I ever should about any child under whatever circumstances." Then, saying that family ties meant little to her, she went on:

Indeed, I actively dislike nearly all my Sayers relations, or at most tepidly tolerate them. I like the Leighs — and of course, my dear, I'm damned fond of you — because you are you — not because you happen to be a cousin. Same with J.A. He seems to be turning out a good sort of kid, and I'm disposed to like him — but for no other reason.

But she was anything but cold and remote. She could love passionately. She had many friends, for whom she openly expressed affection. Her parents cherished her and though she disliked what she called "fuss", she responded warmly to their love.

There was also Aunt Mabel, who had been one of the household ever since Dorothy's childhood. As she seldom wrote letters we have no direct evidence as to her personality. Evelyn Compline (later Mrs Bedford), who took care of her in old age, said she was "a dear little person". She was five feet, three inches tall, pretty and possessed of great charm. She took to Mac immediately and became very fond of him: "an extraordinary fancy", Dorothy called it, writing to Ivy:

> just because he has always been careful to pay considerable attention to her – [she] positively clings to him at parting! It's a very good thing, because if she disliked him – and she does dislike most people's husbands, you know – she could make things very disagreeable for Mother. However, she now won't hear a word against him from anybody, and is always telling Aunt Maud and people like that what a wonderful person he is. It really is rather amusing.

We know a little more about Aunt Gertrude Sayers, for Dorothy unashamedly imitated her epistolary style, underlinings and exclamation marks included (she was a great employer of these herself), in the letters of Miss Climpson, who first appears as Lord Peter's assistant in *Unnatural Death*. Sending her parents a copy of this, her third novel, she says she hopes Aunt Gertrude won't notice. Although the portrait of Miss Climpson is drawn with humour and affection, Dorothy did not really care much for Aunt Gertrude. She found her inquisitive and interfering. In May 1927 she called on Dorothy and Mac at 24 Great James Street, and took it upon herself to discuss the future of Mr and Mrs Sayers. Dorothy wrote to Ivy:

> As usual, she was very keen on running other people's business for them, and had retired Dad and Mother on a pension and set them up in a private hotel or boarding-house in a seaside-resort before I could say "knife". Mother would fall out with the other inhabitants and Dad would be bored to death.

And she drew an amusing sketch of the inhabitants of the boarding-house, queueing up for lunch. She often illustrated her letters in such ways.

Though her aunts sometimes irritated her, she had compassion for them. In a revealing letter to Maurice Reckitt dated 19 November 1941 she wrote:

> I remember my father's sisters, brought up without education or

training, thrown at my grandfather's death into a world that had no use for them. One, by my father's charity, was trained as a nurse; one, by wangling, was received into the only sisterhood that would take her at her age – an ill-run community, but her only refuge; the third, the most attractive [Aunt Gertrude?], lived peripatetically as a "companion" to various old cats, saving half-pence and cadging trifles, aimlessly doing what when done was of little value to God or man. From all such frustrate unhappiness, God keep us!

It was with the fate of such women in mind that Dorothy L. Sayers the novelist created employment for Miss Climpson and her "cat-tery" in *Unnatural Death*.

Dorothy had written regularly to her parents from school and from Oxford. She continued this habit as a married woman, even though she was weighed down by work for Benson's and writing novels and short stories in her spare time. She kept her parents up to date with her and Mac's life together, their achievements and hopes for the future. She was independent financially and glad to be so, but she was still, to some extent, emotionally dependent on their affection, interest and approval.

Her letters were usually addressed to both her parents but it was more often her mother who replied. Her father was busy with his parish duties, but he often sent a present of money, not only at Christmas or for birthdays, and one or two of his letters have survived, written in a small, neat script (like Lord Peter's). He addresses her as "Dearest" and signs himself as "Dad". This is what she called him and, sometimes, "Tootles". The origin of this strange nickname is not known. One might guess that he had taken up a wind instrument in his later years, or perhaps it referred to his habit of tooting the horn of his car frequently, like Mr Venables in *The Nine Tailors*. However that may have been, though Dorothy was closer to her mother, she nearly always addressed her by the formal name of "Mother", or sometimes "Mater". Her collective form of address for them was "Dearest People", which included Aunt Mabel.

In January 1926 Dorothy reported that she had written "a thrilling motor-cycling tale for [Lord Peter] . . . but probably the magazines won't like it, as it has a cut-off head in it. It's a pity my brightest fancies are illuminated by a ghastly red light." This is the story entitled "The Fantastic Horror of the Cat in the Bag". It was evidently turned down by *Pearson's*, which had previously accepted several of her short stories, for it first appeared in the collected volume, *Lord Peter Views the Body*, which was brought out by Gollancz in November 1928. It opens with a description of two motor-cyclists racing north from London:

> The Great North Road wound away like a flat steel-grey ribbon. Up it, with the sun and wind behind them, two black specks moved swiftly. To the yokel in charge of the hay-wagon they were only two of "they dratted motor-cyclists", as they barked and zoomed past him in rapid succession. A little farther on, a family man, driving delicately with a two-seater side-car, grinned as the sharp rattle of the o.h.v. [over-head valve] Norton was succeeded by the feline shriek of an angry Scott Flying-Squirrel. He, too, in bachelor days, had taken a side in that perennial feud . . .

Dorothy knew the exhilaration of motor-cycling at speed when she rode along the same road (now the A1) to visit her parents. She knew the danger of "that abominable and unexpected S-bend across the bridge above Hatfield" and the thrill of "cornering melodramatically, with left and right foot-rests alternately skimming the tarmac". She much preferred this route to the one south of London, to Southend, Brighton and Margate, where she had noticed with distaste drivers

> grinding their way . . . in the stench of each other's exhausts, one hand on the horn and one foot on the brake, their eyes starting from their orbits in the nerve-wracking search for cops, blind turnings and cross-road suicides . . . And all the time the Great North Road winds away like a long, flat, steel-grey ribbon – a surface like a race-track, without traps, without hedges, without side-roads, and without traffic.

Alas for the "without traffic"! That was in 1926.

To make this journey and also the one to Oxford, to visit John Anthony (for which purpose she bought her first motor-cycle, having learned from Bill how to handle one), Dorothy dressed in motor-coat, leggings and boots. She wore gauntlets and goggles and her cropped hair was hidden beneath a leather helmet. Her appearance was startlingly unfeminine. What her parents thought of it we can only guess but someone who saw her arrive attired in such fashion at his father's house outside Oxford described her in very unflattering terms. There is a tough masculinity about her at this time. She must have been quite robust to handle the heavy motor-cycle of the period and she obviously enjoyed the aggressive noise of the engine and the defiant danger of speed. Writing to Ivy in August 1925, she said: "I rode down to Christchurch, and was well received. I hadn't announced myself, and arrived with great éclat after a fine four-and-a-quarter hours' run from town (99 miles)." She considered motor-cars "middle-aged" in comparison with motor-cycles. Not for her the elegant motoring-bonnet and fur wraps of the female passenger of the period who graced the open motor-cars of their begoggled and gauntleted male escorts.

In February (1926) she sends her parents an advance copy of *Clouds of Witness*, saying she doesn't care much for it and fancies the public will care still less. A year previously she had written to Cournos saying that "the cursed book – associated with every sort of humiliation and misery – is actually finished" and that she was about to take it to her agent, Andrew Dakers. "Nobody will like the book", she remarked then too, "though there are good things in it." She had asked him if he thought Americans would be interested in the trial of a Peer in the House of Lords: "Nobody has ever put such a trial into a novel before that I know of (except perhaps an impeachment in a costume novel – I think it's unique in a detective story). It may appeal to their itch for British antiques." She habitually expressed dissatisfaction with her novels when she had just finished them, an example of the post-natal depression which authors are said to experience.

In June she reports that she and Mac have bought the Ner-a-Car already mentioned, which was possessed of "modest climbing powers". They are off on holiday to stay in a country inn. If the weather is fine they will stray about the countryside; if wet, they will remain indoors and write stories, "in the hope of making the holidays pay for themselves". She sends a copy of *Pearson's* (the June volume), in which another of her short stories has been published. This is "The Learned Adventure of the Dragon's Head" which is, she says, "rather dull, but *Pearson's* doesn't like anything really grisly. The old book is a real one. I picked it up for five shillings myself, exactly as described." Here is yet another example of Dorothy's habit of sprinkling her fiction with portions of her everyday life.

In May 1927 she reports that she has been working hard to finish her new novel, *Unnatural Death*. (It was published on 16 September of that year.) The following month she and Mac are planning to go on holiday in Maldon, Essex. They put up at the Ship Hotel, Market Hill. It was their first experience of Essex and they are surprised to find what a pretty county it is: " . . . not nearly so flat as one imagines and beautifully wooded. It has many of the charms of the

Fens (fine skies, good air, etc.) without their drawbacks." She relates from Maldon that "the infernal book" is finished. "It is a bad book and I am not at all satisfied with it. Possibly Gollancz will turn it down altogether. I shouldn't blame him if he did. It was a good idea, but it went wrong somewhere in the working." Her mother replies soothingly that she has read the book and enjoyed it.

It is to her mother, also, that she confides feelings about her appearance. She is dismayed about her "rapidly fattening frame. Too much good living is doing me in completely"; and she has an unmistakable double chin. She is pleased with her decision to cut her hair short (this was one of the watershed decisions for women at that period: to bob or not to bob). She opted for the then fashionable Eton crop, which displayed, she told her mother, her "really fine points, viz. a beautifully shaped head and neat ears". And she is delighted with "a very clever flashlight photograph" which Mac has taken of her, "for press purposes, which shows me as a very handsome woman for the first time in my life – and be damned to it!" From such comments it is plain that for all her satisfaction in striding about in boots and leggings and rejoicing in the use of her muscles she still had a feminine interest in her appearance, though not the resolution to diet.

Above all, she liked creating an effect, the more startling the better. At Somerville she had worn what were considered outrageous ear-rings, designed as miniature cages, each containing a brightly-coloured parrot. Her parents sent her clothes and jewellery and encouraged her to make the most of herself. At Benson's, in the time of her silver wig, she also wore large ear-rings and sported a long cigarette holder. A portrait and a sketch of her by John (later Sir John) Gilroy, with whom she worked on the famous Guinness advertisements, show her as a striking personality, flamboyantly dressed, with a low-cut bodice, displaying the long, graceful neck which had earned her the nickname "Swanny" at school.

In August 1927 her father wrote to tell her of Chesterton's reference to Wilkie Collins in his life of Dickens: "If you are persevering with Wilkie Collins, it has occurred to me that it would be a good idea to get it included in the 'English Men of Letters' series, for so it would be a part of a set of books for which there would always be a sale and demand." A year later he sent her a postcard, on which he quoted from W. H. Hudson's *The Land's End*, which contains yet another reference to Collins. It is evident that she talked over her plans with her father and that, characteristically, he hoped she would proceed with the scholarly project of the biography.

In November 1927 Dorothy attended the wedding of her cousin Gerald to Molly Hutchinson. She wrote a lively description of it in a letter to her father, beginning "Dearest Dad", and ending "Ever yours devotedly". She asserted (perhaps protesting too much) that she did not care for formal weddings, especially deploring the crowd at the reception and the paucity of food and drink. The ceremony had been unusual in that the bride's mother tripped and fell full length on the floor of the chancel. Dorothy noted that the word "obey" was used, but that the words had elsewhere been bowdlerised, "substituting for 'those who have not the gift of continency' an unharmonious and ill-constructed phrase about the regulation of the natural instincts. I don't know why the efforts of modern liturgists should sound so much like a journalese report of a scientific lecture." (She would undoubtedly be a member, probably a Vice-President, of the Prayer Book Society if she were alive today.)

She thanks her father for his letter and for his cheque, which she tells him will pay for a brief holiday in Cornwall, where they are going for Mac's sake. He gets recurrent bad coughs and colds and needs sun and warmth: "We are both working so strenuously that we haven't time to go anywhere or see anybody. I'm depressed about my new book – but then I always am!" This was *The Unpleasantness at the Bellona Club*, which was published in July 1928.

Dorothy and Mac spent Christmas 1927 at Christchurch. They were there again at Easter. In writing to thank her mother for "a splendid holiday" she remarked that she had found them all looking wonderfully well, in spite of "the damnable winter". (Unhappily, as regards her father this was an illusion.) They had stopped at Bluntisham on the way home and called in on old friends in the area. Although she often asserted that she hated going back to the past, she describes this visit with pleasure and affection:

We saw the great Turner on the way back, also poor dear old Blankets who is getting very old, poor old thing, but looks very healthy and happy – rather like an aged white pet rabbit. He was charmed to see us and recognised me immediately. I then looked in at Bryant's – old B. just the same, and his shop looking wonderfully nice and quite up-to-date, with nice, pretty materials and frocks, etc., and all his girls in a charming dull-blue uniform. He says the big stores have not affected him much, as he builds his success on studying his customers' personal requirements, which *they* can't do. I congratulated him on this. Miss Ely and Miss James then appeared – absolutely unchanged from 30 years ago, or so it seemed to me! – standing side by side and giggling like schoolgirls at being specially asked for and remembered. So we exchanged some little pleasantries about the new fashions, and then old Bryant pranced down to the door with me, most attentive, and saying he had read *Unnatural Death*. Everybody particularly wanted to be remembered to you and Aunt Mabel.

In September of that year, 1928, her anthology was published, a major achievement which had involved prolonged and strenuous work. An advance copy was proudly despatched to Christchurch. It was the last of her works her father was to see: on the twentieth of that month he died. For two days he had felt unwell but had nevertheless gone about his parish duties. A doctor was called the next morning and diagnosed pneumonia. Soon afterwards, Mrs Sayers entered the bedroom and found her husband dead.

There was no telephone in the rectory. Someone had to hurry to the village post office to get a message through to Dorothy at Benson's. She came at once, by train, alone, and joined the sorrowing household.

It was her first experience of the death of someone close to her. It had come suddenly, without warning; grief was thus accentuated by shock. Her relationship with her father had been loving and secure. He was a figure of authority, as a priest as well as a father, but an authority of "mild stateliness", the phrase she said best described him. Her childhood memories of him were sunny. He had taught her the violin and practised with her. He had started her on Latin. He had allowed her, conspiratorially, to dress up in his masonic regalia. He had joined in the game of musketeers, playing the part of Louis XIII and putting on a false beard to please her. Still earlier memories recalled him reading to her when she was a four-year-old; and herself, as a toddler, running beneath the arch of his long legs.

She was thirty-five years old when he died. He was seventy-four. For many years he had supported her financially, waiting patiently for her to find her way as a writer. He and her mother had welcomed Mac, the unconventional marriage partner she had sprung on them, and both had been lavish in presents for the London flat. She must have felt, as she stood by his death-bed, that she had been right not to distress him with the knowledge that he had a grandson born out of wedlock. At some cost to herself, she had spared him that.

She felt his loss keenly. "I'm so awfully glad," she wrote later to her mother, "that Dad lived to see me beginning to make good. He did so much for me that I'm thankful to know that he could feel it

Dorothy's father in old age
(Mrs Evelyn Bedford)

wasn't all chucked away on me!" He had lived long enough to read her first four novels and at least to see and handle the Gollancz anthology, with its masterly Introduction, in which he must have taken pride. He had also seen five of her short stories published month by month in *Pearson's*. No doubt she had sent him the excerpts from her translation of *Tristan* which were published in *Modern Languages* in 1920 and of course he had received copies of *Op. I* and of *Catholic Tales and Christian Songs*. Concerning the latter, she had written to assure him that though some people might find them blasphemous they were in fact entirely reverent in intention. Six years after his death, his unworldly and self-effacing personality was to be tenderly evoked in *The Nine Tailors* in the lovable character of the Reverend Theodore Venables, rector of Fenchurch St Paul.

She braced herself to help her mother with the funeral arrangements. Mac did not come, but a number of the Sayers family were present. Dorothy felt bitterly hostile towards them. Writing to Ivy she said: "Lord! How I hated all those Sayerses who turned up for the funeral — noisy, selfish, tiresome, stupid — all spongers and soakers — poor old Dad was the only decent one of the bunch."

Henry Sayers was buried in the churchyard where he had so often presided at the funerals of his parishioners. Strange to say, Dorothy made no arrangements for the grave to be marked. When her mother died she was buried in the same grave, and still no stone was placed. Her inaction was not due to indifference but to indecision. She always intended one day to arrange for a horizontal stone to mark the grave, but time went by and she omitted to attend to the matter. Some years later, independently, it would seem, the parishioners placed a memorial plaque of polished slate on the interior west wall of the church. The inscription reads as follows:

IN GRATEFUL MEMORY OF THE SERVICE OF
HENRY SAYERS, PRIEST:
FROM 1917-1928 RECTOR OF THIS PARISH
AND OF HELEN MARY HIS WIFE
THIS TABLET
IS PLACED BY HIS PARISHIONERS

After the funeral, Dorothy had to return to her job. Mac, whose absence from the funeral may have been due to ill health, went to Christchurch to help and advise Dorothy's mother about furniture and other possessions, for she would soon have to leave the rectory. He and Dorothy then took a brief holiday in order to recuperate. They chose Maldon again and, while there, they decided to look out for a house in Essex which might suit Mrs Sayers and Aunt Mabel. By 10 October Mac had found one and had entered into negotiations. This was the house known as "Sunnyside", later 24 Newland Street, in Witham.

Dorothy wrote her mother an excited and enthusiastic letter: "We think we have made an uncommonly good bargain. Mac found the house and did the bargaining . . . Mac and I are quite in love with it, and have decided to retire to it when we have made our fortunes." Earlier that year her mother's brother, Percy Leigh, who had settled in Australia, had died and left Dorothy a legacy of five hundred pounds. On the advice of a solicitor she decided to buy the house herself, using the legacy and a loan of five hundred pounds from her mother, who would then live in the house as Dorothy's tenant, but rent free. In this manner, death duties would be avoided when her mother died. A favourable description of the house and garden is followed, objectively, by a list of drawbacks. The first of these is that the house is lit only by gas and oil lamps (though electric light is expected to be installed in Witham before long). Some of the bedrooms are dark because the ceilings are low and the windows narrow. The gutters get blocked with leaves. The house is on the main road, but as it is solidly built it does not vibrate to the traffic and there are good old-fashioned wooden shutters at the windows. There is plenty of room and Aunt Mabel need not get rid of any of her possessions: "We have an idea you are going to like Witham." Mac adds a note, beginning "Darling Mother", and supporting all that Dorothy has said.

In fact, it was Mac who played a leading role in the removal. In November he was in Witham, seeing to everything, buying linoleum and putting up shelves. He telephoned Dorothy at her office to suggest that her mother should come to stay with them in London for a few days – Aunt Mabel being looked after temporarily in Christchurch. He will then drive Mrs Sayers down to Witham and install her there. Mrs Sayers agrees and Mac, immensely pleased, sets about

The house at Witham *(Essex County Council)*

"planning a particular kind of fish-pie" for her arrival. She is to catch the 9.59 train from Stonea, the railway station nearest to Christchurch, change at Ely and take a train from there to Liverpool Street, where Mac will meet her and bring her to the flat in a taxi. Mrs Sayers duly complied and all these thoughtful arrangements were carried through.

It appears that members of the Sayers family, in particular Aunt Gertrude, had been advising against all such plans and Dorothy wrote indignantly: "As you say, the Sayerses never have done a single thing for you, and they have no right to poke their noses into our affairs at all. You're *our* Mater and we'll do all the necessary fussing."

Mrs Sayers had become depressed in Christchurch without her husband. ("He bored her to death for forty years", Dorothy wrote to Ivy, "and she always grumbled that he was no companion for her – and now she misses him dreadfully.") Towards the end of November she went down to Witham with Mac to see the house and to choose wall-papers. The visit was not wholly a success. Dorothy wrote to Ivy: "She couldn't seem to see anything but gloom and difficulties, and that depressed poor old Mac (who is suffering badly from nerves) till he almost had a breakdown."

The removal itself, she said, was a nightmare.

Mac is helping them to move in now, and Mother is being dreadful – knocking herself up, and worrying Mac into a nervous breakdown. I can't get there till Saturday – or I could manage her. Between my Mother and my husband with their nerves and worriment, things are too maddening.

In December the elderly sisters, aged seventy-three and eighty-one, were settled. Dorothy went down to Witham on Christmas Eve, "just about in time to prevent Mac from going clean off his head with exasperation!" They spent their holiday hanging up pictures and Dorothy began to love the house. "It really is a very pretty old place."

Aunt Mabel took the move quite well. "She gets younger every day – and consented while we were there to drink a glass of port every night – a thing she always refused when Dad offered it."

Letters to her mother thereafter contain frequent mentions of Mac's ill health. He has a tiresome cough which he gets every winter: " . . . it's the remains of the war gas, I'm afraid"; and he suffers from stomach upsets. He had given up his job with the *News of the World* and was now free-lancing. There is mention of a cookery book for Crosse and Blackwell and of cookery articles for the *Evening News*. The slump in his income depressed him and he became difficult to live with. It did him some good to take holidays in Scotland, in Gatehouse of Fleet in Kirkcudbrightshire, where he had been before he met Dorothy and still had many friends. The climate there is mild and the scenery such as to attract a community of painters, as well as fishermen. Dorothy accompanied Mac on several holidays there and eventually used the surroundings as the setting for *The Five Red Herrings*. In June 1929 she reports that Mac has won eight pounds on a race and bought a splendid new fishing rod. They are off on holiday that month to stay at the Anwoth Hotel, kept by Joe Dignam, that "kindliest of landlords" to whom *The Five Red Herrings* would be dedicated. Dorothy returned to work at Benson's half way through July, but Mac stayed on for another week. In a letter dated 17 July 1929, she tells her mother that she and Mac have rented a small studio in Kirkcudbright, where they plan to stay the following summer. By then she hopes to have left Benson's and so be able to get about more.

This letter is probably the last Dorothy wrote to her mother. A week later Mrs Sayers was taken ill and had to be removed to hospital. The diagnosis was an internal stoppage connected with a small rupture of the bowel. She died on 27 July 1929, having survived her husband by only ten months. "Poor dear", Dorothy wrote to Ivy,

> if only she had called the doctor earlier, something might have been done about it, but she absolutely forbade them to send for the doctor or for me, and when we were sent for, it was too late . . . It seems hard to realise that she has gone – it seems as though she were still about the place which she had grown to be so fond of.

Dorothy had suffered, suddenly and within a short interval, a grievous double loss. The ties which had so long sustained her with a continuing sense of being a much-loved daughter were now gone. There remained Aunt Mabel to be cared for and an increasingly ailing and unhappy husband. There also remained the problem of her son.

211

CHAPTER 15

The Making of a
Detective Story

When, in March 1928, Dorothy L. Sayers was putting the final touches to her Introduction to the first volume of the anthology, she referred to the short stories of Mrs L. T. Meade, who initiated the medical mystery story with her *Stories from the Diary of a Doctor*, published in 1893, which she continued in *The Sorceress of the Strand*, published in 1902. In this volume she collaborated with Eustace Barton, M.D., whose pseudonym was Robert Eustace. Dorothy wished to include an example of their work, in particular the short story "A Handful of Ashes", but the publishers, Ward, Lock and Co., would not co-operate. In the event, she included L. T. Meade's "The Face in the Dark", and Edgar Jepson's "The Tea-Leaf", for both of which "Robert Eustace" as co-author had provided the scientific content.

In writing to him to arrange about royalties, she said how much she admired the "ingenious and delightful medico-legal plots which [he] and Mrs Meade evolved at so comparatively early a date". She asked him if he would care to collaborate with her, if she could invent a new detective. In reply, Dr Barton said how much he admired Lord Peter Wimsey; he hoped she was not thinking of killing him off? She answered on 7 May:

> I am so glad you like Lord Peter. I certainly don't intend to kill him off yet, but I think it would be better to invent a new detective for any tales we do together. For one thing, people would associate his name with mine and be inclined to hand me more than my half-share of the credit for the story, which wouldn't be just. Also it would simplify matters to have somebody with more scientific surroundings, don't you think? Lord Peter isn't supposed to know

213

a lot about chemistry and that sort of thing, and it would mean inventing a doctor or somebody to help him out. Also, I'm looking forward to getting a rest from him, because his everlasting breeziness does become a bit of a tax at times! The job is to invent a scientific character of a new type. There have been so many of them . . . and it's very hard to think of any sort that hasn't been done.

They met, and discussed "the new detective" and a possible method of murder. Barton suggested the addition of the poison muscarine to a dish of otherwise harmless mushrooms. The motive, he thought, would have to arise from an overpowering love affair. Dorothy promised to turn the matter over in her mind, but first, she said, she had to "polish off a number of short stories". A few days later, she wrote:

In this story, as you say, it is obvious that there must be a powerful love interest, and I am going to turn my mind to making this part of the book as modern and powerful as possible. The day of the two nice young people whose chaste affection is rewarded on the final page, has rather gone by . . . Since, in this case, we must have the love to help the plot along, we must do our best to make it as credible and convincing as up-to-date standards require.

Towards the end of May, Dr Barton's ideas had developed and he wrote:

We can introduce some very deep and interesting questions into the mushroom story – the subtle difference between what is produced by life and that artificially produced by man. The molecular asymmetry of Organic Products marks the difference between the chemistry of dead matter and the chemistry of living matter, and this touches on the most fundamental problems of the phenomena of life itself.

He then proceeded to expound the difference between symmetric and asymmetric molecules. Muscarine, a substance derived from the organic tissue of certain poisonous mushrooms, is composed, like all other living substances, of asymmetric molecules. Synthetic muscarine, constituted by artificial means, is composed, like all other inorganic substances, of symmetric molecules.

If light is passed through a crystal, for example, of a form of calcite known as Iceland spar, the vibrations of the ray are brought into one plane, like a flat ribbon, and the result is known as a beam of polarised light. When this beam is passed through an inorganic substance, whose molecules are symmetric, it remains unchanged. The substance is said to be optically inactive. If, however, the polarised beam of light is passed through an organic substance, whose molecules are asymmetric, a spiral effect is produced. The substance is said to be optically active.

The difference can be verified by means of an instrument called a polariscope, resembling a small telescope fixed vertically upon a stand. At the bottom end is a thin plate of semi-transparent mineral, the silicate known as tourmaline, which has a finely foliated structure. This is the polariser. When light is passed through it, that light is brought into one plane, in other words, it is polarised.

Higher up, near the eye-piece of the instrument, is another slice of tourmaline, known as the analyser. When this is turned so that its foliations are parallel to the polariser, light will pass through. If it is turned so that its foliations are at right angles to those of the polariser, no light will show.

If, when the analyser is in this position, a solution of synthetic substance is placed between the two slices of tourmaline, no light will penetrate the foliations of the analyser. If, however, a solution of organic substance is so placed, it will rotate the beam of light, producing a spiral effect by reason of its asymmetric molecules, bringing it into line with the foliations of the analyser and making it visible at the eye-piece.

Dorothy was greatly taken with the possibilities of this scientific phenomenon. On 29 June she wrote: "I think we have got hold of a really fine theme for a story here, and I am most eager to get on with it . . . The religious-scientific aspect of the thing will require careful handling, but ought, I think, to be very interesting to people, if we can succeed in making it clear to them."

She was especially interested in the basic distinction between organic and inorganic matter: was life, then, a question of asymmetry? On 20 August she wrote: "[The idea] touches the very key note of the mystery of the appearance of Life on this planet. There seems no escape from the conclusion that at some wonderful moment in the evolutionary process a Directive Force-from-Without entered upon the scene of Life itself." She asked Dr Barton to supply her with a simple statement of his understanding of the matter. He wrote the following explanation, entitled "A Theory of the Origin of Life on the Planet".

It is necessary for the existence of Life that there should be an asymmetry of molecular structure. Whence rose that asymmetry? As the planet cooled from its gaseous form, purely inorganic compounds were formed, composed of molecules symmetrical in their structure, that is, molecules that had not been formed directly or indirectly from any living tissues. And as such they would have been found to be optically inactive and incapable of rotating the plane of Polarised Light. It is known that light is circularly polarised by the light of the Sun from the surface of the sea and it is probable that when this occurred, when the vapour of the atmosphere condensed, and formed the first seas, an asymmetric agent became present on the face of the globe and by decomposing one antipode rather than another, gave rise to the first asymmetric molecule from which all living tissues arose and following the course of evolution continued to the present day. It is known that Life originated in the sea, and even we mammals retain in our Branchial Clefts the vestigial structures of fishes. May we not then look to the action of sunlight on the first oceans as the agent, through circularly polarised light, that produced the first asymmetric molecule, the starting point of Life on the Planet?

Dorothy was delighted by the phrase "an asymmetric agent became present on the face of the globe", which she accepted as "a modern substitute for 'the spirit of God moved upon the face of the waters'":

By the way, what inspired those old birds who wrote the Bible and the other early accounts to guess that life did start from the waters? That always beats me. It was all too far away and long ago for them to have had a racial memory of it, and it's not the kind of thing that's obvious on the face of it. And yet they got extraordinarily near the correct order of things: light first – and then water – and then earth – and then cattle – and then man – anybody would think they had been given elementary scientific instruction in a board-school! Perhaps the "creeping things" have got a trifle out of place, but even so, what an amazing guess!

Dr Barton could not answer this, but he hazarded the tentative query: "Atlantis?"

At the end of August he went to London to consult medical colleagues at University College Hospital in Gower Street, where an experiment was conducted by means of a polariscope. He sent a vivid description of it:

> [It took place] in a dark lecture theatre, the only light being that of the sodium flame which renders faces literally corpse-like. Perhaps when you were a child you had – as we had – Snapdragon on Christmas Eve, and at the last threw a handful of salt into the burning brandy, and became deathly in colour. With this colour on his face, the great chemist will raise his eyes from the polariscope and utter the words of doom, "The muscarine which killed Mr X was never produced by the living tissues of a fungus!"

He was greatly excited by the whole idea. They must keep it quiet, he urged: "I want it to be the best idea of my life and I feel it is going to be." It has greater depths than he first imagined and will result, he believes, in "a story with elements above the ordinary run of detective fiction, [which] should excite comments in wide circles of thought". He suggests "The Death Cap" as a title, echoing the popular name, "Warty Cap", of the poisonous mushroom *Amanita muscaria*, which the victim will be assumed to have eaten in mistake for the harmless *Amanita rubescens*.

Dorothy was equally enthusiastic:

> The sodium flame scene sounds absolutely great! We must certainly do this story as soon as we can. I am not breathing a word about it to anybody – hardly, even, to my husband – but these things seem to get "into the air", and it would be dreadful to be forestalled. My short stories are nearly finished and then I shall be ready to deal with muscarine.

Later she wrote: "The scene in the laboratory will be very good. I think we might let the Great Scientist do a check experiment with genuine fungus poison first." The scene as she eventually wrote it emerges recognisably from this animated and creative correspondence.

In the novel, Jack Munting, the friend of the murderer, relating this part of the narrative in the first person, describes a visit to the laboratory of the Home Office analyst, Sir James Lubbock, who had previously carried out the analysis of the contents of the victim's stomach and of the dish of fungus. Munting is accompanied by Dr Waters, a scientist to whom he has confided his disquiet about the death of the victim and his fear that his friend Lathom may have been implicated in it. Waters opens the proceedings.

217

"By the way, Lubbock, did it by any chance occur to you to give that muscarine the once-over with the polariscope?"

"With the polariscope? Good heavens, no. Why should it? That wouldn't tell one anything. You know all about muscarine. Dextro-rotatory. Nothing abstruse about it."

Waters persuades Lubbock to check up on the point and asks him to test the control solution of organic muscarine first, so that Munting can see for himself that it rotates the beam of polarised light:

He struck a match and lit a Bunsen burner, the flame of which played upon a small mass of sodium chloride held above it by a platinum projection.

"Sodium chloride," said Waters, "in fact, not to make unnecessary mystery about it, common salt. Shall I switch off?"

He snapped off the lights, and we were left with only the sodium flame. In that green, sick glare a face floated close to mine – a corpse-face – livid, waxen, stamped with decay – sharp-shadowed in the nostrils and under the orbits – Harrison's face, as I had seen it in "The Shack", opening a black mouth of complaint.

"Spectacular, isn't it?" said Sir James pleasantly, and I pulled myself together and realised that I must look just as ghastly to him as he to me. But for the moment the face had been Harrison's, and from that moment, Lathom was nothing to me any more.

When Munting has seen for himself that the organic muscarine allows the light to penetrate to the eye-piece, the synthetic muscarine which killed the victim is then tested:

With maddening deliberation, the analyst set the first cylinder carefully on one side and took up the other. My mouth was dry as I watched him. He put the cylinder into the polariscope and looked. There was a pause. Then a grunt. Then his hand came up, and an exclamation of impatience. Then his eye was jerked back from the eye-piece and his head peered round to examine the exterior of the instrument . . . Then came Sir James's voice, queer and puzzled.

"I say, Waters. There's something funny here. Just have a look, will you?"

Waters applies his eye to the instrument and sees only darkness.

"What do you make of that?" said Sir James.

"One of two things," said Waters, briskly, "either it's a suspension of the laws of Nature, or this muscarine of yours is optically inactive. I hesitate to suggest a suspension of the laws of Nature."

"But how could – " Sir James broke off, and in the corpse-light I watched his face as he revolved the possibilities in his mind. "You know what that means, Waters."

"I might hazard a guess."

"Murder."

"Yes, murder."

Once the murder method and means of detection had been settled, there remained the working out of the story and the selection of suitable characters. Dorothy wrote:

> We shall have to work it powerfully on the emotional side. This is rather a new line for me [she evidently disregarded *Clouds of Witness* in this respect], but it will be very interesting to have a go at it. And we shall have somehow to work the scientific-theological interest solidly into the plot ... I am longing to have a go at this story. I have now finished my set of short stories for Gollancz, so there is now only the Old French poem to compete with our novel.

On 10 September she writes to say that she has decided that the villain must be away when the victim eats the poisoned dish. A week or two later she is trying to think of a way for the murderer to administer the poison. By 19 November she has solved the problem and knows how she can support the alibi by means of a witness:

> I have also been considering the love-affair. I don't want to make the villain too villainous, nor yet must the victim be a villain. I think I shall (with your approval) make the victim a harmless sort of bore, conceited and self-centred and always twaddling about his cookery and so on, and have him married to a sort of Edith Thompson woman, who eggs on the villain to get rid of the husband. That will allow plenty of human nature and furious frustration and all that kind of thing.

Here is a valuable insight into the mechanics of constructing a detective novel. In this case, the detection of the murder, which involves a basic principle of life, dictates the choice of characters, who are manipulated to serve the plot. Their personalities and feelings have a functional purpose and are in themselves of secondary significance. Even the love affair between the murderer and the wife of the victim is introduced only as a motive. It is not a theme of the novel. It has been suggested that the character of the victim, Harrison, was a portrait of Dorothy's husband and that the feelings of the wife towards him represented, to some extent, her own unhappiness. The glimpse behind the scenes in the author's workshop afforded by this revealing correspondence with her collaborator shows how wide of the mark such an interpretation is.

In his medical capacity, Dr Barton was a consultant at a mental hospital in Northampton. From time to time, therefore, in a general way, Dorothy discussed medical and psychological questions with him. With no conscious awareness (at that moment) of any relevance to the plot they were evolving, she told him about a typist in her office who was mentally unstable. She had a foolish preoccupation with sex and seemed unable to make decisions of any kind. Among her symptoms was a craving for kippers. When Dorothy required a neurotic character for the plot, she cast about her; remembering the malady of the unfortunate typist, she used her as a model for the unbalanced companion-help, Miss Milsom, among whose symptoms is a craving for shrimps.

By the end of June she has begun to write: "The characters are coming out quite nice and clearly in my mind. The husband, wife, lover, poet and lady-help are all on the scene together now, preparing to fall in love and poison and generally misbehave. I hope I shan't make a muck of it." At a later stage she wrote:

> We are getting along nicely. The step-son is suspecting the murder and is about to purchase a bunch of compromising letters from a blackmailing charwoman! The novelist is having a dreadful time, torn between his natural good feeling and the fact that he was at the same public school as the murderer. The wife is a dreadful person. The murderer (who has my sympathy) has just discovered this and his feelings of misery and remorse are dreadful, but nobody knows this yet but me.

She was in good spirits about the mechanics of the plot and enjoying manoeuvring the characters to further it. But what really mattered to her was the method by which the murder would be detected. This kindled her imagination to intense excitement. The reader, she said, must realise what has been done and despair of its ever being proved. "Then comes the ray of light – the hand of God – science, life, truth – 'the light that moved on the waters of Chaos' and, somehow, formed the first asymmetric atom on the face of the deep – ready, after millions of centuries to catch the murderer out." She is elated by this cosmic vision. Searching her mind for a title to do it justice (she is not satisfied with "The Death Cap"), she recalls two lines from Omar Khayyám:

And the first morning of Creation wrote
What the last dawn of reckoning shall read.

At 3 a.m. on 9 February 1930, she wrote the last words of the novel, drank a large glass of Bovril-and-milk and staggered away to bed. Later that morning, she re-read the first part and found much to displease her. The following day she went to the Reading Room of the British Museum, in order, as was her habit, at the final stage, to cull a sprinkling of contemporary events from the file of the *Daily Mail*. The work was now entitled *The Documents in the Case* – a lifeless title and a far cry from the powerful vision which had so elated her.

She always felt depressed when she had finished a novel. This time she was bitterly disappointed with herself:

In my heart I know I have made a failure of it. Really and truly I was feeling so nervous and run down last year, what with funerals and other worries, that I ought not to have been writing at all. It has produced a mingled atmosphere of dullness and gloom which will, I fear, be fatal to the book . . . I wish I could have done better with the brilliant plot.

She was right to be disappointed. The book is engaging and ingenious – good Sayers fun, but little more. The most striking and original part comes almost at the end, of necessity, for it involves the solution. This is the discussion between Munting's parson friend and his scientific cronies, which results in the flash of understanding as to how the murder can be proved. Here Dorothy L. Sayers rises to the height demanded by the theme. Her intellect and her imagination are fused and the writing is brilliant. But so light-weight and at times jaunty is the handling of the rest of the work that this profoundly interesting section seems almost an intrusion.

The epistolary form in which she chose to tell the story does not help. It was unfortunate that just while she was planning this novel she was also working on her biography of Wilkie Collins. She admired the brilliance of his technique of first-person narrative in *The*

Moonstone and was moved to emulate him: "I'm rather keen to try the experiment of writing the book in a series of first-person narratives, à la Wilkie Collins. It will be a new line to try." This was a mistake. The basic scientific idea was itself such a novelty, so challenging and requiring such careful structuring, that it was perilous to try out yet another novelty at the same time. The letters which unfold the plot are amusing and, for the most part, slight in style and characterisation, while the impact of the whole is weakened by the continual switching of view-points.

A serious failure, in terms of the awe-inspiring novel Dorothy wanted to write, and might indeed have written, is the affair between Mrs Harrison, the victim's wife, and her lover, Lathom. The situation resembles the Thompson-Bywaters case. In fact, as has been shown, Dorothy told Dr Barton she wanted to make the wife a sort of Edith Thompson woman, who eggs on her lover to murder her husband. This, as it turned out, was another mistake. She said more than once that the plot required a powerful emotional motive and admitted that this would be new territory for her. She must have hoped that the dreary, lower middle-class setting she chose would enable her to tell a passionate love story in a convincing and realistic manner, as she believed up-to-date readers preferred. Unfortunately, in the handling, it turned out a rather shoddy, respectability-obsessed, suburban case of adultery, drawn on too small a scale for the dimensions of the original idea of the book.

This need not have been the case. In his famous essay, "Decline of the English Murder", first published in 1946, George Orwell pointed out the tragic potential of an ordinary domestic murder committed in a semi-detached house in the suburbs: "With this kind of background, a crime can have dramatic and even tragic qualities which make it memorable and excite pity for both victim and murderer." In *The Documents in the Case* we certainly feel pity for the victim, but our horror at the manner of his death wipes out any sympathy we might have for the lovers. Their feelings for each other are too shallow to draw forth any deep response.

The Documents in the Case was published on 4 July 1930 and was at once selected by the Book Guild as the detective story of the year. Undoubtedly, therefore, in relation to its *genre*, its merits were appreciated. Someone who read it was the novelist and criminologist, F. Tennyson Jesse. It occurred to her that she could make a better job of the Thompson-Bywaters case than that; and she did so, in her compelling novel, *A Pin to See the Peepshow*, published in 1934. Here all the passion and tragic inevitability of the affair are realised to their full dimensions. This is the powerful love-story Dorothy was groping for but never grasped, possibly because she had not the courage to do so. It is interesting that F. Tennyson Jesse, perhaps with an intentional and courteous salute to her predecessor, takes the letters of Mrs Harrison to Lathom as models for the letters she herself writes for her character Julia (the Edith Thompson of her novel). When Dorothy read this work, and there is evidence that she did so, she must have noticed both the resemblance and the different effect which Julia's letters have in their stronger context.

She knew quite well what had gone wrong. It was not only that she had had a troubling year, with the death of both her parents and anxiety about Mac's health. She had not yet succeeded in detaching herself sufficiently from her unhappy experience of passionate love to write about it with confidence. She gives this unease to Harriet Vane in *Gaudy Night*. In chapter 4, Harriet is revising three of her books for a new edition – a dismal and depressing task:

> The books were all right, as far as they went; as intellectual exercises, they were even brilliant. But there was something lacking about them; they read now to her as though they had been written with a mental reservation, a determination to keep her own opinions and personality out of view. She considered with distaste a clever and superficial discussion between two of the characters about married life. She could have made a much better thing of that, if she had not been afraid of giving herself away.

When she wrote that, Dorothy L. Sayers had come to terms with a great deal of her past.

Soon after *The Documents in the Case* was published, Dr Barton received a disturbing letter. A reader objected that organic muscarine, not being a protein, though closely related, did not share with proteins the property of being optically active. The solution of the murder was therefore based on a fallacy. Dr Barton was stricken and profoundly apologetic. Dorothy was less perturbed and made the best of the situation in a breezy talk on the radio. A year later, on 17 October 1932, Dr Barton, greatly relieved, wrote to say that all was well, after all:

> I have now got a copy of the *Analyst* and have re-read carefully . . . Dr Hewitt's review, and his most courteous reference to our book, and I gather that although the *structure* of muscarine is still in dispute among these learned gentlemen, there is no doubt about its

optical activity, and that is the whole point so far as we are concerned. It is very comforting after all the agonies and the criticisms we had.

By then Dorothy L. Sayers had moved on.

CHAPTER 16

Under Contract

"A novelist", said Dorothy L. Sayers in a characteristically down-to-earth manner, "is a tradesman who supplies books to the public. Writing books is not a hobby; it is a job, a trade like any other." She was business-like in her relations with publishers, she honoured her contracts, she met her dead-lines and she gave good value for money. She did not go in for mystique, nor did she ever spell art with a capital A.

Whose Body? was first accepted by Boni and Liveright, a firm in New York, who brought it out in May 1923. They had also published John Cournos' book of verse, *In Exile*, so it is possible that he suggested them. The novel was then accepted in England by T. Fisher Unwin, who published it in October of the same year. He also accepted the second novel, *Clouds of Witness*, which came out in February 1926.

For various reasons Dorothy was dissatisfied and wanted to change her publisher. She found an agent, Andrew Dakers, who secured her a contract with Ernest Benn for her next three novels. The first of these was *Unnatural Death*, which came out in September 1927. Victor Gollancz, then a young man, was one of Benn's employees. He much admired what he had seen of Dorothy's work and had faith in her as a coming writer. Towards the end of 1927 he was planning to set up as a publisher on his own and invited her, as we know, to edit an anthology of short stories of detection, mystery and horror. She was free to accept, since her contract with Benn covered novels only. She replied on 25 November:

Yes, rather, of course, like a shot! . . . Indeed I have always yearned after some book of the sort . . . I think it should be kept as far as possible along the lines of mystery and detection and not too much sheer horrors and ghost-grues, because the latter has been done once or twice, whereas, so far as I know, the detective field has scarcely been touched. It ought to be hugely successful – I'm awfully thrilled!

Gollancz was also interested in publishing her own short stories. She wanted to free herself from Benn but he still had a claim on her for two more novels, which she honoured. She pressed forward with *The Unpleasantness at the Bellona Club* while at the same time working on the anthology for Gollancz. Three days after agreeing to undertake this, she wrote: "Twenty volumes of *Strand Magazines* have now arrived and we are having to build a new set of bookshelves."

By early December, she is "buried up to the eyes in old *Strands*". She is also into the ninth chapter of *The Bellona Club* and hopes to have this off her hands soon after Christmas. At the end of January 1928 she sends a list of authors and titles for the anthology and says she is struggling with the Introduction: "I can't get it quite right, but it's shaping." She spends her Saturday mornings in the Reading Room of the British Museum.

Contemporaneously with all this, she was preparing a volume of her own short stories and writing others to bring it up to the desired length. She settled on the title *Lord Peter Views the Body*, although, in her opinion, the best short stories in this collection have no bodies in them. She sent Gollancz "The Footsteps That Ran" and "The Man with the Copper Fingers", two stories which *Pearson's* had rejected, considering them too gruesome. Gollancz, less timorous, included them in her selection.

One of the most chilling stories she ever wrote dates from this period. She intended to construct a series of tales under the collective title "Smith and Smith: Removals", of which, it seems, she completed only two. They concern the mysterious and sinister firm of Smith and Smith who specialise in the removal of unwanted or inconvenient persons, for a consideration. The first, "The House of the Poplars", about the removal of a wife, was never published. The second, "The Leopard Lady", was included in the collection, *In the Teeth of the Evidence*, brought out in 1939. It tells the story of the removal of Cyril, a boy aged five, who is the ward of his uncle, Mr Tressider. If the boy was to die, his uncle would inherit an estate. The first sentence strikes a note of icy horror: "If the boy is in your way," said a voice in Tressider's ear, "ask at Rapallo's for Smith and Smith."

An arrangement is entered into, a signed confession is previously obtained, the boy is "removed" by being pathetically gulled into eating the berries of deadly nightshade, one thousand pounds is paid over, and the incriminating document is returned. Nothing could be neater.

To follow, step by step, the measures Dorothy took to ensure the well-being of her own small son is to realise the gulf that separates a writer's creative imagination from real life. Early in 1928 Ivy had moved from Cowley and now rented a thatched cottage in the village of Westcott Barton, to the north-west of Oxford. Its local name was Cocksparrow Hall but Ivy re-named it The Sidelings. Dorothy had been to see it and recommended her to take it. It had no modern conveniences but it was solidly built of Cotswold stone, with oak-beamed ceilings and stone-flagged floors. There was a large, wild garden for the children to run about in and there were walks to take in the very beautiful surrounding countryside.

The question of her son, despite her many other commitments, was seldom absent from her thoughts. In August 1928 she wrote to Ivy: "I shall have to go seriously into the question of [John's] future before long. Just at present my own future (on which his depends) is occupying the forefront of my attention, and I have hopes of some rather useful developments, if all goes well." Her hopes concerned the securing of lucrative serial rights for her novels.

When her father died the following month, she set about making a will. She wrote an interim letter to Ivy, saying that she was leaving everything to Mac, "who will look after J.A. as though he were his own son". (This was trusting, indeed.) If they were both killed simultaneously, everything was left to Ivy, who was to use the money "for my son, John Anthony Sayers", to hold it, "in trust for him, to feed, clothe, lodge and educate him as far as it will go". She asked Ivy to keep the letter, which constituted, her lawyers had told her, a secret trust. "It is only a temporary arrangement, in case of Mac and myself both being killed off before he can carry out his intention of formally adopting J.A."

The years 1928 and 1929 were astonishingly productive. In July 1928 Benn published *The Unpleasantness at the Bellona Club*; in September Gollancz brought out the first series of *Great Short Stories of Detection, Mystery and Horror*; in November he published the collection, *Lord Peter Views the Body*. During 1929 she was busy writing *The Documents in the Case*, which was owed to Benn, to whom she also offered her translation of the mediaeval French poem by Thomas, *Tristan in Brittany*. He accepted, and published it in July 1929. At the same time she was writing a new Lord Peter novel for

Gollancz. When he enquired, in April 1930, when he might expect it, she replied, by reply, on the twenty-eighth:

> Dear Mr Gollancz,
> *Strong Poison.*
> Yours sincerely,
> Dorothy L. Sayers.

The manuscript accompanied the letter.

Her speed of work and invention is amazing. She was, of course, under great financial pressure. Mac had arrears of unpaid income tax and he was earning very little. His health was also very uncertain. They had incurred extra expense when they took over the upstairs flat. Not only was there redecoration to pay for; they had to buy new furniture and equipment and meet an increase in rent. But they badly needed the extra space. In September 1928 Dorothy wrote to Ivy: "We shan't be so near divorcing each other on account of aggravated propinquity as we were before – and that's a great comfort. Before we got these extra rooms, we really were so awfully on top of one another that we were ready to shriek!"

When Mrs Sayers died, Ivy, ever hopeful of making it possible for John and his mother to see more of each other, suggested coming to live in the house in Witham and helping to look after Aunt Mabel. This would have meant bringing three children with her – John, Isobel and another little girl named Rosemary. Dorothy replied: "I don't think Aunt Mabel would very well be able to stand children about the house, though she's bearing up wonderfully, and carries her great age well." It was not only Aunt Mabel who could not have tolerated a house full of children. Dorothy would have found it difficult too, not to mention Mac, whose temper, like his health, was uncertain.

By August 1929 an agreement with American publishers made it possible for Dorothy to give notice at Benson's. She would leave at the end of the year, after which she and Mac intended to live permanently in Witham, using the London flat as a *pied-à-terre*. She had been a success at her job, helping to create the famous Mustard Club and working with John Gilroy on the memorable Guinness advertisements. But nine years were long enough and she looked forward to having more time for her writing.

Gollancz was pleased with *Strong Poison*, especially with the murder method. Dorothy replied that the idea had been in her mind for about six years, "and to me [it] seems no longer baffling but obvious". This is interesting because it shows, once again, as with *The Documents in the Case*, that it was her habit to begin with a method of murder and construct her plot and characters round that.

She had told Eustace Barton that Lord Peter Wimsey's everlasting breeziness was a bit of a tax at times and that she would be glad of a rest from him. She had considered inventing a new detective for their joint novel but, as the story turned out, she had no need to do so. She did not, in fact, give herself a rest from Wimsey after all, for while working on *The Documents* she was also writing *Strong Poison*. It is true that in this story she makes him less breezy. She also makes him more interesting as a human being, for he falls in love.

She had said in her Introduction to the anthology that some of the finest detective stories were marred by a conventional love-story, irrelevant to the action and perfunctorily worked in. Particularly blameworthy, she considered "are the heroes who insist on fooling about after young women when they ought to be putting their minds to the job of detection". Instances in which the love-story is an integral part of the plot were extremely rare. She cites the "beautiful example" of Wilkie Collins' *The Moonstone*. "E. C. Bentley, in *Trent's Last Case*, has dealt finely with the still harder problem of the detective in love. Trent's love for Mrs Manderson is a legitimate part of the plot."

It may be that she wished to see what she could do with this "still harder problem" herself. Lord Peter's enamourment is not, in fact, necessary to the plot of *Strong Poison*. The murder and the detection of the method would work equally well if he were not in love. The emotional situation, however, puts him in a new light and heightens the suspense, even if it is not technically essential to the solution.

Some years later, in an article entitled "Gaudy Night", writing in her professional *persona*, Dorothy L. Sayers said that when she embarked on *Strong Poison* "it was with the infanticidal intention of doing away with Peter, that is, of marrying him off and getting rid of him". If this is really the case, it would surely have been rather a shock to Victor Gollancz, with whom she had only then signed a contract undertaking to produce one book a year. Presumably he was expecting the remunerative Lord Peter Wimsey to continue. If this was not specified, did she perhaps intend to write a different kind of detective novel from then on? Her mind was always teeming with ideas and it may be that *The Documents in the Case*, even though it did not turn out as well as she wished, had opened up new vistas. She may have hoped, by changing course, to achieve her long-cherished aim of raising the detective story to the level of the novel of manners, from which it had lapsed since the time of Wilkie Collins.

If this is so, it is strange that she should introduce in what was to have been the last of the Wimsey books a promising new character, namely Harriet Vane, the young woman chosen for him to marry. If he was destined to be finished off, then so was she, after making only one appearance. It is difficult to believe that Dorothy L. Sayers, that shrewd craftsman, ever intended to waste such good material.

From the outset Harriet is a more credible character than Peter, being in many respects a projection of the author. A successful writer of detective fiction, she enters upon the scene under a double burden of tragedy. She has recently passed through an unhappy love affair, comparable to Dorothy's own humiliating affair with Cournos. She now stands wrongly accused of poisoning her lover with arsenic and in danger of being hanged. From this fate Lord Peter Wimsey saves her.

We are not given much direct knowledge of Harriet's personality in this novel, for we are shown her almost exclusively through other people's eyes – those of the judge, her friends, her publisher and especially Lord Peter. But what we see of her for ourselves reveals her as independent, lively-minded, witty, and spirited enough to engage, in prison, in animated conversation with Wimsey about an ingenious plot for a murder story. Obviously a woman of originality and character – much too good to throw away in the waste-paper basket.

In the same article, the Dorothy L. Sayers who rather enjoyed pulling the wool over her readers' eyes, said that, much to her surprise, she found herself unable to make her puppets fall into each other's arms at the end of the novel. The situation was false and degrading. Harriet owed too great a debt of gratitude to Wimsey; her creator "could find no form of words in which she could accept him without loss of self-respect". Consequently, she felt it necessary to continue their story through several more novels. But was she really so surprised?

It is doubtful that she was really tired of Wimsey. She found him great fun. In an article entitled "How I Came to Invent the Character of Lord Peter Wimsey" (not entirely accurate, but why should it be?), she said:

Lord Peter's large income (the source of which by the way I have never investigated) . . . I deliberately gave him . . . After all it cost me nothing and at that time I was particularly hard up and it gave me pleasure to spend his fortune for him. When I was dissatisfied with my single unfurnished room I took a luxurious flat for him in

Piccadilly. When my cheap rug got a hole in it, I ordered him an Aubusson carpet. When I had no money to pay my bus fare I presented him with a Daimler double-six, upholstered in a style of sober magnificence, and when I felt dull I let him drive it. I can heartily recommend this inexpensive way of furnishing to all who are discontented with their incomes. It relieves the mind and does no harm to anybody.

Like Harriet Vane, Dorothy possessed the exuberance to rise above her constraints and difficulties. Her mind was continually creative and she revelled in its inventiveness. Her intellect and her imagination were partners in a world which it elated her to enter. She was naturally high-spirited and her sense of fun and enjoyment were unquenchable. She knew how to give pleasure and amusement to her readers. No wonder Victor Gollancz had faith in her.

It may be that he persuaded her not to give up Lord Peter, if indeed she ever really intended to at this stage. After all, she had to continue making a living and was now wholly dependent upon her writing. She was occasionally depressed about her financial situation. On 15 April 1930, she wrote to Ivy:

What is the good of trying to make money when the Government immediately snatches it away from one, I do not know. If it were not that somebody must look after Aunt M., we could cut the cable and go and live abroad, with half the expense and a greatly reduced taxation, but we are tied by the leg and there it is. One can but do one's best.

They still had Evelyn Compline to help them in the house and she had promised never to leave them as long as Aunt Mabel was alive. When Dorothy and Mac went on holiday, reinforcements were called upon to stand by in case of emergencies. In May, for the sake of Mac's health, they went up to Kirkcudbright and again in September. Dorothy was then well on with her new novel. She wrote to Gollancz:

The nuisance is I can't get hold of a good title. As you know, I wanted to call it *The Six Suspects*, but somebody has pinched that. I might call it:
Six Unlikely Persons
The Body in the Burn
The Murder at the Minnoch

The Missing Object
There's One Thing Missing

Eventually she settled for *The Five Red Herrings* – a book which owes a great deal to Mac and his knowledge of painting and fishing and his love of the part of Scotland in which the action is set. He had recently taken up painting, as Dorothy reported to Ivy: "Mac is very busy painting in addition to his ordinary work. He really ought to have been an artist. He seems to enjoy painting more than anything and is really good at it." *The Five Red Herrings* glows with the happiness of a relaxed holiday in congenial and beautiful surroundings. Dorothy particularly requests Gollancz to supply "a large, handsome, clear, well-executed, generous and convincing map ... not like the mean, miserable, petty, small, feeble and unworthy map provided by Collins for Freeman Wills Crofts' book." He complied with her request.

An odd coincidence had occurred in connection with Freeman Wills Crofts, as Dorothy reported to Gollancz:

This book [her own], in which all the places are real and which turns on actual distances and real railway time-tables, is laid in exactly the same part of the country as Freeman Wills Crofts' new

Mac during World War II
(Estate of Ann Schreurs)

book, which also turns on real distances and time-tables! We only discovered this the other day, in the course of a correspondence about something else. The two plots are, of course, entirely different, and it doesn't really matter a pin.

By January 1931 *The Five Red Herrings* was despatched to Gollancz and he wrote to say how pleased he was with it. Dorothy was glad he had agreed that she should try her hand at the "pure puzzle story" just for once:

> I am always afraid of getting into a rut, and like each book to have a slightly different idea behind it. I have also been annoyed (stupidly enough) by a lot of reviewers who observed that in *Strong Poison* I had lost my grip, because the identity of the murderer was obvious from the start (as indeed it is also in *Unnatural Death* and *The Documents in the Case*). Personally, I feel it is only when the identity of the murderer is obvious that the reader can really concentrate on the question (much the most interesting): How did he do it? But if people really want to play "Spot the Murderer", I don't mind obliging them – for once!
>
> They have also grumbled that Lord Peter (a) falls in love, (b) talks too discursively. Here is a book in which nobody falls in love (unless you count Campbell) and in which practically every sentence is necessary to the plot (except a remark or two about Scottish scenery and language). Much good may it do 'em!

The book sold very well. Eighteen months after publication, Dorothy wrote to Gollancz from Kircudbright to say how glad she was that he was reprinting it because there was a great interest in it there:

> You see, what happens is this: even at this distance of time, people arrive in Gatehouse and Kirkcudbright and say they've come to spend their holidays there because they read a book called *The Five Red Herrings*. Whereupon the proprietor says: "Och aye? Weel, the authoress is jist stayin' in Gallowa' the noo – maybe ye'd like tae be meetin' her." So presently I am displayed as one of the local amenities, and the visitor says: "Now, I've just bought a copy of your book – I wonder if you would write your name in it for me." Which I do.

She had promised to return to a less rigidly intellectual formula in *Have His Carcase*, "which will turn on an alibi and a point of medicine, but will, I think, contain a certain amount of human interest and a more or less obvious murderer. But I haven't made up the plot yet." Once again, she began with the method of murder.

The chief human interest in *Have His Carcase* is the development of the relationship between Harriet and Peter. For the first half of the book Harriet is the main character. This time, she is presented directly and we watch her grappling not only with the murder mystery but also with her feelings towards Peter, whom we see mainly through her eyes. They work together on the mystery and solve it, but their own problem still remains to be disentangled.

Dorothy was now well established as a writer of detective fiction and Victor Gollancz had every reason to be pleased. Her family life, however, continued to be worrying. Aunt Mabel died in August 1930, suddenly, while Mac and Dorothy were in Scotland and they had to hurry back. Aunt Gertrude was dying of cancer. Mac was often ill. Dorothy wrote to Ivy: "We seem to have been living in an atmosphere of deaths and illnesses for YEARS. The only person who remains cheerful and no nuisance to anybody is my Lord Peter."

In February 1931 Ivy wrote to say that John, who was now seven years old, wished to open a Post Office savings account. In which name should she arrange for him to do this: John Anthony White, or John Anthony Fleming? Dorothy replied:

When Mac and I got married the understanding was that we should formally adopt J.A., but it's been put off by one thing and another. I can't quite explain. He always says he is going to do it and wants to do it, but naturally I can't push it on to him. He says he doesn't see any objection to the name Fleming being used − (Sayers of course is the only one to which he has any right) − in fact Mac himself suggested it should be Fleming. But I'm damned if I really know. I wish it could be settled one way or another, but it doesn't really lie with me . . . Just at this particular moment I can't speak very decisively. I can't go into all the whys just now, but I'll explain some day.

She suggested that Ivy should open the account in her own name, if this could be done without hurting John's feelings.

In March that year, John went down with scarlet fever. Dorothy said that Ivy was on no account to nurse him at home; it would be too much for her, and the other children would be likely to catch it. She must get him into hospital and send her the bill. He is taken to the Acland Nursing Home, "where", said Dorothy, "they once had the honour of removing my appendix". There is further worry about his ears. Dorothy tells Ivy to consult a specialist, who recommends an operation for the removal of his adenoids and tonsils. The question is, how soon after the scarlet fever should the operation be performed? Dorothy says, "while he still remembers with pleasure his friends at the hospital, if you ask me". He was taken back to the Acland and Dorothy telephoned to know how he was. She reported to Ivy, "I gather he is doing as well as can be expected, poor little wretch." She sent him books to read and kept constantly in touch with Ivy about his progress.

In the meantime she is struggling with *Have His Carcase* – "horribly complicated! But it must be done, under contract, so there's nothing for it but to wire in and work it out." She sends extra money and will settle the bills when they come. She thanks Ivy for conducting all the business with the Acland without mentioning her name, "which is rather well known in Oxford".

I hope you will have no more health worries with J.A. You must be sick of it. I don't mind saying that I am a little weary, of last years, of illnesses and death-beds! I feel it would be nice to have a year go by without anybody's being operated on or buried – just for a change!

She adds that Mac has not been well recently either.

It was not only her publisher to whom she was under contract.

CHAPTER 17

A Labour of Love

In *Gaudy Night* Harriet Vane and Miss de Vine discuss the relation of the mind to the emotions. Miss de Vine asks, "Isn't the writing of good prose an emotional experience?" Harriet replies: "Yes, of course it is. At least, when you get the thing dead right and know it's dead right, there's no excitement like it. It's marvellous. It makes you feel like God on the Seventh Day – for a bit, anyhow."

In the midst of all the problems of her personal life, Dorothy's creative mind survived. Indeed, the more disrupting the problems were, the more resilient her imaginative powers became. Material circumstances compelled her to keep on writing, but there was another, even stronger compulsion – the desire to create. "My proper job", she told a friend, "is making things with my imagination."

In January 1932 her son was eight years old. He was an intelligent little boy. Ivy was teaching him extremely well and he was advanced for his years. Dorothy took pleasure in his progress. She chose toys for him with care and sent him books, about which he wrote to her. She got to know him on her visits. He called her "Cousin Dorothy" but (so he told friends in adult life) from the age of about six or seven he had an idea she was his mother. Observing his passage through childhood, Dorothy was reminded of her own. Suddenly she felt an urge to get it down on paper. She wrote to Ivy: "In a spasm of middle-agedness the other day [she was thirty-seven], I started to write memoirs of my childhood – but I find I don't remember much about it really!"

The spasm resulted in a brief, unfinished account, called *My Edwardian Childhood* – a strange title, since the first eight years of her life were passed in the Victorian era. The manuscript, which is unpublished, does not continue beyond her fifth year. Although she told Ivy she did not remember much, it in fact contains vivid recollections of Brewer Street, Oxford, and of the rectory in Bluntisham.

After a month or so she stopped. The little excursion into her early past had done its work. Memories, released, came flooding forth and took possession of her creative self. On 17 February she tells Ivy that she must now get on with a new book, "which is to be all about a big church in the Fens, and a grave which is suddenly found to have an extra body in it!!" This became *The Nine Tailors*, a work which surpassed anything she had written.

On 19 April she writes to Ivy about it again:

[It is] all about a country parish in the Fens — you will find some reminiscences of Bluntisham in it, I expect, when it is done — though the actual scene in which it is laid is more like Christchurch. It is all about Bell-ringing, which turns out to be a very complicated and difficult subject. I have had to mug it all up! I'm trying hard to get it done by June, and may succeed, if nobody else goes ill on me.

This was too much to hope. Mac was ill again in May, with liver trouble and nerves. Also, the difficult subject of bell-ringing was taking longer to master than she anticipated. She was obliged, therefore, in order to fulfil her contract, to write another novel quickly, which was less demanding as regards specialised information. This was the spirited, witty and light-hearted *Murder Must Advertise*, set in an advertising agency, for which she could draw on her own experience. It is one of her most entertaining novels and says a great deal for her vitality and zest; yet she told Victor Gollancz that she hated it. On 14 September she wrote:

The new book is nearly done. I hate it because it isn't the one I wanted to write, but I had to shove it in because I couldn't get the technical dope on *The Nine Tailors* in time. Still, you never know what people will fancy, do you? It will tell people a little about the technical side of advertising, which most people aren't inquisitive about, and it deals with the dope-traffic, which is fashionable at the moment, but I don't feel that this part is very convincing, as I can't say "I know dope". Not one of my best efforts. *The Nine Tailors* will be a labour of love — and probably a flop!

Connoisseurs of detective fiction consider *The Nine Tailors* a masterpiece. How and from what did she generate the creative power to write it? The phrase "a labour of love" is one key. Another is a renewal of her interest (on this occasion beneficial) in Wilkie Collins.

In March, at the very time when she was planning *The Nine Tailors*, she told Ivy that she was "easing up a little and writing a peaceful biography of Wilkie Collins", on which she had been engaged, on and off, for four years. The "easing up", after finishing *Have His Carcase*, which she called "a beast of a book", and the peaceful pondering on Collins, allowed her mind to range over a wide terrain and new perspectives.

The biography was never completed but the five chapters which exist contain observations on the qualities she most admired and which she set herself to emulate. Collins was "a master of constructional form", above all, "a plot-maker". She praises the "brilliant landscapes" of *No Name* and *Armadale*, and the "solid portrait painting of *The Moonstone* and *Poor Miss Finch*". Like Reade and Dickens, he knew how to draw romance from familiar, homely things, and she quotes approvingly, "Is not the noblest poetry of prose fiction the poetry of every-day truth?" Examining his technique, she observes how skilfully he fixes the story in the reader's own experience, blending the sensational with the ordinary in a way that made possible the rise of the modern English detective story "to its present position of international supremacy". By firmly binding together the novel of plot and the novel of character, the great Victorians, particularly Collins, Reade and Dickens, she considered, had made possible the appearance in English literature of a novel "as closely knit and logical as the plot of a classical drama".

The broad canvas used by Collins, allowing room for significant themes, enlarged her view of detective fiction. *The Nine Tailors*, unlike its predecessors, is a spacious, panoramic work, constructed on a large scale, involving time and change, the seasons and festivals of the year, the menace of natural forces, death and renewal, guilt and retribution. Interwoven with these solemn issues are lovingly drawn pictures of Fenland villagers. The minor character sketches are among the best she ever did. The central figure, eclipsing even Lord Peter Wimsey (as Hone rightly points out), is the Reverend Theodore Venables, rector of the parish of Fenchurch St Paul – a charming evocation of her father, yet not identical with him, "only" (as she wrote to me in 1948) "in the sense that I know how elderly clergymen tend to go on".

Another quality which she admired in Collins was his attention to detail. He took infinite pains to be accurate, understanding that this was the way to predispose the reader to accept the incredible.

How easily [she wrote] the will to believe may be shattered and

239

dispersed is shown by the indignation with which readers of any modern detective story will pounce upon the most trifling inaccuracy. Arnold Bennett declared that he was unable to put any faith in Mr J. J. Connington's story, *The Case with Nine Solutions*, because his confidence was destroyed at the start by an unimportant technical slip about a telephone-bell. In the art of capturing confidence by the preliminary establishing of a reputation for accuracy, Collins was to prove himself a past-master.

Her own attention to detail in *The Nine Tailors* resulted in the construction of a world which the reader enters and re-enters with a delighted sense of realism or, as she later expressed it in another connection, "a vivid conviction of fact". It is achieved, she said, by "a trick of particularity", such as led people to address letters to "Sherlock Holmes, Esq., 221B Baker Street", asking him to solve their problems. She recognised the same quality in Dante, and in Defoe: "We believe in the Inferno as we believe in Robinson Crusoe's island – because we have trudged on our own feet from end to end of it. We are convinced that it is *there*." In the same way, we are convinced that the village of Fenchurch St Paul is there and that if we had the courage of our conviction and called at the rectory, Mrs Venables would receive us with the same "competent tranquillity" with which she received Lord Peter that snowy New Year's Eve, and that Mr Venables would enthuse to us about bell-ringing, waving his muffin in the air, the butter running down his cuff.

She took trouble – and pleasure – in creating a church – an amalgam of St Peter's in Upwell, St Wendreda's in March and Terrington St Clement's near King's Lynn. She engaged an architect to help her, Mr W. J. Redhead, whom she thanks in the Preface for having "designed for me the noble Parish Church of Fenchurch St Paul and set it about with cherubims". The first edition contains as a frontispiece his drawing of the exterior and a section of the angel roof. She also took pains with the complications of the fen dam and sluice system. Some of the finest writing in the book is found in the descriptions of the church and the desolate dyke and drain landscape.

Her notebooks show the intensive work she devoted to the question of bell-ringing. Sixty-three pages exist, containing detailed notes on bells, bell-cages, bell-inscriptions and the care of bells; forty of them are sheets of changes, on which she spent innumerable hours until she could do any method accurately in her head. Her understanding of this difficult subject was entirely theoretical – she had never pulled a rope in her life. She visualised and *felt* through her imagination what it was like to handle a bell and what it meant to have "rope-sight". In the end, she wrote, "the experts could discern only (I think) three small technical errors which betrayed the lack of practical experience". This made her, she confessed, "sinfully proud".

She had every reason to be proud. The Campanological Society of Great Britain invited her to become their vice-president. *The Oxford Companion to Music* refers the reader to *The Nine Tailors* for a lucid explanation of change-ringing. The book has been praised as "one of the finest examples of a mystery story incorporating specialised knowledge".

The power of the work is derived from more than authenticity, however. The bells are personalities, sinister and threatening; the flood, which could have been prevented had it not been for negligence, comes as an inevitable catastrophe, claiming lives; there is crime – robbery and murder – in the background; there are reminders of the slaughter of the battle of the Marne. The parish church, standing upon an elevation which raises it above the flood, is an Ark in which the villagers take refuge.

The rector is well prepared to meet the disaster. "Good lord, sir," said Wimsey, impressed, "anybody would think you'd done this all your life."

"I have devoted much prayer and thought to the situation in the last few weeks," he replied.

His venerable figure takes on a hieratical, almost a divine aspect as the tragedy accumulates:

> In the church, the Rector, with the electoral roll-call of the parish in his hand, was numbering his flock. He was robed and stoled, and his anxious old face had taken on a look of great pastoral dignity and serenity ... Into the ringing-chamber ... streamed light and sound from the crowded church. The Rector's voice, musical and small, came floating up, past the wings of the floating cherubim:
> "Lighten our darkness ... "

The epic quality of the book was inspired by a work for which she had long had admiration. This was *The Nebuly Coat* by John Meade Falkner, first published in 1903. The action is set in a place called Cullerne, situated two miles from the coast and protected from the sea by a dyke with a sluice. At a spring tide and with a strong southwest wind blowing, the sea could pour over the wall and with heavy rainfall could cause extensive flooding. Towering above the land-scape is a large church — the centre-piece of the story. In the background of the plot is a mystery connected with a prominent local family — as there is in *The Nine Tailors*. The present head is Lord Blandamer, whose arms, the "nebuly coat", are depicted in a window of the church — a shield of argent crossed by nebuly sea-green bars. An architect, named Westray, is engaged in examining the state of the tower. There are impressive descriptions of the bells and of bell-ringing, very similar to corresponding passages in *The Nine Tailors*. The organist is found dead in the organ-loft, in suspicious circumstances. The village is assailed by a violent gale, the tower collapses and Lord Blandamer, who is discovered to have usurped the title, is killed amid the rubble. "My own *Nine Tailors*", Dorothy wrote to a correspondent, "was directly inspired by that remarkable book."

Dorothy L. Sayers had now arrived. *The Nine Tailors*, published in January 1934, became a best-seller and was hugely admired. Charles Williams, who had seen an advance copy, wrote to Victor Gollancz:

> Your Dorothy Sayers ... ! Present her some time with my pro-foundest compliments. It's a marvellous book; it is high imagination — and the incomprehensible splendours of the pre-ludes to each part make a pattern round and through it like the visible laws and the silver waters themselves. But farther! do beg her to go farther, along the awful road of Le Fanu and the spirit that was buried in Vallombrosa — even the Stagnum Ignis itself. You won't do a greater book in all your serious novels this year. The end is unsurpassable. (I dare say I exaggerate, but I've only just finished it and I'm all shaken!)

She was sought after and lionised. She was interviewed for the national press, she lunched with celebrities, she was elected a charter member of the newly founded Sherlock Holmes Society, she had for some time been a leading light of the Detection Club, and was at least part author of their amusing initiation ceremony.

Her output since 1931 (to go no further back) had been amazing. In July of that year, Gollancz published her *Second Series of Great Short Stories of Detection, Mystery and Horror*, for which she wrote another Introduction. In December, *The Floating Admiral* was published by Hodder and Stoughton. This was a composite work by several members of the Detection Club, who each contributed a chapter, as the sisters in *Little Women* did with such success,

Dorothy commented when sending a copy to Ivy. Her chapter is the seventh, which contains the solution. In April 1932 *Have His Carcase* was published, followed in February 1933 by *Murder Must Advertise*. She had also been writing more short stories and had invented a new detective – Monty Egg, the jaunty travelling salesman in wines and spirits, with his amusing jingles quoted from *The Salesman's Handbook*. Mere *Passing Show* material, she called him, writing to Gollancz who had said he liked him. *Hangman's Holiday*, her second collection of short stories, appeared in May 1933. In June of that year, another composite work, *Ask A Policeman*, to which she again contributed, was published by Arthur Barker, Ltd. That month she began reviewing detective fiction for the *Sunday Times*, a weekly commitment which she continued for over two years and which necessitated reading two novels a day.

Meanwhile, Dorothy L. Fleming had not been having such a successful time. Mac's health was a continual anxiety. On 20 February 1933 she wrote to Ivy:

> I do wish his health wasn't so bad. It is better in some ways than it used to be, but he has to go terribly carefully about food and everything, and it makes him awfully depressed and "difficult". All these things are really the result of the War, of course, and you'd be surprised at the number of people who suffer from the same kind of trouble. But it does complicate life!

Dorothy had always been sympathetic about Mac's ailments – his cough, his liver trouble, his neuritis, his rheumatism, particularly affecting his stiff knee which had been shattered as the result of a war injury and caused him to walk with a slight limp. "Mac must always be my first consideration," she wrote, explaining to Ivy in 1930 why they were spending so much time in Kirkcudbright.

But Mac's ill health was not the only problem. He was married to a brilliant and increasingly successful wife. He himself had talents – for journalism, photography and painting – but he was out of work and earning almost nothing. It was a classic situation. He bitterly resented being pointed out as the husband of Dorothy L. Sayers. He took petty revenge by making things difficult for her, insisting that meals should always be punctual (he had long ago given up doing the cooking) and his requirements given prior consideration. He found consolation in whisky and this was often a problem. She took to writing late into the night in order to find uninterrupted time. He further distressed her by deferring his promise to adopt her son.

It is not surprising that in November 1933 the doctor ordered her to take three weeks' complete rest. She announced to Ivy that she would be pushing round the country with a friend and would call on her to discuss a bit of business which would not take long.

The friend was Muriel St Clare Byrne, one of the Somervillians with whom she had kept in touch. She was a specialist in Tudor history and a lecturer in drama at the Royal Academy of Dramatic Art. After Dorothy's death, Muriel related something of the three weeks' motoring holiday they spent together. She noticed that Dorothy seemed very depressed – an effect, partly, of a long period of over-work. There was also another reason: she was trying to decide whether to separate from Mac.

Muriel recalled arriving one evening at a cottage in an Oxfordshire village. Dorothy disappeared inside for a short while, then came out again and invited Muriel in. She remembered meeting Ivy and seeing a girl (Isobel) and a boy of about ten years of age. This was John. Muriel had no idea that he was Dorothy's son and she did not see him again until the day after Dorothy's death, when their meeting was indeed dramatic. He arrived on the doorstep of her house in London, a young man of thirty-three, and asked, "Are you Miss St Clare Byrne?" "Yes," Muriel answered. The unknown young man then said, "I am Dorothy Sayers' son. May I come in?"

Thinking back to their first meeting, Muriel recalled that as they left Ivy's cottage she had noticed that Dorothy was in tears.

By the end of the holiday Dorothy had decided that she would not separate from Mac. He had agreed to the adoption – preliminary papers requiring Ivy's signature were despatched that December – and she felt indebted to him for that. Something had been regularised and John's future would be simplified. Their marriage had not been a total failure. The early years had been happy. Mac had then, as she herself had, great zest for life. He had been a good partner, professionally as well as sexually. She had soon got over her distaste for the products of the rubber shop, expressed so uncompromisingly to Cournos. She could not have coped with any more children so she sensibly took precautions. She was prepared to make enquiries as to the best methods available and a letter written in 1929 to her friend Charis Frankenburg (née Barnett), who was an expert on contraception, shows that on her advice she consulted Dr Helena Wright, the well-known gynaecologist, who fitted her with a Dutch cap.

She and Mac were fond of each other but as time went by they got increasingly on each other's nerves. While Aunt Mabel had been alive she had acted as a "buffer state" between them and they maintained a relationship of armed neutrality. Soon after Mabel's death, Dorothy invited another aunt to stay. This was Aunt Maud, the widow of her mother's brother Henry Leigh, who had been a Fellow of Corpus Christi College. Born Alice Maud Bayliss, she had won a scholarship in history to Somerville Hall, as it then was. Her daughter Margaret Leigh, in her autobiography *The Fruit in the Seed*, has described her childhood in Oxford in the company of this impoverished but undaunted woman. In 1932 Margaret was living in the Scottish Highlands and had induced her mother to join her there. Dorothy wrote to Ivy: "I like Aunt Maud and so does Mac – and she is so intelligent and keen on seeing people and talking about things that it's jolly hard she should, in her old age, be banished so far away and have to get all her meat by post!" Muriel St Clare Byrne recalled that when she stayed in Witham it seemed to her that Aunt Maud was very good at keeping the peace between Dorothy and Mac. The old lady was there for Christmas in 1932 and again early in 1934, when she stayed for six weeks. Dorothy offered her a permanent home with them but Aunt Maud felt obligations towards her daughter. It was a family pattern to which Dorothy was accustomed and it may be that she derived psychological support from it. It seems also that Aunt Maud was an agreeable companion, which was no doubt some solace in that household.

They were in domestic difficulties again that year. The young couple whom they had engaged to help them in the house were expecting a baby, "and of course", Dorothy wrote to Muriel, "we are treating the matter with imbecile indulgence, as we knew we should". But how Mac's temper would react to the baby she did not know. He was now suffering from high blood-pressure.

In August there was serious cause for concern. Dorothy had found a letter dating from June, unopened, under a pile of books, which Mac should have forwarded to her at her flat in Great James Street. She reported to Ivy:

Mac is getting so queer and unreliable that it is not safe to trust him to do anything at all, and if he is told that he has forgotten anything, he goes into such a frightful fit of rage that one gets really alarmed. The doctors say that he is getting definitely queer – but there doesn't seem to be much that one can do about it . . .

[It may be] due to some kind of germ or disease or shock or something – probably a result of the War . . . It also makes the financial position very awkward, as he can't earn any money, and what with his illness and the difficulty of managing his odd fits of temper and so on, it isn't easy for me to get any work done regularly or properly . . . I can't explain to you how difficult things are. There seems no remedy for them but patience.

By then Dorothy L. Sayers, whose job it was to make things with her imagination, was already embarked on another masterpiece.

CHAPTER 18

A City Sanctified

Dorothy L. Sayers now basked in admiration and acclaim. As a detective novelist she had attained a new height. Where should she go from here? There remained the unfinished business of Lord Peter Wimsey and Harriet Vane. She had left them, at the end of *Have His Carcase*, hurriedly packing their bags, eager to dine in Piccadilly. Since then, there had been only one fleeting reference to Harriet, and even then she is not named. In chapter 7 of *Murder Must Advertise*, after a telephone conversation with Pamela Dean, who is beginning to show an embarrassing desire for his company, Wimsey says to himself:

> "I hope she isn't going to make an awkwardness. You cannot trust these young women. No fixity of purpose. Except, of course, when you particularly want them to be yielding."
>
> He grinned with a wry mouth and went out to keep his date with the one young woman who showed no signs of yielding to him, and what he said or did on that occasion is in no way related to this story.

As far as *The Nine Tailors* is concerned, Harriet might never have existed.

Dorothy's next task was to pick up the threads of the love-story she had begun in *Strong Poison* and bring it as best she could to the conclusion she had intended. Thus far, her way was plain. But she deferred taking it. Instead, she did something quite unexpected. At the height of her success, she changed course and even changed her name. She began a novel of a totally different kind, under the pseudonym of Johanna Leigh. The title of the work is *Cat o' Mary*. Reference has already been made to it as an indirect source of information concerning Dorothy's early years.

The manuscript, which is unpublished, consists of about 200 pages. The perplexing title is explained at the outset: it is an adaptation of a phrase from a poem by Kipling, "The Sons of Martha".

> The sons of Mary seldom bother; they have inherited
> that good part;
> But the sons of Martha favour their mother of the
> careful soul and the troubled heart.

The book sets out to tell the life-story of a woman named Katherine ("Cat") Lammas who, after marriage and motherhood, will seek fulfilment in the life of the mind. Her unusual surname was perhaps intended to suggest harvest. Like Mary in the New Testament, who chose the better part, and like Hilary Thorpe in *The Nine Tailors*, whose creative imagination will bring benefits in her maturity, Katherine Lammas is destined to reap a harvest in her later life.

The novel is manifestly autobiographical, at least in the first and largest section. This is consecutive as far as the illness which Katherine suffers at boarding-school, corresponding to Dorothy's own at the Godolphin, and there breaks off. There remain two shorter sections, also incomplete, in which Katherine appears as a married woman.

The circumstances and events of Katherine's childhood and schooldays correspond closely to Dorothy's. Names of places and people are barely disguised. Bluntisham becomes Fentisham, Ivy becomes Myrtle, Miss White becomes Miss Green, Violet (Christy) becomes Rose, and so on.

It is not known when precisely Dorothy started on this new story, but towards the end of the manuscript there is an allusion to A. P. Herbert's novel, *Holy Deadlock*, which was published in April 1934. This means that she was still at work on it at that date and perhaps for some time afterwards. The length of the manuscript suggests that it took her about two or three months to write it. She was sufficiently confident of completing it to allow it to be announced as forthcoming in the *New York Times Book Review* of 14 October 1934. It was announced again as forthcoming in July 1935 in a new edition of *Whose Body?* among a list of her works, but this may or may not have been with her consent.

The beginning of the novel is a continuation and enrichment of *My Edwardian Childhood*, which she had begun and left aside two years before. The descriptions of her home in Oxford and in Bluntisham and of the members of her family are extremely vivid, almost tangible, revealing a power of recall and reconstruction for which her detective novels had offered little scope. The nearest she had come to anything comparable is to be found in *The Nine Tailors*, but *Cat o' Mary* is more personal and in consequence more intimate and moving.

The account of Katherine's experience of boarding-school is a brilliant re-creation of adolescent fears, embarrassments, ambition, love, intellectual excitements and religious uncertainties. Parts of this section are as good as anything she ever wrote and show her unrealised potential as an author of the psychological novel.

Although the story follows Dorothy's life so closely, there are enough differences to show that fictionalisation and adaptation have taken place. A marked change occurs in the two sections in which Katherine is an adult. In the first of these she has just discovered she is pregnant and is shown reacting in a brisk, no-nonsense, unsentimental way, resentful of the solicitude of her husband and her mother. In the second, she is shown reacting in an equally brisk, business-like way to the discovery that her husband has a mistress and wants a divorce. Their two children are both almost grown up and Katherine sees this as an opportunity to resume intellectual work. The story breaks off at this point. It has to be said that in these sections Dorothy's touch is less sure. The characters of Katherine and her husband are poorly drawn and their dialogue strikes an unconvincing note.

In the article entitled "Gaudy Night", which has been mentioned, Dorothy L. Sayers explained to her public that, while looking about for some means of putting Harriet on an equal footing with Peter,

> [I was at the same time] playing with the idea of a "straight" novel, about an Oxford woman graduate who found, in middle life, and after a reasonably satisfactory experience of marriage and motherhood, that her real vocation and full emotional fulfilment were to be found in the creative life of the intellect.

This may well have been her original intention, but what she says here does not, in fact, tally with the manuscript of *Cat o' Mary*. All her care and the best of her creative powers have been given to the detailed and beautifully written section on Katherine's early years. This does not in itself conflict with her statement. The difficulty is that this section contains a discordant element which seems to be the main thrust and *raison d'être* of the book. This can be perceived in the full title: *Cat o' Mary: The Biography of a Prig.* The subtitle scarcely prepares the reader for a novel of which the main theme is intellectual fulfilment.

The psychological drive which powered the first section was strange indeed. At the age of forty, Dorothy looks back on the child she was and takes a violent dislike to her. Some of the passages are startling in the self-disgust which they express:

> If egotism, greed, covetousness, cruelty and sloth are sins, then children possess that original sinfulness in high degree . . . When Katherine in later years looked back on the childish figure that had been herself, it was with a hatred of anything so lacking in those common virtues which were to be attained in after years at so much cost and with such desperate difficulty. She saw through no rosy mist of illusion; she must, she knew, have been a disagreeable child. Strangers rightly considered her a prig.

"The judgment", comments Brabazon, "is merciless." So it is, but it does not follow that it is a true one. *My Edwardian Childhood* contains no tone of censure or self-condemnation. Neither do her letters in which she recalls her early years. All her first-person recollections of herself as a child are sunny, amused, tolerant, neither self-admiring, nor unduly self-critical. Yet again and again in *Cat o' Mary* she strikes a blow at the little girl she portrays: "She liked correcting other people, but didn't like being corrected herself, and would argue a point with obstinacy. She had a great opinion of her own cleverness, and to be proved wrong was humiliating." And again: "As time went on, Katherine developed all the faults and peculiarities of an only child whose entire life is spent among grown-up people. She was self-absorbed, egotistical, timid, priggish, and, in a mild sort of way, disobedient." In the summer of 1915, just after going down from Oxford, Dorothy wrote from Bluntisham to her friend Muriel Jaeger, telling her about a young man whom she thought conceited:

> God forgive me for calling anybody conceited – I've suffered too much from the accusation myself. Is a prig the same thing? Because that's what he is. Please tell me next time you write how you define priggishness, and is it conceit, or isn't it rather a kind of inelasticity?

It is not known how Muriel Jaeger replied but it does not seem that at that date Dorothy numbered herself among the prigs.

Why, then, in the first three months of 1934, a triumphant period in her professional life, did she feel this need for self-flagellation? Was she taking refuge from fame? The assuming of a false name and a fictitious *persona* – two masks – suggests that she was. Or could it be that the recent near break-up of her marriage compelled her to examine her character for fundamental flaws? Why was she so unsuccessful in her sexual relations, while at the same time so successful in the use of her mind and her creative talent? The notes she left for the continuation of *Cat o' Mary* appear to indicate that some such problem was troubling her. Concerning the personal relationships of Katherine Lammas, she scribbled: "Get in strongly the feeling that 'inside me I don't really care'." Another note reads: "I have made a muck of all my emotional relationships and I hate being beaten, so I pretend not to care." This is followed by: "It isn't that I've failed and pretend not to care. I don't care; and that is why I have failed." We do not know what made Dorothy plunge so deeply and unhappily into her psyche at this time, but it is fairly clear why she broke off writing *Cat o' Mary*.

On 13 June 1934, her forty-first birthday, she attended a gaudy at Somerville College. Two days before, she had written about it to Muriel St Clare Byrne: did she think that a very dark blue-grey coat and skirt would be suitable for full academical dress? She didn't want to have to buy a black coat and skirt, which would be "a damned nuisance – me being so outsize".

The occasion was the celebration of Miss Mildred Pope's appointment to the chair of French at Manchester. Dorothy was invited to propose a toast to the University of Oxford. Nineteen years had passed since she had qualified for her degree. She was now another person – a successful author, as the world knew her, but, in private, a woman who had betrayed her personal self and was unhappy about it. Making her speech from the dais of the High Table, a large, commanding figure in M.A. gown and hood, she dwelt movingly on all that she felt to be of enduring value at Oxford:

We in this college are this term bidding farewell to a woman who, to all who knew her, has always seemed to typify some of the noblest things for which this University stands: the integrity of judgment that gain cannot corrupt, the humility in face of the facts that self-esteem cannot blind; the generosity of a great mind that is eager to give praise to others; the singleness of purpose that pursues knowledge as some men pursue glory and that will not be contented with the second-hand or the second-best. Mildred Pope would be the first to say that Oxford made her what she is; we say that it is the spirit of scholars like her that has made Oxford anything at all.

Dorothy's visit to Oxford was providential. In the article referred to she says what then occurred:

> While investigating the possibilities of this subject [a novel about the intellectual life], I was asked to go to Oxford and propose the toast of the University at a College Gaudy dinner. I had to ask myself exactly what it was for which one had to thank a university education, and came to the conclusion that it was, before everything, that habit of intellectual integrity which is at once the foundation and the result of scholarship.

She knew then that she had found the solution to the problem of Peter and Harriet: "On the intellectual platform, alone of all others, Harriet could stand free and equal with Peter, since in that sphere she had never been false to her own standards." Secondly, the choice of theme would also solve a problem of her own: "By choosing a plot which should exhibit intellectual integrity as the one great permanent value in an emotionally unstable world I should be saying the thing that, in a confused way, I had been wanting to say all my life." Thirdly, the structural problem of combining theme and plot would likewise be solved: "Finally, I should have found a universal theme which could be made integral both to the detective plot and to the 'love-interest' which I had, somehow or other, to unite with it." The ultimate result of this flash of illumination was the novel, *Gaudy Night*.

The dominant theme of this novel is love. Not only is the love-story of Peter and Harriet brought to a happy conclusion; the whole work is the consummation of the author's long-standing love affair with Oxford.

The rapturous enamourment of her student days which inspired her first volume of poems, the homesickness she felt during her absences, longing for "the curve of the High and Radcliffe Square by moonlight", the "Oxford fever" against which she did battle by playing Bach and Schubert on the piano, her delighted return to "a city sanctified", as she called it, to work for Basil Blackwell, all this had been driven underground by the pressure of overwhelming events.

Some portion of it had been tentatively released in *My Edwardian Childhood*. The opening quotation, "I am a citizen of no mean city", followed by the proud statement that she had been baptised in Christ Church Cathedral (she also mentioned her confirmation in yet another cathedral – Salisbury), had stirred a tremor of long-suppressed emotions. Her severe self-scrutiny in *Cat o' Mary* had brought her face to face with her dissatisfactions. One of Katherine Lammas' problems is that she is never sure what she really feels. Consequently she is fiercely on her guard against being persuaded, or persuading herself, into feelings which she does not genuinely possess. This perplexity also troubles Harriet Vane in *Gaudy Night*. When, in adulthood, Katherine frees herself from family ties and prepares to return to intellectual life, what kind of fulfilment will she find? *Cat o' Mary* does not answer this question. *Gaudy Night* does.

Dorothy's visit to Oxford in June 1934 clarified many things. She had known the destructive power of uncontrolled emotion in her affair with John Cournos. She had known the emptiness of sexual desire without love in her affair with Bill White. For some years, marriage had brought stability and a measure of happiness but was now cracking under the strain of circumstances. As a result of these experiences she did not trust emotion in her personal life and she had also found, in *The Documents in the Case*, that she lacked the courage to handle it in depth as a writer. She had confidence only in her intellect and in her ability to create and construct.

The illumination she experienced at Oxford revealed to her clearly what it was she most valued: a love of learning for its own sake, the impersonal pursuit of truth and, in all things, intellectual integrity. She also discovered that assent to these ideals was in her case no mere cold abstraction. Passionate feeling accompanied conviction. A fusion of mind and heart occurred; what her intellect believed in she also loved. Her self was no longer divided.

This is brought out in a letter she wrote in September 1935 to Muriel St Clare Byrne. She had just completed *Gaudy Night*. Muriel, who had been reading it chapter by chapter, had raised doubts about the average reader's interest in Oxford as it really was. Could Dorothy not write it up in a way to appeal more to the general public? Dorothy replied indignantly:

To make a deliberate falsification for personal gain is the last, worst depth to which either scholar or artist can descend in work or in life: which, as it happens, is what *Gaudy Night* is about. Here, of course, the theme of the plot is also the theme of the book, and, indeed, the whole theme of the Peter-Harriet complication as well: I mean, that no relation can ever be sound that is not founded in faith to the fact. *So that, unless the heart and mind are brought into this relation, they must be kept apart or produce nothing but discord.* [My italics]

Muriel had also said that the book was too autobiographical. Dorothy retorted:

As for "autobiography", it is, of course, autobiographical to pre- cisely the same extent as parts of *The Nine Tailors, Murder Must Advertise, The Bellona Club* and *Five Red Herrings,* in the sense that it deals with a background which I personally know; the whole book is personal (though not autobiographical) in the sense that it presents a consistent philosophy of conduct for which I am prepared to assume personal responsibility.

She knows that people will say (again) that they can't see what Peter sees in Harriet: "Peter has said what he sees – he has told her. He is seen only through her eyes (almost exclusively) and she is the focal point of the book. He is the catalyst, which, itself unchanged, changes everything." She agrees that *Gaudy Night* is not a detective story at all, but a novel of an almost entirely psychological kind, with a mild detective interest: "But the plot . . . is part of the theme. The same fundamental treason to the mind which wrecks a man's career might have wrecked the Peter-Harriet relationship – but they refused to allow it." The conviction which binds the book together is the same bond which unites all the Oxford characters. She adds that she will no longer write what she is expected to write but only what there is to be written.

Dorothy denied that *Gaudy Night* was autobiographical. Indeed, in the Author's Note at the beginning of the book she categorically states, "None of the characters I have placed upon this public stage has any counterpart in real life." This is disingenuous, to say the least. Miss Lydgate has an obvious counterpart in Miss Mildred Pope. The Dean, Miss Martin, is based on another Somerville don, as Dorothy candidly admitted in a letter to me. This is not to say that they are identical with their models. "Most fictitious characters", Dorothy wrote to another friend, "are bits of patchwork – a trait here and a trait there."

Harriet Vane, however, is a great deal more than patchwork and, for that reason, all the more credible. Throughout the novel,

Dorothy's own life, her experience as a writer of detective fiction, her personality, her thoughts and feelings, her very way of talking, even her appearance, run parallel with Harriet's, lending solidity and resonance.

Like Harriet, Dorothy has been separated from her Oxford past, "cut off as though by swords from the bitter years that lay between". Dorothy, like Harriet, is afraid to trust her emotions, finding security only in her work which she has never betrayed. Harriet, and perhaps Dorothy at times, is filled with longing to lose herself in some impersonal, scholarly piece of research, away from the pressures and confusion of an author's life with its continual distraction of publisher's contracts, blurbs, publicity and rivalries. There comes back to her the vision of an old desire, "standing up unmistakable, like a tower set on a hill. 'Once, I was a scholar'". Harriet has immense respect and affection for the community of women dons of Shrewsbury College, as Dorothy had for Somerville. Both enjoy intellectual debate and the civilised exchange of ideas. The conversation at High Table, when Lord Peter comes to dine, which is continued afterwards in the Senior Common Room, while it skilfully serves both theme and plot, is also a *tour de force* in intellectual elegance which can scarcely have been surpassed in modern fiction.

Harriet's thoughts about Oxford are also Dorothy's. She takes pride in her status as a Senior Member of the university: "They can't take this away, at any rate. Whatever I may have done since, this remains. Scholar, Master of Arts; Domina, Senior Member of this University . . . a place achieved, inalienable, worthy of reverence." And she quotes to herself from the mediaeval Latin of the University Statutes: "*statutum est quod Juniores Senioribus debitam et congruam reverentiam tum in privato tum in publico exhibeant.*" (It is laid down by Statute that Junior Members shall both in private and in public show due and suitable respect for Seniors.) Latin phrases are threaded through the work at intervals like a decorative motif, culminating in a proposal of marriage which echoes words from the degree ceremony, thereby joining the love-story of Harriet Vane and Peter Wimsey, both Oxford graduates, to the inalienable privilege they share.

Harriet, listening to the after-dinner speech by the Warden of Shrewsbury, is Dorothy at Somerville exulting in the achievements of women scholars, of one in particular, her beloved tutor, Miss Mildred Pope. "In the glamour of one Gaudy night", thinks Harriet, "one could realise that one was a citizen of no mean city", echoing the very quotation with which Dorothy began *My Edwardian*

Childhood. In still more exalted mood, Harriet continues to contemplate her vision of Oxford: "her foundations were set upon the holy hills and her spires touched heaven".

Harriet's conversations with the ruthlessly intellectual scholar, Helen de Vine, are particularly revealing. It is fatal, says Miss de Vine, to pay the slightest attention to people who expect you to feel what you do not feel. "I never know what I do feel," says Harriet. How is one to know what course to take or what is important? She will know that, Miss de Vine tells her, when it has overmastered her. Harriet looks back on her life. Through all her turmoil, she had somehow stuck to her job of writing. She had written what she felt called upon to write. "It had overmastered her without her knowledge or notice, and that was the proof of its mastery."

Miss de Vine agrees with Harriet as to the difficulties of combining intellectual and emotional interests. "But if", she says, "you are once sure of what you do want, you find that everything else goes down before it like grass under a roller – all other interests, your own and other people's." The problem of reconciling brain and heart comes up also in conversations between Harriet and Peter, for this is one of the impediments in their relationship.

But first something had to be done to convert Lord Peter Wimsey from a Bertie Wooster-Ralph Lynn lightweight to someone acceptable as Harriet's husband. Some measure of development had actually been in progress ever since *Whose Body?* In *The Nine Tailors*, though he is, in his creator's words, "extraneous to the story and untouched by its spiritual conflicts", he has acquired depths of sympathy and sensitivity. But, if he was to match Harriet, it would be necessary "to perform a major operation upon him":

> Peter had got to become a complete human being, with a past and a future, with a consistent family and social history, with a complicated psychology and even the rudiments of a religious outlook. And all this would have to be squared somehow or other with such random attributes as I had bestowed upon him over a series of years in accordance with the requirements of various detective plots.

The operation was successful. The alteration was so skilfully carried out that we are gulled into believing that the Lord Peter, "fair and Mayfair", of the earlier novels is potentially the mature, responsible, believable Lord Peter of *Gaudy Night*. In fact, on re-reading, we unconsciously transfer back from *Gaudy Night* what we know about him there.

In *Gaudy Night* he is deeply in love. Having blundered in *Strong Poison*, he is now aware of the need for patience and restraint. Harriet must have time to recover from the burden of gratitude she owes him for having saved her life. As readers we are involved in their problem and want it to be resolved, as we are involved in Philip Trent's love for Mrs Manderson in E. C. Bentley's *Trent's Last Case*. There had always been a number of similarities, especially in mannerisms, between Trent and Wimsey. Dorothy confessed to E. C. Bentley how ashamed she was to think how much her "poor Peter" owed to his Trent. In *Gaudy Night*, it is Trent's serious qualities which are taken over – his social conscience, his concern for international relations, his fear of a coming war, his distaste for propaganda and special pleading.

The sexual current which runs through *Gaudy Night* like an electrical charge is the more powerful for not being overt and explicit. Harriet spends much of her energy resisting it, running away from Peter, from herself and from her full potential as a writer. On one occasion, her physical feeling for Peter is revealed to her in a dream but her conscious mind brushes it aside. When she sends for him it is as a detective, not a lover. Unable to solve the Shrewsbury mystery, she turns to him for help. He enters the all-female community – a sole male whose attractiveness is as potentially explosive, Harriet later realises, as dynamite in a munitions factory.

He makes no attempt to exert the force of his personality on Harriet; rather the reverse – to her he exposes his weaknesses. Once, when she dines with him in London, he has two cracked ribs, an injury incurred while climbing a wall to escape from an assailant armed with a gun. His condition has the effect of slightly softening Harriet's heart towards him. When he calls on her at Shrewsbury, he has just returned from Rome and Warsaw, where he had been sent on an exhausting and inconclusive mission by the Foreign Office. Harriet notices, with unwonted concern, that he looks tired to death. He reveals to her his misgivings about the international situation and his feelings of guilt at having turned his back on so many traditions which in his heart he still values. Like Harriet, he wishes it were possible to take refuge in Oxford and lose oneself in some obscure piece of scholarship "for the love of the job and nothing more". She is astonished to hear him echo her own thoughts and with so much passion.

They spend the afternoon on the river in a punt. Faultlessly attired in white, they behave towards each other with Edwardian courtesy and decorum. Peter has come provided with a tea-basket; Harriet has brought with her the dossier she has compiled on the college mystery, which Peter studies, reclining against the cushions of the punt. In an unguarded moment, for a second time, Harriet is made aware of the nature of her feelings for him. While he reads, she studies his half-averted face:

> The flat setting and fine scroll work of the ear, and the height of the skull above it. The glitter of close-cropped hair where the neck muscles lifted to meet the head. A minute sickle-shaped scar on the left temple . . . The faint laughter-lines at the corner of the eye and the droop of the lid at its outer end. The gleam of gold down on the cheek-bone. The wide spring of the nostril. An almost imperceptible beading of sweat on the upper lip and a tiny muscle that twitched the sensitive corner of the mouth. The slight sun-reddening of the fair skin and its sudden whiteness below the base of the throat. The little hollow above the points of the collar bone.
>
> He looked up; and she was instantly scarlet, as though she had been dipped in boiling water.

This is the first time that she, and the reader, is aware of him other than as "the familiar intelligence that lived and moved so curiously behind an oddly amusing set of features". She knows what has caused the sudden surge in her blood, and so does he. They make no move, but after a moment's pause, continue to discuss the Shrewsbury affair. Then, putting that aside, they fall silent for a while. When Harriet next looks at him she finds he is asleep.

The term "sub-text" had not been invented then, but that is precisely what Dorothy L. Sayers, so often ahead of her time, here deliberately provides. What might have taken place between Peter and Harriet at this point is as much a part of the scene as their non-action. Such dual awareness was reinforced for contemporary readers by a recent memory of another novel.

Reference has already been made, in connection with *The Documents in the Case*, to F. Tennyson Jesse's handling of a love-story based on the Thompson-Bywaters case in *A Pin to See the Peepshow*, which preceded *Gaudy Night* by three years. At one point, the lovers, Julia and Leo, rest together in a punt on a lake and Leo falls asleep. Julia contemplates him:

> She felt the melting pity that every imaginative human being feels on looking at the helplessness of sleep. "Sleep, the little death". Where had she heard that? It was true, anyway. How helpless and

oddly innocent he looked, his young mouth slightly open and his thick lashes upon his cheeks . . . helplessness in the withdrawing of his mind; of the safeguard, when awake, the mind exercises over the body. It was as though he lay there helpless, at the mercy of anyone who saw him . . . it was as though everyone were helpless in sleep, without the majesty of death. Death was majestic . . . nothing she, or anyone else, could do, could hurt a dead person any more. But a sleeping person lay inviting wounds, ready to be chilled by a breath, yielding, infinitely pathetic.

A comparison with Harriet's reflections as she contemplates Peter lying asleep reveals interesting similarities:

Asleep he undoubtedly was. And here was Miss Harriet Vane, gone suddenly sympathetic, afraid to move for fear of waking him . . . "How wonderful", says the poet, "is Death, Death and his brother Sleep!" And, having asked whether Ianthe will wake again and being assured that she will, he proceeds to weave many beautiful thoughts about Ianthe's sleep. From which we may fairly deduce that he (like Henry who kneeled in silence by her couch) felt tenderly towards Ianthe. For another person's sleep is the acid test of our own sentiments. Unless we are savages, we react kindly to death, whether of friend or enemy . . . Death is the ultimate weakness, and we dare not insult it. But sleep is only an illusion of weakness . . . we look down on the sleeper, thus exposing himself in all his frailty.

This is an intriguing salutation from one author to another. But it is more than that. The difference between the two similar situations is significant. The relationship of Julia and Leo is adulterous and brings them to a hideous end. The bond, as yet unexpressed, between Peter and Harriet, remains in a state of tension until the honesty which solves the Shrewsbury problem removes at the same time all psychological impediments to their union. Their coming together is a matter not only of physical passion but of intellectual conviction, a union of heart and brain. It is also part of Dorothy's vision of Oxford. "There's something about this place", said Peter . . . "that alters all one's values."

Thus it is that when he again proposes to Harriet, promising that this time if she says No he will accept her answer, he finds the form of words which enables her to say Yes.

With a gesture of submission he bared his head and stood gravely, the square cap dangling in his hand.

"*Placetne, magistra?*"

"*Placet.*"

The words "*placetne?*" and "*placet*" ("does it please?" – "it pleases") are uttered at a degree ceremony when a candidate is presented for graduation. The young Dorothy had described just such a ceremony in her letter to Catherine Godfrey many years ago – the occasion when she first set eyes on Maurice Roy Ridley, who was to become, though she had forgotten, a model for Lord Peter. When the degrees are conferred, the Proctors walk round so that anyone objecting may "pluck" the proctorial robes and protest. This did not occur in the case of Harriet and Peter:

The Proctor, stumping grimly past with averted eyes, reflected that Oxford was losing all sense of dignity. But what could he do? If Senior Members of the University chose to stand – in their gowns, too! – closely and passionately embracing in New College Lane right under the Warden's windows, he was powerless to prevent it. He primly settled his white bands and went upon his walk unheeded; and no hand plucked his velvet sleeve.

CHAPTER 19

Joy's Bonfire

In *Gaudy Night* the serious side of Dorothy L. Sayers is uppermost. This had not been given public utterance before. Acknowledging a telegram of congratulations from Victor Gollancz in September 1935, she wrote:

> It is the only book I've written embodying any kind of a "moral" and I do feel rather passionately about this business of the integrity of the mind – but I realise that to make a "detective story" the vehicle for that kind of thing is (as Miss de Vine says of the Peter-Harriet marriage) "reckless to the point of insanity". But there it is – it's the book I wanted to write and I've written it – and it is now my privilege to leave you with the baby! Whether you advertise it as a love-story or as educational propaganda, or as a lunatic freak, I leave to you. It may be highly unpopular; but though I wouldn't claim that it was in itself a work of great literary importance, it is important to me, and I only hope it won't be a ghastly flop!

There had always been a lighter side to Dorothy's nature, which not even the worst moments of her life had extinguished. As many of her letters show and as her friends remember, her sense of fun was irrepressible.

One day, while she was still in the early stages of writing *Gaudy Night*, a sweep was sent for to clear the chimneys at 24 Newland Street, Witham. There is a superstition that chimney-sweeps bring good fortune. This one certainly did. We do not know his name but we know something about his appearance. It must have been winter because he arrived wearing several layers of pullovers which, as he warmed to his task, he peeled off, at intervals, one after the other, to Dorothy's fascinated gaze. He is immortalised as Tom Puffett in her novel *Busman's Honeymoon*:

> He was an exceedingly stout man, rendered still stouter by his costume. This had reached what, in recent medical jargon, is known as "a high degree of onionisation", consisting as it did of a greenish-black coat and trousers and a series of variegated pullovers one on top of the other, which peeped out at the throat in a graduated scale of décolleté.

Mr Puffett removes his coat and reveals his outermost sweater "in a glory of red and yellow horizontal stripes"; later, removing this, he displays a blue one; underneath that is one of emerald green; this is finally peeled off to leave him "arrayed in a Fair-Isle jumper of complicated pattern", in which he renewed his attack upon the chimney.

A few days after this event, Dorothy went to London and called on her friends Muriel St Clare Byrne and Marjorie Barber, who shared a house in St John's Wood. Always a great teller of an amusing tale, she made the most of this one, ending, as she often did, with tears of merriment running down her face. She said what a splendid stage character the sweep would make and how much she would like to put him in a play — for his manner of speech had been as entertaining as his strip-tease act. "Why don't you?" said Muriel.

For some time, Muriel had been helping Dorothy to weed out the numerous attempts that were then being made at putting Wimsey on the stage or screen. Dorothy had herself written a scenario for a film entitled *The Silent Passenger*, but, as is the way of the film world, though she had been promised editorial control, the script was altered beyond recognition. She had felt thoroughly out of her element and resolved never to have anything more to do with films.

The theatre, however, was different. She had always loved the stage, but lacked the technique to write for it. She said she would like to try, but only if Muriel would help her. They began to talk about it at once. From the beginning, what interested them both was theatrical technique and practicality. No moral was intended, no social message, no passionate concern for integrity. This was to be a detective *comedy*. The game was to devise a means whereby the "fair-play" rule, which Dorothy demanded of detective fiction, could be made to work on the stage. The clues to the murder must be as obvious to the audience as to the detective and yet the final solution should come as a dramatic revelation.

It was not unusual for Dorothy to work on more than one book at a time. (According to one of her secretaries, she kept her separate working papers in different rooms of the house.) While writing *The Documents in the Case*, for instance, she was also at work on *Strong Poison*. Also products of a twin gestation were *Murder Must Advertise* and *The Nine Tailors*. So now, while writing her deeply committed, idealistic novel *Gaudy Night* ("the book I wanted to write"), Dorothy L. Sayers, the maker of solemn speeches at college dinners, was also light-heartedly engaged in the stage-craft of comedy. Muriel provided professional expertise, tightening the dialogue, sharpening a climax, strengthening the dramatic impact of the end of an act. Dorothy thought out the method of murder and devised the action. They worked joyfully together, respecting each other's complementary skills. The play they produced was *Busman's Honeymoon*, the predecessor of the novel of the same title.

They were already at work on it in February 1935. By the middle of March they had sketched out Act II. That was the month when Dorothy, invited to lecture on "Aristotle and the Art of Detective Fiction", went to Oxford and, entering the lecture room, came face to face with Roy Ridley. "My God!" she said to herself, "it's Peter Wimsey!" And she wrote (as has been quoted) to Muriel, expressing her heart-broken regret that he was not an actor but the chaplain of Balliol.

On 15 March, back in Witham, she is eager to get on with the play, "as soon as I have succeeded in removing Harriet from the College gate, where she is at present standing, poor girl, first on one leg and then on the other, while Wimsey and the porter exchange war reminiscences." This shows that she had then reached chapter 17. The action of *Busman's Honeymoon*, in which Peter and Harriet are married, was running far ahead of the novel. It would take another six chapters to get them engaged. They were not making it easy for her. As late as June, she wrote: "Peter and Harriet are the world's most awkward pair of lovers – both so touchy and afraid to commit themselves to anything but hints and allusions!" The craftsmanship involved in writing a comedy was giving her immense pleasure and satisfaction. Concerning construction, she wrote to Muriel on 1 April:

By the way, with what curious and (to me) unconscious symmetry we have builded to make, not only one, but all the masks come off, one after the other, in Act II, scene 1 – Bunter, Crutchley, Miss Twitterton and finally Harriet and Peter, by whose central sincerity all the rest are, as it were, put to the proof! . . . I was simply thinking of making a dramatic contrast in the two love scenes, and put the Bunter bit in for sheer fun — but the thing seems to have made its own symbolism as it went along, which appears to me to be the right way about.

Holding a balance between the detective plot and the emotions of the characters was not easy, but the problem fascinated her. On 30 March she had written:

I think that in this scene [the dialogue between Kirk and Sellon in Act II] my mind has been so closely set upon the construction of the thing — the making it water-tight — that I have probably missed some of the necessary emotion. This, as you know, is the prime difficulty of detective denouements.

I have also been worried by keeping the balance between the comedy note — which must be kept going — and the tragic note — which is bound to creep in if a real murderer is going to be really detected and hanged. The least tip the wrong way, and the thing will become either heartless or really grim. I think Miss Twitterton's attitude is fairly well worked out, in outline. She has got to be rescued from the Crutchley-complex and the inferiority complex, if she is not to be left as a tragic figure. Hence the insistence upon the importance and grandeur of the funeral. For country people, a funeral simply DOES make all the difference. It comforts and sustains them in a way you and I would find preposterous. I remember a woman who had lost a son in the war and who said to my Mother, at the end of a Memorial Service which Dad had held for all the fallen, in a packed church: "It's almost worth while to lose a son, to have such a beautiful service held over him." That is a fact. But I can well believe that with my mind fixed on establishing the when, how and where of the crime, I may have failed to get these things over. Please don't mind altering anything at all that seems to you weak or inadequate. I trust your judgment quite implicitly.

Her new experience was releasing a surge of happiness. This was reinforced at home by the enjoyable company of Aunt Maud, who played an important part in Dorothy's life at this time and not only as a buffer between her and Mac. On 6 May 1934 she had written to Ivy: "We enjoy having her [Aunt Maud] with us — in fact we get on remarkably well together. Just hurrying to town to the Detection Club. I'm taking Aunt Maud, who is quite pathetically delighted at the idea of a party!" She describes her as "very sporting and intelligent" and, in a letter to E. C. Bentley, as "a woman of great ability and an immense appreciation of beautiful writing". Dorothy evidently discussed *Gaudy Night* with her, for she tells Muriel that she is taking a sympathetic interest in the breaking down of Harriet's inhibitions. In September 1935, when the novel was finished, it was Aunt Maud whom Dorothy chose as a companion to rejoice with. She describes the occasion in a letter to Muriel: "Aunt Maud and I went up to town for a couple of nights to celebrate Peter's engagement with a binge and two theatres." They saw an open-air performance of *Love's Labour's Lost* in Regent's Park: "glorious sunshine, warm air, good seats, outburst of blossom in the rosery, a good performance . . . Why do people call *Love's Labour's Lost* a bad play? [It must be] one of the most *réussi* things of its kind ever made . . . it's all pure fairy-tale; and some of the loveliest lines in the lyrical-witty mode ever written."

By then the play *Busman's Honeymoon* had been completed. It was sent to Maurice Browne, the theatrical producer, who kept it until January 1936, trying to find financial backing. He did not succeed. It was then sent to Anmer Hall, who did. Dennis Arundell was cast as Lord Peter and Veronica Turleigh as Harriet, or "Lady Peter Wimsey", as she had then become. Rehearsals began in November 1936.

Dorothy was now in her element. A new phase of her life had begun which was to bring her much happiness and some prosperity. She found herself in the uninhibited world of actors. "There was I", she once said to me, talking about this period of her life, "stiff in my ways with strangers, suddenly plunged among people who called each other 'darling' at first sight and immediately embraced without the slightest embarrassment." She loved it and responded warmly. She found herself once again able to enjoy life and to indulge in fun.

She had recently made two new friends who were to become important to her. One was the novelist Helen Simpson, whose witty conversation and letters delighted her. Born in Australia, of a French mother, Helen had inherited a Gallic cast of mind. One of her short stories, "A Posteriori", is so French in outlook as to seem almost a translation. She stood (unsuccessfully) as a Liberal candidate for the Isle of Wight, doing the canvassing driving round in a donkey-cart. She was married to Denis Browne, a surgeon. She was a visitor at the house of Muriel and Bar [Marjorie Barber], where Dorothy may have met her. To all three friends Dorothy dedicated the novel *Busman's Honeymoon*, which she wrote soon after the play. The form of the dedication shows the comradeship she was then enjoying, reminiscent of the Mutual Admiration Society at Somerville over twenty years before.

Dear Muriel, Helen and Bar,

   With what extreme of womanly patience you listened to the tale of *Busman's Honeymoon* while it was being written, the Lord He knoweth. I do not like to think how many times I tired the sun with talking — and if at any time they had told me you were dead, I should easily have believed that I had talked you into your graves. But you have strangely survived to receive these thanks.

   You, Muriel, were in some sort a predestined victim, since you wrote with me the play to which this novel is but the limbs and outward flourishes; my debt and your long-suffering are all the greater. You, Helen and Bar, were wantonly sacrificed on the altar of that friendship of which the female sex is said to be incapable; let the lie stick i' the wall! . . .

The other new friend was Wilfrid Scott-Giles. An expert in heraldry, he wrote to her in February 1936 to say that in his view the arms of the Wimsey family (sable, three mice courant argent, with a domestic cat as crest and two Saracens as supporters) had the appearance of antiquity. In the interest of some future antiquarian who around the year 1990 might wish to write a monograph entitled "Lord Peter Wimsey: Man or Myth?", should not some opportunity be found to explain that the arms were in fact ancestral, and only by chance reflected Lord Peter's interest in criminology?

Dorothy, delighted, replied at once with similar mock seriousness:

The original arms of the Wimseys are held to have been, Sable, three plates. Tradition asserts that the Baron Fulk de Wimsey (or Guimsey) encouraged King Richard I to persist in the siege of Acre, quoting to him the analogy of the patience of a cat at a mousehole; and that after the fall of the city the plates were changed into silver mice in recognition of the baron's good advice, the crest being assumed at the same time . . .

A lively correspondence developed, in which the family history of the Wimseys was gradually "discovered". Scott-Giles found the mediaeval ancestors, in particular those of heraldic interest. Dorothy discovered Wimseys of the Tudor and later periods. An excellent draughtsman, Scott-Giles made drawings of the arms, of the monumental brass of Gerald First Baron Wimsey, of the effigy of the tomb of the fifth Baron and of his equestrian seal. Mrs Scott-Giles, who was also an artist, contributed a charcoal drawing of Thomas, tenth Duke of Denver.

In April 1936 Wilfrid Scott-Giles and Dorothy L. Sayers met for the first time. The occasion was a lunch, at which Muriel St Clare Byrne and Helen Simpson were also present. They too had been drawn into the game. The amount of "historical" material which they had accumulated between them was already impressive. They discussed the possibility of publishing extracts from it for the amusement of their friends. The result was a pamphlet entitled *Papers Relating to the Family of Wimsey*, edited by Matthew Wimsey, who acknowledged the help given to him by Lord Peter Wimsey, Dorothy L. Sayers, Muriel St Clare Byrne, Helen Simpson, Wilfrid Scott-Giles and his wife. It was privately printed "for the family" by Humphrey Milford.

In March 1937, Wilfrid Scott-Giles, who was a member of the historical society, *Confraternitas Historica*, of Sidney Sussex College, Cambridge, arranged a meeting at which four papers on the Wimsey family were delivered. He himself dealt with the mediaeval background and with heraldry. Muriel St Clare Byrne examined the theory that some of the plays attributed to Shakespeare were written by the Elizabethan Duke of Denver in association with the Earl of Oxford. Helen Simpson read extracts from an eighteenth-century Household Book kept by Mary Wimsey, whose descendants lived in New Zealand. Dorothy presented a paper relating the story of Lord Mortimer Wimsey, the Hermit of the Wash, "who in the rationalistic 1800s conceived himself to be one of the fish netted by St Peter the Apostle, and lived many years alone in a hut on the sea-coast of Norfolk, wholly mute and eating nothing but shrimps and seaweed". Dorothy was enjoying herself immensely. "Our beautiful game", she called it in a letter to Scott-Giles.

In the meantime, there was the production of *Busman's Honeymoon*. She attended rehearsals and travelled round with the company when the play was tried out in the provinces. She worked hard at improving it, altering the dialogue and making cuts as seemed advisable. It opened finally in London at the Comedy Theatre on 16 December 1936. It had good notices and ran for nine months. Dorothy had achieved a West End success.

Her personal life was also improving. Mac's health and moods were still uncertain but the situation concerning her son was working out well. In July 1935 she had discussed with Ivy the need that would soon arise to send him away to school. She was not enthusiastic about preparatory schools, which, in her opinion, turned out a "stereotyped product". Ivy had fostered John's personality, and she was grateful for this. Nevertheless, if he was to gain entrance and, if possible, a scholarship to a public school, he would have to be sent first to a tutor for a year's intensive coaching and then to a preparatory school in order to be brought up to the standard of the Common Entrance examination. She was looking out, through her lawyers, for "one of those excellent clergymen who undertake this sort of job", as indeed her father had done, in the rectory at Bluntisham. She wrote on 16 July:

> I have put things off a little because I didn't want to take him away from you while he was the only one you had; but now, I think, it can perhaps be done without too much hardship on either side. He has got on very well and I am terribly grateful to you for your care of him. Both he and you will feel the parting very much, I'm sure – but of course, these things have to happen. I am letting the lawyers handle the preliminaries as far as possible (in the circumstances it is better, as, for reasons I have mentioned before, I find it difficult to discuss these matters with Mac).

In December 1934, although arrangements had been made about adoption, she was still signing her letters "Cousin Dorothy". In September 1935 he was told that he had been adopted by Cousin Dorothy and Cousin Mac and that his surname would now be Fleming. Dorothy wrote to Ivy:

> Better warn J.A. to leave "Dorothy L. Sayers" out of it. Mrs Fleming is unknown, but "Sayers" will be the signal for autograph-hunting and nuisance. Explain to him that professional writers want their business and private affairs kept separate – which is true enough, God knows! I spend my time in Witham choking off the bores who want to call on Mrs Fleming for the sake of seeing Miss Sayers, confound them!

As to how John should now address her in his letters: "'Dear Mother' will be all right – but don't let the poor kid bother himself writing to me more than once a month or so. It is to you that he will want to write."

She gives thought to his requirements. There are new clothes to be bought. He will also need "a good, stout penknife, a reliable watch and a fountain-pen – these things lend importance. If you need more money let me know. They must be good ones."

He goes off to the home of a rector in Combe Florey in Somerset, who runs a small school for boys. Excellent reports of his progress arrive. Dorothy writes: "That John should be doing so well reflects very great credit indeed on your love and care for him. Believe me that I am grateful to you from my heart." The headmaster dies and John is transferred to a school in Bideford, Devon. This proving unsatisfactory, he is sent next to a school in Broadstairs, Kent, which Dorothy goes to inspect in person. She writes to him regularly, signing her letters "Your loving Mother, Dorothy L. Fleming". She sends him a tuck box, congratulates him on doing so well in his work, agrees to his having piano lessons. Later on he asks if he may learn to ride and she replies "Yes, I think the Exchequer can rise to riding lessons." Occasionally she meets him in London and takes him out before putting him on the right train to Oxford or to Kent. "It was so jolly seeing you the other day," she writes. On 28 October 1936, when he is nearly thirteen, she sends him a lively account of her adventures with *Busman's Honeymoon*, which is being put on in Birmingham:

Every day we go into the theatre at 11 and work furiously till past 1 o'clock – then snatch hasty food somewhere, and bolt back at 2, and then on again till 5. And after that, either one has to go and consult about alterations in the play, or rush off with the stage designer to see about furniture and "properties"; or go to a tailor or dressmaker to give an opinion about the costumes, or interview the Press, or tell the management how to write the advertisements – and if one isn't doing that, one is taking agitated actors and actresses out to dinner and telling them how marvellous they are, and what a wonderful performance they are going to give, and generally soothing their shattered nerves and encouraging them, poor dears! So at the end of the day, one tumbles exhausted into bed, thinking of new things to do to the play . . . We've got a grand cast, and it's going to be a splendid show, I hope. I expect it will be on in Town during the Christmas holidays, and you and Aunt Ivy will be able to come and see it. It is tremendous fun doing it – rather like a grand dressing-up game with grown-up people; only every so often, of course, one stops and thinks, "Gosh! this is serious; and if it's a flop, these poor people won't get any salaries, and how guilty one will feel, having let them down." But we hope it's going to be a success.

The play *Busman's Honeymoon* is a detective comedy constructed round the central mechanism of the plot. The novel uses the same plot and the same characters, but subordinates them to a different purpose. This is made plain in the sub-title, which reads: "A Love-Story with Detective Interruptions". In the concluding paragraph of the dedication, Dorothy also indicates the alteration in emphasis:

> It has been said, by myself and others, that a love-interest is only an intrusion upon a detective story. But to the characters involved, the detective-interest might well seem an irritating intrusion upon their love-story. This book deals with such a situation. It also provides some sort of answer to many kindly inquiries as to how Lord Peter and his Harriet solved their matrimonial problem. If there is but a ha'porth of detection to an intolerable deal of saccharine, let the occasion be the excuse.

The narrative is set, as in a frame, between a Prothalamion (a song sung before a wedding) and an Epithalamion (a song sung in praise of the bride and groom). The centrepiece is a celebration of Peter and Harriet's marriage, "with detective interruptions".

"I have been facing one fact for some time", said Harriet to Miss de Vine in *Gaudy Night*, "and that is, that if I once gave way to Peter, I should go up like straw."

"That", said Miss de Vine, drily, "is moderately obvious."

Paul Delagardie, Peter's uncle, who had taken him in hand as a young man and superintended his sexual education, says to his sister, the Dowager Duchess of Denver, "I was wondering how long Peter would last before he let the bars down."

Their surrender to each other releases not only passion but an exaltation of the spirit, which gives an idyllic quality to the book. Their mood is shaken at one moment by Harriet's temptation to persuade Peter not to investigate the murder which has occurred in their honeymoon retreat. "Must he, in such circumstances . . . ?" Together they overcome this danger of marital blackmail and mutual trust is restored.

The love-scenes in *Busman's Honeymoon* are exultant. The surprising, and original, thing about them, for a novel, is that they are love-scenes between a husband and wife. Despite the deterioration of her own marriage, Dorothy L. Sayers the writer has allowed herself to visualise Hymen as a god of joy. Romantic sentiment, which she had so long distrusted, here comes triumphantly into its own.

The book ends with a quotation from John Donne's "Eclogue for the Marriage of the Earl of Somerset", an ecstatic celebration of married love:

> Now, as in Tullia's tomb one lamp burnt clear
>> Unchanged for fifteen hundred year,
>> May these love-lamps we here enshrine,
> In warmth, light, lasting, equal the divine.
>> Fire ever doth aspire,
> And makes all like itself, turns all to fire,
> But ends in ashes; which these cannot do,
> For none of these is fuel, but fire too.
> This is joy's bonfire, then, where love's strong arts
> Make of so noble individual parts
> One fire of four inflaming eyes, and of two loving hearts.

CHAPTER 20

Canterbury

Dorothy was now on the brink of a new creative experience which would totally alter her career.

In 1928 George Bell, the Dean of Canterbury Cathedral, had taken a bold and momentous step: he had brought drama back into the Church. Ever since the days of Oliver Cromwell, acting had been prohibited in ecclesiastical precincts. In the nineteenth century clerical attitudes had begun to relax and by 1897 Sir Henry Irving was permitted to give a dramatic reading of scenes from Tennyson's *Becket* in the Chapter House at Canterbury. Another thirty years of reappraisal and debate had yet to pass, however, before the Dean and Chapter would feel justified in sanctioning an actual performance. The production of John Masefield's *The Coming of Christ* in the very nave of the cathedral launched a series of religious dramas which over a period of twenty years formed part of the Canterbury Festival.

Of these the best known is T. S. Eliot's *Murder in the Cathedral*, first presented in 1935. This was followed by Charles Williams' *Thomas Cranmer of Canterbury*. On 6 October 1936 Margaret Babington, the Festival organiser and steward and treasurer of the Friends of Canterbury Cathedral, wrote to Dorothy, asking her if she would consider writing a play for the following year. In the light of subsequent developments this would seem to have been an obvious thing to do. At the time it was not obvious at all.

By then the name of Dorothy L. Sayers was renowned, certainly, but only as a writer of detective fiction. At that point, she had neither written articles nor given talks on religious subjects: that phase of her work was all in the future. Though the theatre had long been one of her enthusiasms, she had made no public pronouncement of her views on drama, religious or secular. Few people were aware that she had written a play: *Busman's Honeymoon* had not even gone into

273

rehearsal when Miss Babington made her approach. What, then, prompted her to do so?

She said that she wrote at the suggestion of Charles Williams. He and Dorothy were certainly in contact by November 1935, and perhaps even in 1934, soon after he wrote his rapturous letter to Victor Gollancz about *The Nine Tailors*. They enjoyed each other's work and used to meet now and then in London for a drink or a meal. They may have discussed religious drama, especially at the time when Williams was writing *Cranmer*. As has been shown, he had read and admired her early morality play, *The Mocking of Christ*. Listening to her views, and knowing that she had recently co-authored another play – albeit a secular one and a comedy – he may have said, "Why don't you have a shot yourself at writing a religious drama?" All this is speculation and would seem in any case to offer only slender reasons for Williams to propose her to Miss Babington as the next playwright for Canterbury. Nevertheless, propose her he did.

Dorothy replied:

Dear Miss Babington,

Thank you very much for your letter. I hardly know what to say about this invitation to write you a play for Canterbury. Naturally I am much honoured at being asked, and should like very much to try my hand at it; but as you will realise, it is rather out of my line and there is also the very serious question of whether I could possibly find the time to devote to it . . .

Although she knows she will be extremely busy with the forthcoming production of *Busman*, she invites Miss Babington to come to see her in her flat in London.

She began by saying that she wasn't keen "to mug up the history of kings and archbishops". Miss Babington assured her that a historical play was not called for. The theme of that year's Festival was to be the celebration of artists and craftsmen. This at once caught Dorothy's imagination. On returning to Canterbury Miss Babington was sufficiently hopeful to follow up the interview by sending off that same day a Latin chronicle which told the story of the burning and rebuilding of the choir in 1174. She also sent a copy of her own book, *The Romance of Canterbury Cathedral*, "wherein you may see at a glance the sort of thing the fire was". And she forwarded a photograph of the Chapter House in which the play would be performed.

From her letter acknowledging all this, it is evident that Dorothy, though greatly tempted, had not yet committed herself. In the "rather agitated week" which she sees ahead of her (*Busman's Honeymoon* has gone into rehearsal in Birmingham and is due to open the following month), she will try to look at the material and see whether there is anything which to her mind suggests a play. She promises to make a decision as soon as possible and concludes: "Believe me . . . if I see any prospect of being able to do it I should like, above all things, to have a shot at it." She is eager now to get on with something new.

Early in November *Busman's Honeymoon* opened, to good notices, and the next step was to find a theatre in London. Despite all her commitments, so vividly described in her letter to her son, Dorothy had found time and energy to think about the Canterbury project and had hit on a general scheme, "which I think may work out quite well":

I fear, however, that mine will be but a simple and unimpressive kind of play compared with the fine verses and elaborate mysticism of Eliot and Charles Williams. However I will do my best and send you shortly a suggested outline of the thing, and perhaps a few specimen passages so that you may see what you think of the idea.

By now, 14 November, she was committed to the new project. Miss Babington expressed delight and assured her that the Festival Committee did not wish her play to be "in any way or in any degree similar to the plays of the last two years". This meant no disparagement to Eliot or Williams; it was simply that a change was considered desirable.

Anmer Hall succeeded in booking the Comedy Theatre for *Busman* and rehearsals were about to begin. Dorothy, who always regarded herself as a working playwright, attended them all, in order to make cuts or alterations in dialogue if necessary. Despite such distractions, her new creation was leaping into life. By 27 November, when she wrote again to Miss Babington, she was already visualising costumes and décor:

I find that the story of the building of the Choir, which seems to me to afford admirable material for a play, is going to land us with rather a sombre company of black monks [of the order of St Benedict]! I shall do what I can to get in as many brightly coloured laymen and women as possible, and am rather proposing to let myself go over a kind of explanatory chorus consisting of the Recording Angel and the three Archangels! If we can get these really effectively costumed in the manner of the early primitives, with something of the wing effects used by Tyrone Guthrie in *Tobias* [*and the Angel*], they ought to lend a good deal of splendour to the scene.

The "admirable material" was the story of William of Sens, the architect appointed by the Chapter to rebuild the choir. The monk Gervase, author of the chronicle, relates that architects were invited from France and England to submit plans. They disagreed as to the best way to proceed, some recommending complete demolition, others repair of the ruins. A Norman architect, William of Sens, was chosen, under whose direction the work went well for four years. Then, using a machine he had himself invented, he ascended with his assistants to fix the keystone of an arch. The scaffolding collapsed and William fell fifty feet to the stone floor below. No-one else was hurt, but William's injuries left him severely crippled. He strove heroically to continue directing the work but was forced at last to hand over to another architect.

The event is symbolic as well as tragic, but what made it potentially dramatic, to Dorothy's mind, was a cryptic comment by Gervase: "Either the vengeance of God or the envy of the Devil, wreaked itself on him alone." This offered scope for the exploration of character in relation to fate.

Writing novels is a lonely business. She had welcomed the fun of collaboration with Muriel St Clare Byrne and of involving herself with a theatrical company. Now, to her delight, she was again a member of a team, though it was of a different kind, being mainly amateur and serving a religious audience. Her ideas about drama were directed along new lines and she found it stimulating. The name of Elizabeth Haffenden, who had designed the costumes for Williams' *Cranmer*, had been put forward and accepted. As regards a producer, two names were proposed: Bridges Adams and Harcourt Williams. Dorothy preferred the latter, whose work she had seen at the Old Vic and whose style, her theatrical friends advised her, would be well suited to the scenic effects she was visualising.

In December she met Laurence Irving (the son of H. B. Irving and grandson of the great Sir Henry). He had designed the permanent sets in the Chapter House against which the play would be acted. She was eager to have his advice and help at an early stage. They met at her flat in London and she showed him her draft for the opening scene.

He suggested shortening it and advised aiming at a duration of an hour and a quarter for the whole play. She at once obliged with a revised beginning and a scheme for varying the dialogue with versicles and responses, to be intoned, and an interlude, adapted from Ecclesiasticus, for which she hoped special music might be written. This brought in Gerald Knight, the cathedral organist, with whom she worked structurally from the beginning.

It was Laurence Irving who thought of the title: *The Zeal of Thy House*. Miss Babington wrote to congratulate Dorothy on it, saying she had got no further in her own mind than *Builders and Makers*. She replied: "It was Mr Irving's inspiration, and though I sat grinding my teeth with jealousy for two hours, I could not think of anything half as good!"

The phrase is taken from Psalm 69:9, where the psalmist, despairing at unjust treatment on the part of cruel and suspicious men, proclaims that he has subordinated all personal interests to the glory of the God of Israel: "For the zeal of thine house hath eaten me up". The implication that perhaps God owed the psalmist something for his zeal may have led Laurence Irving to make his suggestion. Certainly it focused on Dorothy's presentation of the character of the architect and reinforced the dramatic conflict between his mounting hubris and the growing concern of the monks. *The Church Times* was to call it "a forbidding title" and *The Times*, likewise, found it "unattractive". Nevertheless, it met with general approval at Canterbury.

In January 1937 Dorothy approached Elizabeth Haffenden about the designs for costumes. At that stage the plan was for the play to culminate in a pageant – "a tableau full of colour and splendour bringing in all the various craftsmen and so on who contribute to the building and furnishing of the church". She anticipates that they can have some fun with this, but a difficult problem is presented by

> . . . certain gigantic angelic figures forming a kind of chorus to the Play about which we shall have to talk . . . What I particularly want is to find out from you how far one may go in the matter of fantastic design, and how far angels could be expected to move about when encumbered by, what I understand will be, large quantities of gold American cloth!

Laurence Irving, who was enthusiastic about the pageant, had asked for two further sections to be added. Dorothy wrote to Miss Babington on 23 January 1937: "It is now getting pretty long and I don't think we ought to put in anything more until the composer and producer have seen what they can do with it."

Her approach to Mr Knight was tactfully modest and gave nothing away: "I should like to leave the selection of the music to you really, since my own musical knowledge is very small ... " This from someone who had sung in the Oxford Bach Choir, who played the violin, at one period almost to professional standard, and whose father was a musician as well as a churchman! She went on:

> I can make a few suggestions in answer to some of your questions. Generally speaking, what we have to aim at is swiftness and dramatic effect, avoiding as much as possible long passages of Gregorian plain song which the audience is apt to find dull, and which take an unconscionable time to sing. I ought to warn you that as the play is rather on the long side, some of the musical interpolations may have to be considerably cut down or omitted for performance in Canterbury, so I think it would be better not to spend too much energy upon them until Mr Harcourt Williams has been able to run through the play and see what cuts will have to be made, both in the music and the text.

From the beginning she relied on Harcourt Williams for advice in shaping the play. Her first draft was completed by the end of February He wrote on 4 March to say that he liked it, was willing to produce it and would be happy to play the part of William, but would need a good deal of help if he was to do both. In due course, Frank Napier was therefore engaged as assistant producer. Williams said at once that he could see no reason for the pageant: "The play ends finely on [the Archangel] Michael's speech and if the play has made its proper effect the pageant could only be an anti-climax." He asked for a general meeting for discussion, which took place on 19 March, and a rehearsal was fixed for April.

William of Sens is presented as a brilliant architect, but a man of moral weaknesses, prepared to compromise in the matter of financial dealings; for the sake of the work, for example, he fudges the accounts in order to get the best materials, for which the treasurer of the Chapter is reluctant to pay. He also allows himself to become amorously entangled with a wealthy patron, the Lady Ursula de Warbois, taking no trouble to be discreet. This scandalises monks and workmen alike. His chief weakness is pride: he sees himself as indispensable to God. Over-confident and heedless, he trusts his safety to an inattentive workman and to a monk who, the one amused, the other outraged by the presence of Lady Ursula, allow themselves to be distracted while inspecting a rope which is to bear William's weight. A flaw is overlooked, with the result that William crashes to the ground.

Dorothy confessed that she found it difficult to make the situation between William and the lady definite enough to be interesting without giving offence to the Dean and Chapter. The supernatural presence of the Archangels also presented problems of production. In keeping with the tradition established at Canterbury, the play was partly in verse, partly in prose. This called for a modulation of tone and style, from the "committee meeting" of the monks in the opening scene, to the sublime poetic utterance of the Archangel Michael at the end of the play.

Harcourt Williams was her guide and collaborator from the beginning. An acting copy of the play shows clearly the extent to which he recommended cuts and minor alterations which tightened the action. She was immensely grateful, not only for his experienced guidance but for his interpretation of the part of William, considered by some critics to be the finest performance of his long and distinguished career. He was also to produce her second Canterbury play, *The Devil to Pay*, and to act the leading role of Faustus, both at Canterbury and at His Majesty's Theatre, London. Her joy in this collaboration is expressed in one of her finest poems:

To the Interpreter HARCOURT WILLIAMS

Sound without ear is but an airy stirring,
Light without eyes, but an obscure vibration,
Soul's conference, solitude, and no conferring,
Till it by senses find interpretation;
Gold is not wealth but by the gift and taking,
Speech without mind is only passing vapour;
So is the play, save by the actor's making,
No play, but dull, deaf, senseless ink and paper.

Either for either made: light, eye; sense, spirit;
Ear, sound; gift, gold; play, actor; speech and knowing,
Become themselves by what themselves inherit
From their sole heirs, receiving and bestowing;
Thus, then, do thou, taking what thou dost give,
Live in these lines, by whom alone they live.

279

The sonnet is preceded by a quotation from Shakespeare's dedication of *The Rape of Lucrece* to the Earl of Southampton: "What I have done is yours; what I have to do is yours; being part in all I have, devoted yours." Dorothy was deep in love with her brave new world that had such people in it.

On 12 June 1937 *The Zeal of Thy House* had its first performance. Special trains from Victoria Station were laid on during the run of the Festival. Dorothy arranged for a private party of her guests to travel down together. Among them were Helen Simpson and her husband Denis Browne, Muriel St Clare Byrne, Marjorie Barber, Mr and Mrs Scott-Giles, and, of course, Mrs H. D. Leigh (Aunt Maud). Dorothy was unable to travel with them herself, having to be in Canterbury for the dress rehearsal, but she arranged for her secretary to be at the barrier at Victoria, holding conspicuously a copy of the novel *Busman's Honeymoon*, in its bright yellow jacket. Lunch would be provided on the train and further transport for the pilgrims would be laid on at Canterbury. Commenting on these princely arrangements, Mr Scott-Giles characteristically wrote to say that he thought they ought all to go on foot, like true pilgrims, "but the old road has been renamed, classified and trunked since I walked it – twice – twenty years ago."

Dorothy in 1937. This is the photograph that she gave to members of the cast of *The Zeal of Thy House*. *(Estate of Anthony Fleming)*

The occasion was in every way festive. An hour after the performance a Service of Arts and Crafts was held in the cathedral. This ceremony of thanksgiving and dedication was also an acknowledgment that the artist's exercise of his art was a religious act, a concept Dorothy was to make more and more her own. After the entry of the mayors of a number of Kentish boroughs came a procession of architects, painters, sculptors, writers and musicians. Among them was Dorothy L. Sayers. It was the eve of her forty-fourth birthday.

Sadly, one person who had not been on the pilgrims' train or present at the performance of *The Zeal of Thy House* was Dorothy's husband. Her professional and her married life had now little to do with one another.

CHAPTER 21

Words of an Archangel

The Canterbury experience created a new Dorothy L. Sayers. From then on, she became a public person, a figure of authority, whose opinions would be increasingly sought, not only on detective fiction, which had long been the case, but, more important, on religious drama and the tenets of the Christian faith.

The challenge of writing *The Zeal of Thy House* had uncovered a neglected well-spring of poetry. It had also awakened her to the dramatic power of Christian dogma. These two disclosures, in combination, resulted in a work possessing beauty of both structure and expression. Architecture had long been a source of inspiration to her. Her earliest years were passed among beautiful buildings. She had been taught by her father to admire the Early English style of church architecture. As an adult her love of Oxford was heightened by its structural glories. Building and writing, both forms of making, were linked in her mind from the beginning ("I will build up my house from the stark foundations"). Some of the finest passages in *The Nine Tailors* and in *Gaudy Night* are the expression of a mind elated and energised by noble construction.

The work of any maker – architect, craftsman, poet – was for Dorothy a sacramental act. Thus, in *The Zeal of Thy House*, the Archangel Raphael accepts the work of William in lieu of neglected prayer:

> . . . True as a mason's rule
> And line can make them, the shafted columns rise
> Singing like music; and by day and night
> The unsleeping arches with perpetual voice
> Proclaim in Heaven, to labour is to pray.

But William's work is not his alone. That is his great error: he sees himself, and all human makers, as indispensable to God:

> . . . This church is mine
> And none but I, not even God, can build it.
> Me hath He made vice-gerent of Himself,
> And were I lost, something unique were lost
> Irreparably; my heart, my blood, my brain
> Are in the stone; God's crown of matchless works
> Is not complete without my stone, my jewel,
> Creation's nonpareil.

The words are terrifying in their hubris and are soon followed by catastrophe.

The theological issues involved in the mounting pride and in the fall of William, his confession and repentance and his ultimate surrender, opened up vistas which Dorothy had not yet taken into consideration as a writer. She experienced a return of the vision she had had as a child, of the relatedness and wholeness of things, of an interlocking pattern of logic, of cause and effect, of rationality. Her mind focused on the central belief of Christianity – the Incarnation – and she saw how all else flowed from it. She would later define a Christian drama as "a play . . . which can be fully understood and accepted only by those who understand and accept the act of God in history which we call the Incarnation." When William is at last brought to see that God, incarnate as Christ, left His work to be finished on earth by others, he finds it possible to admit his sin of pride and leave the completion of his work to another architect. The final words of the Archangel Michael express the community of work and its symbolic relationship with the triune God:

> Look then upon this Cathedral Church of Christ: imagined by men's minds, built by the labour of men's hands, working with power upon the souls of men; symbol of the everlasting Trinity, the visible temple of God.

Dorothy was vividly and creatively aware that her Canterbury play owed its being to the collaboration of all who had worked with her to honour the cathedral: the actors, the producer, the composer and the choir, the designer of costumes and all who gave life to her words. There was a third element: the audience, who responded. Meditating on this, she was visited by a revelation: not only the building of the cathedral, not merely the production of a play, but every act of creation had a triune structure which mirrored the Trinity. The words she gives to the Archangel are the expression of her new vision:

> Children of men, lift up your hearts. Laud and magnify
> God, the everlasting Wisdom, the holy undivided
>   and adorable Trinity.
> Praise Him that He hath made man in His own
> image, a maker and craftsman like Himself, a
>   little mirror of His triune majesty.
> For every work of creation is threefold, an
>   earthly trinity to match the heavenly.
> First: there is the Creative Idea; passionless,
> timeless, beholding the whole work complete
> at once, the end in the beginning; and this
> is the image of the Father. Second: there is the
> Creative Energy, begotten of that Idea, working in
> time from the beginning to the end, with sweat and
> passion, being incarnate in the bonds of matter; and
>   this is the image of the Word.
> Third: there is the Creative Power, the meaning of
> the work and its response in the lively soul; and
>   this is the image of the indwelling Spirit.
> And these three are one, each equally in itself
> the whole work, whereof none can exist without
> other; and this is the image of the Trinity.

In the first production at Canterbury this final speech was omitted. The play ended with William of Sens being carried from the cathedral on a stretcher and the singing by the choir of the Latin hymn, "O quanta qualia sunt illa sabbata". Harcourt Willliams no doubt had his reasons, though he had earlier admired the original ending; but Michael's speech contained, beyond anyone's knowing at the time, the germ of one of Dorothy's most influential works.

The play was an undoubted success and reviews were excellent. It was largely responsible for the profit which the Festival made that year. Complimentary letters poured in. Canon F. J. Shirley, headmaster of the King's School, Canterbury, in whose house Dorothy had been a guest during the Festival Week, wrote as follows: "Canon Lanchester – who dined on the 'last night' with us, and who is really one of the most learned men in our Church – was much moved by your Play, and said it was the work of a genius. If ever you want the critique of a cleric, let him do it." Many who saw it spoke of its freshness and originality. Some critics expressed surprise at the difference between the play and the Wimsey books, hardly believing that it could have been written by the same author. Dorothy was exasperated. It seemed to her obvious that the theme of *Gaudy Night* and *Zeal* were fundamentally one and the same — the overriding importance of work itself, be it the pursuit of truth or the building of a cathedral.

It was not obvious to everybody. Dorothy's discerning friend, Dorothy Rowe, who had read the play in typescript, saw the connection at once:

Thank you ever so much for the MS: I've read it with immense pleasure and enjoyed it greatly. Oh, how comely it is and how reviving to the spirits of just men long oppressed to find a plot based on inexorable logic; the scene of the rope testing is first-rate, and the whole argument, culminating in the speech of Michael on the threefold nature of the works of creation is not only vital in itself but an admirably "stiff bourdon" to the "integrity" motif of *Gaudy Night*.

Miss Rowe had a genius for seeing the point: her observation hits the target whang in the gold. Dorothy replied:

I am frightfully glad you really think well of the Canterbury play, in spite or because of its "logic". I do feel that if one has to write a play on a religious subject, the only way to do it is to avoid wistful emotionalism, and get as much drama as one can out of sheer hard dogma. After all, nothing can be more essentially dramatic than Catholic doctrine; but it is all lost if one surrounds it with a vague cloud of let-us-all-feel-good-and-loving-and-God-won't-mind-anything-much.

Her realisation of the dramatic nature of Christian dogma was to dominate her thinking and her creative work for years to come.

Having seen two plays through production, Dorothy was badly in need of a holiday. Marjorie Barber invited her to join her on a month's cruise along the Dalmatian coast, stopping in Venice on the way there and on the way back, and finishing with a few days in Paris, where they hoped to see some plays. Dorothy accepted and told Miss Babington she was going to abandon all thoughts of work, "even of *The Zeal of Thy House*".

Before she left England the play was published, including the final words of the Archangel Michael. These caught the eye of an elderly cleric, Father Herbert Kelly of the Society of the Sacred Mission at Kelham Hall, Nottinghamshire. He was moved to write her a letter which was destined to have far-reaching results. He began by saying how wonderful and delightful it was to find a writer "of your influence who actually realises and can state the vital force of a Christian faith in God and His Christ, not in the abstract fashion which is all we theologians can teach, but in a living, pictorial fashion which common people can follow". He then asks her a question: "I wonder if you recognise, or are interested in recognising, how closely your book images the principles of the Athanasian Creed – the two-fold necessity of faith in the Trinity of God, and the Incarnation." Thus Father Kelly was the first theologian to recognise the import-ance of the Archangel's speech for Trinitarian theology.

In her reply, dated 4 October 1937, Dorothy expresses delight at receiving a letter from someone who understands that the play is about "that dusty and disagreeable thing, Christian Dogma". And she goes on to say:

> The neglect of dogma is the curse of nearly all religious plays, from the playwright's point of view. The dogma of the Incarnation is the most dramatic thing about Christianity, and indeed, the most dramatic thing that ever entered into the mind of man; but if you tell people so, they stare at you in bewilderment . . .
>
> In this case, there was no doubt at all about the dramatic effect of the final scene in which Michael argues the matter out with William. It held the house attentive and excited, though there was no movement on the stage and the whole drama is contained in the dogmatic argument.

Some members of the cast, she told him, had found the idea of a Suffering God "a staggering novelty" and thought she must have invented it. She had tried to explain – "doing my best to steer clear of all the . . . terrifying heresies which lie in wait for amateurs who try to explain things over the lunch-table . . . that the doctrine really was that Christ was always and equally God and Man." The actor who played the Recording Angel Cassiel had been brought up a Unitarian and,

> being condemned, poor dear, to stand and listen for an hour-and-three-quarters, immovably trussed up in a pair of wings, while the

characters argued about the nature of Christ, he could at first make neither head nor tail of what was going on. But, having a very sensitive and intelligent mind, he applied himself to working the thing out, and found it most surprising and interesting.

She was astonished to find that the central tenet of the Christian faith should take people so much by surprise. She did not think this was due to lack of intelligence or interest. (Indeed, she had been amazed to find that the stage-hands, the call-boy, and members of the cast stood in the wings night after night to listen to the theological debate.) She attributed it to the fashion among clergy of over-emphasising the "Human Jesus", a tendency she deplored:

That attractive and picturesque figure has almost succeeded in pushing the Divine Logos off the stage altogether, with the result that God the Father appears as the villain of the piece, which isn't orthodox . . . Of course, the minute Michael puts his finger on the seat of the trouble, William is up in arms. God has no right to take that attitude. And, after all, if it wasn't for the Incarnation, I don't know that He would have the right. But if God has really been through the whole grim business Himself, then He's fairly won the right and one must give in – and that's why it's so exciting and dramatic, and why anybody should think that sort of doctrine DULL passes my comprehension. You may call it a fairy-tale, but it's ridiculous to call it dull.

Father Kelly's reference to the Athanasian Creed prompted the following important statement:

One thing that interested me was to discover a new application of that much-disputed Athanasian statement that "this is the Catholic faith, which except a man believe faithfully, he cannot be saved". Artistically speaking, it turns out to be a plain statement of fact. I mean that, unless you keep the God-Man idea properly balanced, your play, as a mere piece of dramatic structure, falls to pieces and makes no artistic sense: which brings me to the defence of my thesis; because the play is really chiefly "about" the Christian dogma as it presents itself to the creative artist.

Dorothy now had a new platform and she stood on it squarely, centre stage. In April 1938 the *Sunday Times*, for which she had reviewed detective fiction for over two years, now invited her to contribute an article for Passion Sunday. She wrote "The Greatest

Drama Ever Staged is the Official Creed of Christendom". This article and its companion, "The Dogma is the Drama", published that same month in *St Martin's Review*, are a digest, in some places a reproduction word for word, of her letters to Father Kelly. Both articles, especially the first, which reached a wider public, met with enthusiastic response. One reader wrote: "The article by Miss Dorothy L. Sayers is the most practical, condensed and thorough exposition of our religion expressed in plain English which I have seen or heard during eighty years of Church membership and attendance." Encouraged by many such letters, and not only from the elderly, the editor of the *Sunday Times* commissioned another article for Easter Sunday. This was "The Triumph of Easter", which deals with the problem of sin and evil and redemption through the Crucifixion and Resurrection of Christ.

In the meantime Dorothy was busy organising a tour of *The Zeal of Thy House*. Despite the enthusiastic approval of the play in church circles, the ecclesiastical authorities did not see their way to backing it financially. Dorothy invested her own money in it and even raised more by writing advertising copy for Horlicks, without, however, introducing the figure of Lord Peter Wimsey. *The Times* rebuked her humorously for this in its "fourth leader", an item devoted to light and witty comment, a feature which has now, sadly, disappeared Dorothy replied:

Sir – My attention has been drawn to your leading article of yesterday, "Whither Wimsey?" You are curiously out of date in your information if you suppose that this is the first time that either Peter Wimsey or myself has been connected with the advertising profession. Peter was himself an advertising copy-writer for a short time with the firm of "Pym's Publicity" (is it not written in the book called *Murder Must Advertise*?), while I for nine years held a similar position with Messrs S. H. Benson, Limited . . .

It may be of interest if I add that I undertook this advertising job when a small amount of capital was needed to finance the provincial tour of my play *The Zeal of Thy House*, and I had already invested in it as much as I could justifiably contribute from my revenue as a writer. Since no assistance was forthcoming from the Church for a play written and performed in her honour, I unblushingly soaked Mammon for what I could get in that quarter. *Et laudavit Dominus villicum iniquitatis.* [And the lord commended the unjust steward.]

The tour of *Zeal* was not a financial success. It opened in Norwich on 8 October in 1938. The Munich crisis hit it badly. In Southport tempest and flood did its best to kill it: the leading man was obliged to take off his shoes and socks and wade ankle-deep into the theatre. Dorothy travelled round the country with the cast, enjoying herself enormously, despite set-backs. "Mac is getting very cross", she wrote to Ivy, "because I am never at home." The tour ended in Birmingham on 12 December 1938. Dorothy was down several hundred pounds.

By then the B.B.C. had invited her to write a nativity play for Children's Hour. This gave her an opportunity to try out yet another conviction which was by then uppermost in her mind. The way to bring home the Incarnation to people – and the need to do so had been forcefully drawn to her attention by comments made to her during the production of *Zeal* – was to use the language of every day, to show that "His Manhood was a real manhood, subject to the common realities of daily life; that the men and women surrounding Him were living beings, not just characters in a story; that, in short, He was born, not into 'The Bible', but into the world." Apart from the prologue and the epilogue, which present the Magi in fairy-tale and poetic style, the play, *He That Should Come*, is entirely realistic, set in a crowded inn, with bustling, quarrelling travellers, talking like ordinary people of the present day.

Listeners to radio had never heard anything like it. The story came to life for them as never before. Letters, some protesting about irreverence, but the majority rapturous, showed how effective the realism had proved:

As the play progressed the whole scene became amazingly vivid, and the people "came alive". None of us realised before how much we had just accepted the story without properly visualising it. It gave us a new vision of it all and the tiny infant's cry brought home to us as never before the real humanity of Jesus . . .

The sincerity and beauty of your Nativity Play are so free from sentimentality. Moreover, many references to politics and serious questions of those times might apply equally well to today . . .

Letters like these gave Dorothy a new view of herself and of her role as a writer. She experienced an increase in confidence and a surge of creative power which enabled her to rise, when the moment came, to the greatest challenge of her professional life, the invitation to write a series of plays for radio on the life of Christ.

CHAPTER 22

The Challenge of War

World affairs and the menace of totalitarianism were the predominant concern of the late 1930s. After the Munich crisis of the autumn of 1938, when false hopes of peace had been aroused, events moved so rapidly that well-informed observers knew that war was inevitable.

People still hoped, however. The Friends of Canterbury Cathedral planned yet another Festival for the summer of 1939. The success of *The Zeal of Thy House* led them to invite the author to write them a second play. She accepted.

The subject she chose was the problem of good and evil, set forth in the story of Faust – "one of the great stories of the world . . . a perpetual fascination to the poet, whose task is to deal with the eternities". The Faust of legend sells his soul to the Devil for worldly power and the satisfaction of intellectual curiosity. In Marlowe's play, he is damned in accordance with the bond and goes to Hell. Goethe, unable to accept that the pursuit of knowledge could be evil, allows him to cheat the Devil by using his power for good; his Faust goes to Heaven.

Dorothy was aware of the presumption of attempting to follow two such masters. She justified herself on the grounds that she had a contemporary Faust to offer. In the Preface to her drama, *The Devil to Pay*, she observed, with dry humour: "I do not feel that the present generation of English people needs to be warned against the passionate pursuit of knowledge for its own sake: that is not our besetting sin." "Looking with the eyes of today", she saw in Faust the figure of the revolutionary, impatient of facts, eager to put the world to rights by a sudden overthrow. Once in power, such a man becomes a dictator: and his followers, as she conceived them, denying all value to growth and time, take flight in fantasy, in the primitive and in the unconscious.

291

This was a contemporary aspect of the problem of evil — the rejection of adult responsibility and a retreat into infantilism. The story, however, given its supernatural nature, called, Dorothy decided, for the setting and machinery of the mediaeval stage, with the traditional mansions, Hell-mouth and Heaven and diabolic masquerade. This gave her and her colleagues a great deal of fun. In the concluding scene they perhaps over-reached themselves. When Mephistopheles claims the soul of John Faustus it is found, owing to its retreat from responsibility and adulthood, to have shrivelled to the form of a black dog — and an actual dog was produced on the stage. The Devil is tricked again, but this time Faustus goes, not to Heaven, but to Purgatory, with the hope of ultimate salvation.

The play was transferred from Canterbury to London to His Majesty's Theatre in the Haymarket in August 1939. Presented by the Daniel Mayer company, it was excellently produced, with costumes designed, once again, by Elizabeth Haffenden and with Harcourt Williams in the part of Faustus. Reviews were not enthusiastic, the one by James Agate being particularly peevish. Whatever the play's fortune might otherwise have been, it was killed outright by the declaration of war on 3 September. It has never since been professionally performed and is now very little known.

This is to be regretted for the play deals in an original way with the problem of evil. The question is raised first of all in the Preface:

At the base of [the legend] lies the question of all questions: the nature of Evil and its place in the universe. Symbolise Evil, and call it the Devil, and then ask how the Devil comes to be. Is he, as the Manichees taught, a power co-equal with and opposed to God? Or, if God is all-powerful, did He make the Devil, and if so, why, and with what justification? Is the Devil a positive force, or merely a negation, the absence of Good?

In the first scene, Faustus, who has resolved to conjure up Mephistopheles, says: "There must be some meaning in this tormented universe, where light and darkness, good and evil forever wrestle at odds . . . " And in the final scene, when Mephistopheles puts forward his claim for the soul of Faustus in the court of Heaven, Faustus challenges him to speak the truth:

> . . . Thou, Mephistopheles,
> Answer again, and this time all the truth,
> Art thou God's henchman or His Master? Speak!
> Who made thee?

Mephistopheles replies: "God, as the light makes the shadow." In himself he is nothing. Evil is the "non-being" which every being automatically creates, negative and inactive unless and until in the exercise of human freedom it is made the mainspring of consciousness and will. Dorothy L. Sayers continued in her Preface: "Has Evil any real existence, viewed *sub specie aeternitatis*? I have suggested that it has not; but that it is indissolubly linked with the concept of value in the material and temporal aspect of the universe." Or, as Mephistopheles continues in his reply to Faustus:

> I am the price that all things pay for being,
> The shadow on the world, thrown by the world
> Standing in its own light, which light God is . . .
> Nothing myself, except to give a name
> To these three values, Permanence, Pleasure, Good,
> The Godward side of matter, life and knowledge.

Another important concept of this new work – and one which the author would bring more and more into her writings – was that of the passing of time, the relation of the past to the present: what has happened has happened, the past cannot be undone, only redeemed and made good. As she wrote in the programme note to the London production:

> Faustus, the sensitive and impatient humanist, now as then, sells his soul to the Devil. No longer for knowledge and power – for he comes to despair of them – but for a way of escape from the burden of self-consciousness. Yet the knowledge of good and evil, once gained, can never be renounced with impunity; the wheel of time cannot be turned back; the luring phantasy of primal innocence only makes Faustus, still more surely, a tool in the Devil's hand. Waked from his golden dream, he goes "to find reality" and to be faced with final, ineluctable choice between the evil and the good.

The same concept is powerfully expressed by the Judge at the end of the play:

> All things God can do, but this thing He will not;
> Unbind the chain of cause and consequence,
> Or speed time's arrow backward . . .
>   Adam sinned, indeed,

And with him all mankind; and from that sin
God wrought a nobler virtue out for Adam,
And with him, all mankind . . .
                    [and] from the griefs of time
Wrought out the splendour of His eternity.
There is no waste with God; He cancels nothing
But redeems all.

During the spring of 1939, while Dorothy was writing *The Devil to Pay*, thoughts concerning growth, maturity and time were uppermost in her mind. On 9 April, the *Sunday Times* published yet another of her articles, entitled "The Food of the Full-Grown", which was republished the following June by Hodder and Stoughton and renamed *Strong Meat*. This, brief as it is, is one of the most personally revealing things she ever wrote. Starting from the words of St Augustine of Hippo, "I am the food of the full-grown; become adult and thou shalt feed on Me", she challenges the prevalent tendency to take refuge in nostalgia for youth and to regard the passing of the years as bringing only deterioration. This is to overlook the soul's development in time, "the vigorous grappling with evil that transforms it into good, of the dark night of the soul that precedes crucifixion and issues in resurrection". The only way to deal with the past is to accept it as a whole and, by accepting it, to change its meaning. She had recently read T. S. Eliot's *The Family Reunion*, which had been published the previous month. In this play, Harry, Lord Monchensey, haunted by hereditary evil and a confused sense of his own guilt, seeks refuge in the past of his childhood. The more he tries to escape, the more his guilt, manifested as spectral figures (the Furies), pursues him. It is only when he turns to face and accept them that they become the Eumenides and he is liberated. The relevant lines are quoted in the article:

                           . . . Now I know
That the last apparent refuge, the safe shelter,
That is where one meets them. That is the way of spectres . . .
                       And now I know
That my business is not to run away, but to pursue,
Not to avoid being found, but to seek . . .
It is at once the hardest thing, and the only thing possible.
Now they will lead me. I shall be safe with them;
I am not safe here . . .
I must follow the bright angels.

She also quotes from Charles Williams' work, *He Came Down From Heaven*, published in 1938, describing it as "brilliant and exciting" and praising its "beautiful and imaginative treatment" of the problem of the knowledge of good and evil and the resolution of evil into good. In these references and in the article itself, we have a glimpse of the main-spring of her soul and of her spiritual energy.

In May 1939, foreseeing the coming emergency, she took the initiative and offered her services as a writer to the Director of Public Relations for the War Office. The result was an invitation to serve on the Authors' Planning Committee of the Ministry of Information. Their brief was to advise how various authors might best be put to work in case of war. In July she was appointed to an advisory sub-committee. She found the organisation inefficient and made radical suggestions for its improvement. At the beginning of September she was given the task of reporting on two secret pamphlets, but the Ministry found her difficult to work with and she was dropped. This was just as well as she had more important things to do.

Her first war-time publication was a letter to *The Times* of 6 September, signed jointly by herself and Helen Simpson, urging that the churches should be kept open during the war, even if the theatres had to be closed. Her second was an article in the *Sunday Times* of 10 September, entitled "What Do We Believe?" The theme of this article is creativity, a subject to which she will give increasing prominence in her writings from now on. "Man is most god-like and most himself when he is occupied in creation . . . Our worst trouble today is our feeble hold on creation." To allow ourselves to be spoon-fed is to "lose our grip on our only true life and our only real selves . . . If we truly desire a creative life for ourselves and other people, it is our task to rebuild the world along creative lines; but we must be sure that we desire it enough."

That same month, Victor Gollancz asked her to write a Christmas message for the nation. He perhaps had in mind a short pamphlet. What she wrote was a book of 160 pages. While considering what to say, she read yet another work of Eliot's. This was *The Idea of a Christian Society*, which was published that October. It consisted of three lectures, delivered in June of that year at Corpus Christi College, Cambridge. They had been preceded by a broadcast talk, given in February 1937, in a series on "Church, Community and State", and published in the *Listener*, a paper which Dorothy read regularly. Two statements in this talk had caught her eye. One was: "It is not enough simply to see the evil and injustice and suffering of this world, and precipitate oneself into action. We must know, what only theology can tell us, why these things are wrong." The second made an especially forcible impact. Criticising the predominantly economic and commercial organisation of society, Eliot said, "The acquisitive, rather than the creative and spiritual instincts are encouraged."

In *The Idea of a Christian Society* Eliot visualises the setting up of a Community of Christians, of clergy and laity, who shall speak with authority, contesting heretical opinion and immoral legislation, individually and collectively setting themselves to form the conscience of the nation. The lectures were written and delivered before war was declared but the coming conflict was present in his mind. In the published volume, he adds a note, dated 6 September: the reality of the conflict presented us clearly with the inescapable issue: we had before us the alternative of Christianity or paganism. The situation was now urgent: "We cannot afford to defer our constructive thinking to the conclusion of hostilities." Dorothy pounced on this: she now had the thrust and the title of her book for Gollancz: *Begin Here*.

The book is not one of her best. She herself said it was written in "indecent haste" and later wrote to Father Kelly, who enquired about it: "The book is dead now, thank God! and will never, I hope, be resuscitated." It is of interest, however, as providing evidence of trends in her thinking which were to lead on to more important works. The first is a continuing emphasis on time: the future is here and now; the past is irrevocable; what has gone wrong cannot be undone, it can only be redeemed. The second is her concept of Creativity: God, the Creator, created Man in His own image; it follows that we are never so truly ourselves as when we are actively creating something. The third is her conviction that a mechanised society has diminished the essential nature of human beings with the imposition of repetitive work. The fourth is her belief that the prevalently economic structure of society has degraded education by directing it to commercial ends. Underlying all these themes is a concern for individual freedom and responsibility.

Her own sense of responsibility was titanic. She took part in conferences, she gave talks to the Forces, she broadcast, she wrote letters to the press, she wrote articles, she formed a group for knitting socks and sweaters for trawlermen (and took the Government to task for their inefficient distribution of the right kind of knitting wool), she became an air-raid warden and took her share of fire-watching. From November 1939 to January 1940 she wrote eleven letters for the *Spectator*, in which members of the Wimsey family and their friends discussed the black-out, food rationing, the housing shortage,

During the war *(Estate of Anthony Fleming)*

evacuation and other war-time conditions. The ostensible aim was to amuse and to boost morale, but there was the underlying serious purpose of directing readers' minds to the aims of peace, reconstruction, educational and social reform and the preservation of traditional values. In the last letter, she gives to Wimsey, who is "somewhere in Europe" (as the phrase then went), the expression of some of her most deeply held beliefs. He writes to Harriet:

> You are a writer – there is something you must tell the people, but it is difficult to express. You must find the words.
>
> Tell them, this is a battle of a new kind, and it is they who have to fight it, and they must do it themselves and alone. They must not continually ask for leadership – they must lead themselves. This is a war against submission to leadership, and we might quite easily win it in the field and yet lose it in our own country.
>
> I have seen the eyes of the men who ask for leadership, and they are the eyes of slaves. The new kind of leaders are not like the old . . .
>
> It's not enough to rouse up the Government to do this and that. You must rouse the people. You must make them understand that their salvation is in themselves and in each separate man and woman among them . . . They must not look to the State for guidance – they must learn to guide the State . . .
>
> I can't very well tell you just how and why this conviction has been forced upon me, but I have never felt more certain of anything.

On 5 February 1940 the Rev. Dr J. W. Welch, Director of Religious Broadcasting, wrote a letter to Miss Dorothy L. Sayers which had momentous consequences.

> Dear Madam,
>
> I am writing to ask whether you could help us in our work of religious broadcasting to the children . . .
>
> I have long been conscious that some consistent Christian teaching might be given in dramatic form and I have long wanted to find someone who could write a series of thirty-minute plays on the Life of Our Lord. The children we have in mind are those between the ages of seven and fourteen. I had thought either of a dramatic retelling of the Gospel story, or even the dramatic imaginative telling of Our Lord on earth today. I feel that we might rightly and reverently use direct speech, but my mind is not quite made up

about this yet. You may well imagine the good that such a series of about twelve plays might do, broadcast regularly to millions of children and adults. It seems to me a wonderful opportunity which ought to be taken. I believe that you are probably the only person who could take it . . .

On 18 February Dorothy replied:

The sort of series you suggest, of little dramas from the New Testament, is a thing I have frequently thought I should like to do, but it would, of course, entail a good deal of very careful thought and, consequently, a good deal of time. Your suggestion is exceedingly tempting, and if you are not in a great hurry for the series, is just the sort of thing I should enjoy attempting, but it would not be honest to accept it without warning you that I should not be able to get down to it for the next two or three months at the earliest.

One prior commitment was the plan to revive *The Zeal of Thy House* for the Canterbury Festival of 1940. Arrangements for this absorbed a good deal of her time, but the Festival was cancelled because of the threat of invasion. Another, much more demanding, was the ambitious undertaking to edit, with the collaboration of Muriel St Clare Byrne and Helen Simpson, a series of books for Methuen, on social, moral and theological subjects, aimed at encouraging the public to think creatively and constructively about the future. Dorothy planned to start the series off with a book of her own on the subject of "Creative Mind", later to be entitled *The Mind of the Maker*, a work of startling originality which was to have widespread influence.

Dorothy's activities at this period were so many and various that it is not possible to deal adequately with them in chronological order. Some idea of what she had undertaken in 1940 alone may be gained from a letter dated 27 July, in reply to the Bishop of Chichester (Dr George Bell), who had invited her to lecture in Brighton. She lists the things she has recently contracted to do:

> write a book on the Creative Mind
> give 2 broadcasts on Christianity
> give 1 broadcast on keeping up morale
> select and edit a vast religious anthology
> write 12 plays on the life of Christ
> write a paper for the Malvern Conference

write an anti-Russian pamphlet for the Ministry
    of Information
give a talk at Chatham House

In her first letter to Dr Welch, Dorothy had said that she would wish to introduce the person of Christ as a character and to use the same kind of realism as in her nativity play, *He That Should Come*:

> I feel very strongly that the prohibition against representing Our Lord directly on the stage or in films . . . tends to produce a sense of unreality which is very damaging to the ordinary man's conception of Christianity. The device of indicating Christ's presence by a "voice off", or by a shaft of light, or a shadow . . . tends to suggest to people that He was never a real person at all, and the impression of unreality extends to all the other people in the drama, with the result that "Bible characters" are felt to be quite different from ordinary human beings.

She had no doubt that a realistic presentation of the humanity of Christ as God Incarnate was orthodox theologically, but she foresaw difficulties, especially with regard to the choice of language. Fortunately, from the very beginning, Dr Welch gave her his unreserved support:

> To make the Gospel story live for . . . children is our object, and I feel tempted therefore to say that not only should I welcome modern speech from the Biblical characters you mention but also from Our Lord Himself . . . These dramatisations take on a new importance when we think that the completely realistic presentation, including modern speech from all the characters, may give religious teaching to a multitude of listeners to whom the Gospel story is largely unknown and who could not be reached so effectively in any other way.

Dorothy thus had a powerful ally, in no less a person than the Director of Religious Broadcasting who had in the first instance commissioned the plays.

By the end of July she had chosen a general theme: the kingship of Christ. This led to her choice of title, *The Man Born to be King*, remembered, she said, from an old fairy tale. The Kingdom of God would be shown in conflict with the earthly ideal of government and each separate play, complete in itself, with its own dramatic unity, would at the same time be an integral part of the entire theological and historical structure. She asked for adequate rehearsal time (not usually granted to Children's Hour programmes) and said she would very much like Val Gielgud to be the producer. They had worked well together over the production of *He That Should Come* and they understood each other.

Dr Welch regretted he could not grant her request. The plays would be the responsibility of the Children's Hour Department (then evacuated to Bristol), the director of which, Derek McCulloch ("Uncle Mac"), would be the producer. He asked if she would go to Bristol to meet him and the other members of his staff who would be concerned with the production. She asked to be excused the journey, for which she had neither time nor energy (war-time travelling was no joke). In any case, she is not keen to talk too much about the plays at this stage: "It is my experience that to talk over any work which one is doing has the curious effect of destroying one's interest in the work itself." (This was not true as regards her intimate friends, with whom she often found it stimulating to talk over her books while they were in the making; indeed, it seemed often to be a necessity.)

She will finish the first play and send it to Dr Welch. If he passes it from the religious point of view, then the only person she will want to see is the producer and if necessary she will go to Bristol to meet him. Later on, she will try to get to rehearsals and make herself useful. "Discussion beforehand is apt to get in the way of the job." She hopes he will understand and will not think her ungracious. It is significant that from the very beginning Dorothy is on her guard against being managed by a committee.

Dr Welch perfectly understood. In October she received her first letter from Derek McCulloch. He refers to an article of hers he had read in March in the *Guardian*, entitled "Divine Comedy", in which she had wittily put the case for the realistic, natural production and acting of religious plays. Mr McCulloch writes:

As a guide to producers and authors of religious drama alike, it is crammed with irrefutable advice. I particularly like the line, "At the name of Jesus, every voice goes plummy" — we have been on our guard against this danger of humbug for more years than I care to remember.

Your article, in fact, is a synopsis of what you, as author, and I as your producer will aim at. Your attitude to the whole difficult subject is, if I may say so, so exactly right that it makes me look forward all the more to seeing your first script. The dramatic, dynamic reality is just what we want.

This was encouraging indeed. Dorothy replied on 11 October, saying she looked forward very much to working with him. She asks his advice about the problem of writing for children. Dr Welch has told her that the range of ages they envisage is from seven to fourteen. She thinks it is better to write a little above the heads of the youngest rather than give them what the older ones will find babyish. She also understands that it is hoped to attract adult listeners as well. She is trying to make the political situation clear. Herod is in an awkward position and intelligent children should be given a chance to understand this. "I know that when I was a child it was never really explained to me why Herod should have been so angry about the birth of a Messiah and it would have made the whole story much more intelligible if somebody had told me." Mr McCulloch thanks her for her "delightful letter" and goes on to express agreement. Yes, she should write for the older children, following the advice of an enlightened headmaster, who said to a visiting preacher: "Talk to the Sixth Form and let the others pick up what they can." Dorothy is gratified and tells Dr Welch that she thinks she and Mr McCulloch will be able to work together very well.

On 5 November 1940 she sends off a copy of the first play, accompanied by a long letter explaining her aims. She writes also to Dr Welch, saying that she has stressed the theological aspect:

> Even for children I do not think one can quite reduce the Christian thesis to a doctrine of universal kindliness . . . When I was a child I liked a bit of mystery and the sense of something larger than life; and that I feel is what one loses by presenting Christianity so exclusively in terms of morality.

Dr Welch agrees with her absolutely. His reply is dated 14 November:

> Your point about reducing the Christian thesis to a doctrine of universal kindliness is constantly in my mind, and about which I personally am often troubled, in regard to religious broadcasting during the Children's Hour . . . It will be a relief if your plays err on the side of religion instead of on the side of morality.

Mr McCulloch acknowledged receipt of the play – only one copy had been sent, for fear others might be destroyed in an air-raid, and he has not been able to read it yet, "as my staff tore it from me to read in relays, but judging from their excited remarks the general opinion seems to be 'favourable', as publishers with their extreme caution are fond of saying." Everything was looking most promising and Dorothy began work on the second play. Then disaster struck.

Mr McCulloch had been obliged to go to Glasgow for a few days – an unlucky visit. In his absence he had asked his assistant director, Miss May Jenkin, to write to Dorothy about the play. She began by saying: "We have now all read it and let me say at once that we are quite delighted with it. It seems to us admirably dramatic, and both profound and beautiful." So far so good. She then went on to say that, in their opinion, certain speeches would be right over the heads of children, especially since there was no spectacle to help them and they had to rely on their ears alone. She also said that in one or two places the idiom was too modern and suggested other changes in style.

> We wonder if you will allow us discreetly to edit! If you would prefer to make these small alterations yourself, I will send you the play back, but we are anxious not to delay having the copies duplicated and posts are so slow at the moment. We would, of course, get your O.K. for every change before the broadcast.

Dorothy was very angry and said so. Her basic point through all the long dispute which followed was that the plays had been commissioned by Dr Welch and Mr McCulloch had been appointed producer. She resented, as a professional writer, the suggestion that she should take advice from an editorial committee. Mr McCulloch, arriving back after a nineteen-hour train journey from Fife, wrote in reply to her letter to Miss Jenkin, all of whose suggestions he supported. He asked Dorothy to go to Bristol and visit them: "You do not know us, but we flatter ourselves that by meeting each other we might soon sweep away all obstacles".

"Oh, no, you don't, my poppet!" Dorothy replied:

> You won't get me to do three days of exhausting travel to Bristol in order to argue about my plays with a committee. What goes into the play, and the language in which it is written is the author's business. If the Management don't like it, they reject the play, and there is an end of the contract.

In her previous experiences as a dramatist she had prided herself on her excellent relations with producer and cast:

> If travelling is at all possible, I am ready to meet the Producer and
> the Actors *in rehearsal*. Then, if there is any line or speech which,
> *in rehearsal*, I can hear to be wrong, or ineffective, or impossible to
> speak aloud, I will alter it, if I think the objection is justified . . .
> You are the producer. Where production is concerned, I will
> respect your authority. But this is not a matter of production. It
> falls within the sphere of my authority, and you must respect mine.

On the same day, 28 November, she also wrote to Dr Welch, saying
she had reached an impasse:

> Unfortunately, while [Mr McCulloch] was away, an excessively
> tactless letter from a Miss Jenkin [she referred to it elsewhere in
> her letter as "a blazing impertinence"] obliged me to insist on the
> author's right to be sole judge of matter and style where his expert
> work is concerned. Mr McCulloch (who is, as I quite understand,
> bound to back up his subordinate) now seems to have stepped out
> of the part of a producer into that of a Director, and to think it is
> part of his business to teach me how to write.

Dr Welch was exceedingly distressed:

> All that seems supremely important at the moment is that we
> should broadcast to the children of the nation as perfect a picture
> of Our Lord as possible through the medium of your plays, in the
> belief that [they] will get a picture which may be decisive for
> them in determining their attitude to Christ and the Church.

He deeply regrets the breakdown in her relationship with Mr Mc-
Culloch:

> When [he] wrote to you as producer, you and he seemed to
> understand each other, and everything seemed to augur well for a
> happy and successful production. My own suggestion is that we
> should ignore the comments made on the play as a work of art,
> that you and McCulloch should pick up where you were before
> Miss Jenkin's letter, and that McCulloch should make such com-
> ments as he wishes – including those made by Miss Jenkin – during
> the production itself.

Dorothy climbed down and agreed to meet Mr McCulloch in London:

By all means let us pretend that Miss Jenkin never happened, and return to the starting-point. When the next plays come along, I will send a copy direct to you (I should have done so before, but I rather gathered you had handed the whole thing over). Then, if you have any blasphemy, heresy or schism to complain of, we will get it mended, and the script can go to Mr McCulloch as producer, without any committees, for his technical criticism about production. To that I'm always ready to listen.

So all seemed well. In view of air-raids and the damage done to Broadcasting House by a land-mine in December, it was suggested that the meeting between Mr McCulloch and Dorothy should be deferred until the New Year. Dorothy was quite happy about this and continued work on the second play, in the meantime serenely writing letters to Dr Welch about the capacity of children to understand a great deal more than adults gave them credit for.

Unfortunately, Miss Jenkin, who had seen the correspondence which had passed between Dorothy, Dr Welch and Mr McCulloch, felt moved to defend herself against the charges of "impertinence, tactlessness and literary ignorance" which Dorothy had levelled against her. In the course of a lengthy letter, she outlined her career and experience of drama. Even then, all might have been saved, had she not taken it upon herself to point out that in the absence of Mr McCulloch it would be her responsibility to take over the production. And she concluded:

The responsibility for the Children's Hour programme rests firstly with Mr McCulloch and in his absence with me. Therefore we cannot delegate to any author, however distinguished, the right to say what shall or shall not be broadcast in a Children's Hour play.

I am desperately keen to have this Life of Christ in the Children's Hour, but the prospect of a series of heated wrangles over rehearsals fills me with horror. Frankly, I do not see how the plays can be produced at all, unless you will give us the credit of knowing our job, and will pull with and not against us.

Two days before Christmas, 1940, Dorothy replied:

Dear Miss Jenkin,

THE MAN BORN TO BE KING

Under the circumstances you outline, I have no option but to cancel the contract. Kindly return all scripts of *Kings in Judaea* immediately. My agents will communicate with you.

Yours faithfully,

Dorothy L. Sayers.

The envelope containing the letter was full of tiny torn-up pieces of the contract.

CHAPTER 23

Creativeness

The misunderstanding with the B.B.C., though distressful at the time, was no more than a minor skirmish, soon in any case to be resolved. Far more important was the development which had been taking place in the mind of Dorothy L. Sayers. The years 1940-41 saw the consummation of her creative powers and the production of her two greatest works, *The Mind of the Maker*, followed by *The Man Born to be King*.

Several factors combined to bring about these new dimensions in achievement. One was the war, which gave a different trend to her thinking and activity. Another was her growing conviction that the salvation of society lay in the encouragement of creativeness. A third was personal: she was in her late forties. Not enough is made in biographies written about women of the dynamic effects of the menopause. It often happens that the change in hormonal balance and the realignment of psychic forces result in a clarification of purpose and a redirection of heightened energy.

T. S. Eliot's concept of "a Community of Christians", which she had met in *The Idea of a Christian Society*, lodged in her mind. Here was something to be done and she at once set about doing it. She talked matters over with her friends Muriel St Clare Byrne and Helen Simpson – and carried them along with her in the momentum of her vision. On 1 December 1939, before even *Begin Here* was published, she wrote to B. C. Boulter, of the Guild of Catholic Writers: "I am engaged . . . in getting together a group of people, mostly writers, to do books, articles, lectures, etc. about national reconstruction and a creative spirit, not precisely under the Christian banner, but certainly on a basis of Christian feeling."

She enclosed a "rough draft of aims and intentions". This is one of the earliest mentions of the plan to publish a series of books on social reconstruction, collectively entitled *Bridgeheads*. It is important to notice that from the beginning the theme of creativeness was uppermost in her mind, as it was in *Begin Here*. In fact, the Statement of Aims of the series, written by the end of September, is an anticipation of this work. The scope is vast and shows the dimensions of the vision which inspired the undertaking. The immediate purpose of the editors was to prepare people for reconstruction in peace. The overall programme was majestic: "We shall try to quicken the creative spirit which enables man to build ... systems in the light of his spiritual, intellectual and social needs. *We aim at the Resurrection of Faith, the Revival of Learning and the Re-integration of Society.*" [My italics]

Early in 1940 Dorothy was in correspondence with E. V. Rieu, then on the staff of Methuen, about publishing the series. The proposition was accepted and advertising material was prepared, stating that the aim of the forthcoming volumes was to help readers to discover for themselves that creative power which constitutes their real claim to humanity. They would be based on the assumption that "no social structure can be satisfactory that is not based upon a satisfactory philosophy of man's true nature and needs". The hope of the editors was that the books would prove useful to "the re-makers of civilisation" in their efforts to "throw forward their pioneering works".

The first of these volumes, of which only three were brought to fruition, was Dorothy's own, *The Mind of the Maker*, on which she worked throughout the autumn of 1940. On 22 November, she reported to her agent that the book was "ready, all but the last chapter", with which she was having difficulty. It was completed soon afterwards but war-time conditions held up publication until July 1941.

Sending a copy to Maurice Reckitt, she explains the purpose of the series and the place of her contribution in it:

It is the first volume of a series called *Bridgeheads*, edited by M. St Clare Byrne and myself, of which the general idea is to deal with this business of "Creativeness" – both in theory and in practice. The object of this particular book is to start us off on the right lines by trying to examine, in the light of theology as interpreted by the writer's experience, what Creativeness is and how it works, because the word is rapidly becoming one of those catch-phrases which people use without always understanding them very well.

In a letter to Lord David Cecil, dated 28 November 1941, she said: "Our job is rather to build our 'bridge' between one set of thinkers and another than to attempt reconstruction inside any particular sphere of thought. (Thus, in my case, I was trying to bridge the gap between theory of art and theory of religion . . .)" It is important to bear in mind Dorothy's own understanding of her book and the purpose for which she wrote it. It was not primarily, in intention, a book about theology. While she was writing it, she always referred to it in her letters as "a book about Creative Mind", never as "a book about the Trinity". As it turned out, however, the book did fulfil a secondary purpose, which was theological. Writing to Monsignor Ronald Knox on 26 August 1941, she said: "[I wanted to show] that the Trinity doctrine did mean something closely related to what one was doing . . . I thought the artist's way of making might be useful material for the Trinitarian theologian."

Dorothy's belief that creativeness is an essential part of our true nature is based on her understanding of two lines from Genesis: "In the beginning God created", and "God made Man in His own image". Since, according to Trinitarian theology, God is from everlasting Father, Son and Holy Ghost, it follows, as she later said, that "all three persons of the Trinity are essentially concerned in creation". In order to explain how human creativeness works, in the particular case of a writer, she states the doctrine of the Trinity and shows how the threefold structure may be seen mirrored in human creative activity.

She had arrived at this vision as a result of her experience of the writing and production of *The Zeal of Thy House*. It was first expressed, as has been shown, in the concluding words of the Archangel Michael: " . . . every work of creation is threefold, an earthly trinity to match the heavenly". Developing this concept, she had identified in a work of human making the Creative Idea (imaging God the Father), the Creative Energy (imaging God the Son), and the Creative Power (imaging the Holy Ghost).

Father Herbert Kelly had asked her if she had had St Augustine's work on the Trinity in mind when composing this speech. If so, he points out, St Augustine identifies the Three Persons somewhat differently: Being (the reality of an existent mind), Thought (an idea formed in the mind) and Activity (by which the Thought is carried out). Father Kelly was aware of both the similarity and the difference between the analogies drawn by St Augustine and by Dorothy L. Sayers. The basic distinction between them is that St Augustine uses the human mind for his analogy, whereas she uses the human work.

Thus the originality of the Sayers analogy is that it explores the possibility of a doctrine of human creativity.

Dorothy had entered joyfully into this discussion in her letter to Father Kelly of 4 October 1937:

> The speech about the Trinity . . . isn't meant to be a restatement of St Augustine . . . It is, I'm afraid, only an effort of my own to make an illustration of three-in-oneness familiar to every creative artist and drawn from his own experience . . . St Augustine says that God, in making Man, made an image of the Triune. I am trying to say that Man (made a craftsman in the image of the Master-Craftsman) in making a work of art presents also an image of the Triune, because "every work of creation" is threefold . . . I wasn't just jumbling up St Augustine but trying to work out a little picture of my own – very limited, naturally – of an earthly three-in-oneness which I know by experience to exist and which may therefore serve as an inadequate analogy of the Divine Three-in-Oneness. There may be several illustrations of the same thing, mayn't there? – though I absolutely refuse to accept St Patrick's shamrock! Each leaflet of the shamrock isn't equally by itself the whole leaf, and you can't reasonably say that any one of them is begotten of, or proceeds from, another, because they all proceed alike from something quite different!

To explain herself more clearly, she takes as an illustration the experience of writing a book. There are always, she says, simultaneously, three books: The Book as You Think It, The Book as You Write It, The Book as You and They Read It . . . "But Idea, Energy, Power – it is always the same book; at least, it would be in an ideally perfect book, though, as William of Sens truly observes, 'no man's work is perfect', and often the Idea is feeble, the Energy ill-directed and the Power conspicuously lacking." Here in essence, already in 1937, is the book she will write in 1940, brought into potential existence by questions put to her in a letter out of the blue by an elderly and insightful theologian, Father Herbert Kelly.

The Mind of the Maker, "this brief study of the creative mind", as she defines it in the Preface, is in itself a brilliantly creative book. This is not to say that Dorothy L. Sayers here breaks new ground in theology by suggesting an analogy between the divine and the human maker. No less a predecessor than St Thomas Aquinas had said, "God's knowledge stands to all created things as the artist's to his products". G. K. Chesterton, too, had drawn an analogy between

310

literary work and God's creation. Her originality lies elsewhere. As a writer, she was conscious of creation as a simultaneously threefold experience. This led her to reconsider the doctrine of the Trinity in the light of that activity. She discovered that the statements in the Creeds concerning God as Creator were an exact description of the human mind when engaged in an act of creative imagination. By examining this similarity, she throws light on the meaning of the doctrine in terms of human experience and on the process by which a work of art is produced.

To date, her own experience of creativity comprised poetry, detective fiction, a detective comedy, a nativity play and two other religious dramas. Her great series of radio plays on the life of Christ, except for the first, had yet to be written, and was to gain immeasurably from this searching analysis of the Creeds.

The revelation of the creative process is one of the most remarkable achievements of the work. The relationship between a novelist and his characters is described as follows:

> [An author] in a manner separates and incarnates a part of his own living mind. He recognises in himself a powerful emotion – let us say, jealousy. His activity then takes this form. Supposing this emotion were to become so strong as to dominate my whole personality, how should I feel and how should I behave? In imagination he becomes the jealous person and thinks and feels within that frame of experience, so that the jealousy of Othello is the true creative expression of the jealousy of Shakespeare.

But a character who is merely the mouthpiece of the author is not a living creation:

> The creative act is here one of extreme delicacy and in studying it we gain a kind of illumination upon the variety and inconclusiveness of the world about us . . . The vital power of an imaginative work demands a diversity within its unity; and the stronger the diversity, the more massive the unity.

She had found in writing for the stage that her capacity to create a diversity within a unity had been severely tested:

> Let us say that the situation calls for a dialogue among four or five persons. It is probable that the central character will, so far as he goes, represent a true act of creation: the author will have "entered

into him", and his words will be a lively expression of his creator's emotion and experience. But some or all of the other personages may be mere dummies, whose only function is to return the verbal ball to the chief speaker's hand. In that case, the creative act is a failure, so far as they are concerned; in them, the Energy is not incarnate.

Since "no man's work is perfect", the threefold nature of the creative act is often made clear to us in and through imperfections. In the brilliant and entertaining chapter entitled "Scalene Trinities", examples are given of artistic failures, analysed in terms of faulty Trinitarian doctrine. As imperfect apprehension of the being of God results in heresies, so imbalance between Idea, Energy and Power in the creative act results in a work that is "father-ridden", "son-ridden" or "ghost-ridden". The relation of theological heresy to artistic imperfection, an almost certainly original insight, is explored with characteristic humour and zest.

The concept of an author's energy incarnate in his characters is pursued also in relation to the reader, in whose mind the work "re-incarnates itself with ever-increasing Energy and ever-increasing Power". This is the moment of Pentecost, the Power of the Holy Ghost.

The Energy of the creative mind, as Dorothy experienced it, is "mysterious and terrible". Though its manifestations can be analysed, its source is not to be defined:

> The artist's knowledge of his own creative nature is often unconscious; he pursues his mysterious way of life in a strange innocence. If he were consciously to pluck out the heart of his mystery, he might say something like this: I find in myself a certain pattern which I acknowledge as the law of my true nature, and which corresponds to experience in such a manner that, while my behaviour conforms to the pattern, I can interpret experience in power.

All her life she had been aware of a strong urge to create. This was the law of her nature and she conformed to it, through all her vicissitudes, creating her own world, marked with her mind and personality, varied but consistent: "I find . . . that the same pattern inheres in my work as in myself; and I also find that theologians attribute to God Himself precisely that pattern of being which I find in my work and in me." She did not believe she was unique in this.

On the contrary, she concluded that "the pattern directly corresponds to the actual structure of the living universe". If this is true, then there is something gravely wrong with our organisation of society – a mismanagement to which *Bridgeheads* was planned to draw attention:

> If we conclude that creative mind is in fact the very grain of the spiritual universe we cannot arbitrarily stop our investigations with the man who happens to work in stone, or paint, or music, or letters. We shall have to ask ourselves whether the same pattern is not also exhibited in the spiritual structure of every man and woman. And, if it is, whether, by confining the average man and woman to uncreative activities and to an uncreative outlook, we are not doing violence to the very structure of our being.

This paragraph states the essential purpose of the book and of the series to which it was intended to serve as an introduction. Six titles, in addition to *The Mind of the Maker* were announced by Methuen: U. Ellis-Fermor, *Masters of Reality*; Denis Browne, *A New Charter in Medicine*; M. St Clare Byrne, *Privilege and Responsibility*; A. P. Herbert, *The Point of Parliament*; G. W. Pailthorpe, *The Social Value of Surrealism*; Helmut Kuhn, *Encounter with Nothingness*. The enterprise was beset with misfortune. Helen Simpson, one of the three editors, died in 1940. Her husband, Denis Browne, was so stricken by her loss that he found himself unable to write the book he had promised. Muriel St Clare Byrne made no progress on hers. Una Ellis-Fermor's was published in 1942. In part a descant on *The Mind of the Maker*, it is now out of print but deserves to be better known than it is. A. P. Herbert's contribution, most of which had already appeared in *Punch*, came out in 1946. G. W. Pailthorpe's work was never written. Helmut Kuhn's work was eventually published by Methuen in 1951, but not as part of *Bridgeheads*, which had by then been discontinued.

The failure of *Bridgeheads* as a collective undertaking was a disappointment. It was redeemed, however, by the success of *The Mind of the Maker*, which far exceeded Dorothy's own expectations. She herself was mockingly disparaging about it. On 9 September, when she had begun work on it, she wrote to Father Kelly (their correspondence continued for over ten years, until 1950, when he died at the age of ninety): "People won't understand it, and will think it silly or blasphemous, but it is a true record of experience as far as it goes." To Maurice Reckitt she wrote on 8 May 1941, before the book was published: "I have produced a curious book called *The Mind of the Maker* – a sort of exercise in Applied Theology."

On 26 August, having just received an excellent review by the Rev. Dom R. Russell of Downside, she wrote self-deprecatingly to Monsignor Knox: "The more Catholic and orthodox the critic, the more sympathetic to my curious caperings on theological territory." Disavowing theological competence, she went on to say: "I only know the Creeds and bits of St Augustine" – and she quoted against herself:

> I'm like the Old Man of Thermopylae
> Who never did anything properly.

She was prepared, however, when readers misunderstood her meaning, to take the trouble to explain herself in full. An undated fragment of a letter to an unknown correspondent reads as follows:

> I think you have read hastily the passage . . . which compares the "threefoldness of the work" to the threefoldness of the mind from which it derives; and proceeds to infer that, as the book is threefold because it derives from the mind of the human maker, which is threefold, so the mind of the human maker is threefold because it derives from the God who is Himself triune; and that, in fact, the triune structure of God's nature runs through all His works, whether created immediately or indirectly.

It is to be hoped that the unnamed correspondent was enlightened by this closely reasoned clarification.

At the time of its publication the book was acclaimed, by theologians as well as laity, as a lucid analysis of the Trinity and a help to belief. The Rev. V. A. Demant wrote at once: "Whatever priests may say, I think that is the way theology should be written. It is the way it was written in the formative periods of the Church." Sir Richard Acland said, "*The Mind of the Maker* is the first book I read which made the doctrine of the Trinity seem real and sensible." The composer Armstrong Gibbs wrote on 10 January 1942 to say that the book had greatly helped him. He had been able to draw parallels which applied to the creator of music, "a genuine and often sadly puzzled seeker after true religion".

More recently, Richard T. Webster, a philosopher who has done some up-dating of classical metaphysics, has commented:

[Hers] is precisely the sort of vision which overcomes the usual abysmal separation between theology and life . . . Unfortunately *The Mind of the Maker* has not yet received the attention it deserves [from philosophers]; even to the comparatively few who know the author as a religious writer, as well as for her novels, the book does not seem to be known for its precise philosophical significance.

Canon John Thurmer, who, among theologians, has given authoritative attention to the work, similarly regrets that various factors, such as the book's prominence in literary criticism, have diminished its theological impact. He regards it as being "of overwhelming importance for the analogy of the Trinity". He considers too that the world created by the novelist or the playwright is "a particularly useful analogy for God's creation . . . [since] creation in words is particularly appropriate as the analogy of God who creates and reveals by his Word, especially his Word-made-Flesh". His magisterial comment sums up a theologian's view: "*The Mind of the Maker* is unique in being a developed and confident appeal to something in human experience corresponding to, or providing a direct analogy of, the Holy Trinity."

As regards the book's value to literary criticism, Maurice Browne, the Director of Religious Drama, wrote to Dorothy on 23 January 1947 to say that in his view *The Mind of the Maker* ranked with Aristotle's *Poetics*: "Even if you had never written anything else, this alone, it seems to me, would put you among the very few who have thought, and therefore, written clearly on the craft of writing and all which that implies."

The book's prominence in literary criticism is well established in academic circles in the United States. Professor Catherine Kenney, in her admirable work, *The Remarkable Case of Dorothy L. Sayers*, has stated that she has many times directed students to it, always with beneficial results. For her, *The Mind of the Maker* manages not only to make Christian doctrine more intelligible and believable but also to make aesthetic theory relevant to everyday life.

On the subject of the work's usefulness to literary criticism, the final word must be left with Richard L. Harp: "I can see no kinds of literary works to which her book could not apply. Basically, Sayers provides us [with] a starting point for any work of criticism, and it is the most liberal and generous imaginable: the heart of the creative act . . . Sayers' book communicates in Power." Dorothy L. Sayers was shortly to communicate in Power beyond all expectation.

CHAPTER 24

Incarnation

Dr James Welch, the Director of Religious Broadcasting, was a man of vision, courage and diplomacy. It is thanks to him that the project of *The Man Born to be King* was rescued and set going again. Dorothy, on her side, had in fact left the door open: "Possibly you may be able to make another arrangement more satisfactory to all parties", she hinted in a letter explaining why she had torn up her contract. After all, it was he who had commissioned the plays in the first place. He replied firmly on 30 December 1940:

> Nothing, no one matters, compared with the prime importance of revealing the character of the Son of God to the younger listeners of this country. To me, that is "religious education" . . . I cannot accept the cancellation of these plays, which means the denial to the children of an entirely fresh portrayal of the life and teaching of Our Lord.

Dorothy, though still smouldering, replied at once: "If I am to go on, I must ask that there shall be *one* management, *one* producer who is not a secondary management, and *one* responsible contracting party, who understands the nature of contractual obligation. This ought not to be impossible."

Dr Welch was eager to open negotiations with the Controller of Programmes, Mr B. E. Nicolls, but he, poor man, had been injured in an air-raid and was still convalescent. Dr Welch then had the misfortune to slip on an icy pavement and break his collar-bone. As soon as these set-backs were out of the way, arrangements were made to remove the plays from the Children's Hour Department and to broadcast them on a national network on Sundays but at a

listening time suitable for children. All this required delicate nego-
tiation. Dorothy agreed to continue writing with children in mind
but with the added consideration that there would now be listeners
of all ages. This suited her very well. Even further to her satisfaction,
Val Gielgud had been engaged as producer. This was what she had
wanted all along. She was now happy to make a fresh start.

It was settled that the first play would be broadcast on 5 October
1941 and she agreed to do her best to have six plays and a lay-out
synopsis of the whole series of twelve ready by the beginning of
August. She warned, however, that she might not manage it all by
that date, because, she said, she seemed to be spending most of her
time "haranguing Baptist Ministers and the Royal Air Force about
the Christian religion".

In actual fact, the second play was not written for another four
months. Astonishingly, at this point in the proceedings, the B.B.C.
asked her to do something else. Perhaps they required a breathing-
space, or possibly Val Gielgud did. On 2 February, the Rev. Eric
Fenn, another member of the Religious Broadcasting Department,
and so presumably with the knowledge of Dr Welch, invited her to
take part in a series of ten-minute talks on the Forces Programme on
the subject of the Nicene Creed. Would she be willing to give six talks
on the second section dealing with the Son of God? She agreed.
Whatever reason lay behind this untimely invitation, it had, on the
other hand, the very timely effect of obliging her to scrutinise
the theology of the Incarnation before making her presentment
of the Incarnate in her plays.

By the end of March she has done a rough draft of her first two
talks. Writing to Fenn, she says she finds that the Nicene Creed
bristles with technical terms. It will be difficult to explain them in
everyday language to the Forces. Will the previous speaker, who is to
deal with the section on God the Father, bring in the Trinitarian
formula, or will she be left to introduce it without preparation? On 4
April she writes indignantly about an article by Ivor Brown in *The
Literary Guide*:

It shows pretty clearly that the expression "God the Son" is one he
has never separated from the historic Jesus. He is, of course, an
old-fashioned and ignorant "rationalist" of THE FREETHINKER
type, brought up on Robert Blatchford; but his ideas are the ideas
which his generation has handed down to the younger generations
as being the Creed of Christendom.

She is particularly on the alert for such views, having, as she announces, "just written an entire book on Trinitarian analogy". In a letter to her, Fenn had used the phrase "Father and Son", but this, she suspects, misleads people into visualising two personalities. "The point towards which I am getting is rather two personae with one personality." She adds that she is busy lecturing up and down the country and does not know how she is to get her six talks on the Creed written and recorded in time. Work on the plays has obviously been shelved for the time being.

By the middle of May she is in difficulties with the clause "Who for us men and for our salvation came down from Heaven". This requires, she says, preliminary instruction on the nature of man and the nature of sin. The whole concept of sin is unfamiliar and unconvincing to modern people, but there is nothing she can do about that. Her job, as she sees it, is to explain what the clauses of the Creed actually mean. After some discussion, she decides on a general title for her six talks: not "The Son of God", which she considers misleading, but the more plainly incarnational phrase, "God the Son": "There seems to be very little danger that anybody will confound the Persons in these days; what they all do is to divide the Substance disastrously." By early June she has completed four talks. She has been having a correspondence, she reports,

with a "middle-aged public-school" man, on whom it has just broken, as a totally new idea, that it is just possible the Church really supposes Christ to be GOD, and not some kind of human sacrifice. I hope my scripts made it clear that GOD is just what Christ is correctly supposed to be nothing else but!!!

By the middle of July her talks were finished and recorded and she was free to turn to the plays. She was relieved to learn that the first would not be broadcast until late in December. She resumed work on the second and was soon in correspondence again with Dr Welch:

Nobody, not even Jesus, must be allowed to "talk Bible" . . . [The thing must] be made to appear as real as possible, and above all . . . Jesus should be presented as a human being and not like a sort of symbolic figure doing nothing but preach in elegant periods, with all the people round Him talking in everyday style. We must avoid, I think, a Docetist Christ, whatever happens – even at the risk of a little loss of formal dignity.

The part played by Dr Welch at this formative period of the plays was of vital importance. From the very beginning he gave her his full support and expressed total confidence in what she was trying to do. His role was that of "management" and also of theological editor. He did not, however, have an entirely free hand: it was his duty to keep the Central Religious Advisory Committee of the B.B.C. informed. After the broadcast of the first play, it would be necessary to obtain their sanction to proceed and to submit to them the text of every play. It is not certain how soon Dorothy was aware of this — she had stipulated one management; the most delicate and difficult part of Dr Welch's task lay ahead.

His immediate step, on receipt of the second play, *The King's Herald*, was to discuss it with his colleagues in his department. It contains the scene of the baptism of Jesus and the theophany, or manifestation of God. He reported to Dorothy that the naturalistic and truly incarnational manner in which she had treated this had startled them all, but after a second or third reading they had accepted it: "Your idea of Our Lord, born of the travail of your mind with the medium of broadcast drama, the Gospel narrative and the Creeds, is really new ... We are all excitement to meet this new Jesus." She replied on 17 September. What Dr Welch had said about her treatment of the theophany touched on the central point of what she was trying to show: that the people at the time had no idea that the world's history was changing. Thus she makes them chatter to Jesus after the baptism as though nothing had happened. That is "the thing that is so dramatic and so convincingly 'real'".

By then the third play, *A Certain Nobleman*, was ready. This contains the episode of the wedding at Cana. One problem here was to present the Virgin Mary as a believable person, not as someone superhuman, for that would produce a static, undramatic effect: "No character in a play can be made effective unless it experiences something in the course of the action." She was determined that every play should be a play, not a scripture lesson with dialogue to improve the minds of the young. Another problem had been the need to show the effect on the disciples of the human and practical results of the divine mission: they had just witnessed the first miracle. Technical considerations had necessitated some rearrangement of details of text. She hoped Dr Welch would find this acceptable. He found it completely justified and considered this play the best so far.

He was beginning to think about publicity, convinced that the more listeners the plays attracted, the better. Dorothy agreed and was willing to co-operate. Accordingly, on 10 December 1941, a press conference was called at the Berners Hotel, Berners Street, where twenty-six years before a young Dorothy L. Sayers had been interviewed by Miss Elliot and offered a teaching post in Hull. This occasion had more dramatic consequences. Dr Welch addressed the assembled journalists and Dorothy read aloud a long statement she had prepared on certain aspects of the plays – the impersonation of Christ and the use of modern English being the two most important. She was then asked to read a few examples of the dialogue and she consented. This had not been previously arranged or agreed to by the Director of Publicity, Kenneth Adams, and he may have had something to say about this afterwards.

One of the scenes she chose to read was the beginning of the fourth play, *The Heirs to the Kingdom*. Matthew the tax-collector has joined the disciples. In her Notes to the Producer she described this character as she had conceived him to be and suggested that he should be played with a Cockney accent. In the opening dialogue, being the astute man of business he is, he is shocked by Philip's simplicity in having allowed himself to be cheated of six drachmas:

Andrew: Six drachmas! Well, really, Philip!
Philip: I'm very sorry, everybody.
Simon: I daresay you are. But here's me and Andrew and the Zebedees working all night with the nets to get a living for the lot of us – and then you go and let yourself be swindled by the first cheating salesman you meet in the bazaar –
Philip: I told you I'm sorry. Master, I am very sorry. But it sounded all right when he worked it out.
Matthew: Fact is, Philip my boy, you've been had for a sucker. Let him ring the changes on you proper. You ought to keep your eyes skinned, you did really. If I was to tell you the dodges these fellows have up their sleeves, you'd be surprised.

This was jam for the journalists. The *Daily Mail* came out the following morning with the headline: B.B.C. "LIFE OF CHRIST" PLAY IN U.S. SLANG. Other papers also reported sensationally on the impersonation of Christ and the use of modern English. There was an uproar. The Lord's Day Observance Society and the Protestant Truth Society mounted a determined opposition. The Secretary of the former body, the Rev. H. H. Martin, launched a campaign, on which he was prepared to spend up to one thousand two hundred pounds, against this act of "irreverence bordering on the blasphemous". Petitions were sent to the Prime Minister and to the Archbishop of Canterbury, urging them to use their influence to get the plays banned. The Parliamentary Secretary to the Minister of Information was asked in the House of Commons if he was "taking steps to revise the script of a series of plays on the life of Jesus . . . so as to avoid offence to Christian feeling". The Secretary replied that it was hardly the business of the Ministry to tell the B.B.C. what to do, but added that the matter had been referred to the relevant advisory committee. The public became more and more hysterical. The desks of newspaper editors were deluged. Leaflets of protestation were distributed and handed out in public places. One such document read:

At [a church] in Bedford, the whole congregation stood, without one dissentient, in solemn protest, on a recent Lord's Day morning, at the request of their Minister, and a letter was written, signed by the Pastor and Deacons, and sent to the Lord's Day Observance Society . . . We must go on protesting. Readers are now urged to write to their M.P.s, asking them to support the growing movement in the House of Commons for more authority over the B.B.C.

When Singapore fell to the Japanese the event was interpreted in the Press as a sign of God's judgment on Britain for allowing such blasphemy to be committed.

Most of the protests were made even before the first play was heard on the air. Dorothy's telephone rang incessantly and she received letters of abuse. She found it difficult to concentrate on writing the other plays. In a letter to Val Gielgud, dated 13 January 1942, she said:

I should like some peace about this show . . . I wish [the uproar] didn't make one so self-conscious about the job. I wish one didn't see Mr Kensit [the Secretary of the Protestant Truth Society] lurking behind every page of the Authorised Version. I wish one hadn't had to fight desperate rear-guard actions with the Press, trying to shut them up, and yet not to alienate them so hopelessly that they would start a fresh campaign of hate against the next play. When we go to Heaven all I ask is that we shall be given some interesting job and allowed to get on with it. No management; no box-office; no dramatic critics; and an audience of cheerful angels who don't mind laughing.

Dr Welch remained calm. Two days after the storm had burst, he wrote:

I entirely support you in your determination to cast the whole play into modern language and to make the characters real. Actually, the vulgar reporting of papers like the *Daily Mail* is really playing into our hands, because when the interested readers tune in to satisfy their curiosity, they will see that the reporting has been entirely false ... I can only be thankful that public interest has been aroused because these plays are going to say something that all our religious broadcasting has failed to say, and are going to say it in a way which is entirely beyond our present powers.

Dorothy replied formally on 15 December, making her position clear:

Under the terms by which I am contracted to the B.B.C., I have the right to insist that the plays shall be performed as I have written them, subject only to your personal approval (which I have already received in writing) and the technical requirements of the production. If there is to be any question of tinkering with the general presentment, or with isolated passages, in order to appease outside interests, I shall be regretfully obliged to withdraw the scripts, under the terms of the contract.

You will understand, I am sure, that I could not consent to complete the series, or permit any parts of it to be broadcast, under conditions which would interfere with the integrity of my work; since this would be fair neither to yourself nor to me, nor to the producer.

This was the May Jenkin situation all over again, but writ large, on a national scale.

The first play, *Kings in Judaea*, was scheduled to be broadcast on 21 December. Before that could happen, however, Dr Welch felt obliged, in view of the storm of protests, to consult the Central Religious Advisory Committee. There was no time to call a meeting, but he sent copies of the second and third plays to all thirteen members, asking them to comment by post, telephone or telegram. It did not seem necessary to consult them about the first play, which deals with the Nativity; no impersonation of Christ is involved, not even the cry of an infant. What Dr Welch hoped for was the Committee's sanction to proceed with the rest. He received it. The replies came: "Plays magnificent . . . go ahead" (from an Evangelical); "The plays are excellent – go ahead" (from a Jesuit priest). Only one member expressed doubt and he was later won over. Reassured by such enthusiastic approval, the B.B.C. felt justified in broadcasting the first play.

Letters of quite a different kind now began to arrive – not of abuse but of praise and gratitude. Writing to congratulate Dorothy on what a correspondent had called "quite the most lovely rendering of the Nativity I have ever experienced", Dr Welch went on to comment on the protest, which was still raging:

What [it] has revealed to me quite clearly is that at heart most of us are Arians; we are prepared for Our Lord to be born into the language of the A.V., or into stained-glass or into paint; what we are not prepared to accept is that He was incarnate. *Incarnatus est* is a phrase; we bow when we say it; but how many of us are prepared really to believe it? I believe this defective belief in the Incarnation is due to Puritanism and not to the influence of Karl Barth; and it goes along with an exaggerated emphasis on the Atonement – I say that in the full belief that a recovery of some faith in the Atonement is the crying need of modern theology. What has always thrilled me about your plays has been this combination of Christology with a full belief in the Incarnation.

The most difficult part of Dr Welch's task was now approaching. He had to persuade the Central Religious Advisory Committee to approve each play, one by one, and he had to persuade Dorothy to accept any alterations to which they might attach particular importance. This was perilously like writing plays by committee. Would she find herself, once again, regretfully obliged to withdraw her scripts and cancel the contract? He was in an awkward position and he knew it:

I love a fight. But I am a bit depressed about the ignorance and stupidity of people, about cold feet in higher quarters and about the possibility that we may lose these plays for no adequate reason. How to combine firmness with diplomacy is enough to give me a headache; my job is to get these plays on the air; yours is to safeguard the integrity of your work; and Val's is to produce the plays without being irritated to death by interfering people.

The Central Religious Advisory Committee met on 8 January

1942. Present were, in addition to the thirteen members, the Chairman of the B.B.C., the Director General, the Controller of Programmes and Dr Welch. The meeting was chaired by the Bishop of Winchester, Dr Cyril Garbett. Dr Welch sent Dorothy a full account that same evening. The meeting had gone extraordinarily well. The position was that the Committee had not the authority to prevent the B.B.C. from broadcasting the plays, but it was advisable to have the Committee's approval if possible. They, for their part, felt they could not give a blank cheque and asked to be allowed to read the plays and comment on them in advance. Dr Welch said he would gladly receive criticism but made it plain that the author reserved the right to withdraw the plays if the integrity of the work was put at risk. Every member of the Committee supported the series, raising no objection to the impersonation of Christ by an actor or to the use of modern English. One or two expressed the hope that extremes of slang would be avoided, but not to the detriment of the naturalness of the dialogue. The Committee represented all denominations and there was not one dissentient voice.

Dr Welch was immensely gratified and heartened. All that remained now, it seemed, and this was still a ticklish matter, was to coax Dorothy to accept minor alterations to meet the "sensibilities of honest, simple Christians whose alarm arises solely from a personal devotion to Our Lord, and not from stupid prejudices". He was convinced that the Lord's Day Observance Society had helped the situation by angering the Committee, one member of which said he hoped the B.B.C. would not allow the Ministry of Information to interfere.

Dorothy was mollified. On 13 January she wrote to Val Gielgud: "I do think Dr Welch has fought a courageous and skilful fight. And the unanimity of the Committee was really rather a triumph."

The second play, *The King's Herald*, was broadcast on 25 January. The following day Miss Jenkin sent a generous note to Dr Welch: "What an entrancing production! It was extraordinarily moving throughout and beautifully simple . . . And to think that we ran a risk of losing all this beauty! I have sent a line to Val proffering homage." There is no evidence that any such note was sent to Dorothy.

Dr Welch was not yet out of the wood. Dorothy was at first as good as gold, accommodating herself with hardly a murmur to minor alterations suggested by the Committee. But then a crisis occurred. The Bishop of Winchester raised objections to the informality of some of the dialogue in the fourth play, *The Heirs to the Kingdom* (the play which had led to such trouble after the press conference).

On 19 February Dorothy wrote to Dr Welch:

> Look here; I rather think the time has come when I must dig my
> toes in a little ... I cannot deal with the Bishop as I should deal
> with Miss Jenkin ... But I am frankly appalled at the idea of
> getting through the Trial and Crucifixion scenes with all the "bad
> people" having to be bottled down to expressions which could not
> possibly offend anybody. I will not allow the Roman soldiers to
> use barrack-room oaths, but they must behave like common
> soldiers hanging a common criminal, or where is the point of the
> story? Nobody cares ... nowadays that Christ was "scourged,
> railed upon, buffeted, mocked and crucified", because all those
> words have grown hypnotic with ecclesiastical use. But it does give
> people a slight shock to be shown that God was flogged, spat
> upon, called dirty names, slugged on the jaw, insulted with vulgar
> jokes, and spiked up on the gallows like an owl on a barn-door.
> That's the thing the priests and people did – has the Bishop
> forgotten it?

Dr Welch replied, "How right you are! I am taking the matter over
the Bishop's head to Caesar [the Director General of the B.B.C.]. I
will do my *utmost*."

Then, providentially, it must have seemed, came the announcement that Dr Garbett was to become the Archbishop of York. Dr
Welch expected him to resign from the Committee, of which he had
been Chairman for twenty years. Then, when the new Chairman was
appointed, he hoped they might all three meet and arrive at a clear
understanding about "not watering down the crudity, indeed the
truth, of the Prosecution, Trial and Crucifixion".

As it turned out, Dr Garbett remained as Chairman of the Committee and Dr Welch suggested that Dorothy should go and see him.
She was doubtful about the usefulness of this but she was willing to
try. On 17 March she wrote to him direct, putting to him

> the necessity of making the characters and behaviour of the per-
> sons who brought about the Trial and Crucifixion of Christ real to
> the listener, even at the cost of some slight shock to the pious ...
>
> My Lord, the people have forgotten so much. The thing has
> become to them like a tale that is told. They cannot believe it ever
> happened ... How can it honour God to make His enemies seem
> less cruel, less callous, less evil than they were?

On 30 March Dorothy did visit the Archbishop-elect and though, as was to be expected, they did not see eye to eye on every point, he made fewer criticisms of the plays from then on. Towards the end of the series, on 22 September 1942, having by then been enthroned at York, he wrote to thank her for writing the plays, apologising for having sometimes had to ask for alterations: "I should like to add how greatly moved I was at listening yesterday to the Crucifixion play. I shall be very interested to see if I have any letters about it." He told Dr Welch that he found it more moving than Oberammergau and expressed the wish that it might be broadcast again on Good Friday.

The nation-wide response to *The Man Born to be King* was overwhelming. Appreciative, even rapturous letters poured in from listeners of all ages, of a wide range of professions and callings, from laity and from clergy of all denominations. Thousands are still alive who heard the broadcasts when they were young and whose lives were lastingly affected by them. When the series was concluded, the Controller of Programmes wrote to thank her "for providing one of the great landmarks of broadcasting". As regards the religious value of the plays, the vision and faith of Dr Welch had been abundantly justified. It was a great evangelistic undertaking, an unprecedented achievement in religious education and one which has never since been equalled.

For Dorothy, one of the greatest satisfactions of the whole enterprise was that it had been a joyfully communal effort. In her Introduction to the published version of the plays, which first appeared in May 1943, she pays eloquent tribute to Val Gielgud and to Dr Welch and his colleagues, to the Central Religious Advisory Committee and to Dr Garbett, who as Chairman, "drew on himself the enemy's heaviest weight of fire and the most violent barrage of abuse" in what she characteristically calls "the Battle of the Scripts".

But it is in her gratitude to the whole cast that her deepest feeling is conveyed:

It was a wonderful company to work with. It was large and it was brilliant, and it worked with an energy and an enthusiasm that can seldom, I should think, have been equalled in any studio. The work was hard, too — exacting, exhausting, and repaid by nothing except the satisfaction of work well done, since no actor received any publicity either in the announcements or in the press. [Except that Robert Speaight's name was disclosed beforehand as that of the actor playing the role of Jesus, "to forestall a flood of random and distracting speculation".]

She also praised the Crowd:

> Only real enthusiasm and devotion to the job can keep crowd and small-part actors on their toes the whole time; and unless they do keep on their toes, the principals have nothing to work to. That devotion and enthusiasm never once flagged . . . They said they enjoyed the work, and certainly they behaved as though they meant it . . . To all the company, then

> I owe a debt of love
> Which I will pay with love.

The Introduction to the plays is itself an important theological statement, being a forceful and moving essay on the gospels and their central character. She expressed herself, characteristically, from the standpoint of a writer:

> I am a writer and I know my trade; and I say that this story is a very great story indeed, and deserves to be taken seriously. I say further (and here I know what I am saying and mean exactly what I say) that in these days it is seldom taken seriously. It is often taken, and treated, with a gingerly solemnity: but that is what honest writers call frivolous treatment . . . It is, first and foremost, a story – a true story, the turning point of history . . .

In statements such as this, as well as in the plays themselves, Dorothy L. Sayers revealed herself as a biblical scholar and critic of great insight, pointing forward to modern developments in theology. Her coherent visualisation of the story, both as theologian and as dramatist is summed up in a further masterly statement: "The history and the theology of Christ are one thing: His life is theology in action, and the drama of His life is dogma shown as dramatic action."

The story was not quite ended. The noble Dr James Welch, who himself merited an award for valour, wrote on 18 June 1943 to the Archbishop of Canterbury, Dr William Temple, to ask if he would consider conferring on Dorothy L. Sayers the Lambeth Degree of Doctor of Divinity for her "fine piece of Christian evangelism". He considered that such an honour would have the support of Church people throughout the country.

The Archbishop replied that he would take soundings to see

whether such a suggestion was possible. He agreed with Dr Welch that the plays were "one of the most powerful instruments in evangelism which the Church had had put into its hands for a long time past". Having assured himself of the support and approval of several clerics, including the Archbishop of York and the Bishop of London, he wrote to ask Dorothy if she would allow him to confer on her the Degree of D.D. "in recognition of what I regard as the great value of your work, especially *The Man Born to be King* and *The Mind of the Maker*". On 7 September Dorothy replied:

Your Grace,
Thank you very much indeed for the great honour you do me. I find it very difficult to reply as I ought, because I am extremely conscious that I don't deserve it. A Doctorate of Letters – yes; I have served Letters as faithfully as I knew how. But I have only served Divinity, as it were, accidentally, coming to it as a writer rather than as a Christian person. A Degree in Divinity is not, I suppose, intended as a certificate of sanctity, exactly; but I should feel better about it if I were a more convincing kind of Christian. I am never quite sure whether I really am one, or whether I have only fallen in love with an intellectual pattern.

After saying that she is unlikely to remain as a writer on the austere level of *The Man Born to be King* and *The Mind of the Maker*, and might therefore bring disrepute to the honour she is offered, she says that she will leave it to the Archbishop's judgment: "If you tell me that I ought to accept, I will."

The Archbishop replied that he saw no harm in a Doctor of Divinity writing detective stories or any similar literature. The object he has in view would not quite be met by a D.Lit. and he hopes very much she will accept the D.D. She asked for two or three more days in which to think the matter over.

During that time she consulted friends whose advice she thought would be valuable and with their help she came to the conclusion that it would be better for her not to accept. Apart from her reluctance to sail under anything that might look like false colours, she had been influenced by the consideration that any good she could do in the way of presenting the Christian faith would be hampered if she wore any sort of ecclesiastical label. Further, she anticipated, since women are "news", there might, from time to time, be unwelcome publicity in the sensational press – "some of which does not love me very much". This apprehension would impose a constraint upon her secular writing: "there would always be the strain of an obligation to be innocuous and refrain from giving offence, and that is a strain under which no writer can work properly".

Dr Temple was very understanding. He replied in a way which Dorothy must have found helpful and consoling:

I think I do fully understand the situation; indeed you have persuaded me that if I were in your position I should have reached your conclusion. Meanwhile I am still glad that I made the proposal and that you are willing for me to mention it to some of those who have been eager that the Church should show some real recognition of the great value of your Plays and also the book *The Mind of the Maker*.

CHAPTER 25

Reluctant Prophet

Dorothy L. Sayers was now a national figure. The public, the press, the B.B.C., the Church looked to her to make pronouncements. Dr Welch said, "We must make you a prophet to this generation and hand you the microphone to use as often as you feel able."

She did not feel comfortable about this. She had explained to the Archbishop of Canterbury, when declining his offer of a Lambeth Doctorate of Divinity, that she was reluctant to sail under anything that might seem like false colours. She began gradually to feel more and more that in writing and lecturing on the Christian religion she was straying from her proper job, which, as she told Father Kelly, was "to show in story form, and not to argue and exhort".

Ever since the production of *The Zeal of Thy House* and the publication of her trenchant articles, "The Greatest Drama Ever Staged", "The Dogma is the Drama" and "The Triumph of Easter", various religious bodies had been seeking her out. The Church Assembly asked her advice about religious drama. Dom Bernard Clements, the vicar of All Saints, Margaret Street, where she attended Mass when she was in London, asked for her support in setting up a Guild of Catholic Writers, with the object of helping journalists and writers to relate their work to their religious life. She was present at a meeting in May 1938 and there she met for the first time the Rev. V. A. Demant, who invited her to lecture to his parish in Richmond on "Our Reading, Listening-in and Play-going". She did so, with misgiving: "I do not know that I am much good at speaking about religious life, being a great deal stronger on doctrine than on practice!"

The Guild of Catholic Writers was affiliated to the Church Social Action Group, of which the Secretary was Father Patrick McLaughlin, who became a friend. (Dorothy was to be closely associated with him in connection with St Anne's House, Soho, an enterprise which absorbed a great deal of her time and energy in her later years.) The Social Action Group set themselves to keep a watch on newspapers and journals in order to seize suitable opportunities of combating anti-Christian views. Dorothy agreed to take part and was allotted the task of keeping an eye on *John o' London's Weekly*.

Her first action was to challenge an article by Julian Huxley entitled "Life Can be Worth Living", intervening with a letter dated 2 January 1939 protesting against pronouncements by scientists about dogma, "which are dangerous to the uneducated mind". Reporting to her colleagues, she complained indignantly: "They insidiously take for granted propositions which never have formed part of orthodox doctrine and then proceed to refute them with a remarkable air of plausibility." Father Kelly drew her attention to a programme drawn up by Dr J. H. Oldham, calling on writers "to keep the Christian flag flying during the war". Dorothy wrote to him at once, saying that they must not only keep it flying, but "bring it out and carry it ostentatiously down the street":

> Materialism is dead, and the people who have been busy for the last fifty years secularising everything are now thoroughly frightened by the results when they see the idea carried to its full conclusion. Even the intellectuals, whom the Church was foolish enough to lose, seem to be wavering in their self-confidence.

The war, she asserted, provided an opportunity to bring Christian doctrine into relation with reality and the Church should now say something loud and clear. Dr Oldham asked to meet her. He had decided to publish a weekly Christian newsletter and had enlisted the support of the two Archbishops and a number of other clergy. Would Dorothy help? She would, and eagerly enlisted his support for *Bridgeheads*, enclosing the statement of aims, which she had just drawn up. Her letter is dated 2 October 1939, which shows how speedily she set to work on this project. Dr Oldham invited her to contribute an article to the newsletter on the meaning of Christmas. She agreed to do so but warned: "I always get hauled over the coals for talking about Him as though He was somebody real." Her article, entitled "Is This He That Should Come?", was published as a supplement to the Christmas number of the newsletter of 1939.

The Archbishop of York (then William Temple) wrote to Dr Oldham: "How magnificent Dorothy Sayers is!" The Rev. Dr James Parkes also wrote: "Dorothy Sayers is superb, magnificent. The

Christian newsletter would have justified its existence on that supplement alone."

Meeting with such approval and acclaim, she found it difficult to
refuse invitations to continue. At first she looked on her new role as
part of her war work, but in August 1940 she was already writing to
the philosopher Donald Mackinnon: "I've got wound up accidentally into this theological business, and I feel more and more
ridiculous as it goes rollicking along. I only started by writing a play
and trying to make its theology coherent and orthodox, and look
what's happened to me!"

That same month, sending the Rev. J. C. Heenan the scripts of two
broadcast talks on the Sacraments, she said that she was trying to do
as little religious speaking and writing as possible, "for fear of being
classed as a religious writer, but it's difficult to refuse":

> So few parsons are really trained in the use of words . . . The result
> is that when the trained writer restates an old dogma in a new form
> of words, the reader mistakes it for a bright new idea of the
> writer's own. I spend half my time and a lot of stamps telling
> people that I have not been giving them a fancy doctrine of my
> own . . . Typical of this is a woman who writes to say: "I can't
> agree with you that Christ is the same person as God the Creator".
> One can only say: "It isn't a question of agreeing with me. I have
> expressed no opinion. That is the opinion of the official Church,
> which you will find plainly stated in the Nicene Creed, whether or
> not you and I agree with it."

She considered the teaching and preaching of the Church inadequate.
The result was that people were bewildered and "in a nightmare of
muddle out of which [they] have to be hauled by passing detective
novelists in a hurry and with no proper tackle". Preachers will not
define terms or say what the doctrine is.

In September she was invited to attend a meeting of clerics and
laity at the B.B.C., "who were trying to work out plans for some sort
of 'call to religion' with musical and dramatic accompaniments". She
was not enamoured of what she called "propaganda art-forms" and
considered that it would be better to begin by making a work of art
for its own sake and let the moral emerge from it, not the other way
round. She came away from the meeting very depressed. To Canon
Cockin, a member of the committee, she wrote, "It sent me out in a
mood for a stiff gin-and-tonic and the robust company of my heathen
friends." She wrote at length about it to Father Kelly:

The wretched pacifist question boiled up at once, and these people always contrive to put one into an awkward position, as though one was completely corrupted by Caesar, while they sit loftily on the Mount with Christ and Mr Gandhi. And the clergy, who were not pacifist, but showed a great reluctance to fight the issue, all seemed disposed to believe that it was the chief business of the Church to advocate socialism and economic reform. It's so easy to say "Lets have the simple Gospel and consider what Christ would have done." But what is the "simple Gospel"? And whatever Christ "would have done", there's one thing He would have resolutely refused to do, viz. to sit on committees and argue about politics . . . Perhaps the people who sit on B.B.C. committees are the wrong kind of clergymen. They don't seem able to keep the Law and the Gospel distinct in their minds.

They all made me feel very gloomy, including the Socialist parsons, who all seem to think that the difficulties of labour will be smoothed away by getting wages right, never mind what happens to the work. I tried to suggest to them (along the lines of the little section on Work in "Creed or Chaos?") that it was necessary, along with the wages question, to get a right attitude to the work. They thought this very novel and constructive . . . which shows how hopelessly we have all got wound up into the "economic theory" of society.

They babbled, she went on, about European Federation, which in her opinion is no more likely to work than the League of Nations or the temporal sovereignty of Rome. "The one Federation that does work – i.e. the British Commonwealth – they have no use for."

One parson on the committee of whom she approved was Father John Groser, the celebrated East-End socialist reformer. Eric Fenn wrote to her about him after one meeting: "Groser is a most uncomfortable creature, isn't he? I've known him well for years and he always makes me feel I really know nothing about the love of God at all!" Dorothy replied:

I know what you mean about Father Groser, though oddly enough before getting your letter I said to a friend of mine that he was the person with whom I felt most comfortable. I think this is because, although he is obviously right out of our sphere as regards saintliness of heart, he has the quality, which I can appreciate with my head, of coming straight to the essentials of any question without being distracted or bamboozled by a clutter of secondary considerations.

She had delivered the talk "Creed or Chaos?" the preceding May, in Derby, at the Biennial Festival of the Church Tutorial Classes Association. The section entitled "Work", about which she had spoken to the committee, contains the very essence of her thinking on a Christian society:

> Nothing has so deeply discredited the Christian Church as her squalid submission to the economic theory of society . . . I believe, however, that there is a Christian doctrine of work, very closely related to the doctrines of the creative energy of God and the divine image in man. The modern tendency seems to be to identify work with gainful employment; and this is, I maintain, the essential heresy at the back of the great economic fallacy which allows wheat and coffee to be burnt and fish to be used for manure while whole populations stand in need of food. The fallacy being that work is not the expression of man's creative energy in the service of Society, but only something he does in order to obtain money and leisure . . .
>
> If man's fulfilment of his nature is to be found in the full expression of his divine creativeness, then we urgently need a Christian doctrine of work, which shall provide, not only for proper conditions of employment, but also that the work shall be such as a man may do with his whole heart, and that he shall do it for the very work's sake.

In January 1941, Archbishop Temple presided over a conference to consider what role the Church should play in the social reconstruction which would be needed after the war. One of the ten speakers – and the only woman – was Dorothy L. Sayers. She was asked to address two questions:

1. Is the Church's witness concerned with the possibility of a breakdown of civilisation, and with the economic and political causes of such a breakdown? If so, upon what grounds?

2. Does the present situation derive in any degree from the fact that the modern Church has been more concerned to raise the moral level of social effort rather than to discover and correct falsity in the dominant purposes of corporate life?

The conference was held in Malvern, to be out of the way of air-raids. Dorothy opened the second session on 8 January. Her paper was entitled "The Church's Responsibility". She began:

> It is always with some embarrassment that I approach any

question about the Christian Church. When challenged, I am never quite sure how to identify it or whether, in anything but the technical sense, I feel myself to belong to it. In practice, when writing articles for instance about Church doctrine, I get along fairly well by confining myself as far as possible to the Creeds, and I interpret them by something which my intellect recognises as . . . the authentic voice of the Church . . . self-consistent [and] offering a complete and rational explanation of the universe, and by the fact that it reconciles to itself various other experiences of truth with which I am more or less familiar − such as the artist's truth . . .

They had put the hammer in her hand and, after this modest preliminary disclaimer, she wielded it.

If the Church is concerned with civilisation, or with politics and economics, it can only be on the grounds of a realistic and sacramental theology of the Incarnation. For this means that the whole of man's humanity, at its most vital, developed, and characteristic, is the vehicle of the divine part of his nature . . . A Church which takes up this fully sacramental position must not confine her concern with civilisation to the political and economic aspects of civilisation. If she undertakes to sanctify humanity, it must be the whole of humanity. She must include within her sacraments all arts, all letters, all labour and all learning . . . For she stands committed to the assertion that all human activity, whether of spirit, mind or body, is potentially good − not negatively, by repression, but positively, and as an act of worship. Further, she must include a proper reverence for the earth and for all material things; because these also are the body of the living God.

On the resentment of the common man against the intrusion of politics into the pulpit, she delivered some shrewd blows:

The Kingdom of Heaven is not of this world; and the attempt to yoke it to any form of secular constitution is treason . . . If . . . the Church commits herself . . . to the support of any particular form of political government . . . she will find herself insensibly adopting and maintaining . . . its underlying assumptions, which may be very strongly in conflict with her theology.

She stated that the Church had too limited an understanding of morality, "deforming the very meaning of the word by restricting it to sexual offences". She had put this pithily in her letter to Professor Mackinnon in August 1940: "The Church is uncommonly vocal about the subject of bedrooms and so singularly silent on the subject of board-rooms." She expressed concern about intellectual corruption and considered that the Church had neglected its duty in not denouncing it. She saw the besetting sins of society as pride, avarice and intellectual sloth:

> The grave error of the institutional Church has been that she has supposed it her business to administer the Law. For this reason, her dealings with the world have partaken too much of the nature of the Law – negative, restrictive, codified, cautious; moral rather than spiritual, resigned rather than enthusiastic, given to omission rather than to excess, instructive rather than inspiring, organising rather than leading, resisting evil rather than overcoming evil with good . . .
>
> If the Church is to find her common soul, she must contrive to root it in a common integrity. I do not mean that she must be uninterested in the social, political and moral sphere of the Law, but that she must be disinterested . . . But I find in the Church as a whole very little reverence for intellectual integrity. . . . For the general tendency today, among the rank and file of Christendom, is to a religion divorced from theology – a religion that is a denial of the divinity of the Word.

Bernard Causton, one of the organisers of the conference, said: "Miss Sayers' paper . . . summed up so much that people have waited for years to hear stated from a Christian standpoint." W. G. Peck, whose task it was to make synopses, wrote to tell her that hers was quite the best, "excellent, and entirely on the right lines". In her reply, dated 9 December 1941, she said that she agreed that there is a "tendency to link the Church up with political -isms, generally socialism, under the impression that she must atone for her sins in the past by committing fresh ones in an opposite direction". Her own comment, in writing to a friend immediately afterwards, was that her speech had been "directly centred about the whole question of intellectual integrity". Later that year she told Donald Mackinnon that she had found it extremely difficult to write: "When I am doing this kind of thing, I am visited by a powerful sensation that it is not my proper job, and that I am doing something perilously like violating my own integrity." To Father Kelly she confessed, writing to him on

15 May 1941, that she had "an irritating sensation that my time is being wasted and a strong sensation of guilt for allowing it to happen ... I am not called to be a fisher of men."

Pressure on her increased. On 19 January 1942, the Rev. J. C. Heenan wrote to her:

> I wonder if you realise your own important position in the Christian world. I know your views on your work and I know nothing would persuade you, even for the sake of religion, to use your genius as propaganda. All this I take for granted but, at the same time, I feel keenly that you are about the only woman of letters (how you'll love that expression!) who is forthright and belligerent in calling the bluff of self-styled intellectuals who are too clever to bow before mysteries. You make an extremely good case for humility of the mind. I know, because you have told me, that it would be a bad thing if you became a religious writer yet I can't help thinking that you could produce a very powerful challenge to shabby thinkers if you wrote just one short *ex professo* religious work. Please don't say that you have already done so. I don't mean anything like that you have already done. I mean a real 100 per cent broadside.

No reply to this letter is extant.

In June 1943 she made a determined resolve to resist all such pressure. A cleric by the name of H. C. Marsh had written to ask her to contribute a paper to a religious conference at Alnwick. She wrote to thank him, but said:

> I have ... decided, after careful consideration, for the present at least, that it will be advisable for me to give up speaking on religious subjects. I have been giving addresses of this kind, off and on, for about three years, and this is about as long as it is wise for any speaker to air his views on any subject in which he is not professionally qualified; and it is, I think, particularly true when that subject is theology or religion.

She had resolved to refuse all such invitations "during the coming year at any rate".

She did not succeed in breaking free. As late as 1955, on 25 March, she wrote to G. R. Collings of Penguins:

> Alas! yes – I have got labelled as a "writer of Christian Apolo-

getics", but God knows it is the last thing I ever wished to be. For the last fifteen years or so I have been reluctantly bound to this Ixion wheel, from which I ceaselessly struggle to escape. I like writing plays and stories, I like doing literary criticism, I like translating verse; but I do loathe making the direct attack by way of argument and exhortation. It is ruinously bad for one's proper work, and it lands one in a false position – that of seeming to be an evangelist when one is not. Also it fosters an irritable and domineering temper.

Pressure was also put upon her to write more Peter Wimsey books. This, too, made her irritable. On 24 October 1949, writing to Sir Henry Aubrey-Fletcher, who wrote detective stories under the name of Henry Wade, she said:

As for writing detective stories – there are a thousand and one reasons why I can feel no desire for it; but the chief one is that, like Conan Doyle, I have been so much put off by being badgered to do it when I was wrapped up in other things that the mere thought now gives me a kind of nausea. When I started on my plays in 1937, I fully intended to do another novel some day – though novels are terribly slow and tedious after the briskness of stage work. But the infernal nuisance of writing letters to sentimental Wimsey-addicts, telling editors that I cannot switch my mind off any job to write crime-stories for them, and I dare not start it up again, even if I wanted to . . . ! A new mystery story now would probably run me into super-tax – so brilliant is this government in devising discouragement for the dollar-earners. But the chief reason is, as I have said, that I have become sickened by importunity, and that the thought of being pushed and halloooed into the old routine fills me with distaste.

She had also come to the conclusion that detective stories tended to have a bad effect on people, making them believe that there was one neat solution for all human ills and she would have no more part in encouraging such an attitude.

Nevertherless, Lord Peter and his world stayed alive in her mind. In her article "Gaudy Night", published in 1937, she had described him as being "a permanent resident in the house of my mind. His affairs are more real to me than my own; his domestic responsibilities haunt my waking hours, and I find myself bringing all my actions and opinions to the bar of his silent criticism."

In 1936 she had already started a new novel, entitled *Thrones, Dominations*, in which the Wimsey marriage was to be contrasted with that of two other couples. It was left unfinished, but it is clear from what exists that it was to have been yet another murder story. One short story, "The Haunted Policeman", published in the *Strand Magazine* of March 1938, brings the Wimsey saga up to the birth of their first son. Another short story written in 1942, but not published during Dorothy's life, shows the Wimseys in war-time, evacuated to Talboys (the house which featured in *Busman's Honeymoon*), and already the parents of three sons. They were to have five children in all. Viscount St George (Jerry), Lord Peter's charming nephew and the heir to the dukedom, was, alas! shot down and killed in the Battle of Britain, though this sad event, like the size of Harriet's family, was disclosed only orally to friends. At the beginning of the war, as has been shown, she enlisted Lord Peter and his associates to write letters to the *Spectator* to help in boosting public morale. That is the last we hear of them.

On 13 June 1943 Dorothy L. Sayers was fifty years old. She had decided to give up writing and lecturing, for a time at least, on religious subjects. She had resolved to write no more Wimsey novels, at least until the war was over. Her productivity during the past twenty years had been enormous. She had achieved world fame. Apart from the promotion of *Bridgeheads*, she had no immediate plans for the future. She had earned a rest. Now was the moment, surely, to pick up the unfinished biography of Wilkie Collins and work "peacefully" at that, as she had once described herself as doing.

Two months later, Faber and Faber published a book by Charles Williams, entitled *The Figure of Beatrice*. It was to give yet another new direction to her creative life.

CHAPTER 26

Seeing It Through

John Anthony was growing up. Dorothy had every reason to be proud of him. He did extremely well at his preparatory school in Broadstairs and duly won a scholarship to Malvern College. Still signing her letters, "with best love, your affectionate Mother", she began now to treat him like the intelligent young adult he was. They discussed books, ideas and world affairs. When he was fourteen he wrote to tell her that he had been reading Eddington. She replied: "He isn't exactly easy reading, but he does end up with an attempt to deal with what you were speaking of – from how few assumptions one can build up a coherent universe." That same year, soon after the Munich crisis, she wrote to him: "Actually, I think the Germans were abominably treated at Versailles and afterwards." She recommended E. Wingfield-Stratford's *The Harvest of Victory*, which she said was "written with great fairness", and promised to try to find a copy for him in London.

If he asked for advice she gave it, but seldom otherwise. Finding he had a talent for writing, he tried his hand at a play, which he sent to her, asking for comments. She took the time and trouble to make constructive and encouraging suggestions. At Malvern he began to do well at mathematics and asked how one could tell if one was a "real" mathematician or a "real" writer. She replied that she would call a "real" mathematician someone who was creative in the subject, "not just a clever worker in figures", in the same way as the creative writer is quite unlike the man of letters, "whose talent is critical and interpretative". And she added: "Of one thing you can be sure: if you are a creator in any particular medium, you will end by discovering the fact. Nothing can prevent the genuine creator from creating, or from creating in his own proper medium." She expressed the hope that if he decided to specialise in mathematics or science he would also keep up with the humanities: "Scientists in these days tend to work in isolation from the general body of thought . . . I believe there will be a reaction, in the next few generations, to a synthesis of science and philosophy, which will help to correct the present disjunction of the two activities."

In the summer of 1940, when there was talk of invasion, and he asked what he should do, she advised him to stay in Oxfordshire; he was probably as safe there as anywhere.

> If I should be killed in an air-raid, you and Aunt Ivy must at once get into communication with my solicitors, who have my will and will know how to act. There will not be very much money, I am afraid — nobody will have much money when this is over, even if all goes as well as we can hope. It is not possible to plan out anything for the future. I shall try to pay the school fees as long as is necessary.
>
> In the event of a German occupation of this country, which is possible, though I think not probable, be careful not to advertise your connection with me; writers of my sort will not be popular with the Gestapo. If there should be any question of evacuating to the Dominions, on the other hand, I will take what measures I can. But we are in the front of the battle now, and the great thing is to stay put and work at whatever the defence requires . . . You have done well at school . . . do well in this business.

He had told her earlier that he found history difficult and she had explained that the politics of the present would be history to future generations, just as the politics of the past were now history to us. And the same situations kept recurring:

> Look now at the history you used to find so difficult. England is back in the centre stream of her tradition — she is where she was in 1588 and 1815. Spain held all Europe, France held all Europe; they broke themselves upon England; we have to see that the same thing happens to Germany.

She had urged him to keep on with history, for the study of contemporary events, unless based on the past, was shallow and dangerous. She quoted from T. S. Eliot's *The Family Reunion*:

> . . . because everything is irrevocable,
> Because the past is irremediable,

Because the future can only be built
Upon the real past. [Her italics]

And she added, "The 'directed' education of Nazi Youth is absolutely dependent on their being kept from any knowledge of the 'real past'."

She took pleasure in telling him about her work. Before *The Mind of the Maker* was even published, she sent him a copy of the advance proofs. He was then seventeen. He wrote a long letter about it and she replied, also at length, answering his questions and helping him to understand the analogy she had drawn between human creation and the Trinity.

In December 1941 he won a scholarship to Balliol (Lord Peter Wimsey's college). She wrote: "Best congratulations . . . I thought you would pull it off all right. Well done." His tutor was to be Roy Ridley. John had asked his advice about taking a war job before beginning to work for his degree and Ridley had discouraged this. What did his mother think? Her reply was that his tutor naturally considers that he would do better at college than doing war-work "and passionately rebuts the suggestion that Oxford is behaving in a remote and academic way". She thought that the loss of a term would not really matter. "You have brains enough to catch that up": "Nobody loves the Universities more than I do – but a war-time Oxford isn't the real Oxford, and that's what's wrong with it . . . I know, because I had a war year of it last time. It has neither its own virtues nor the virtues of the world." Whatever he decides to do, she will make the necessary financial arrangements.

In the event, he signed on with the Technical Branch of the Royal Air Force and it was to be several years before he went up to Oxford. He was now living at close quarters with working men and he found this a startling change after Malvern College. Dorothy commented:

Yes, I wondered how you would feel about that . . . The workers of this country are damned good stuff, take them all in all; though it's an error to suppose that, merely by being a worker, a man becomes endowed with infallible virtue and wisdom. That's not the case, though a great many socialist Utopias are built on that curious assumption. The intelligent humanist is liable to make a major divinity of the proletariat – but they are merely human beings, with their own virtues and follies and vices like other people.

343

He finds the work monotonous and she reminds him that war is won, not only by armaments, but by a nation's ability to withstand boredom and inconvenience. It is easy to feel one's work is important when it involves excitement. "By the way," she added, in reply to an assumption he had made, "I don't think I do take a gloomy view of the war. I am inclined to take a gloomy view of the peace." She spends her time, she tells him,

> writing letters to people imploring them not to imagine that the "Post-War World" is going to be a time of peace, plenty and expanding markets . . . I'm not sure, but I think we are going to see mass production come full circle and destroy itself – not in my time . . . but probably in yours. That will be interesting . . . I think (again) that, after the aristocracy of managers, the next thing will be an aristocracy of technicians. You will probably come in for that.

As regards his own future, she advised him to look out for something on the technical side of aeronautics or radio, where he would be likely to meet with intelligent colleagues. She then allowed herself to reach back into the past. She recalled that he was, after all, the son of a motor engineer and might well have inherited his genes: "You would be in contact with the really intelligent British mechanic, who is a person worth knowing. And it would be something real." He was in no position, then, to catch the drift of that remark, for he never knew, in his mother's lifetime, who or what his real father was.

She was aware that he had practical skills and when he asked her for a capital sum to enable him to build himself a house, she agreed. She encouraged him to open a bank account and trusted him to manage his own money. She kept up a generous allowance and frequently sent him something extra, "for fun", or "to make whoopee with", though begging him not to spend it all on "gin and girls". And she counselled him: "One thing . . . I do want to say with very great emphasis. If you get into any serious trouble, let me know, and I will extricate you if I can. But do not, whatever you do, get into debt."

She took him into her confidence about her domestic difficulties and about Mac's moods. In May 1943 she wrote:

> Your father has been rather more uncertain-tempered than usual just lately, and it's extraordinarily difficult to discuss anything when he's there, because he never listens to anything anybody says,

but just walks away from the whole thing and is very cross afterwards. He is really rather a difficult person.

When John finally went up to Oxford in the autumn of 1945, she wrote, in reply to enquiries he had made: "I think your best plan, if questioned, is to say that you are our ward and adopted by us, and leave it at that. Which reminds me that you ought to have a copy of your adoption papers – if you haven't got it, I will get the lawyers to send you one." He had a Government grant which would cover his tuition and College fees. In addition she guaranteed him an allowance of two hundred pounds a year for the next three or four years. After that, she proposed to hand over a capital sum of five hundred pounds, "in a lump to get started with". "That is what I have in mind to do. Naturally, it will depend on how things pan out; I mean, I couldn't do it if I fell ill and couldn't work, or taxation becomes any more savage."

During the last year of Mac's life, she was particularly hard pressed. John had asked for a lump sum and she had sent him five hundred pounds, with difficulty, since Mac's visits to hospital and a convalescent home had cost her about a thousand guineas:

If my health cracks up – as it might do with all the worry and strain – then that is just too bad and we have all had it. But before the end of the year I hope to know better whether the strain will ease, or whether I have to face the fact that I shall be landed with a permanent invalid and a permanent heavy expense.

She hoped he would enjoy Oxford:

Remember that it is a gossipy sort of place, and Roy Ridley a gentleman of a very unbridled tongue. A pleasant man, but remarkably silly. I once happened to say that he had a profile like Peter Wimsey, and he started a host of rumours, the reverberation of which has not yet died down – giving himself out to be the original of that character, though in fact I never met him till all the books were written.

She had completely forgotten, and was never to remember, the rapturous occasion in 1913 when she had seen and heard the young Maurice Roy Ridley recite his prize poem at the degree ceremony in the Sheldonian.

In March 1948 she wrote to congratulate her son on winning

fifteen guineas for a poem on Blake. She noticed he had used the signature "Anthony Fleming": "Do you prefer that name? I rather like it myself, except that it appears to have become suddenly fashionable and every second person is Anthony – I can't think why." This was, in fact, the form of his name which he adopted from then on, though his mother continued to call him John.

In his last year at Oxford he wrote to say he was suffering from "Schools fever" (he was reading Modern Greats – Philosophy, Politics and Economics) and she advised him to go on the river:

> The most brilliant language student in my year sat riveted to her books all day, got Schools fever in its most virulent form, went stale, suffered a nervous collapse and took a Fourth. (Whereas I, who had consistently cut lectures and concentrated all my attention on the Bach Choir, took a First, which was very unjust, but there you are!) A lot of it is luck.

When the results came out, the name of John Anthony Fleming was among those who had achieved a first class degree. His mother wrote:

> Dear John,
>   Many thousand congratulations on your class. You must have worked like a beaver – and indeed, I felt sure you were doing so and am not really surprised, though much delighted with the result.
>   Yours joyfully,
>   D.L.S.

She enclosed a cheque for ten pounds towards a holiday.

It was a landmark. Looking back over the twenty-four years during which she had made herself responsible for her son's well-being, she could indeed allow herself some feeling of joy. With Ivy's help, she had given him everything possible, except the acknowledgment of him as her son among her friends. It has been said that he resented this in later life. If so, it was something she had also denied herself. She could never indulge in the pleasure of introducing or referring to "my son at Balliol", or "my son, who has just taken a First at Oxford". In a conversation I had with him a few months before his death, at the age of sixty, Anthony Fleming said: "She did the very best she could." As her letters show, she continued to do so until her death, in 1957. Under her will, he was her sole beneficiary.

Mac had died suddenly, on 9 June 1950, aged sixty-eight, of a cerebral haemorrhage. He had been suffering for several years from high blood-pressure and arterial degeneration. For six months previous to his death, Dorothy had hovered anxiously, unable to do any sustained work. "Poor dear old Mac", she called him, replying to letters of condolence. To one friend she wrote:

> Thank you very much for your sympathy. It is quite true that my husband had a great zest for life in the old days, and it was when it grew obvious that he had altogether lost it, and lost all his resilience, that it became clear that there was something very seriously wrong. He said that he would be "glad to be out of it all", and so, for his sake, I am glad he is.

He had asked to be cremated and that his ashes should be scattered near his birthplace in Scotland. This was done by the local doctor who had attended him. Travelling by car, he stopped outside an inn named the Fleming Arms and then at a nearby church the ashes of Oswold Arthur Fleming were returned to his native soil. On the death certificate Dorothy identified him professionally as "artist", a touching tribute to all that she had most admired in him.

Dorothy's robust sense of individual responsibility was heightened by the world crisis. Though she tried to resist pressure on her to speak and write on religion, she thought it her duty to make known her views on public affairs. The war brought out her Englishness. She told me that when filling in a form she always wrote "English" (never "British") in a column headed "nationality".

Her speeches and articles about the immediate pre-war period, the war itself and plans for reconstruction emphasise, again and again, the rights and obligations of the individual: she regards this as a recognisably English stance. On the pre-war policies of appeasement and disarmament, on socialist Utopias and on "Progressive Humanism" her views are sweeping and scathing: "I have no use whatever for Enlightened Opinion, whose science is obsolete, its psychology superficial, its theology beneath contempt and its history nowhere." For her, Winston Churchill symbolised the country's reawakening from a twenty-years' sleep:

> [He] had always been obstinately unenlightened. He was English and aristocratic, and had the bad taste not to be ashamed of his origins ... He had always stubbornly affirmed that some things were worse than war ... He believed in History – even English

history. He affronted the highbrows, with vulgar outmoded virtues, such as patriotism, courage, honour, loyalty, cheerfulness and high spirits; he defied the plain, practical low-brows by using the sort of language which a Raleigh would not have thought unbecoming. He not only was, in a symbolic and spiritual manner, a bulldog . . . he looked like a bulldog – the cartoonist's delight, an endearing mascot . . . He was England.

She drew an affectionate cartoon of him herself in a letter to Muriel St Clare Byrne, dated 20 March 1941:

Dorothy's view of Winston Churchill *(Marion E. Wade Center)*

[Churchill is someone] whom the common Englishman promptly recognises as the real thing – gent, scholar, wit, foul-mouthed, *bon vivant*, and all the rest of it ... I say, the old boy's been on the binge, hasn't he? Trotting away to see the world, running through convoys, dropping in at Reykjavik for a quick one, and refusing to come home! When there was such a long and awful silence, I really began to think they'd lost him and were wondering how to break the news. It seems to need a cartoon in Tenniel's domestic manner.

And here she drew one (reproduced on page 348). She added, "There ought to be Stalin and Musso and Pétain looking out of the windows, but I can't draw them."

This is the pugnacious, defiant, forthright Dorothy of the war years. Large, square, mannish in dress (except on gala occasions) – flat shoes, tailor-made suits, a pork-pie or a wide-brimmed felt hat – her appearance from her fifties on disconcerted friends and foes alike. Of bulldog breed herself, like Churchill, she knew her own mind and spoke it forcibly.

When the journalist William Connor ("Cassandra" of the *Daily Mirror*) attacked P. G. Wodehouse, accusing him of treason for broadcasting to America while interned by the Germans in France, she sprang indignantly to his defence, a lone voice amid the uproar, protesting against the general assumption, unconfirmed, that he had been giving comfort to the enemy.

Her brush with Tom Driberg, the Labour M.P., was characteristic of her somewhat testy personality at this period. She had supported him in 1942 when he stood as a candidate in the Maldon by-election, as he himself recalled:

> At the King's Head in Maldon the splendid elderly landlady ... rallied all sorts of unexpected help. Dorothy L. Sayers, who lived at Witham, lent furniture for our committee room there. (She thought better of it later; when I asked her in 1945 to help again, reminding her that we had been to Mass in London together, she replied that I appeared to be inviting her to commit inverted simony.)

The full story is revealed in the Sayers correspondence. In September 1944, the vicar of the local church wrote to invite her to take the chair at a meeting of the Witham Branch of the Maldon Constituency Association at which Tom Driberg and Vernon Bartlett would be speaking on post-war reconstruction. Dorothy replied:

> Though I have no personal quarrel with Mr Driberg, whom I knew
> in another connection before he adventured into politics, I disap-
> prove so heartily of everything he has done since he was elected to
> the House of Commons that it would be highly incongruous for
> me to take the chair at his meeting. Even if bloodshed were
> avoided, a wordy conflict between the chairman and the principal
> speaker can have an air of indecorum about it. I must beg leave,
> therefore, to decline your kind invitation.

Her letter was passed on to Driberg, as she knew it would be, and
in June 1945 he wrote her a letter of six hand-written pages, asking
for her support in the forthcoming election. He said he did so with
apprehension, knowing that she did not share his political views, but
since she had been kind to him at the time of the by-election of 1942
he wished to say how distressed he had been to learn that she had
disapproved of every single thing he had said and done since his
election to Parliament. He reminded her that the first question she
had put to him then was "Are you standing for a Christian programme?" His views, being of the Left, he knows must be repugnant
to her, but since she put that question to him she must, he assumed,
regard it as more important than their secular differences. He went
on to recount all that he had done in the House to defend the
interests of the Church. Would it not be a pity if the Church of
England were seen to be the preserve of one party only?

This was grist to Dorothy's mill. In her reply she admitted that she
disliked his politics, "both the hedge on which you were sitting and
the side on which you appear to have come down". Why had she
asked him that question? Because she prefers to know the worst in
advance: she has a profound distrust of "Christian" political programmes: "The suggestion that one should vote against one's
political conscience for the sake of securing ecclesiastical reforms is
interesting; I do not quite know the name of the particular sin
involved – it is a sort of inverted simony: the sale of the world to the
church." Driberg had asked what questions she considered most
important in the present world situation. She answered: "If you want
to know what questions interest me, I will tell you: British Armed
Power; Imperial Foreign Policy; the responsibility of the State to the
Nation; the maintenance of the rights of citizens under the Common
Law."

Her renown brought added responsibilities. She was influential and other influential people took notice of what she said. A striking example was the Prime Minister of Canada, Mackenzie King, to whom she wrote on 12 May 1944 to thank him for his "great and heartening speech" at Westminster. Her letter is an impassioned statement of her patriotism and of her vision of her country's role in history:

England is very small and very old. It is very easy for the old to be persuaded that they are useless and out-of-date, and that their smallness ought to relegate them to a back seat. In the years between the Wars we were very nearly talked into believing that we were an anachronism, and no longer fit to call ourselves the centre of a great Empire.

What the talkers had forgotten, and we seemed to have forgotten, was our history and our position on the map. Small as we are, we are the keepers of the gate. If that gate is once slammed and bolted, there is no road into Europe and no road out. The power that shuts the gate of England could be tyrant of all Europe and perhaps of all Asia too.

For nearly nine hundred years we have kept the gate of Europe open. We hold the sea-way and we hold the air-way. But the gate is getting too heavy for us to hold alone; this time it almost slipped from our hands before help could come. Yet, when we saw the enemy in the Channel Ports, we felt a great lifting of the heart, because then we knew for a certainty that what people had been saying about us was not true. We knew again who we were, and what we were for . . .

When peace comes, the others may forget again, and so may we . . . The heart of man is desperately wicked and the end of tyranny is not yet . . . Don't let us forget — we need aircraft, fleet, merchantmen, faith and courage.

The situation in Europe is going to be very complicated, dangerous, and hard; and something tells me that we shall be greatly hated, and that neither the vanquished nor yet our Allies will find it easy to forgive us our existence — for we have no illusions that gratitude can endure very long in people who have been rescued from a humiliating position; it is not in human nature.

Mr Mackenzie King was so moved and impressed by this letter that he quoted it in the Canadian House of Commons.

Another channel through which she communicated her views was the Christendom Group, founded by Maurice Reckitt, who enlisted her support and invited her to write articles for the journal which he edited. Her correspondence with him is a further gauge of her involvement in the formation of opinion. One passage must suffice as an example. In the course of a long letter on the subject of war crimes and post-war defence policy, dated 6 October 1945, she said:

> I just record my opinion that it would be wholly disastrous, at this juncture, for any influential section in this country to do or say anything which would encourage aggressors to think that we should again [be] unwilling to endure or use all available power in the defence of a just cause. Do we want some truculent foreign minister to report home that nations can be oppressed with impunity because the British are again going to be inhibited by moral scruples from interfering in the only swift and effective way? We did so much harm by that sort of thing last time, and all to no end, except to make the war longer and bloodier.
>
> I can hardly expect you to agree with me, but between the wars I held my tongue for fear of appearing to be a war-monger. So this time I must make amends by speaking what I believe to be the truth.

Speaking what she believed to be the truth – this she regarded as a duty. Was it, however, to use her own phrase, her "proper job"?

CHAPTER 27

Gaudium

For the last fourteen years of her life, the creative imagination of Dorothy L. Sayers was caught up in a new enchantment: the *Divine Comedy* of Dante. I have already told in full the story of this, her last enamourment, in another book, *The Passionate Intellect: Dorothy L. Sayers' Encounter with Dante*. What follows here shows how this unforeseen development was related to her mind and character and in particular to her capacity for joy.

It is significant that her interest in Dante was first aroused by Charles Williams. His admiration for *The Nine Tailors*, expressed in rhapsodic terms in a letter to Gollancz, had naturally endeared him to her. They met, and enjoyed each other's company. Like many people, she found his conversation stimulating and inspiring. She admired his novels, his works of criticism and his theological writings. He talked with her about his play on Cranmer. He suggested her name to the organisers of the Canterbury Festival as a possible playwright. This led, as has been shown, to *The Zeal of Thy House* and to all that followed. Now, for the second time, he gave a new direction to her career.

In August 1943 a review of his book, *The Figure of Beatrice*, appeared in the *Sunday Times*. Dorothy bought a copy, not, she said, because it was about Dante but because it was by Charles Williams. It made her resolve to read Dante – her knowledge of him having been fragmentary till then – but a year went by before she did so. She was, after all, busy with other matters. Then, one night in August 1944, the air-raid siren sounded. She snatched up a book she had set aside for reading and took it down to the shelter with her. It was Dante's *Inferno*.

The effect was dynamic. Neither the review of Williams' book nor the book itself had prepared her for what she found: a story of compelling power. It was a revelation. She later described her experience:

> I can remember nothing like it since I first read *The Three Musketeers* at the age of thirteen . . . However foolish it may sound, the plain fact is that I bolted my meals, neglected my sleep, work and correspondence, drove my friends crazy, and paid only a distracted attention to the doodle-bugs which happened to be infesting the neighbourhood at the time, until I had panted my way through the Three Realms of the dead from top to bottom and from bottom to top.

The mention of herself at the age of thirteen is revealing. The creative talent she had then for living vividly in an imagined world had not deserted her. In the intervening years she had created worlds of her own, captivating readers in her turn. Now, suddenly, after nearly forty years, her mature imaginative and intellectual powers were rejuvenated by an epiphany of delight.

The first result was an outpouring of remarkable letters to Charles Williams. These, more vividly than anything she later wrote, show the rapture of which her mind was capable. She rejoices in Dante's skill as a narrator, his lucid style, his pictorial similes, the dramatic power of the *Inferno*, his delicate use of colour in *Purgatory*, the gradations of light in *Paradise*. Most characteristic is her astonishment at Dante's picture of celestial joy:

> Was there ever a heaven so full of nods and becks and wreathèd smiles, so gay and dancing? or where the most abstract beatitude was so merrily expressed? Surely nobody ever so passionately *wanted* a place where everybody was kind and courteous, or carried happiness so lightly.

Later, her intellect came to grips with the theology and moral grandeur of Dante's poem. That was after she had yielded to the temptation to translate and expound it for Penguin Classics, a series recently created for book-hungry post-war readers. This was her last great undertaking. She was to die before finishing the third volume, *Paradise*, but her first two, *Hell* and *Purgatory*, especially the Introductions and Notes, as well as the many lectures on Dante which she gave between 1946 and 1957, have proved a lasting legacy. Her translation, like many others, has met with criticism. Unlike all the others, it has made Dante come alive to millions of English-speaking readers.

She felt herself called to this new task. In 1947 the Dean of Chichester invited her to write a play for the cathedral. She replied that she was too busy translating Dante. The Dean pointed out that many people can translate Dante and had indeed done so, "but there is hardly anybody with your particular dramatic gift in England". To this she answered: there were indeed those who had translated Dante, "but how many people read him in their translations?" It was possible for Penguins to reach an enormous reading public because their volumes were so inexpensive and their distribution so effective. She believes that Dante "has more to say to our present diseases than any editor of the Liberal-Humanist era could possibly foresee". She is trying to present him as helpfully as possible to the many who want to learn something about him. And then she makes a revealing and decisive comment: "I feel it is, as Tennyson observed, 'one clear call for me'."

Her new undertaking, therefore, was not only a creative and intellectual self-fulfilment: it was a theological and educational mission, as important as she hoped *Bridgeheads* would prove as a contribution to post-war moral reconstruction. Dante, the greatest Christian poet, the pre-Tridentine Catholic European, had a vital message, in her eyes, for the modern world. It was not sufficient that he should be accessible only to those who could read Italian, or to a closed society of scholars. Her lectures on Dante, delivered between 1946 and the year of her death, were also marked by this serious approach. She took Dante, as she took the gospel story, seriously. In this she was unique.

When she spoke on Dante at the University of Manchester in 1956, Professor R. D. Waller wrote to thank her for a lecture that "had heart in it", by which he meant, he said,

> that it was about something humanly interesting and that you were humanly interested in it . . . I don't see why professors and lecturers shouldn't try to give lectures like yours and so put a bit of heart into their universities . . . I think you do a good thing giving lectures like that when you can in universities . . . University people have grown shy of committing themselves to anything, especially in the presence of their colleagues, for fear of being proved wrong, or perhaps of being thought naïve for having any beliefs or enthusiasms.

She had found a way of speaking out on matters of moral and social concern while at the same time doing her "proper job", namely, using her literary and critical skills.

The Figure of Beatrice revealed to her a vision of Dante which she made her own. Williams' system of romantic theology, known as the Affirmative Way, stressed the value of the things of this world as images of the Divine. She was already familiar with this concept through his other writings. Now, linked with Dante's experience of transfigured reality, it illumined for her the nature of what Williams called "the Beatrician vision", a phrase she adopted for the ability to perceive the immortal in the mortal, the eternal in the temporal. Many years before, in the talk she gave in Hull entitled "The Way to the Other World", she had intimated that she understood what this dual vision was:

> One must remember that though in one sense the Other World was a definite place, yet in another the kingdom of gods was within one. Earth and fairy-land co-exist upon the same foot of ground. It was all a matter of the seeing eye . . . To go from earth to faery is like passing from this time to eternity; it is not a journey in space, but a change of mental outlook.

To someone of her temperament, with such earthy zest for life, the Affirmative Way as mapped by Charles Williams was a liberating sanction. Enjoyment, gaudium, elation of the soul, was a virtue she did not find difficult to practise.

Her sense of humour and her love of fun are evident in many of her writings, especially in her letters to friends. Even domestic mishaps and inconveniences are topics for comic narration. Her letters about cats and kittens, hens and pigs, floods through the roof, are small masterpieces. Bad weather on holiday is not usually a theme of merriment, but here is an excerpt from a letter she wrote to Helen Simpson in September 1937:

> Marjorie Barber and I had a lovely holiday in Venice, along the coast of Dalmatia and in Paris – full of comic relief and entertaining incidents. For comedy and thrill let me recommend to you being caught in a cloudburst in an open gondola at a spot where there is only one extremely narrow bridge under which you rock perilously while the gondoliers scream unintelligibly over your heads like cats on a midnight roof!

It is no wonder her friends enjoyed her company. Helen Waddell

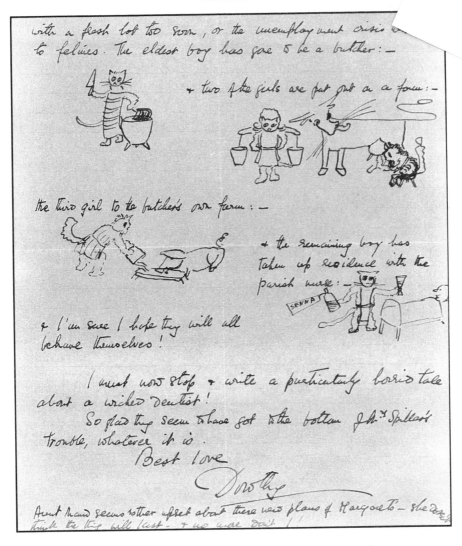

From a letter about homes for kittens (*Marion E. Wade Center*)

once wrote, inviting her to dinner: "It is so long since I heard you laugh!"

On their second visit to Venice in August 1938 she and Marjorie rented an apartment for three weeks. This time there were thunderstorms. When they couldn't go out, Dorothy spent the time writing a light-hearted comedy, set partly in Venice. Entitled *Love All*, it was written, she said "just for fun . . . in a rather irresponsible mood" – a holiday romp, in other words, and a relaxation from her serious works. It has been interpreted as a feminist tract (mistakenly in my view), for the reason that the women characters get the better of a somewhat ineffectual man. Dorothy was never a feminist and said so clearly more than once. In 1936, writing to her agent about an invitation to give a talk to a women's group, she said: "I have a foolish complex against allying myself publicly with anything labelled feminist . . . The more clamour we make about 'the women's point of view', the more we ram into people that the women's point of view is different, and frankly I do not think it is – at least not in my job."

There has been speculation as to what view she would have taken about the ordination of women as priests. I once asked her what she thought about this and she said in her opinion it was wisest to stick to traditional practice. She explains why in a letter to C. S. Lewis, who approached her on the subject on 13 July 1948. He wrote:

> News has just reached me of a movement (starting, I believe, from Chinese Anglicans) to demand that women should be allowed Priests' Orders. I am guessing that, like me, you disapprove of something which would cut us off so sharply from all the rest of Christendom, and which would be the very triumph of what they call "practical" and "enlightened" principles over the far deeper need that the Priest at the Altar must represent the Bridegroom to whom we are all, in a sense, feminine. Well, if you do, really I think you will have to give tongue. The defence against the innovation must if possible be done by a woman: but when the job demands "ANGLICAN (woman): effective dialectical powers: established literary reputation essential", who can we turn to? Write an article (or at the very least a letter) to something – and swear at me as much as you please while doing it.

Dorothy replied:

> Oh, Lord! Look here, are you sure, of your own knowledge, that this precious "movement" has any weight behind it? I should have thought it could be trusted to perish on the barricades of prejudice before arriving at the citadel.
>
> Obviously, nothing could be more silly and inexpedient than to erect a new and totally unnecessary barrier between us and the rest of Catholic Christendom. (It would be rather a link than otherwise with some of the Free Churches, as tending to emphasise a ministry of the Gospel rather than a ministry of Sacraments and as involving a break with Apostolic tradition.)

I fear you would find me rather an uneasy ally. I can never find any logical or strictly theological reason against it. In so far as the Priest represents Christ, it is obviously more dramatically appropriate that a man should be, so to speak, cast for the part. But if I were cornered and asked point-blank whether Christ Himself is the representative of male humanity or all humanity, I should be obliged to answer "of all humanity"; and to cite the authority of St Augustine for saying that woman is also made in the image of God . . .

It would be a pity to fly in the face of all the Apostolic Churches, especially just now when we are at last seeing some prospect of understanding with the Eastern Orthodox, and so on . . . The most I can do is to keep silence in any place where the daughters of the Philistines might overhear me.

She regarded the intellect as androgynous – neither male nor female, but human, and she took pleasure in using it, as she did in using her writing skills. She rejoiced in the English language and in the right use of it by others. In a letter to Father Kelly, dated 15 May 1941, she discussed Bunyan –

his lovely lucid style, which most people only attain after years of training through involved and elaborate writing, before they learn to discard everything but the essential . . . [His] every word [is] like a living thing, full of light and moving in its place like a dancer; but one has to love [words] before they will dance a step – love them, I mean, not for what one can compel them to do but for what they are in themselves.

She enjoyed her fame, but was irked by journalists who reported her falsely or who asked stupid questions: "Miss Sayers, did you have anything special in mind when you wrote *The Man Born to be King?*" But she lent herself to publicity from time to time and thoroughly enjoyed the occasion in June 1950, at S. H. Benson's, when she was asked to unveil a plaque commemorating the staircase down which the victim fell in *Murder Must Advertise*. The photograph taken at the time shows that she was quite willing to do honour to the event in the matter of dress. That same year she was made an Honorary Doctor of Letters by the University of Durham. Describing the ceremony to the Dante scholar, J. D. Sinclair, she wrote: "I never saw such a flower garden of different robes and gowns before." That too gave her immense pleasure and she asked

Dorothy at Benson's in 1950 *(Estate of Anthony Fleming)*

that the letters D.Litt. should be printed after her name whenever appropriate.

This raises the question of her insistence that her professional name should always be given as Dorothy L. Sayers. Much has been made of this as though it were some idiosyncratic whim. She explained the matter patiently to a correspondent in 1936:

> The name as it stands on the title page . . . is part of the author's "publicity". This, of course, applies alike to men and women. For instance, the college friend whom I in private refer to as "Muriel Byrne" would, if I were writing a review of her work or announcing her to speak at a public dinner, always be "M. St Clare Byrne". Similarly, "E. C. Bentley" (not "Edward Clerihew" or "Edward C.", still less "Jack", though that is how I personally address him) . . .
>
> The form "Dorothy L. Sayers" is . . . more commonly used for women than men, and has, for women I think, nothing particularly American about it – "Charlotte M. Yonge" and "Ethel M. Dell" are firmly established.
>
> My personal objection to "Dorothy Sayers" is that it invites the pronunciation of "Sayers" as an ugly spondee [i.e. SAY-ERS, instead of SAIRS]. My old headmistress always pronounced it so, and gave me a distaste for the form that I cannot get over. I cannot object to it in private, but in public I think it is not too much to ask reviewers, etc. to take the trouble to discover how I prefer to be called.

She was especially annoyed when the B.B.C. gave her name as "Dorothy Sayers", as they quite often announced another "Dorothy Sayers", who was a variety artiste who sang and played the guitar. Dorothy L. Sayers sometimes received *her* letters, press-cuttings and invitations to perform in music-halls. The confusion was aggravating, but she could speak of it with humour, as she did once to me: "What I'd like to happen is that the other Dorothy Sayers should die first. Everybody would think it was me and I'd be able to read my own obituaries."

She enjoyed gala occasions, such as dinners of the Detection Club, for which she dressed with splendour. At home, she tended to neglect her appearance and took little care of her health. She smoked heavily and put on a great deal of weight. "The elephant is crated," she said self-mockingly, as she crammed herself into a friend's car. She enjoyed good food and Amontillado sherry too much to do anything about it.

Most of her energies in her last years went on her translation of Dante – and of the *Chanson de Roland*, which she undertook as well, disconcertingly, at this period. She was also much involved in the activities of St Anne's House, Soho, a centre for lectures and discussions on religion, literature, the arts and science.

Even so, she had immense stores of creativeness in reserve. Two major dramatic opportunities occurred, to which she rose with her customary vigour and panache. One was an invitation to write a religious play for Lichfield Cathedral in 1946. This was *The Just Vengeance*, on the theme of Atonement and inspired by a passage in Dante's *Paradise*, from which the title is derived. The other was *The Emperor Constantine*, a chronicle play written in 1951 for the Colchester Festival, of which the climax is the formulation of the Nicene Creed at the Council called by Constantine in Nicaea. Between these two events, there was a revival in Canterbury in 1949 of *The Zeal of Thy House*.

Dorothy was personally involved in all three of these productions, as Norah Lambourne relates in her article "Recollections of Designing for the Religious Plays of Dorothy L. Sayers". Dorothy attended rehearsals, as she always loved to do, and participated in overcoming many of the practical difficulties. In the run-up to *The Emperor Constantine*, one room in her house was given over as Norah's work-

A scene from *The Just Vengeance (Ford Jones, Lichfield)*

place. Another was used to store costumes. Together they pored over books of Byzantine style and "vied with each other amid laughter in inventing strange garments for some of the bishops who come from remote parts of the Christian world". The house became a workshop for the production of stage properties – brooches, necklaces, head-dresses, rings. Dorothy, who had always been skilful with her hands, made a hand-mirror and a prayer book with an illuminated page. This was the teenage Dorothy still alive, making props and costumes for her plays at Bluntisham.

Her friends loved her humour and quoted her sayings. John Betjeman wrote to ask her for the correct version of four lines of verse which were in circulation and attributed to her. They were:

> As years come in and years go out
> I totter toward the tomb,
> Still caring less and less about
> Who goes to bed with whom.

She added the following textual criticism: "The alliteration in the second line lends, I feel, a kind of rickety dignity to the whole, as of one tapping slowly along on two sticks; and the rhyme and enjambement at the end of the 3rd line seem to me to usher in the final pronouncement with a more breathless solemnity."

She had fun also writing satirical sketches on invented saints and celebrations of the secular society. Known as *The Pantheon Papers*, they were published in *Punch*, a distinction she now shared with her celebrated great-uncle, Percival Leigh. Several of these are similar in thrust to *The Screwtape Letters* by C. S. Lewis, a work she greatly enjoyed. One of her letters to him is an imitation, from a demon named Sluckdrib, complaining to his superior about the unfortunate effect which certain religious plays are having on atheists. He is, however, gratified by the effect that writing them has had on the author's character:

> I have already had the honour to report intellectual and spiritual pride, vainglory, self-opinionated dogmatism, irreverence, blasphemous frivolity, frequentation of the company of theatricals, captiousness, impatience of correction, polemical fury, shortness of temper, neglect of domestic affairs, lack of charity, egotism, nostalgia for secular occupations, and a growing tendency to consider the Bible as literature.

Her work on Dante progressed but she was beginning to feel tired and sometimes hinted that she wondered if she would live to finish it. When she died suddenly on 17 December 1957, she had completed only two-thirds of the last volume, *Paradise*.

The weekend before her death had been a happy one. On the Friday she had attended a baptism in Cambridge, becoming a god-mother, a sacramental act which gave her quite evident joy. On the following Sunday, at home in Witham, she had received a visit from her much loved friend, Val Gielgud. After her death he wrote, "She was her usual brisk, vital, amusing, almost exuberant self, full of plans for the future . . . "

On the following Tuesday, 17 December, she went to London to do some Christmas shopping, giving instructions for gifts to be sent to her friends. She was tired and was tempted to stay overnight in town but felt she must get back. Her usual driver, Jack Lapwood, met her at Witham station and drove her to her house. She went upstairs, threw her hat and coat on the bed and went down to feed her hungry cats. She fell dead at the foot of the stairs, where she was found the next morning.

As a young woman, while still at Oxford, she had written a poem entitled "Hymn in Contemplation of Sudden Death". Though immature, it speaks with a strange prescience for the whole of her life:

> Lord, if this night my journey end,
> I thank Thee first for many a friend,
> The sturdy and unquestioned piers
> That run beneath my bridge of years.
>
> And next, for all the love I gave
> To things and men this side the grave,
> Wisely or not, since I can prove
> There always is much good in love.
>
> Next, for the power thou gavest me
> To view the whole world mirthfully,
> For laughter, paraclete of pain,
> Like April suns across the rain.
>
> Also that, being not too wise
> To do things foolish in men's eyes,
> I gained experience by this,
> And saw life somewhat as it is.

Next, for the joy of labour done
And burdens shouldered in the sun;
Nor less, for shame of labour lost,
And meekness born of a barren boast.

For every fair and useless thing
That bids men pause from labouring
To look and find the larkspur blue
And marigolds of a different hue;

For eyes to see and ears to hear,
For tongue to speak and thews to bear,
For hands to handle, feet to go,
For life, I give Thee thanks also.

For all things merry, quaint and strange,
For sound and silence, strength and change,
And last, for death, which only gives
Value to every thing that lives;

For these, good Lord that madest me,
I praise Thy name; since verily,
I of my joy have had no dearth
Though this night were my last on earth.

CHAPTER 28

The Woman Who Was Dorothy L. Sayers

"What a woman! Brilliant, erratic, rude and impatient as only dedicated writers and artists can be, earnest, hard-working, loving, yet never achieving settled love, deeply religious, with a flair for expressing old truths in new words, funny as well as witty, eccentric, curious in appearance, scholarly, a woman who knew her own mind and knew, too, that it was as good as any man's; a fighter who could be a worthy opponent in any kind of controversy – there's a list!"

Thus wrote Rosamund Essex in 1979, reviewing a biography of Dorothy L. Sayers. It is a list which adds up to the conventional, long-accepted portrait of her. It omits, however, several traits which are needed to bring the portrait to life.

Of these the most important is intellectual ardour. This is apparent in many of her writings: in *Gaudy Night*, in her articles on creativeness and on the Christian faith, in her religious plays and in her interpretation of Dante. It is also apparent in her letters.

There is one in particular which contains a key passage for the understanding of her inner life. The circumstances in which she wrote it are as follows. In 1954, a fellow-member of St Anne's House, the scientist and theologian John Wren-Lewis, took her to task for being interested only in the dogmatic pattern of Christianity and for being unwilling to commit herself personally in presenting the faith to atheists and agnostics.

Dorothy reflected on his reproach. On the following day, which was Good Friday, she wrote a long, extremely candid, soul-revealing letter. She admitted that she was not by temperament an evangelist:

I am quite without the thing known as "inner light" or "spiritual experience". I have never undergone conversion. Neither God, nor (for that matter) angel, devil, ghost or anything else speaks to me out of the depth of my psyche ... It follows naturally, perhaps, from this that I am quite incapable of "religious emotion".

This, she said, had its good as well as its bad side. It meant that she was not liable to mistake aesthetic pleasure in ritual or architecture for moral virtue, or to dismiss religion as a sublimation of sex, "because I know perfectly well that it is nothing of the sort". She had a moral sense, but was not sure that it derived from religious belief:

Of all the presuppositions of Christianity, the only one I really have and can swear to from personal inward conviction is sin. About that I have no doubt whatever and never have had. Neither does any doctrine of determinism or psychological maladjustment convince me in the very least that when I do wrong it is not I who do it and that I could not, by some means or other, do better.

There follows a statement which explains the individual nature of her mind and which also shows how clearly she understood herself:

Since I cannot come at God through intuition, or through my emotions, or through my "inner light" (except in the unendearing form of judgement and conviction of sin) there is only the intellect left. And that is a very different matter ... Where the intellect is dominant it becomes the channel of all the other feelings. The "passionate intellect" is really passionate. It is the only point at which ecstasy can enter. I do not know whether we can be saved by the intellect, but I do know that I can be saved by nothing else.

This combination of intellectual light and spiritual ardour is something which she recognised in Dante. His phrase for it was "the mind in love". It was a gift which Dorothy had possessed all her life.

Another trait omitted from the list is kindness. In the same letter to Wren-Lewis, Dorothy said: "The lack of religious emotion in me makes me impatient of it in other people, and makes me appear cold and unsympathetic and impersonal. This is true. I am." Here she does herself an injustice, as her letters prove. Again and again, she took time and trouble to write, often at great length, sometimes to total strangers, at other times to friends, who asked her for guidance in religious matters. To take one example: in 1937, when Canon Shirley, the headmaster of King's School, Canterbury, asked her opinion on a paper on religious faith which he had drawn up for his pupils, she replied in a deeply personal letter of eight hand-written pages, communicating her own difficulties in distinguishing between "eternal life" and "survival in time", and giving her understanding of the immediate effect of the Resurrection:

The reason why the Resurrection made such a change in the Disciples [was] that everything then suddenly acquired meaning for them. It showed them the life of Christ whole – with its great tragic shape in time and its triumphant eternal meaning . . . They also saw the double meaning of the Kingdom of God – (a) as something to which one strode forward in time and (b) as something with which every individual soul could be in relation at every moment . . .

It is precisely because of the eternity outside time that everything in time becomes valuable and important and meaningful. Therefore, Christianity . . . makes it of urgent importance that everything we do here (whether individually or as a society) should be rightly related to what we eternally are. "Eternal life" is the sole sanction for the values of this life. The revelation in Christ is the means by which we get into touch with what the eternal pattern is.

To take another example: in 1946, in reply to a letter from Maurice Browne, enquiring what she thought being a Christian signified, she spoke still more directly and simply, out of her inner self:

God is a Person from the beginning (the same Person that was manifested as a man in Christ), and He has made us persons in His own image . . . Sin, by turning the self away from God, depersonalises us; our real selves are rooted in God . . . He wants to call us His friends and His children; we are privileged to stand with Him on terms of mutuality and exchange . . .

Christianity is as plain and common as bread. The simplest person or the youngest child can be a Christian, by faith and baptism. The faith is faith in a Person; the baptism is baptism into His Body.

Her kindness was also manifested in a number of practical ways, as her friends remember. Her concern for her old piano teacher, Fräulein Fehmer, is a moving example. She had kept in correspondence with her, sending her copies of her novels as they came out. After the war, discovering that she was living in great poverty in the French zone of Germany, she sent parcels to her through the organisation "Save Europe Now". This took a lot of time and the bureaucratic restrictions were exasperating. "Can you tell me", she asked the organisers, "whether the British Empire would fall to pieces if I sent my old lady a bit of soap?" She sent tins of cooking fat, beef-steak pudding, plum pudding and dried apricots. Using her woman's understanding of Miss Fehmer's everyday needs, she also sent buttons, reels of cotton, sewing needles, mending wool, a zip fastener, suspenders, pins, hairpins, knitting wool and knitting needles. She also sent her some of her own clothes – a marocain dress with a coat to match, a scarf, a georgette dress, having, she said, no need for them, as she wore only a coat and skirt nowadays. Remembering how much Miss Fehmer loved German Romantic poetry and hearing that she had lost all her books in an air-raid, she sent her volumes of Goethe and Schiller. And she wrote her long, entertaining letters, at a time (1947) when she confided to a friend, "Between translating the *Divine Comedy* and standing in fish queues, I don't seem to have time and energy left for other things."

Like most people, she could be inconsistent. She felt great concern for others but disliked being the object of concern herself. She confessed to her son:

> I cannot altogether explain my violent dislike of personal interest, except that I connect it with the atmosphere of solicitude which surrounded me in childhood and from which I have been trying to rid myself ever since. So much so that I cannot be civil if I am told that I am missed when I am away or welcomed when I return, or that I ought to take care of my life because it is precious to other people.

She maintained that she disliked dwelling on the past; and yet she twice began a work of reminiscences and went out of her way in her novels to introduce details from her early years. She said she disliked children; and yet she had wanted children by Cournos (three sons, she fantasised!), and she took an affectionate interest in those she knew, writing letters to them and choosing presents for them with care. She disapproved vehemently of the biographical approach to literature and yet she was at work on a biography of Wilkie Collins and lamented that not enough was known (then) of his personal life. Her own individual life, for all her fierce denials, does illumine her writings, for it reveals them to have been, if not strictly autobiographical, at least deeply personal.

"A wonderful friend was Dorothy Sayers," wrote Doreen Wallace in an obituary note. Indeed, friendship was one of the most important features of her life, more reliable than marriage, more lasting than sex. She was linked to her friends by a vast network of letters, by many festive occasions and, above all, by work shared and undertaken in common. *That* was where she found happiness: "I do not know of any success worth having except the ability to do a job in which one is interested and to obtain a living sufficient to enable one to go on doing one's work." Or, as she expressed it to her friend and colleague, Val Gielgud:

When we go to Heaven all I ask is that we shall be given some interesting job and allowed to get on with it. No management; no box-office; no dramatic critics; and an audience of cheerful angels who don't mind laughing.

Notes

CHAPTER 1

2 *St Michael's College, Tenbury*: Established by Sir Frederick Arthur Gore Ouseley, later Professor of Music at Oxford, to improve standards of church music.

"small demons with angel voices": *The Teaching of Latin: A New Approach*, 1952. (Alternative title: *Ignorance and Dissatisfaction*.)

4 *someone who knew her*: Mrs Evelyn Bedford (née Compline).

6 *"The Five Red Herrings"*: Chapter 20.

7 *"rhyme or rhythm"*: Letter to Rev. Dr James Welch.

in her perambulator: Said to me by D.L.S.

8 *she vividly remembered . . . winter aconites*: *The Teaching of Latin: A New Approach*.

9 *family joke*: Related to me by D.L.S.

"The Fruit in the Seed": London, 1952.

12 *The garden was a place of delight*: the description is taken from E. Peake, *Birds in a Rectory Garden* (W. H. Smith, Huntingdon, n.d.). The Rev. E. Peake was rector at Bluntisham from 1921.

13 *"my tearful aunt"*: Related to me by D.L.S.

"Have His Carcase": Chapter 16.

14 *a charming account*: *The Teaching of Latin: A New Approach*.

15 *the "old" pronunciation*: Latin was pronounced with a "local" accent until modern times. In the 1870s reformers began to "restore" what they took to be the authentic ancient Roman pronunciation. The "old" English pronunciation continued in use longest at Oxford; it is still in use amongst doctors, lawyers and botanists.

16 *Cyrus the Persian*: See "A Vote of Thanks to Cyrus", *Unpopular Opinions*, (Gollancz, 1946, pp. 23-8).

the metal corners of the tennis court: See Appendix.

17 *Little Arthur's History of England*: By Lady Callcott, first published 1835.

18 *I dramatised myself . . .* : *My Edwardian Childhood*.

19 *old enough . . . a real companion*: *Cat o' Mary*.

21 *She identified herself with Athos*: The American author, Willa Cather (1873-1947), likewise regarded the musketeers as real characters ("her three best friends"). See Sharon O'Brien, *Willa Cather: The Emerging Voice* (Fawcett Columbine, New York, 1987), pp.82-3.

23 *Oliver Locker-Lampson*: He was elected M.P. for North Huntingdonshire in 1910 and went on to have a distinguished political career. Born in 1880, he died in 1954.

25 *Lewis Waller*: William Waller Lewis, 1860-1915.

CHAPTER 2

28 *It has been suggested*: By James Brabazon.

30 *own view of the matter*: See note to p. 349.

31 *Ernst Lengyel*: His surname suggests that he was Hungarian.

stiffly built . . . like bells: Quoted by Hone, p. 8. Fräulein Fehmer had trained as a professsional pianist and had given recitals in Milan.

There is a particular nocturne . . . : From the poem "Target Area", published in *Fortnightly*, March 1944.

32 *she died in 1948*: See chapter 28.

35 *Saint George Suite*: Composed by George Saint George (1841-1924). Born in Leipzig of English parents; his music was popular with violin students.
Spero Nursing Home: Formerly in Campbell Road, Salisbury, near the School. It no longer exists.

36 *hardly bearable*: Hone, p. 10.
what she felt about it: Brabazon, p. 39.

39 *"hugely admired"*: Henry Sayers composed new settings for several hymns, which were sung by the choir at Bluntisham and Christchurch.

40 *In her letters home . . . detested compulsory games*: Brabazon, p. 33.

42 *Ground in the slow mills . . .* : D.L.S. is referring to the French scholastic exercise known as *"critique de texte"*.

43 *nervous breakdown*: Suggested by Brabazon, p. 41.

CHAPTER 3

47 *Christian Social Union*: Founded in 1899 by Brooke Foss Westcott, Charles Gore and Henry Scott Holland.
As soon as I took residence in Oxford . . . : *Latin Teaching: A New Approach*.

48 *by no means unresponsive*: In 1945, Dr L. A. Willoughby, then Professor of German at University College, London University, was to invite his famous ex-pupil to lecture to the English Goethe Society. "How pleasant to hear from you after all these years," she replied in her letter of acceptance. She spoke on "The Faust Legend and the Idea of the Devil" and had tea with Professor Willoughby beforehand. Her paper was published in the proceedings of the Society and reprinted posthumously in *The Poetry of Search and the Poetry of Statement*, Gollancz, 1963, pp. 227-41.

50 *Hugh Percy Allen*: Organist, conductor and musical administrator (1869-1946). In 1907 he became conductor of the London Bach Choir. In 1918 he was appointed director of the Royal College of Music and professor of music at Oxford. He was knighted in 1920. He died in Oxford, as a result of being run down by a motor-cyclist.
Allen was a handsome man, well above medium height, strongly built and broad-shouldered. He had piercing grey-blue eyes, a prominent chin and a moustache cut to almost military brevity. In his unbounded vitality, the source of his creative power, he resembled D.L.S. She was not alone in finding inspiration in his exuberant activity and passionate music-making. See Cyril Bailey, *Hugh Percy Allen*, O.U.P., 1948.

52 *Gaudy Night*: Chapter 12.
Have His Carcase: Chapter 18.
the Boston: A new form of the waltz. By a strange chance, Maurice Reckitt, with whom D.L.S. was later to correspond on serious matters, also learnt the Boston in his youth. He has described it as follows: "Perhaps the essence of the new development lay in the abandonment of the purely rotatory movement of the old waltz and of the three steps of virtually equal length on which it was based, in favour of more tangential glides and even swoops." (John S. Peart-Binns, *Maurice B. Reckitt: A Life*, Bowderdean and Pickering, 1988, p. 94).
aboulia: sloth.

53 *"Earl Ulfric" and "Peredux"*: Poems written in Bluntisham.

54 *Dante thirty years later*: See "And Telling You a Story", *Further Papers on Dante* (Methuen, 1957, p. 7).

55 *the Public Orator*: Alfred Denis Godley, author of "a noble poem", as D.L.S. termed it:

What is it that roareth thus?

Can it be a motor-bus?
Yes! The reek and hideous hum
Indicant motorem bum.

56 *"Placet-ne? . . . Placet"*: See chapter 18, end.

The chaplain of Balliol: Kenneth Garlick, a former pupil of Roy Ridley, writes as follows: "He had a fine aristocratic profile and a beautiful speaking voice, wore a monocle and spats and, usually, lovat tweeds. His normal form of addressing one was 'Old thing'. He was aware that in profile he somewhat resembled Dante and a bronze medallion profile of Dante hung over his mantelpiece. The works of Dorothy Sayers were prominent on his shelves." Robertson Davies, another former pupil, writes: "Ridley was the only clergyman I ever saw celebrate Holy Communion wearing a monocle."

58 *her indebtedness to Chesterton*: D.L.S. wrote to his widow on 15 June 1936: "I think, in some ways, G.K.'s books have become more a part of my mental make-up than those of any writer you could name."

a friend: John Wren-Lewis.

59 *"A bouncing and exuberant . . . "*: op. cit., 1933, p. 105.

CHAPTER 4

65 *Sometimes they proposed . . .* : From personal knowledge; one of them was my mother.

"We were none of us chaste": From a conversation with Eric Whelpton.

66 *"I that am twice thy child"*: "Lay (II)", *Op. I*, p. 21.

a sick persistence: op. cit., chapter 1.

68 *T. W. Earp*: "When he arrived at Oxford, he was a shy provincial boy noted for his awkward ways and known as the twerp (T. W. Earp), a word which became a mild term of abuse and is now established in the English language." (Eric Whelpton, *The Making of a European*, Johnson, London, 1974, p.124).

69 *Op. I*: For an appreciation of the early poetry of D.L.S., see Ralph E. Hone, "Sayers' Singing Voice: The Oxford Phase", an address given to the Dorothy L. Sayers Society, 4 August 1985.

Giles Dixey: Harold Giles Dixey published close on twenty slim volumes of poetry, of which the most recent is dated 1971. Like D.L.S., he had been born in Oxford and he shared her love of it.

71 *It is all black . . . in a most fetching manner*: Letter to Dorothy Rowe.

72 *I'd never been . . . to a neophyte*: The same letter, which contained a drawing of the moving staircase and the old lady leaping down it.

73 *"don't know what they're doing"*: From a conversation with D.L.S.

She was vividly remembered: See Janet Hitchman, *Such a Strange Lady*, New English Library, 1975, pp. 454-60

74 *"teach children"*: Quoted by Hone, p. 24.

75 *"very bad"*: "The Translation of Verse", *The Poetry of Search and the Poetry of Statement*, ed. cit., p. 127.

larger stipend: In the 1920s the living at Bluntisham was worth eight hundred and forty pounds a year and that of Christchurch was worth one thousand five hundred and forty pounds. (See Geoffrey Lee, *Proceedings of the Dorothy L. Sayers Society*, 1980 Seminar, p. 47.)

76 *Doreen Wallace . . . her demesne of joy*: Hone, p. 25.

80 *the oboe or the flute*: She later took up the saxophone and played at staff dances at Benson's. (Janet Hitchman, *Such a Strange Lady*, ed. cit., p. 63.)

CHAPTER 5

87 *The Making of a European*: Johnson, London, 1974, p. 126.

had "nobbled him": From a letter from Doreen Wallace to Eric Whelpton.

88 *taken literally here*: cf. "Everything is going wrong with the Detection Club Dinner, and I am thinking of cutting my throat." (Letter to Aunt Ann, dated 30 April 1934.)

90 *Mr Sayers was an excellent host . . .*: From *The Quest for Wimsey*, an unpublished memoir by Eric Whelpton.
   the Boojum and the Snark: See Lewis Carroll, "The Hunting of the Snark".

91 *to join in quartets with them*: Francis J. Hill later became music master at Marlborough College. He wrote to Dorothy when she had become famous, saying he hoped they would meet again. In reply, she asked him if he had ever introduced anyone to Bach's B Minor Mass (she had once lent him her copy): "If so, for that deed your sins should be forgiven you."

93 *which splashed her thighs*: Tristan, in love with the first Iseult, has not consummated his marriage with Iseult of the White Hands. Out riding with her brother, she tells him that the water has reached higher than ever Tristan reached.

94 *During our hours together . . .*: From a letter from Eric Whelpton.

95 *"Whose Body?"*: Chapter 7.
   saga of Sherlock Holmes: See "Studies in Sherlock Holmes", *Unpopular Opinions*, ed. cit., pp. 134-78.

CHAPTER 6

97 *and he had refused*: From a letter from Eric Whelpton.

98 *"Gaudy Night"*: Chapter 8.

99 *It may even be that she sold some*: One was entitled "Bonds of Egypt: Film Drama in Three Parts". It was written at Verneuil.

100 *three former pupils*: Lu Christian, Gwen Walter, and Winnie Caldin.

101 *Shrewsbury Gaudy*: See *Gaudy Night*, chapter 1.

105 *Sir Arthur Marshall*: (1870-1956) He was called to the bar in 1904 and served as Liberal M.P. for Wakefield from 1910 to 1918 and for Huddersfield from 1922 to 1923. For several years he was a Liberal Whip. He was knighted in 1918.

106 *a woman friend*: Probably Muriel Jaeger.
   "gas and gaiters": Dickens, *Nicholas Nickleby*.

CHAPTER 7

110 *spells Art with a capital A*: Compare *The Documents in the Case*, first letter from Jack Munting: "The old boy is not a bad old bird, but an alarming bore on the subject of Art with a capital A."

113 *"Philip wasn't the sort of man . . . "*: *Strong Poison*, chapter 4.

114 *"rather a defeatist sort of person"*: See preceding note.

CHAPTER 8

120 *salesman in bicycle pumps*: *Clouds of Witness*, chapter 13. Miss Meteyard in *Murder Must Advertise*, chapter 1, also enjoys obscene limericks.

121 *"adjusted and happy together"*: From a letter to Cournos.
   "demnation bow-wows": Dickens, *Nicholas Nickleby*. Mr Mantalini actually says "demnition bow-wows".
   the possibility of abortion: From a conversation with Eric Whelpton.

122 *In England adoption . . .*: The law was changed to admit both adoption and legitimation in 1926 following reforms in title and succession to land effected by the 1925 legislation – a theme taken by D.L.S. as the cornerstone of the plot of *Unnatural Death*.
   Southbourne, Hampshire: Southbourne is now counted as being in Dorset, since 1974.

123 *novel about Dante and his daughter*: See Barbara Reynolds, *The Passionate Intellect: Dorothy L. Sayers' Encounter with Dante*, Kent State University Press, 1989, pp. 191-206.

124 *She let her flat*: Information from a letter to Ivy Shrimpton.

CHAPTER 9

129 *happens after childbirth*: Having breast-fed the baby for three weeks, she would have had to express milk from her breasts for some time afterwards, probably wearing a nursing brassière to protect her clothing. This would tend to make her look fatter.

"Nothing in the commercial world . . . ": Brabazon, p. 92.

133 *"Uncle Pandarus"*: Lord Peter calls his uncle, Paul Delagardie, "Uncle Pandarus". See *Busman's Honeymoon*, Prothalamion, Extracts from the Diary of the Dowager Duchess, 5 October.

135 *"I hope Anthony . . . "*: She calls her son Anthony in her letters to Cournos, but always John or J.A. in her letters to Ivy. When addressing him or writing to him she always called him John. As an adult he adopted the name Anthony.

137 *as if her circumstances had suddenly altered*: She may have met Mac Fleming by then.

article by G. K. Chesterton: See Barbara Reynolds, "G. K. Chesterton and Dorothy L. Sayers", *The Chesterton Review*, 9, no. 2 (May 1984), pp. 136-57.

139 *wanted desperately to marry*: Cournos obviously impressed people as being immensely able. His rise in the newspaper and literary world, his success with Gordon Craig, his employment with the Foreign Office and the Ministry of Information all suggest this.

CHAPTER 10

141 *"The Meaning of Purgatory"*: *Introductory Papers on Dante*, Methuen, 1954, pp. 73-100.

143 *arranging for guardians*: Probably her firm of solicitors.

144 *sending her presents*: Sad to say, Isobel (Tovey) was to die at the age of about twenty of endocarditis. This was a matter of great grief to Ivy and to John, who was then in his early teens. Dorothy was aware of the disturbing effect the loss of Isobel had on him and was much concerned about it.

CHAPTER 11

153 *Fleming was of medium height . . .* : His daughter, Mrs Ann Schreurs, remembered him as handsome, with hair that curled behind his ears, and a sudden, charming smile. She recalled also that he had a soft voice, though others have spoken of it as vibrant.

156 *". . . forty-two"*: The marriage certificate gives his age as forty-three.

161 *pattern inspired by the coat of the tabby cat*: Evidence that Dorothy copied the pattern of her cat's coat in knitting socks for Mac is supplied by a letter from an American visitor named Ralph Allan, who wrote on 12 December 1929, recalling how he had seen her transferring "the design of your cat's lustrous markings to a pair of your husband's socks. I drank quantities of very excellent dark brown sherry. I sampled mysterious and delicious salad dressing." She had presented him with a copy of *The Unpleasantness at the Bellona Club* "with an inscription and an authentic cigarette burn".

162 *Parry Thomas*: J. G. P. Thomas, prominent in motor-racing in the 1920s and successful in short-distance races.

Pendine Sands: in Wales, near Tenby.

added at a later stage: It was her habit to add news items covering the period of a novel when she had finished it. See chapter 15 of the present work.

164 *"Riverside Nights"*: From a conversation between D.L.S. and Alfred Reynolds.
"Nebuchadnezzar": Included in *In the Teeth of the Evidence*.
later to collaborate with him: In connection with *Bridgeheads*. See chapter 23 of the present work.

165 *"The Vindictive Story of the Footsteps That Ran"*: Included in *Lord Peter Views the Body*.

166 *Adelbert*: this cat was lost as a kitten and found under a mattress. D.L.S. later used the episode in a short story, broadcast over the radio, in which Lord Peter, as a small boy, goes to consult Sherlock Holmes about the disappearance of his kitten.

CHAPTER 12

171 *"The Entertaining Episode . . . "*: Included in *Lord Peter Views the Body*.

173 *"How I Came to Invent . . . "*: Published in *Harcourt Brace News*, New York, vol. 1, 15 July 1936, pp. 1-2.

175 *"Murder Must Advertise"*: Chapter 1.
attempts have been made . . . : See the amusing article by Elizabeth Trembly, *Sidelights*, vol. XXXIII (The Dorothy L. Sayers Society).
character of Philip Trent: In a letter to E. C. Bentley, D.L.S. wrote: "Trent is the only modern detective of fiction I really ever wanted to meet (except, possibly, Father Brown . . .)." See Barbara Reynolds, "The Origin of Lord Peter Wimsey", *The Times Literary Supplement*, 22 April 1977, p. 492.
George Horace Lorimer: See Mark and Lynn Venrick, "The Milligan Papers", *Sidelights on Sayers*, vol. XXXVII, March 1992 (The Dorothy L. Sayers Society).

177 *Jewishness*: Attempts have been made to prove that D.L.S. was anti-Semitic, but this is hard to reconcile with her passionate desire to marry John Cournos.

181 *hailing taxis, top-hatted*: London taxis are still required by law to be large enough to make it possible for a gentleman to enter one wearing a top hat.
Michael Arlen: Novelist who enjoyed a great vogue in the 1920s. Born in 1895 in Bulgaria of Armenian parents, he became a naturalised British subject in 1922. His most famous novel, *The Green Hat*, was published in 1924.

183 *Imagining that he really existed*: See *Encounters with Lord Peter*, edited by Christopher Dean, published by the Dorothy L. Sayers Society, 1991.

CHAPTER 13

185 *"I still have it . . . "*: "The Translation of Verse", *The Poetry of Search and the Poetry of Statement*, Gollancz, 1963, p. 127.

187 *The Prime Minister*: David Lloyd George.
an honorific position: She delivered her presidential address on 5 January 1939. Entitled "The Dictatorship of Words", it was a protest against propaganda.

188 *Burd Ellen*: "Burd" is the feminine equivalent of "Childe" and is derived supposedly from Old English "byrde" (embroidress). In ballads Burd Ellen is the sister of Childe Roland.
"The Nine Tailors": See "The Second Course: The Bells in Their Courses". Emerging from the church, Lord Peter turns to his right, "knowing that it is unlucky to walk about a church widdershins".
one of R. H. Benson's stories: "Father Meuron's Tale".

189 *Unnatural Death*: Chapter 3.
Lewis Thorpe: "Dorothy L. Sayers as a Translator of *Le Roman de Tristan* and *La Chanson de Roland*" in *As Her Whimsy Took Her*, edited by Margaret Hannay, Kent State University Press, 1979, pp. 109-22.

191 *"lots of lovely illustrations"*: Quoted from a letter to me.
William Morris: See *The Earthly Paradise*. (D.L.S. was reading this at school in 1909.)

195 *"The Fascinating Story . . ."*: Included in *Lord Peter Views the Body.* Since Cournos despised crosswords as a frivolous waste of time, it is interesting that her first short story should be a celebration of frivolity and of crosswords.

197 *E. R. Gregory*: Dorothy L. Sayers, *Wilkie Collins: A Critical and Biographical Study* (The Friends of the University of Toledo Libraries, 1977).

CHAPTER 14

200 *Maurice Reckitt*: See note to p. 308.

202 *unflattering terms*: The poet, E. H. W. Meyerstein, wrote to John Freeman in May 1925, describing D.L.S.'s arrival at his parents' house, "on a steed shaped like a monstrous stag-beetle, with handlebars instead of antennae, and the manufacturers' device of a sphinx on the sheath protecting the front wheel . . . When she removed her overall . . . we were really surprised . . . Have you ever really considered the juxtaposition on a young woman of tight breeches, high yellow draw-on boots, and a low-necked jumper?" Her hair was cut short and she wore a khaki bandana kerchief. (*Some Letters of E. H. W. Meyerstein*, ed. Roland Watson, London, 1959, Letter No. 50.)

204 *"Possibly Gollancz will turn it down . . ."*: Victor Gollancz was then still working for Benn.

206 *sorrowing household*: From a conversation with Mrs Evelyn Bedford (née Compline), who worked in the rectory at the time.
"mild stateliness": From *My Edwardian Childhood.*

208 *a horizontal stone*: From a conversation with Mrs Bedford.
24 Newland Street; D.L.S. later bought the house next door, known as Chantry Cottage, and had the party wall removed, thus making the two houses into one.
Percy Leigh: She had written of him with affection to her mother, saying how glad she was that she had remembered to send him copies of her books and to know that he enjoyed them. He had left a legacy to Ivy Shrimpton also.

CHAPTER 15

217 *In the novel*: No. 52. Statement of John Munting.

222 *a sort of Edith Thompson woman*: See Filson Young, Notable British Trials Series, *Trial of Frederick Bywaters and Edith Thompson* (Hodge, 1923).
psychological questions: See note to p. 349.
draw forth any deep response: It is striking that at the same period D.L.S. was working on her translation of the powerful love-story of Tristan and Iseult.

223 *the letters of Mrs Harrison*: The letters of Edith Thompson to her lover Bywaters are the ultimate source for those of Julia and of Margaret Harrison.
breezy talk on the radio: "Trials and Sorrows of the Mystery Writer", *The Listener*, vol. VII, 6 January 1932, p. 26.

CHAPTER 16

227 *the gulf that separates*: D.L.S. insisted on the difference between imagination and fantasy. See *The Mind of the Maker*, chapter 10, note A.

228 *another little girl called Rosemary*: She was another example of Ivy's success as a teacher; she won a scholarship to a grammar school.
the memorable Guinness advertisements: One of the most memorable was a drawing of a toucan with its beak arched over two glasses of Guinness. Underneath was the following verse by D.L.S.:

> If he can say as you can
> Guinness is good for you
> How grand to be a Toucan
> Just think what Toucan do.

229 *"Gaudy Night"*: Published in *Titles to Fame*, edited by Denys Kilham Roberts (Nelson, 1937, pp. 73-95).

230 *"How I Came to Invent . . . "*: See note to chapter 12, p. 173.

232 *Freeman Wills Crofts*: The novel is entitled *Sir John Magill's Last Journey*. D.L.S. amuses herself by referring to it in *The Five Red Herrings*, chapter 21, here Strachan says he has been reading it – "a very nice book, all about a murder committed in this part of 'the country". This is another example of her habit of adding details at a final stage.

CHAPTER 17

237 *"Yes, of course it is . . . "*: *Gaudy Night*, chapter 9.
"My proper job . . . ": From a letter to Father Herbert Kelly.
an idea she was his mother: From a conversation with me.

240 *"We believe in the Inferno"*: "And Telling You a Story", *Further Papers on Dante* (Methuen, 1957, p. 10).

241 *In the church, the Rector . . .* : *The Nine Tailors*, The Second Part. The Waters Are Called Home.

242 *a correspondent*: Mr Lakin, editor of the *Sunday Times*.
Second Series: A third series, published in 1934, contained yet another Introduction by D.L.S.

243 *reading two novels a day*: See Ralph E. Hone, "Dorothy L. Sayers: Critic of Detective Fiction", *SEVEN: An Anglo-American Literary Review*, vol. VI, 1985, pp. 45-71.

244 *After Dorothy's death, Muriel related*: All details from a conversation with me.

CHAPTER 18

247 *Johanna Leigh*: This was the name of an ancestress on D.L.S.'s maternal side. She was painted by Sir Joshua Reynolds as Rosalind, in 1775. She married Richard Bennett Lloyd, a captain in the English Life Guards.

250 *"The judgment is merciless"*: Brabazon, p. 14.

252 *love affair with Oxford*: In a letter dated 13 November,1935, addressed to a "Mr Hopkins" (a relation of Gerard Manley Hopkins), D.L.S. wrote: "Oxford did mean something beautiful and valuable to me, beyond the 'dreaming spires' kind of beauty, and it offends me to the soul when disgruntled young men and women write about it as though it was nothing but a futile kind of opium vision on the one hand or a nest of perversions and repressions on the other."
"a city sanctified": "Lay, II", *Op. I*.

254 *"a background which I personally know"*: As regards *The Unpleasantness at the Bellona Club*, her knowledge must have been indirect, probably through her husband.

256 *"extraneous to the story"*: From the article "Gaudy Night", ed. cit.
"Peter had got to become . . . ": See above.

257 *revealed to her in a dream*: *Gaudy Night*, chapter 6.

258 *"The flat setting . . . "*: *Gaudy Night*, chapter 15.
"She felt the melting pity": A Pin to See the Peepshow, Book III, "The Dream", Virago Press, 1979, pp. 259-60.

259 *"Asleep he undoubtedly was . . . "*: *Gaudy Night*, chapter 15.
"How wonderful", says the poet . . . : Shelley, *Queen Mab*.

260 *"no hand plucked his velvet sleeve"*: At the graduation ceremony it was the custom for two proctors to walk within reach of the congregation, any member of which might pluck the sleeve of their gowns if it was desired to raise an objection. In an address to the Association of Booksellers in Oxford, D.L.S. said, "All the associations of Oxford are put – quite deliberately – behind the words '*Placetne, magistra?*'"

CHAPTER 19

261 *Tom Puffett*: A friend of D.L.S. wrote to tell her that in their family circle stripping off a sweater had come to be known as "doing a chimney sweep".

262 *"He was an exceedingly stout man . . . "*: Chapter 4.

"Why don't you?" said Muriel: The conversation was related to me by Muriel St Clare Byrne.

266 *"I tired the sun with talking . . . "*: An echo of the lines by William Johnson Cory (1823-92): "They told me, Heraclitus, they told me you were dead,/ They brought me bitter news to hear and bitter tears I shed./ . . . How often you and I/ Had tired the sun with talking and sent him down the sky."

the family history of the Wimseys: Later compiled from their correspondence by Wilfred Scott-Giles in *The Wimsey Family*, Gollancz, 1977. For W. Scott-Giles' illustrations of D.L.S.'s translation of Dante, see Barbara Reynolds, *The Passionate Intellect*, ed. cit., pp. 61-81, 99-100, 109-10, 132-3.

267 *Lord Mortimer Wimsey*: A spoof pamphlet about him was written by D.L.S., with the spurious date of 1816. Sending a copy to Basil Blackwell, dated 30 May 1941, she wrote: "Graham Pollard [author of *The Forged Victorian Pamphlets*] supervised the format for me, and I think he has made a fairly good job of it, down to the wholly fictitious and misleading imprint."

270 *"I have been facing one fact . . . "*: *Gaudy Night*, chapter 22.

CHAPTER 20

273 *Canterbury Festival*: See Kenneth Pickering, *Drama in the Cathedral*, Churchman Publishing Ltd, 1985.

278 *"The play ends finely on Michael's speech . . . "*: In view of this comment, it is strange that Harcourt Williams omitted this speech in the first production.

280 *Mr Scott-Giles characteristically*: He was an authority on roads. See his *The Road Goes On: A Literary and Historical Account of the Highways, Byways and Bridges of Great Britain*.

CHAPTER 21

286 *"stiff bourdon"*: A reference to Chaucer, *Canterbury Tales*, Prologue, 673: "This somnour bar to him a stif burdoun,/ was never trompe of half so greet a soun." A bourdon is a low accompaniment to a melody. Chaucer's word "stif" means strong, or loud. Like Father Kelly, Dorothy Rowe immediately recognised the structural importance of Michael's speech.

287 *Father Herbert Kelly*: Herbert Hamilton Kelly (1860-1950) was the founder of the Society of the Sacred Mission and a considerable influence on the Church of England, partly through his own writing, partly through the community in its missionary work and the training of ordinands. Kelly owed a great debt to F. D. Maurice (1805-1872), the "Christian Socialist" who had moved away from Unitarianism because he came to see the Trinity not as the denial of God's unity but as its true expression. Kelly wrote of him, "I learnt almost everything from Maurice; then I learnt it over again – several times." (*The Gospel of God*, 1928). I am indebted to Canon John Thurmer for this note and also to his book, *A Detection of the Trinity*, Exeter, Paternoster Press, 1974, in which he explores D.L.S.'s insight into the doctrine of the Trinity in *The Mind of the Maker*.

288 *"ridiculous to call it dull"*: D.L.S. repeated this challenge in her article, "The Greatest Drama Ever Staged" (included in *Creed or Chaos?*): "If this is dull, then what, in Heaven's name, is worthy to be called exciting?"

289 *her letters to Father Kelly*: Extracts from the Sayers-Kelly correspondence were published in the *Journal of the Society of the Sacred Mission*, May 1983.

290 *"His Manhood was a real manhood . . . "*: Note to Producers, preceding *He*

That Should Come (Four Sacred Plays, Gollancz, 1948).

CHAPTER 22

306 *torn-up pieces of the contract*: See Janet Hitchman, *Such a Strange Lady*, p. 152.

CHAPTER 23

308 *Maurice Reckitt*: The founder of the Christendom Group. See *Maurice B. Reckitt: A Life*, by John S. Peart-Binns (Bowerdean and Pickering, 1988).

310 *doctrine of human creativity*: Once again, I am indebted to Canon John Thurmer. See his *A Detection of the Trinity*, ed. cit., pp. 48-51.

313 *a true record of experience*: Not limited to D.L.S. Writing to Muriel St Clare Byrne on 8 August 1941, she said: "Lascelles Abercrombie [*Theory of Poetry*] is right on to lots of *The Mind of the Maker* stuff. I ought to have quoted him there – but I'm glad I didn't read the book earlier. I should have suspected myself of being influenced by what he said – especially about the return of the idea through the Son to the Ghost – almost identical with mine in other words."

314 *The Rev. V. A. Demant*: Vigo Auguste Demant, associated with the Christendom Group and a friend of Maurice Reckitt.
Richard T. Webster: Author of *New Dialogue with Anglo-American Philosophy* (Officium Libri Catholici, Rome, 1972); *The Very Idea Of Ultimate Reality and Meaning* (Toronto, 1989) and many articles in English and Italian on the same subjects. See his article "*The Mind of the Maker*: Logical Construction, Creative Choice, and the Trinity" in *As Her Whimsey Took Her*, edited by Margaret Hannay, Kent State University Press, 1979, pp. 165-75.

315 *Canon John Thurmer*: I quote from *A Detection of the Trinity*, ed. cit., pp. 59, 60, 11. See also the same author's "The Theology of Dorothy L. Sayers" in *Church Quarterly Review*, 1967.
Catherine Kenney: Kent State University Press, op. cit., pp. 245-68.
Richard L. Harp: See "*The Mind of the Maker*: The Theological Aesthetic of Dorothy Sayers and its Application to Poetry" in *As Her Whimsey Took Her*, ed. cit., pp. 176-99.

CHAPTER 24

318 *Ivor Brown*: Leader-writer for the *Manchester Guardian* and dramatic critic on the *Saturday Review* (1891-1974).
Robert Blatchford: Journalist; author of *God and My Neighbour* (1903) and editor of *The Clarion* (1851-1943).

319 *a Docetist Christ*: According to the Docetist doctrine, Christ's body was either a phantom or a celestial substance.

324 *most of us are Arians*: The heretic Arius (fourth century) denied that the Son was consubstantial with the Father. For an illuminating discussion of Arianism, see D.L.S.'s play *The Emperor Constantine*, especially the scene of the Council of Nicaea.

330 *"I think I do fully understand the situation"*: It has been suggested (by Brabazon and others) that the main reason for D.L.S.'s refusal of the offer of the degree was her fear that word might get out of her illegitimate son. The reasons she gives in her letters to the Archbishop are sufficient as they stand and he accepted them as such. As William of Occam advised, "*Entia non sunt multiplicanda praeter necessitatem.*"

CHAPTER 25

332 *St Anne's House, Soho*: See note to p. 362.
  Rev. Dr James Parkes: Author of *The Jew and his Neighbour*, 1930; *The Jewish Problem in the Modern World*, 1939; *God in a World at War*, 1940.

334 *Father John Groser*: See *John Groser, East London Priest*, edited by Kenneth Brill, Mowbray, London and Oxford, 1971. I am indebted to the Rev. Frank Lewis for drawing my attention to this book. D.L.S.'s comments on Father Groser are important as showing the range of her spiritual response, which was independent of her political convictions.

340 *Talboys*: A name frequently given to Elizabethan houses and chosen by Muriel St Clare Byrne. This explanation was given by D.L.S. in reply to a correspondent who enquired whether the name was connected in her mind with the character Mr Tallboy, in *Murder Must Advertise*. (Letter to Miss B. S. Sturgis, 9 March 1937.)
  five children in all: From a conversation with D.L.S.
  disclosed only orally to friends: To Muriel St Clare Byrne and Marjorie Barber, to whom D.L.S. announced one day, during the Battle of Britain, "I'm afraid Jerry [i.e. Gerald] has had it." (Related to me by Miss Byrne.)

CHAPTER 26

347 *Mac had died . . .* : Nine months after Mac's death, Ivy Shrimpton also died, of broncho-pneumonia and measles. She had been suffering from myocardial degeneration and was seventy years of age. She had willed everything to D.L.S. (about four thousand pounds), which D.L.S. passed immediately to her son.

349 *mannish in dress*: Questions have been raised from time to time concerning the sexual orientation of D.L.S. This is probably due to her style of dress in later years. A passage in one of her letters to Dr Eustace Barton sheds interesting light on the matter. Writing to him on 23 November 1928, she asks him for information about sexual inversion and perversion, as a matter of interest, not out of personal concern: "As a matter of fact, inverts make me creep, but that is no reason why one shouldn't face the facts . . . Besides, the normal person often makes the invert creep; I have a friend who was rather that way – a very fine person of powerful intellect – but she won't see, speak or write to me now I'm married, because marriage revolts her. So there you are. The trouble is that these poor wretches have to fall in love with normals, and that is bad for the normals. If only the male women and the female men could pair off together, nobody would care what they did to each other, because that would be part of the 'sanctities of married life'. Well, well!"
  Six days later, she returned to the subject: "A woman doctor I know, who specialises in sexual problems . . . is particularly anxious to know what really authentic cases there are of a really normal person (so far as anybody can be called normal) being 'seduced' by an invert. In 'The Well of Loneliness', it is quite clearly stated that this can be the case; but I think she is anxious to know whether the 'seduced' people are not mostly border-line cases and semi-inverted already. I was wondering whether your experience would be of assistance to her in this matter. (Dr Barton was in charge of a mental hospital in Northampton.) She is a serious sort of person, keen to collect reliable statistics . . . I'm so pleased when I find an ordinary practitioner who takes what I call a reasonable, common-sense interest in the matter – it oughtn't to be left entirely to the Freudians."
  "At the King's Head in Maldon . . . ": Francis Wheen, *Tom Driberg. His Life and Indiscretions*, London, Chatto and Windus, 1990, pp. 175-6. I am indebted to Professor Brinley Thomas for drawing my attention to this quotation. Tom Driberg, created a life peer (Baron Bradwell) in 1975, was a

journalist, lecturer and broadcaster. He was M.P. for Maldon, Essex from 1942 to 1955. Born in 1905, he died in 1976.
Vernon Bartlett: Author, broadcaster and political commentator (1894-1983).
351 *W. L. Mackenzie King*: Prime Minister of Canada, born 1874, died 1950.

CHAPTER 27

353 *"The Passionate Intellect"*: Kent State University Press, 1989.
Charles Williams: After his death, in an undated letter addressed to a Miss Falkin, D.L.S. said: "I was a friend of Charles Williams; but I should not describe myself as belonging to any kind of 'circle' or 'group'. Neither have I any particular interest in occultism or agnosticism, except that, like Charles Williams himself, I know enough about them to know their dangers, and that no Christian may or can tolerate them. Of Steinerism, I can say that I have seen it destroy the body and impair the mind of one of my best friends, and should advise those who value their physical and mental health to steer clear of it."
354 *the doodle-bugs*: The popular nickname for Hitler's guided missiles.
359 *She enjoyed her fame*: She did not always enjoy publicity, however. On 7 March 1951, she wrote to the editor of the *East Anglian Daily Times*, saying that she would grant an interview if the dramatic critic would confine his questions to the play and the production [*The Emperor Constantine*] and "promise to eschew resolutely all gossipy details about me, my house, household, personal habits and appearance, and every other irrelevancy".
stupid questions: From a conversation with D.L.S.
362 *St Anne's House, Soho*: Founded as a centre of liaison between the Christian faith and the secular intellect. The Church of St Anne, from which it was named, was destroyed by bombs. Only the tower was left standing. The ashes of D.L.S. are buried there.
The Just Vengeance: See Barbara Reynolds, *The Passionate Intellect*, ed. cit., chapter 6.

CHAPTER 28

367 *reviewing a biography*: The biography in question is Alzina Stone Dale's *Maker and Craftsman: The Story of Dorothy L. Sayers*, Eerdman, Grand Rapids, Michigan, 1978. The review was published in the *Church Times*, 2 March 1979.
candid, soul-revealing letter: For an important discussion of this letter, see E. L. Mascall, "What happened to Dorothy L. Sayers that Good Friday?", *SEVEN: An Anglo-American Literary Review*, vol. III, March 1982, pp. 9-18.
368 *Dante*: "*la mente innamorata*", Paradiso, XXVII, 88.
371 *I do not know of any success*: From a letter to the Rev. E. Parry Jennings, dated 13 January 1947.

Appendix

EUCLID'S TENNIS COURT

In *Cat o' Mary*, Dorothy L. Sayers attributes to Katherine Lammas a discovery she herself experienced on the tennis court at Bluntisham Rectory:

The back lawn at the Rectory was tree-shaded and rather damp, and the grass grew fast and lush there. It was not an ideal lawn for tennis, but it was the only one that was level, and it did well enough for the children. But that spring had been rainy and the two iron sockets that took the net-posts, together with the permanent metal corners of the court, had sunk out of sight beneath the close roots of the turf. After prodding about for some time, Mr Lammas found one of the sockets, and paused to wipe the perspiration from his forehead, for it was a hot day. Mrs Lammas had retrieved from some drawer the set of measurements, and Mr Lammas, measuring from the socket in what he took to be the right direction, began to prod the ground again for the missing corner.

Katherine watched the series of prods, extending in a direct line towards the mulberry tree.

"I didn't think it was so far this way," said Mr Lammas.

"You're going wrong," asserted Katherine, positively. "You want to make a circle, not a straight line."

Mr Lammas, whose natural intelligence may have been a little confused by the heat, queried this.

"It's Euclid," said Katherine, and proceeded to enunciate the properties characterising the radius of a circle.

"All right," said Mr Lammas, abandoning the string and the garden knife. "See if you can find it."

By a kind of miracle, Katherine did find it (by the peg-and-string system) using the Euclidean method, in a very few seconds. If the court had not been precisely laid out in the first instance, she might have had more difficulty, but the corner being accurately placed, the laws of geometry held good. In her heart of hearts, Katherine was awe-stricken. To see a prophecy made on paper fulfilled on the back lawn is a very enlarging experience . . . Mrs Lammas, having, in the meantime, discovered the second socket by trial and error, with the point of a sunshade, Katherine went on to find the next corner, exactly where it should have been, at the point of intersection of two circles. After this, there was no holding her . . . She had been brought face to face with beauty. It had risen up before her . . . the lovely satisfying unity of things: the wedding of the thing learned and the thing done: the great intellectual fulfilment . . . Nothing would ever quite wipe out the memory of that magnificent moment when the intersecting circles marched out of the pages of the Euclid book and met on the green grass in the sun-flecked shadow of the mulberry-tree.

EXPLANATION

The solution depends upon the principle that all points on the circumference of a circle are equidistant from the centre. Mr Lammas having found the first post-hole by trial and error, on Mrs Lammas' supplying the dimensions of a tennis court "from some drawer", he attempts to locate a corner-iron by pacing the appropriate distance from post to corner and, failing to find it, walks *in a straight line*, presumably parallel to where he thinks the net would be. Katherine sees the error: in order to find the corner of a certain distance from the post-hole, one must inscribe a *circle*. This she does by placing a peg, to which a length of string equal to half the long side of the court is attached, in the post-hole and then prodding along the arc of the circle traced by the end of the piece of string. Meanwhile Mrs Lammas has found the second post-hole by trial and error, so the second corner can be located more expeditiously by employing the first and a second piece of string (equal in length to the width of the court), inscribing arcs centred on the second post-hole and the first corner respectively. The corner is found where the two arcs intersect. The process can then be repeated to find the last two corners.

Principal Sources

UNPUBLISHED

My Edwardian Childhood
Cat o' Mary
Letters of Dorothy L. Sayers

The first two items and the majority of the letters are in the possession of the Marion E. Wade Center, Wheaton College, Illinois. Some of the letters are in private hands.

PUBLISHED

Colleen B. Gilbert, *A Bibliograpby of the Works of Dorothy L. Sayers* (Macmillan, 1978).
Ralph E. Hone, *Dorothy L. Sayers. A Literary Biography* (Kent State University Press, 1979).
James Brabazon, *Dorothy L. Sayers. The Life of a Courageous Woman* (Gollancz, 1981).
John Thurmer, *A Detection of the Trinity* (Exeter, Paternoster Press, 1984).

Other sources are indicated in the text or in the notes.

Acknowledgments

My thanks are due in the first instance to Miss Sylvia Bruce, who read the book in its formative stages and whose help and advice I found most valuable. I also thank Miss Carolyn Caughey, Miss Jane Osborn and Mrs Christine Casley of Hodder and Stoughton for their guidance and professional expertise. Mrs Marjorie Lamp Mead, Associate Director of the Marion E. Wade Center, Wheaton College, Illinois, gave me every possible assistance, enabling me to make full use in a short time of the collection of letters and photographs in her care.

Many other people have also given generous help. Mrs Fortuna Fleming invited me to stay in her house in Florida for ten days and allowed me to make notes on letters in her possession; she also lent me several photographs. The late Mrs Ann Schreurs, the daughter of Mac Fleming, gave me information about her father and also supplied photographs. Canon John Thurmer, whom I consulted about the chapters involving Christian doctrine, enlightened and clarified my understanding. Several others read the book, or parts of it, in typescript, and made helpful suggestions: Mr Adrian Thorpe, Mr Andrew Lewis, Mrs Kerstin Lewis, to whom I owe the explanation of Euclid's tennis court, Mrs Lucile Contamin, Lt. Col. Ralph Clarke, Mrs Eileen Bushell, Baroness James of Holland Park (P. D. James), Dr Catherine Storr, Professor Brinley Thomas, Mrs Barbara Whelpton, the Rev. Frank Lewis, and Mrs Eunice Lewis. Miss Norah Lambourne, who knew Dorothy Sayers well, encouraged me by her assurance that the portrait I was presenting was a living one. Professor Ralph E. Hone, whose biography I much admire, read the whole of the present work and gave it his generous encouragement. To Mr Philip L. Scowcroft, Research Officer of the Dorothy L. Sayers Society, I owe special thanks, as always, for his meticulously

389

accurate information. I have benefited also from the advice and encouragement of Mr Bruce Hunter of David Higham Associates.

Others whom I have consulted on particular points are Mr James Sabben-Clare, headmaster of Winchester (on Henry Sayers as a Wykehamist), Dr J. B. Cottis, Archivist, Magdalen College, Oxford (on Henry Sayers as a member of the college), Miss Pauline Adams, Archivist of Somerville College, Lt. Comdr. Donald M. Andrew (on Henry Sayers as a Freemason), Mr Allan H. Mottram, headmaster of Christ Church Cathedral School, the Rev. Colin Backhouse, rector of Bluntisham, who drew my attention to a rare and charming pamphlet describing the rectory garden as it was when Dorothy Sayers knew it, the Rev. Hugh Reid, rector of Christchurch, Cambridgeshire, Mrs Evelyn Bedford (née Compline), who shared with me her memories of the Sayers household and lent me photographs, Mr Kenneth Garlick and Mr Robertson Davies (on Maurice Roy Ridley as they remember him), Lu Christian, Gwen Walter and Winnie Caldin (former pupils of Dorothy L. Sayers at Clapham High School), Professor William Phemister (on matters relating to musicology). In this last connection I must not forget to mention the generous hospitality I enjoyed for a month in the Phemister household while I was working on manuscripts at Wheaton College.

To all these people, and to any others I may have inadvertently omitted, I offer my acknowledgments and thanks.

I acknowledge with thanks permission to quote from the following authors: Dorothy L. Sayers, granted by David Higham Associates on behalf of the Estate of Anthony Fleming, unpublished material © Harbottle and Lewis; Charles Williams, granted by David Higham Associates on behalf of the copyright owner, Michael Williams; C. S. Lewis, granted by Cambridge University Press, extract from unpublished letter by Curtis Brown, London; T. S. Eliot, granted by Faber and Faber; James Brabazon, granted personally; Norah Lambourne, granted personally; Rosmund Essex, granted by the *Church Times*. For permission to reproduce a photograph of Roy Ridley, I thank the Master and Fellows of Balliol College; for permission to reproduce a photograph of Leonard Hodgson and a group photograph of Henry Sayers and contemporaries, I thank the President and Fellows of Magdalen College.

Barbara Reynolds

Index

Abercrombie, Lascelles, n. to 313
Acland Nursing Home, 79, 234, 235
Acland, Sir Richard, 314
Adams, Kenneth, 321
Adele, 94, 95, 96
Aeneid: see Virgil
Aesop, 194
Agate, James, 292
Ahasuerus, 16
Allan, Ralph, n. to 161
Allen, Sir Hugh Percy, 50–52, 64–65, 74, 75, 79, 80, 84, n. to 50
"And Telling You A Story", n. to 54, 240
Arbuthnot, the Hon. Freddy, 178, 181
Aristotle, 315
"Aristotle And The Art Of Detective Fiction", 56, 263
Arlen, Michael, 181, n. to 181
Arundell, Dennis, 265
Aubrey-Fletcher, Sir Henry: see Wade, Henry
Auden, W. H., 70–71
Ask a Policeman, 243
Austin, Frederick, 164

Babington, Margaret, 273–275, 277, 286
Bach, Bach Choir: see Oxford Bach Choir
Ball, Sir Robert, 17
Balliol College, 52, 56, 167, 343, 346
Barber, Marjorie, 262, 265, 280, 286, 356, 357, n. to 340
Barnett, Charis, 71–72, 113, 244
Barry, Florence, 100
Bartlett, Vernon, 349, n. to 349

Barton, Eustace, 213–217, 220, 222, 223–224, n. to 349
B.B.C., 290, 298–299, 300–306, 307, 317–328, 333–334, 361
Beddoes, Thomas, 23
Bedford, Mrs: see Compline, Evelyn
Bedier, Joseph, 185, 189
The Beggar's Opera, 163–164
Bell, Rt. Rev. George (Dean of Canterbury, later Bishop of Chichester), 273, 299
Begin Here, 295–296, 307, 308
Benn, Ernest, 190, 225, 227, n. to 204
Bennett, Arnold, 240
Benson, Monsignor R. H., 188
Benson's, S. H., 106, 117, 119, 123, 124, 129, 144, 161, 164, 167, 185, 206, 211, 228, 289, 359 nn. to 80, 188
Bentley, E. C., 138, 175, 229, 257, 362, n. to 175
Berners Hotel, 72, 321
Betjeman, Sir John, 363
Biggs, Sir Impey, 0
Black And White, 156
Blackwell, Sir Basil, 64, 68, 69, 76, 78, 80, 81, 84, 85–86, 252, n. to 267
Blake, Sexton, 95, 171–173, 174, 176, 196
Blake, William, 345
Blatchford, Robert, 318, n. to 318
Bluntisham, 7–13, 17, 27, 28, 36, 41, 57, 61, 65, 67–68, 90, 104, 158, 166, 205–206, 238, 248, 250, 268, 363
Boiardo, Matteo, 190–191
Boni and Liveright, 108, 225
Boston, the (a dance), 52, n. to 52

391

Boulogne-sur-Mer, 162–163
Boulter, B. C., 307
Bournemouth, 32, 70. 73, 99, 105, 111, 122, 142
Boyes, Philip, 113–114, 131
Brabant, Frank, 46–47, 85
Brabazon, James, 36, 39, 40–41, 129–131, 250, nn. to 28, 39, 40–41, 43, 129, 250, 330
Brittain, Vera, 59, 61, 98, n. to 59
Bridgeheads, 299, 307–308, 309, 313, 332, 340, 335, n. to 164
Broadstairs, 6, 269
Bronte, Maria, 15
Brown, Ivor, 318, n. to 318
Browne, Denis, 265, 280, 313
Browne, Maurice, 265, 315, 369
Browning, Robert, 75
Bruce, the Hon. Pamela, 61
Bunter, Mervyn, 92, 154, 179
Bunyan, John, 359
Busman's Honeymoon (Play), 56, 76, 173, 263–265, 267, 269–270, 273–274, 275 (Novel) 262, 265–266, 270–271, 280, 340, n. to 133
Butler, Samuel, 23–24
Byrne, Muriel St Clare, 56, 76, 244, 245, 251, 253–254, 262–264, 266, 267, 280, 299, 307, 313, 361, nn. to 244, 262, 313, 340

Caldin, Winnie, n. to 100
Cambridge, 27, 36, 48, 75, 364
Cambridge University, 97
Canterbury Cathedral and Festival, 82, 273–282, 283–285, 291–292, 299, 353, 362, n. to 273
Carroll, Lewis, 7, n. to 91
Cassiel, Recording Angel, 287
Cather, Willa, n. to 21
Catholic Tales And Christian Songs, 80–82, 207
Cat o' Mary, 28, 29, 30, 38, 39, 40, 41, 42–43, 122–123, 158, 247–251, n. to 19
Causton, Bernard, 337
Cecil, Lord David, 309
Chance, Dr Alice, 87, 121, 122, 123
La Chanson De Roland, 75, 185, 362
Chapman, Annie, 9
Chapman, Bob, 9, 13, 158
Chapman, Elizabeth, 9, 21, 22
Chapman, John, 9, 21
Chase, Eleanor, 48–49

Chaucer, n. to 286
Chesterton, G. K., 38, 41, 52, 58, 81, 108, 137–138, 204, 310, nn. to 58, 137
Childe, Wilfred, Rowland, 81, 82
Christchurch, suburb of Bournemouth, 124
Christchurch, Cambridgeshire, 74, 83, 89–90, 102, 104, 110, 122. 124, 127, 145, 149, 158, 203, 205, 206, 208, 209
Christ Church, Oxford College, 4, 7, 46
Christ Church Cathedral, 1, 124, 253
Christ Church Choir School, 1, 2–3, 15
Christendom Group, 351, n. to 314
Christian, Lu, n. to 100
Christian Social Union, 47, n. to 47
Christy, Violet, 28, 29, 30, 34, 248
Church Assembly, 331
Church Social Action Group, 331–332
Church Tutorial Classes Association, 335
Churchill, Sir Winston, 154, 347–349
Clapham High School, 100–101, 192
Clements, Dom Bernard, 331
Climpson, Miss, 30, 99, 200, 201
Clouds Of Witness, 102, 105, Ill, 120, 123, 147–148, 149, 171, 203, 225, n. to 120
Cockin, Canon, 333
Colchester Festival, 362
Cole, G. D. H., 68, 93
Cole, Margaret, 93
Collings, G. R., 338
Collins, Wilkie, 11, 138, 169, 196–197, 204, 221–222, 229, 230, 238–239, 240, 340, 370
Compline, Evelyn, 200, 231, nn. to 4, 206, 208
Connington, J. J., 240
Connor, William, 349
Contamin, Louis, 162
Cooke, Guy, 15–16
Cooper, James Fenimore, 196
Cory, William Johnson, n. to 266
Cournos, John, 107–116, 117, 118, 119, 121, 124, 131–13, 141, 148, 154, 160, 163, 169, 185, 203, 225, 230, 244, 253, 370, nn. to 121, 135, 139, 177, 195
Cowley, 142, 148, 150
Craig, Gordon, 108, n. to 139
Creed Or Chaos?, n. to 288
The Criterion, 108

Crofts, Freeman Wills, 232–233, n. to 232
Cromwell, Oliver, 10, 273
Crichton, Charles, 92, 93, 173, 181
Cyrus, 16, n. to 16

The Daily Mail, 321
The Daily Mirror, 349
Dakers, Andrew, 105, 106, 203, 225
Dale, Alzina Stone, n. to 367
Daniels, Nurse, 162
Dante, 43, 53, 54, 141–142, 183, 240, 353–356, 362, 364, 367, 368, 370, nn. to 54, 56, 368
Davey, Norman, 106, 110, 119–120
Dean, Christopher, n. to 183
Defoe, Daniel, 240
Delagardie, Paul, 270, n. to 133
Dell, Ethel M., 361
Demant, V. A., 314, 331, n. to 314
Denver, Duchess of, 177–178, 270, n. to 133
Denver, Duke of, 153
Detection Club, 242, 264, 361
The Devil Is An English Gentleman, 112, 114–116, 132–136
The Devil To Pay, 291–294
Dickens, Charles, 239, nn. to 106, 121
"The Dictatorship of Words", n. to 187
Dignam, Joe, 211
Dixey, Giles, 46, 52, 64, 69, 76, 85, n. to 69
Dixey, Roger, 82–83, 85
The Documents In The Case, 159, 161, 192, 213–224, 227, 229, 233, 253, 258, 263, n. to 110
Donne, John, 270–271
Douglas, Alice Mary, 27, 35, 37, 40, 41, 42, 43, 361
Douglas, Lucy, 27
Doyle, Sir Arthur Conan, 339: see also Holmes, Sherlock
Driberg, Tom, 349–350, n. to 349
Drinkwater, John, 162
Dumas, Alexandre, 21, 23, 24: see also *The Three Musketeers*
Durham University, 359

"Earl Ulfric", 53, n. to 53
Earp, T. W., 68, n. to 68
Ecole Des Roches, 88, 90–93, 192
Eddington, Sir Arthur, 341
Edmondson, Molly, 37
Egg, Monty, 243

Eliot, T. S., 273, 275, 294, 295–296, 307, 342
Elliott, Miss, 72–73, 74, 76, 321
Ellis-Fermor, Una, 313
The Emperor Constantine, 362–363, nn. to 324, 359
Encarnia (Oxford Degree Ceremony), 55–56
Encounters With Lord Peter, n. to 183
"The Entertaining Episode of the Article in Question", 172, n. to 172
Essex, Rosamund, 367
Eustace, Robert: see Barton, Eustace
The Evening Standard, 160

Falkner, John Meade, 241–242
"The Fascinating Story Of Uncle Meleager's Will", 195, n. to 195
Faust, Faustus, 291–294
Fehmer, Miss, 31–32, 369–370
Fenn, Rev. Eric, 318, 319, 334
Fentiman, George, 164
The Figure Of Beatrice, 340, 353, 356
Fisher, H. A. L., 53
The Five Red Herrings, 6, 211, 232–233, 254, nn. 6, 232
Fleming, John Anthony, 37, 124–128, 131, 136, 141–151, 167, 199, 202, 211, 227, 228, 234–235, 237, 244, 267–269, 341–346, 370, nn. to 135, 347
Fleming, Oswold Arthur ("Mac"), 153–169, 183, 185, 200, 201, 203, 205, 206, 207, 208, 209–211, 227, 228, 232, 234, 235, 238, 264, 268, 282, 290, 344, 345, 346–347, nn. to 137, 153, 161, 254, 346
The Floating Admiral, 242
Ford, Ford Madox, 108
Forrest, Arthur, 52
Frankenburg, Mrs Sydney: see Barnett, Charis
Further Papers on Dante, nn. to 54, 240

Garbett, The Rt. Rev. Cyril, Archbishop of York, 325, 326–327
Gaudy Night, 52, 55, 59, 65, 66, 98, 197, 223, 237, 252–260, 261, 263, 265, 270, 283, 286, 367, nn. to 52, 66, 101, 237, 257, 258, 259, 270
"Gaudy Night" (article), 229, 230, 249, 339, nn. to 98, 229, 256
George, David Lloyd, n. to 187
Gibbs, Armstrong, 314

Gielgud, Val, 301, 318, 322, 325, 327, 364, 371
Gilbert and Sullivan, 53, 82
Gilroy, Sir John, 129, 204, 228
Girton College, 47, 48, 114
Godfrey, Catherine ("Tony"), 48, 54, 55, 57, 58, 66, 67, 71, 72, 74, 77, 89, 260
Godley, A. D., 55, n. to 55
Godolphin School, Salisbury, 27–43, 47, 179, 248
Goethe, 291, 370, n. to 48
Gollancz, Victor, 160, 163, 188, 191, 196, 202, 204, 225, 226, 227, 228, 229, 231, 232, 233, 234, 242, 261, 274, 295, 296, n. to 204
Gourmet's Book Of Food And Drink, 160
"The Greatest Drama Ever Staged", n. to 288
Great Short Stories of Detection, Mystery and Horror, 137, 167, 193–196, 225–226, 229, 242, n. to 242
Gregory, E. R., 197, n. to 197
Groser, Rev. John, 334, n. to 334
The Guardian, 301
Guild Of Catholic Writers, 307, 331
Guinness, 228, n. to 228

Haffenden, Elizabeth, 276, 277, 292
Hall, Anmer, 265, 275
Hamilton, Miss, 21, 22, 24
Hangman's Holiday, 243
Hammersmith, 162, 163, 164
Harp, Richard L., 315, n. to 315
Harrison, Mrs Margaret, 222, 223, n. to 223
Have His Carcase, 13, 23, 52, 159, 233–234, 235, 239, 243, 247, nn. to 13, 52
Heenan, Rev. J. C., 333, 338
Henderson, Elsie, 50, 53, 54, 59, 61
Herbert, A. P., 164, 248, 313, n. to 164
Herodotus, 194
He That Should Come, 290, 300, 301, n. to 290
Hill, Francis, and Mrs Hill, 91, 96, n. to 91
Hitchman, Janet, nn. to 73, 80, 306
Hodgson, Leonard, 77–79
Hodgson, Ralph, 108
Holmes, Sherlock, 95, 180, 183, 194, 195, 196, 240, nn. to 95, 166
Holmes, Sherlock, Society, 242

Hone, Ralph E., 36, 76, 122, 239, nn. to 36, 69, 74, 76, 243
Housman, A. E., 175
"How I Came to Invent the Character of Lord Peter Wimsey", 173, 230–231, nn. to 173, 230
How to See the Battlefields, 154
Hudson, W. H., 204
Hull, 72–73, 75, 76, 100. 185, 186, 187
Hutchinson, Cyril, 25, 65
Hutchinson, Sir William, 102
Huxley, Aldous, 68
Huxley, Sir Julian, 332
"Hymn in Contemplation of Sudden Death", 364–365

Ibanez, Vincent Blasco, 99
The Ingoldsby Legends, 19, 149
In the Teeth of the Evidence, 206, n. to 164
Introductory Papers on Dante, n. to 141
Irving, Sir Henry, 276
Irving, H. B., 276
Irving, Laurence, 276–276
Isobel (Tovey), 143, 146, 149, 151, 228, n. to 144

Jaeger, Muriel ("Jim"), 53–54, 55, 66, 67–68, 70, 72, 74, 77, 81, 87, 88, 91, 95, 99, 1O2, 104, 147, 176, 185, 186, 187, 196, 250, n. to 106
James, M. R., 81
Jenkin, May, 303–306, 322, 325, 326
Jepson, Edgar, 213
Jesse, F, Tennyson, 222–223, 258–259, n. to 258–259
John Bull, 162
John o'London's Weekly, 108, 332
The Just Vengeance, 362, n. to 362

Kelly, Rev. Herbert, 287–289, 296, 309–310, 313, 332, 333–334, 337, 359, nn. to 237, 286, 287, 289
Kenney, Catherine, 315, n. to 315
Kensit, Mr, 322
King, Mackenzie W. L., 350–351, n. to 350
Kipling, Rudyard, 248
Kirkcudbright(shire), 161, 211, 231–232, 233, 243
Knight, Gerald, 277, 278
Knight, Dame Laura, 162
Knox, Monsignor Ronald, 309, 314
Kuhn, Helmut, 313

Labiche, Emile, 37
Lambourne, Norah, 362–363
Lang, Andrew, 190
Lapwood, Jack, 364
"Lectures on Poetic Form", 192–193
Lee, Geoffrey, n. to 75
Leigh, Henry, 14, 245
Leigh, Johanna, 247, n. to 247
Leigh, Mabel, 6, 7, 8, 9, 14, 15, 16, 17,
    118, 121, 145, 150, 158, 159–160,
    161, 199–200, 201, 208, 209, 210,
    211, 228, 231, 234, 244
Leigh, Margaret, 6, 9, 14, 18, 29, 38,
    46, 245
Leigh, Mrs Maud, 14, 46, 50, 52, 80,
    145, 200, 245, 264–265, 280
Leigh, Percival, 3, 123, 363
Leigh, Percy, 208, n. to 208
Lengyel, Ernst, 31, n. to 31
Lewis, C. S., 193, 358–359, 363
Lichfield Cathedral, 362
The Listener, 295, n. to 223
The Literary Guide, 318
Little Arthur's History Of England, 17,
    n. to 17
Locker-Lampson, Oliver, 23, n. to 23
The London Mercury, 106
Lord Peter Views the Body, 202, 226,
    nn. to 172, 195
"Lord Mortimer Wimsey", 267, n. to
    267
Lorimer, George Horace, 175, n. to 175
Love All, 357
Love's Labour's Lost, 265
Lubbock, Sir James, 217–219
Lydgate, Miss, 59, 254
Lyric Theatre, Hammersmith, 163, 164

McCulloch, Derek, 301–303, 304, 305
McLaughlin, Rev. Patrick, 331
Mackinnon, Donald, 333, 336–337
Magdalen College, 1, 75
Maldon, 203–204, 208, 349, n. to 349
Malvern, 85
Malvern College, 167, 341
Malvern Conference, 299, 335–337
The Man Born to be King, 48, 139, 191,
    290, 298–306, 307, 317–330, 359
Mannering, Cyril, 99
Marlowe, Christopher, 291
Marsh, H. C., 338
Marshall, Sir Arthur 105, n. to 105
Martin, Rev. H. H., 321
Masaryk, President, 108

Mascall, Rev. E. L., n. to 367
Masefield, John, 108, 273
May, Herbert 47, n. to 47
Maynard, Theodore, 81, 82
Meade, L. T., 213
"The Meaning of Purgatory", 141, n. to
    141
Mephistopheles, 292–293
The Merchant Of Venice, 36
Meyerstein, R. H. W., n. to 202
Michael, Archangel, 278, 285, 286, 287,
    288, 309, n. to 286
Middlemore, Amphy, 53, 76–77
Milsom, Agatha, 161, 220
Milton, John, 23
The Mind of the Maker, 23, 79, 299,
    307, 308–315, 329, 330, 343, nn. to
    227, 313
Ministry of Information, 108, 295, 300,
    325, n. to 139
"The Mocking Of Christ", 81, 82, 274
Modern Language Association, 186,
    187
Modern Languages, 98–99, 186, 187,
    207
Moliere, 22, 23, 34, 35, 37, 42–43, 74
The Moonstone: see Collins, Wilkie
Morris, William, 191, n. to 191
"The Mousehole", 174
Munting, Jack, 159, 217–219, nn. 110,
    217
Murder Must Advertise, 129, 131, 175,
    176, 238, 243, 247, 254, 263, 289,
    359, nn. to 120, 175, 340
The Mustard Club, 164–165
Mutual Admiration Society, 53, 54, 68,
    69, 70, 76–77, 97
"My Edwardian Childhood", 4, 237–
    238, 248–249, 250, 252–253, nn. to
    18, 206

Napier, Frank, 278
"Nebuchadnezzar", 164, n. to 164
New College, 50, 51, 62, 260
News of the World, 153, 154, 156, 162,
    211
The New Witness, 81, 82, 95
Nicolls, B. E., 316
The Nine Tailors, 102, 188, 201, 207,
    239–242, 247, 248, 249, 254, 256,
    263, 283, 353, nn. to 188, 241
Norton, Sybil: see Satterthwaite, Helen
    Kestner

Oldham, Dr J. H., 332
Op.I, 54, 68–70, 74, 75, 77, 81, 207,
   nn. to 66, 69, 252
Orthodoxy: see Chesterton, G. K.
Orwell, George, 222
Osborne, Betty, 15, 21, 70
Oxford, Oxford University, 1–3, 4–5,
   6, 7, 9, 12, 14, 27, 41, 45–62, 63–73,
   74, 75, 76–84, 85–88, 92, 97–98,
   101, 111, 114, 121, 123, 156, 167,
   175, 179, 185, 186, 190, 195, 201,
   202, 227, 235, 238, 245, 248, 249,
   250, 251–256, 257, 259–260, 263,
   283, 343, 344–346, 364, nn. to 69,
   252, 260
Oxford Bach Choir, 50–51, 52, 69, 74,
   79, 278, 346
Oxford Magazine, 52, 74
Oxford Outlook, 64

Pailthorpe, G. W., 313
The Pantheon Papers, 363
Paris, 90, 94, 95, 286, 356
Parker, Charles, 95, 102, 120, 160, 164,
   177, 182
Parkes, Rev. James, 332, n. to 332
The Passionate Intellect, 82, 353, n. to
   123
Peake, Rev. E., n. to 12
Pearson's, 201, 203, 207
Peck, W. G., 337
Pendine Sands, 162, n. to 162
"Peredux", 53, n. to 53
Pickering, Dr Kenneth, n. to 273
Playfair, Sir Nigel, 163–164
Poe, Edgar Allen, 195
The Poetry of Search and the Poetry of
   Statement, nn. to 48, 75, 185
Pope, Alexander, 23
Pope, Mildred, 59, 62, 75, 98, 185, 186,
   251–252, 254, 255
Pound, Ezra, 108
Prayer Book Society, 205
Puffett, Tom, 261–262, n. to 261
Punch, 62, 164, 313, 363

"The Queen's Square", 164

The Rape of Lucrece, 280
Raphael, Archangel, 283–284
Reade, Charles, 239
Reckitt, Maurice, 200, 308, 313, 351, n.
   to 52, 200, 308, 314
Redhead, W. J., 240

Reynolds, Alfred, 164, n. to 164
Reynolds, Barbara, nn. to 123, 137,
   175, 266, 353, 362
Reynolds, Sir Joshua, n. to 247
Rhys, Sir John, 187
Ridley, Maurice Roy, 56, 93, 173, 260,
   263, 343, 345, n. to 56
Rieu, E. V., 308
Riverside Nights, 164, n. to 164
Romance of Tristan: see Tristan in
   Brittany
Roubaud, Monsieur, 35, 37
Rowe, Dorothy, 67, 69, 70, 73, 92, 99,
   100, 105, 110, 122, 286, nn. to 71,
   72, 286
Russell, Dom R., 314

St Anne's House, Soho, 331, 362, 367,
   n. to 362
St Augustine of Hippo, 294, 309–310,
   314
St George, Viscount, 340
St Martin's Review, 289
St Matthew, 321
St Michael's College, Tenbury, 2, n. to 2
Sadler, Michael, 93
Saint George Suite, 35, n. to 35
Salisbury, Salisbury Cathedral, 27, 32,
   33, 34, 35, 156, 179, 253
Salisbury, New South Wales, 32
Satterthwaite, Helen Kestner, 131
Saturday Westminster Review, 75
Sayers, Mrs, grandmother, 8, 9, 14, 15,
   17
Sayers, Annie, 58–59
Sayers, Cecil, 156, 161
Sayers, Dorothy (variety artiste), 361
Sayers, Dorothy L. passim
Sayers, Dorothy L., Society, nn. to 69,
   75, 175, 183
Sayers, Eleanor, 47, 57, 58
Sayers, Gerald, 18, 46, 149, 205
Sayers, Gertrude, 6, 9, 21, 33, 104–105,
   200, 201, 210, 234
Sayers, Mrs Helen Mary, mother (chief
   references), 1, 3–4, 5–6, 7, 9, 10, 11–
   12, 13, 14, 18, 21, 27, 29, 35, 41, 45,
   47, 63, 67, 68, 83, 90, 96, 101, 102,
   103, 104, 106, 109, 110, 111, 117–
   118, 121–122, 124, 127, 143, 145,
   149, 150–151, 156–158, 159, 161,
   165, 166, 199, 200, 201, 204, 205,
   206, 207, 208–211
Sayers, Rev. Henry, father (chief

references), 1–3, 7, 8–9, 10, 13, 14–15, 21, 27, 30, 32, 33, 34, 35, 36, 38, 39, 45, 47, 157–158, 159, 160, 161, 166, 200, 201, 204, 205, 206–208, 210, 227, 278, 283, n. to 39

Sayers, Raymond, 18, 33, 68, 73

Schiller, 484, 370

Schreurs, Ann, 154, n. to 153

Scott, Walter, 158

Scott-Giles, Wilfrid, 173, 266–267, 280, nn. 266, 280

Scruggs, 6, n. to 6

Shackleton, Sir Ernest, 32–33

Shaw, G. B., 52

Shelley, 193, n. to 259

Sherlock Holmes Society, 242

Shirley, Canon F. J., 285–286, 368–369

Shrimpton, Amy, 123, 127, 143, 149

Shrimpton, Ivy, 17, 18–26, 28, 37–38, 53, 56, 65, 91, 102, 123, 125–128, 129, 131, 142–146, 148, 149, 150–151, 155, 158, 167, 199, 200, 207, 210, 211, 227, 228, 231, 234–235, 237, 243, 244, 245–246, 248, 268, 342, nn. 124, 208, 226, 346

Simpson, Helen, 265–266, 267, 295, 299, 307, 313

Sinclair, J. D., 359

Singapore, 322

Sitwell, Osbert and Sacheverell, 83

Somerville College, 27, 43, 45–62, 67, 68, 72, 98, 114, 185, 186, 189, 204, 251, 254, 255

Southbourne, 122, 124, n. to 122

Speaight, Robert, 327

The Spectator, 296–298, 340

Spero Nursing Home, 35, n. to 35

Squire, J. C., 166

Strand Magazine, 24, 226, 340

Strong Poison, 112, 113–114, 131, 175, 228, 229, 233, 247, 256–257, 263, 263, nn. to 113, 114

"Studies in Sherlock Holmes", n. to 95

Such A Strange Lady: see Hitchman, Janet

Sunday Chronicle, 156

The Sunday Times, 243, 288, 289, 294, 295, 353

Swinnerton, Frank, 191–192

"Target Area", 31, n. to 31

Temple, Rt. Rev. William, Archbishop of Canterbury, 328–330, 331, 335, n. to 330

Tennyson, 273, 355

Terrington, Lord, 162–163

Thackeray, 21

Thomas, Parry, 162, n. to 162

Thompson, Edith, 219, nn. 219, 223

Thompson-Bywaters Case, 222, 258, n. to 219

Thorpe, Lewis, 189, n. to 189

The Three Musketeers, 21–22, 354

Thrones, Dominations, 339–340

Thurner, Canon John, 315, nn. to 287, 309, 315

The Times Literary Supplement, 108

The Times, 108, 157, 289, 295

"The Tooth Of Time", 5

Tours, 60–61

"The Translation of Verse", nn. to 75, 185

Trembly, Elizabeth, n. to 175

"Trials and Sorrows of a Mystery Writer", n. to 223

Tristan in Brittany, 93, 106, 186, 189–190, 194, 207, 227, n. to 93

Turleigh, Veronica, 265

Unnatural Death, 30, 121, 138, 159, 162, 171, 189, 200, 201, 203, 225, 233, nn. to 122, 189

The Unpleasantness at the Bellona Club, 87, 158, 162, 164, 226, 254, nn. to 161, 254

Unpopular Opinions, n. to 95

Unwin, T. Fisher, 225

Vane, Harriet, 13, 52, 65, 66, 101, 113–114, 131, 197, 223, 230, 231, 234, 247, 252, 253, 254–256, 257–260, 263, 265, 270, 298, 340

Venables, Rev. Theodore, 207, 239, 241

Venice, 286, 356, 357

Venrick, Mark and Lynn, n. to 175

Verneuil, 88, 90–96, 186, 192, n. to 99

"The Vindictive Story of the Footsteps that Ran", 165

Vine, Helen de, 237, 256, 261, 270

Virgil, 98, 194

Wade, Henry, 339

Wadhan College, 83, 85

Wallace, Doreen, 76, 80, 86–87, 89, 92, 370, nn. to 76, 87

Walpole, Hugh, 108

Waller, Lewis, 25–26, 29, 30, n. to 25

Waller, Professor R. D., 355

Walter, Gwen, n. to 100
"The Way to the Other World", 187–189, 356
Webster, Richard T., 314–315, n. to 314
Wegner, Fritz, 190
Welch, Rev. James, 298–302. 304, 305, 316–329, 331, n. to 7
Wells, H. G., 60, 108
Westcott Barton, 227
Weyman, Stanley, 23
Whelpton, Eric, 65, 84, 86–96, 97, 99, 108, 110, 121, 158, 173, 181, 191, nn. to 65, 68, 87, 90, 94, 121
White, Miss, 29, 30, 34, 39, 42, 43
White, Bill, 117–121, 129, 132, 135, 143, 144, 145, 162, 253, 344
White, John Anthony: see Fleming, John Anthony
Whitelock, Major, 79
Whose Body?, 101–103, 105, 106, 110, 115, 123, 171, 174, 175, 176–183, 225, 248, 256, n. to 95
Wigton, Earl of, 159
Wilde, Oscar, 1–2
Wilkie Collins: A Critical and Biographical Study, n. to 197
William of Sens, 276, 278–279, 283–284, 285, 287, 288
Williams, Charles, 81–182, 242, 273, 274, 275, 276, 295, 340, 353, 354, 356, n. to 353

Williams, Harcourt, 276, 278, 279–280, 285, 292, n. to 273
Williams, Harold, 108
Willoughby, Professor L. A., 48, n. to 48
Wimsey, Lord Peter, 56, 65, 75, 92, 93, 95, 99, 101–103, 105, 110, 1l3, 120, 126, 147–148, 164, 165, 167, 169, 171–184, 188, 189, 195, 200, 201, 213–214, 229–231, 233–234, 239, 240, 241, 247, 249, 252–253, 254, 255, 256–260, 261, 263, 265, 266, 267, 270–271, 289, 298, 339–340, 343, 345, nn. to 166, 183, 188
Winchester College, 1
Wingfield-Stratford, E., 341
Witham, 208, 209, 210, 261, 349, 364
Wodehouse, P. G., 175, 349
Wood, Mrs Henry, 23
Wordsworth, 17, 30
Wren-Levis, Professor John 58, 367, n. to 58
Wright, Dr Helena, 244
Wrong, E. M., 193, 194

Xerxes, 16

Yeats, W. B., 108
Yonge, Charlotte M., 18, 361

The Zeal of Thy House, 273–282, 283–290, 309, 331, 353, 362